THE SUPREME COURT OF CANADA

History of the Institution

Unknown and uncelebrated by the public, overshadowed and frequently overruled by the Privy Council, the Supreme Court of Canada before 1949 occupied a rather humble place in Canadian jurisprudence as an intermediate court of appeal. Today its name more accurately reflects its function: it is the court of ultimate appeal and the arbiter of Canada's constitutional questions. Appointment to its bench is the highest achievement to which a member of the legal profession can aspire.

This history traces the development of the Supreme Court of Canada from its establishment in the earliest days following Confederation, through its attainment of independence from the Judicial Committee of the Privy Council in 1949, to the adoption of the Constitution Act, 1982. The authors describe the politics of the judicial appointments and document the internal struggles and tensions between the justices. Central to the story is the attitude of successive federal governments to the need for a strong and intellectually vibrant court. Not all prime ministers and ministers of justice took an interest in the Court, and some of their appointments were of less than outstanding quality. Only in recent times have appointments been of consistently high calibre.

Until 1982 the Supreme Court of Canada played a minor role in the history of the Canadian political structure. The Charter of Rights and Freedoms has thrust new responsibilities on the Court, and as those responsibilities are increasingly exercised in the years ahead the Court will become a major participant in our national life. This book explores the foundations on which that participation will be built.

JAMES G. SNELL is a professor in the Department of History at the University of Guelph.

FREDERICK VAUGHAN is a professor in the Department of Political Studies at the University of Guelph.

D0842045

Interior of the present Supreme Court building

The Supreme Court of Canada

History of the Institution

JAMES G. SNELL
and
FREDERICK VAUGHAN

Published for The Osgoode Society by
University of Toronto Press
Toronto Buffalo London

©The Osgoode Society 1985
Printed in Canada
Reprinted 1986

ISBN 0-8020-3417-9 (cloth)
ISBN 0-8020-3418-7 (paper)

Printed on acid-free paper

Canadian Cataloguing in Publication Data

Snell, James G.
The Supreme Court of Canada
Includes bibliographical references and index.
ISBN 0-8020-3417-9 (bound). – ISBN 0-8020-3418-7 (pbk.)
1. Canada. Supreme Court – History. I. Vaughan,
Frederick. II. Osgoode Society. III. Title.
KE8244.S66 1985   347.71'035   C85-098533-1

Picture credits: all pictures are from the Supreme Court photographic collection except the following: Duff – private collection of David R. Williams, Q.C.; Rand – Public Archives of Canada PA47691; Laskin – Gilbert Studios, Toronto; Dickson – Michael Bedford, Ottawa.

This book has been published with the help of a grant from the Social Science Federation of Canada, using funds provided by the Social Sciences and Humanities Research Council of Canada.

For Tricia and Karen Snell
and Geoffrey and Kevin Vaughan

Contents

Illustrations

Foreword

THE OSGOODE SOCIETY

The purpose of The Osgoode Society is to encourage research and writing in the history of Canadian law. The Society, which was incorporated in 1979 and is registered as a charity, was founded at the initiative of the Honourable R. Roy McMurtry, former attorney-general of Ontario, and officials of The Law Society of Upper Canada. Its efforts to stimulate legal history in Canada include the sponsorship of a fellowship and an annual lectureship, research support progams, and work in the field of oral history. The Society publishes (at the rate of about one a year) volumes of interest to the Society's members that contribute to legal-historical scholarship in Canada, including studies of the courts, the judiciary, and the legal profession, biographies, collections of documents, studies in criminology and penology, accounts of great trials, and work in the social and economic history of the law.

Current directors of The Osgoode Society are Brian Bucknall, Archie G. Campbell, Martin Friedland, Jane Banfield Haynes, John D. Honsberger, Kenneth Jarvis, Laura Legge, Allen M. Linden, James Lisson, R. Roy McMurtry, Brendan O'Brien, and Peter Oliver. The annual report and information about membership may be obtained by writing The Osgoode Society, Osgoode Hall, 130 Queen Street West, Toronto, Ontario, Canada, M5H 2N6. Members receive the annual volumes published by the Society.

Canadians know little about the history and traditions of their highest court. In providing the first comprehensive history of the Supreme Court of Canada, James Snell and Frederick Vaughan make a significant contribution to Canadian history. Their study deals with such central concerns as the Court's relationships with government and politicians, the perception of the Court on the part of the bar and the public, and the Court's internal administration and personnel. Leading cases are discussed in their historical context to illustrate the main tendencies in the Court's jurisprudential evolution.

Throughout, the authors emphasize the relationships between the Court and the larger society. Often the story they tell is a startling one, especially with respect to the all but crippling problems the Court faced during the first half-century of its life. This is not an account of steady or automatic progress but rather of gradual growth in stature in the face of many obstacles. In this history, Professors Snell and Vaughan demonstrate that the life of institutions, like that of individuals, is complex and uncertain.

With the Charter of Rights and Freedoms in place as part of the constitution, the Supreme Court now plays a vastly expanded role in Canada's system of government. This book adds greatly to our understanding of our judicial heritage and governmental traditions.

Brendan O'Brien
President

Peter N. Oliver
Editor-in-Chief

PUBLICATIONS OF THE OSGOODE SOCIETY

1981 David H. Flaherty, ed. *Essays in the History of Canadian Law*, volume I

1982 Marian MacRae and Anthony Adamson *Cornerstones of Order: Courthouses and Town Halls of Ontario, 1784–1914*

1983 David H. Flaherty, ed. *Essays in the History of Canadian Law*, volume II

1984 Patrick Brode *Sir John Beverley Robinson: Bone and Sinew of the Compact*

1984 David Williams *Duff: A Life in the Law*

1985 James G. Snell and Frederick Vaughan *The Supreme Court of Canada: History of the Institution*

Preface

Given the relatively lengthy life of the Supreme Court of Canada and given the emphasis of Canadian historians on political history and constitutional development, it is surprising that no basic history of the Court has been written. This volume is an attempt to fill that gap.

Rather than examine in depth one theme or one specific problem, we have tried to write a chronological history of the institution. This has been accomplished by examining the personnel of the Supreme Court, its position in the Canadian polity, its relationship with its political masters, the intellectual environment and representative aspects of the jurisprudence of the Court, and the way in which the institution has been perceived by the public and the legal profession. In short, this is a history of an institution.

Some basic themes emerge throughout the study. A judicial conservatism has long dominated the Supreme Court of Canada. Judicial conservatism is defined here as 'a tendency literally to conserve or maintain existing law by strictly, even mechanistically, applying established rules and precedents. The conservative judge is unwilling to modify rules and thus little interested in policy arguments about the effect of his decision or the social function of a rule.' Justices of the Supreme Court of Canada actively and knowingly adopted strict construction because they believed 'in the principle that changing the law is the province of the legislature, not the judge,' a sentiment in keeping with Canadian judicial and political culture.[1]

There has traditionally been a lack of consistent government support for the Court. Initially, Canadian political leaders intended the Supreme Court of Canada to occupy a significant position within the national political structure, providing a unified system of law and jurisprudence that would help to unite a country of disparate regions and needs. But very quickly and for a variety of reasons, government support in meeting those institutional goals weakened. Over the succeeding decades government interest in the Court was sporadic and often half-hearted. At the same time, however, the government was more than happy to make use of the Supreme Court and its members. The Court and the justices, together or individually, have fulfilled functions that ranged well beyond their normal judicial duties.

In general, the Supreme Court of Canada has not been highly regarded for the quality of its judicial work; this book confirms the accuracy of that assessment. But it is only fair to point out that such a court can only be as good as the environment in which it exists. A strong and effective court, wrote A.C. Cairns, is dependent on a variety of supporters.

It must be part of a larger system which includes first class law schools, quality legal journals, and an able and sensitive legal fraternity – both teaching and practising. These are the minimum necessary conditions for a sophisticated jurisprudence without which a distinguished judicial performance is impossible. Unless judges can be made aware of the complexities of their role as judicial policy-makers, and sensitively cognizant of the societal effects of their decisions, a first-rate judicial performance will only occur intermittently and fortuitously. In brief, unless judges exist in a context which informs their understanding in the above manner they are deprived of the guidance necessary for effective decision-making.[2]

Such conditions have not existed throughout the history of the Supreme Court of Canada.

Until the 1950s legal training in Canada was dominated by an overwhelming emphasis on practical training, largely in law offices where aspiring students observed and participated in the daily activities of lawyers and learned the mechanics of legal practice. The philosophy of such an education was expressed by one commentator in 1923: 'There is a tendency in many, in this utilitarian age in which we live, even amongst those aspiring to practise one or other of the learned professions, to despise all learning that does not appear directly to be of assistance in making money.'[3] This attitude was not unique to the legal profession.

Training in all professions in Canada emphasized the mastery of practical matters rather than an understanding of ideas and principles. An English doctor arriving in Canada in 1908 was struck by the intellectual atmosphere: 'It was not merely that I found myself back in the Biblical and Victorian atmosphere of my boyhood – that would have been bad enough to someone bent on emancipation – but it was the dead uniformity that I found so tedious: one knew beforehand everyone's opinion on every subject, so there was a complete absence of mental stimulation or exchange of thought.'[4] But if Canadians were not truly anti-intellectual, our culture certainly stressed the practical, everyday aspects of life. The country's long-standing colonial status, climatic and geographical characteristics, and emphasis on material development all tended to discourage intellectualism.

This has certainly been an important influence on the character of the legal profession in Canada. The move toward university-based education in the 1950s was not in itself a guarantee of a more intellectually rigorous training. Today, Canadian legal education, though undoubtedly improved, is still dominated by an interest in practical training.[5] This in turn has a direct impact on the Supreme Court. The training of justices, the quality of decisions and reasoning, the amount of good scholarly analysis by academics, and the character of arguments put before the Court are all affected by the way in which our lawyers are trained. In the past decade two Supreme Court justices have criticized the quality of counsel and their argument. Justice Pigeon, while pointing out that the problem was not a general one, nevertheless argued that the number of poorly prepared cases was increasing, particularly among counsel representing governments or large corporations.[6]

Our objective is not to single out different elements of the legal profession for criticism. But it is important to emphasize Cairns's point that a court is dependent upon its supporting systems. If the Supreme Court of Canada has been subject to considerable criticism over the century of its existence – and it has – the responsibility for its weaknesses ought not to be laid solely at the feet of the justices. The Court and its members are the products and reflections of the character and quality of the Canadian legal culture and profession.

Implicit in much of our discussion of the Court and in much of the public debate about the institution over the years is an evolving definition of the judicial function. Expectations and perceptions of the proper and desired role of the justices and the Court have changed markedly during the history of the Court. As a result of the pressures exerted by those expectations and perceptions, the role of the Supreme Court in the judicial and national structure, and indeed in Canadian society, has altered considerably. At present, the independent Court is separated from the political executive, and is expected to play a major role as constitutional arbiter and defender of individual civil liberties. But for much of its history the Court was neither prepared for nor expected to play any such major role. Much of the Court's history, in fact, has been an extended prologue to its present position of significance.

We hope that this book will be of use and interest to lawyers, political scientists, historians, and the general public. Because of the wide range of potential readership we have deliberately eschewed the use of academic and legal jargon so common in law books and journals.

One major omission must be explained. No quantitative analysis of cases or judges is presented in this book. We originally set out to include such information; Sidney Peck and Peter Russell very generously made available to us their machine-readable material on the reported judgments of the Supreme Court from 1875 to 1968. However, we found that the information had not been recorded in such a way as to answer effectively the sorts of questions we wanted to pose. Lacking the funds to cope with this situation (and with a manuscript already very lengthy), we opted to leave it to someone else to apply this approach.

At a very early point we divided our responsibilities. Snell, a historian, examined the personnel, government policy, and public attitudes; Vaughan, a political scientist, studied the case law, the judgments of the Judicial Committee of the Privy Council, and other historical material relating to jurisprudential issues.

In carrying out our work we have enjoyed much support. The Social Sciences and Humanities Research Council funded most of our research. As usual, the staff of the Public Archives of Canada were very supportive. The registrar of the Supreme Court of Canada, Bernard Hofley, and his staff aided our research substantially and responded to a number of specific queries. After the intervention of Chief Justice Laskin on our behalf, the minister of justice granted access to some of the records held by the Department of Justice. J.W. Pickersgill and G. Pearson allowed limited access to the Louis St Laurent papers and the Lester Pearson papers respectively. The staff of the Judicial Committee of the Privy Council made us very welcome and placed their facilities and records at our disposal. The Barristers' Society of New Brunswick granted access to its records. We are grateful to Gordon A. Goldrich, the registrar of the Wellington County Court, and Joseph Berry of the Wellington County bar for their generous assistance. A number of individuals, particularly former Justice Douglas Abbott, were liberal with their time and their knowledge.

Richard Gosse shared his research notes on Supreme Court justices sitting on the Judicial Committee, and David Williams allowed us to quote excerpts from his biography of Lyman Duff, then in draft manuscript. Gerry Stortz provided significant research assistance.

The Osgoode Society was of great help in the later stages of this project. After a first draft of the manuscript was written, the society's editor-in-chief, Peter N. Oliver, arranged a very useful conference at Osgoode Hall in 1983, which gave us an opportunity to discuss the work in progress with members of the Osgoode Society and others. John Cavarzan, Brian Crane, John English, Martin Friedland, Peter Russell, and Kathy Swinton were present and contributed many valuable ideas; and we are well aware of our intellectual debt to these scholars. This book is undoubtedly much the better for their efforts.

We are grateful to Kathy Johnson, who did her best to improve the quality of our prose.

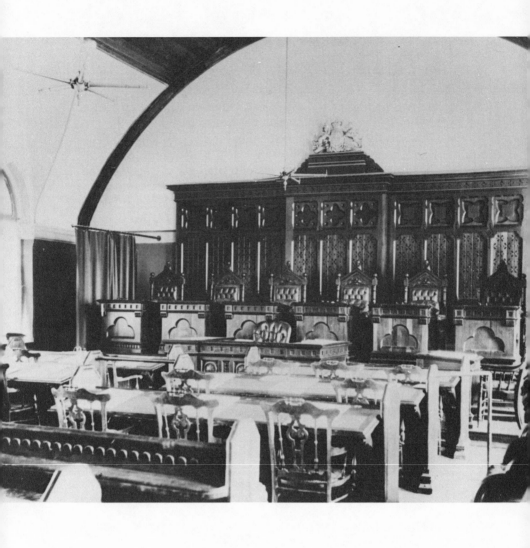

Interior of the old Supreme Court building

The Supreme Court of Canada:

History of the Institution

1

The Founding of the Court

1867–1879

The founding of the Supreme Court of Canada began in ambiguity. At the end of almost three years of Confederation debates and sporadic negotiations, three British colonies joined together on 1 July 1867 to form the Dominion of Canada. No one would claim that the British North America Act, the legislative instrument of unification, was without vagueness or apparent contradiction; it seemed to leave much to ongoing development and change. Among the elements of the political structure that were not detailed in the act was the new dominion's judicial system.

Instead, the existing courts of civil and criminal jurisdiction were maintained; provincial governments were given legislative jurisdiction over 'the Constitution, Maintenance, and Organization' of those courts, as well as over civil procedure (criminal procedure being the responsibility of the central government). Although the provinces controlled the courts, the central government was given authority over the judiciary. Six brief sections of the act, under the general heading 'Judicature,' set out the jurisdiction over the judiciary. Most innovative was the last of those clauses, section 101: 'The Parliament of Canada may, notwithstanding anything in this Act, from Time to Time, provide for the Constitution, Maintenance, and Organization of a General Court of Appeal for Canada, and for the Establishment of any additional Courts for the better Administration of the Laws of Canada.' By this clear-cut allocation of legislative authority, the central government too could establish courts. But the clause is strikingly vague and of little help in leading to an understanding of the prospective aims and purposes of any such 'General Court of Appeal.' It is clear that the role and functions of such a court were not particularly well thought out at the time.

The architects of Confederation had for some time assumed that the new dominion would require a central appellate court. The Canadian proposals of 1858 envisaged 'a Federal Court of Appeal,' and both the Quebec (1864) and London (1866) resolutions called for the establishment of a 'General Court of Appeal.' The records of some of the discussions behind these statements suggest that at least some politicians recognized the need in a federal structure for judicial review – that is, they accepted the idea, somewhat foreign to British practice, that courts would be needed to arbitrate among the various governments of Canada. Both the Judicial Committee of the Privy Council in England and the existing colonial courts were expected to fill that role.[1] Little concrete discussion of the proposed appellate court actually took place; nevertheless, an examination of the sections of the British North America Act dealing with the courts is suggestive of the thinking behind the provision for a general court of appeal.

The fathers of Confederation clearly envisaged a dominion in which there would exist considerable uniformity in law and jurisprudence; this would be one means by which a broader, extraprovincial focus or identity would be created. Section 96 gave the central government the exclusive authority to select the judicial personnel at the county court level and above; those judges would be paid by the central government, and superior court judges could be impeached only by an address from Parliament to the governor-general (sections 99 and 100). At the same time, a centralized jurisdiction over the law was contemplated. Ottawa was given exclusive legislative jurisdiction in the field of criminal law (section 91 (27)). Sections 94 and 97 anticipated that in the future 'the laws relative to Property and Civil Rights in Ontario, Nova Scotia, and New Brunswick, and the Procedure of the Courts of those Provinces' would be 'made uniform' upon provincial agreement. Since property and civil rights were purportedly areas of exclusive provincial jurisdiction (section 92 (13)), the most obvious and consistent way in which this uniform body of law could be articulated was through a unitary system of courts. Given the explicit statements and the implicit attitudes of these clauses, section 101 of the constitution is both appropriate and fitting. It was surely natural that 'a General Court of Appeal for Canada' would be established to co-ordinate the pivotal work of the various provincial-level courts. The call for such a central court, however poorly articulated, was no mere afterthought.

In the decade following the birth of the dominion, there was basic agreement between the two major political parties that section 101 ought to be taken up and a central court of appeal constituted. Such a court was seen as an essential element in establishing the credibility, authority, and status of the polity of the new nation. S.M. Lipset has described the establishment of national authority as the first, essential task facing any new nation.[2] The adherence of the economic élites to the new Confederation was assured by the evolving national policy, which also underlined the prominent role of the central government in the new political structure. A supreme court would have several similar functions. It would force the members of the country's legal fraternities to shift their focus beyond provincial boundaries to a new central court, located in the capital, which would establish a common body of jurisprudence for the whole dominion. Such a court was part of the trappings of nationhood, a means of emphasizing the legitimacy and the power of the young central government. As Alexander Mackenzie put it, a supreme court 'was a necessary complement to our system of self-government in this country ... it [was] desirable that there should be a Canadian tribunal of the highest character, to which our people would appeal ...' One commentator portrayed the court's proponents as arguing that a central court of appeal 'was necessary to complete Confederation, to put the keystone to the arch of Confederation.'[3] These covert functions were important factors in the efforts of the Macdonald and Mackenzie governments to create a supreme court.

Less than a year after Confederation, Sir John A. Macdonald, who was then both prime minister and minister of justice, took the initiative regarding the creation of a supreme court. He entrusted the task of drafting the first legislation to a friend and legal adviser, Henry Strong of Toronto. Throughout the summer of 1868 the two men discussed various ideas as to what the bill should contain. Strong's task was not as easy as he had first expected. Because he found the model of the United States Supreme Court useful, he copied several items from that court's establishing legislation and unsuccessfully sought funds from the prime minister for a trip to Washington to study the work of the American Supreme Court and circuit courts.[4] The model proved to be of limited help, however.

Part of Strong's problem lay in the confusion regarding the character and jurisdiction of the proposed Canadian court. Section 101 of the British North America Act was too vague to provide any guidance. Macdonald himself, for example, complained that 'this provision is very important; very brief; and not a little obscure.' Some legal authorities argued that a supreme court could hear only those cases arising out of the laws of the central government; the court could have no jurisdiction over provincial law. This view was unacceptable to Macdonald. At one point he considered abolishing provincial courts of appeal and providing for appeal directly from the lower courts to a supreme court, but reluctantly concluded that the provincial governments would not consent to such an arrangement.

Macdonald had high hopes for the central court: 'I think this new Court should stand as regards the Provinces in a position analogous to that of the Queen in Council as regards the Colonies generally: and that the procedure should be assimilated as far as possible to that of the Judicial Committee.'[5] This was vintage Macdonald: the imperial government was to the Ottawa government as the Ottawa government was to the provincial governments, and this relationship was to be replicated in the judicial structure.

By February 1869 Henry Strong had finished drafting the legislation; it was submitted to the second session of the First Parliament in May. The bill described a court with a wide range of duties to be performed by seven justices, with no required distribution between those trained in the common law and those trained in the civil law. The court would hold appellate jurisdiction in all civil and criminal cases across Canada. As well, the court would have 'exclusive original jurisdiction' to determine the constitutionality of provincial statutes, decide any question involving enforcement of dominion revenue statutes, hear disputes arising out of treaty obligations, and deal with admiralty matters. The court would be allowed to exercise its original jurisdiction only during special sittings, which would be held in the capitals of the four provinces.[6]

Macdonald seems to have used this bill as a means of engendering discussion. He explained that this first bill 'was rather more for the purpose of suggestion and consideration than for a final measure which [the] Government hoped to become law.' When objections to the bill were raised, the legislation was withdrawn from the House, but the proposal was not allowed to die. Macdonald sent copies of the bill to various judges in the four provinces during the summer of 1869, seeking comments and suggestions for improvements.[7]

Among the responses was one from Oliver Mowat, at that time a member of the Ontario Court of Chancery and a future premier of Ontario. Mowat expressed a common reaction when he objected to the clauses involving original jurisdiction. Given the central government's power to disallow provincial legislation and to appoint lieutenant-governors and judges of provincial superior courts, it was unnecessary, Mowat argued, to limit constitutional and other matters to the new court; surely the central government already had enough influence in this area.[8]

That Macdonald (and Strong) would project such a powerful role for the new court is indicative of the essential function anticipated for the institution. In the same way, the prime minister's revised supreme court bill presented to Parliament in March 1870 (just ten months after introduction of the first legislation) is a sign of his commitment to the court. The new bill contained a number of changes, many of which were of only minor consequence; for example, the justices of the court would now be required to live in or near Ottawa. But there were several major revisions. There was now an explicit statement that the establishment of the court did not interfere with any subject's right to appeal to the foot of the throne. The scope of the reference procedure was expanded from consideration of provincial statutes to include any matters whatsoever submitted by the governor-in-council.[9] Exempted from possible reference, however, were acts or bills of the Parliament of Canada; Macdonald clearly intended the court to be an instrument in overseeing the provinces but not the central government. Nevertheless, the prime minister accepted Mowat's pointed comments and dropped the court's exclusive original jurisdiction in constitutional issues and several other matters.[10]

The supreme court envisaged by this second bill remained a powerful institution (if less so than in 1869) and fitted well into Macdonald's constitutional scheme. There was still no special protection for Quebec's civil-law tradition, nor was there protection for areas of law coming under exclusive provincial jurisdiction. This court was designed to deal with an inferior level of government and to be used as an instrument of homogenization and centralization. In the end, despite its complementary role in Macdonald's constitutional plans, this bill too was withdrawn.[11] Although the prime minister was committed to the establishment of a supreme court, for the next three years his government was too busy with other matters to return to the problem.

However, the Liberal party was also interested in establishing such an institution. The Liberals formed a government late in 1873; provision for a central court of appeal was part of the party's campaign platform in the ensuing 1874 election. The court was mentioned in the speech from the throne in the subsequent session of Parliament. Although the proposal was not introduced in that 1874 session, the department of justice was actively preparing the legislation.[12]

The Supreme Court Bill was introduced by Télesphore Fournier, the minister of justice, in February 1875. The legislation actually proposed to establish two courts with one stroke: a supreme court and an exchequer court. Fournier explained that the Mackenzie government hoped to remove the objections to original jurisdiction that had beset Macdonald's two earlier bills. The 1875 bill provided for 'two courts, one of appellate jurisdiction, the Supreme Court of Appeal; and another, a tribunal of first instance, composed of the same members but being a totally different court.'[13] Any one of the six judges – the chief justice or a puisne justice – would sit alone as judge of the Exchequer Court; appeals from this institution would proceed to the Supreme Court sitting as a panel of the remaining five judges.

Fournier's bill severed the Supreme Court's original jurisdiction in revenue matters; that area was now the responsibility of the Exchequer Court. The jurisdiction of the Supreme Court of Canada was to be strictly appellate. Subject to some limitations, 'an appeal shall lie to the Supreme Court from all final judgments of the highest Court of final resort, whether such Court be a Court of Appeal or of original jurisdiction ... in such cases in which the Court of original jurisdiction is a Superior Court.'[14] Such a broad jurisdiction combined with relatively easy access gave the Court considerable scope for judicial review. Implicit as well was the Court's responsibility to supervise courts at the provincial level.

It is worthy of note that the bill recognized Quebec's difference in certain areas of law. The bill stated that 'no appeal shall be allowed from any judgment rendered in the Province of Quebec, in any case wherein the sum or value of the matter in dispute does not amount to two thousand dollars.' No other province was accorded the same or an equivalent monetary factor in appeals at that time. The bill also contained an explicit provision requiring that at least two members of the Supreme Court be chosen from the bar of Quebec.[15]

One of the most controversial features of the 1875 Supreme Court bill was the continuation of appeals to the Judicial Committee of the Privy Council. Fournier drew attention to the absence of any mention of appeal to the Judicial Committee. He denied a desire 'to put any unnecessary obstacle in the way of exercising the right of appeal.' However, he expressed the hope that appeals beyond the new Supreme Court of Canada would soon end. One reason for such a hope was the recent passage by the imperial Parliament of a Supreme Court of Judicature Act, which proposed to transfer the Judicial Committee's authority over colonial appeals to the new Court. This change, said Fournier, would constitute a major and undesirable innovation; the Supreme Court of

Judicature would be a court of law and not a court of prerogative, as the Judicial Committee was.[16]

The 1875 bill retained the right of the governor-in-council to refer provincial acts for advisory opinions, but now specified the right of the provinces or other interested parties to appear before the Supreme Court in any such case. The governor-in-council was given the power to seek advisory opinions on 'any matter whatsoever as he may think fit.' In addition to making special provision for minority opinions in such cases, the final legislation permitted the Senate or the House of Commons to send private bills or petitions for private bills to the Supreme Court.[17]

As Fournier explained at length upon introducing the bill, the government was intent on making good its throne-speech claim that a supreme court was especially desirable for the settlement of constitutional questions. There is evidence that some federal politicians were becoming unhappy with disallowance as an instrument of constitutional arbitration (dealing only with provincial legislation) and felt the need to establish a new instrument of greater perceived impartiality. Fournier pointed to the provisions that permitted in some cases and required in others that any matter touching the constitutionality of a federal or provincial law should be sent as soon as possible to the Supreme Court for a ruling. The important change, of course, was that the Court was no longer designed simply to keep a consitutional check on the provinces; it now had jurisdiction to examine the legislation of the central government as well.[18]

In general terms, appeal to the Supreme Court of Canada was permitted from the court of last resort in any province. Appeals in a case arising for or upon a writ of habeas corpus (other than in a criminal case) or a writ of mandamus, or in a case in which a municipal by-law had been quashed by a court or a rule for quashing it had been refused, could go on appeal to the Supreme Court as of right. In criminal matters the court was given concurrent jurisdiction with provincial judges to grant writs of habeas corpus.

The parliamentary criticisms directed against the bill by Conservatives and a few Liberal backbenchers were brief compared with the more sustained attacks that began in 1879. The 1875 debates did reveal some basic concerns, however. Some critics were disturbed by the growth and increasing complexity of the judicial system and procedure as part of a more general concern regarding the expansion of government. 'There is not much public sympathy,' it was said 'for measures tending to promote additional litigation.' It was felt that if the government had so much money to spend, it could be put to better use. One future Conservative cabinet minister, J.-A. Mousseau, 'considered the Supreme Court was entirely unnecessary ... This court would cost from $80,000 to $100,000; and he thought it would be much better to husband our resources, and employ them in carrying on and completing our great public improvements, such as the enlargement of the Welland and St.Lawrence Canals, the building of the Pacific Railway.'[19] Other members feared that provincial control over property and civil rights and Quebec's distinct system of law would be undermined; amendments were moved to reduce judges' salaries, to remove jurisdiction over property and civil rights, and to require ratification by the Quebec legislature. More basic still was the concern about the character and nature of the Canadian political structure; some felt that such powerful centralization as embodied in the bill was going beyond the terms of Confederation. Other politicians were disturbed by the prospect of a court capable of reviewing federal legislation and thus challenging directly the supremacy of Parliament. All these criticisms were to be heard again in the near future and in more detail. In the meantime, they were not enough to defeat the bill.

Once introduced, the 1875 Supreme Court Bill received bipartisan backing, although support from the Conservative opposition was somewhat limited. In fact, the Conservatives were badly split over the issue of establishing a supreme court; perhaps this is the explanation for the surprising withdrawal of Macdonald's 1870 bill. In 1875 the proposed legislation faced five roll-call votes, and on those votes the Conservatives divided sharply. Anywhere from 33 to 45 per cent of the Conservatives voting were out-of-step with their party colleagues (see table 1). What is more, on all but the last vote the majority of Conservatives demonstrated that they were opposed to the sort of powerful institution envisaged by the bill. This opposition was concentrated in central Canada; on the second motion, for example, the thirty-two affirmative votes were distributed as follows: sixteen from Quebec, fourteen from Ontario, and one each from New Brunswick and Nova Scotia. The split within the federal Conservative party over the Supreme Court may represent a major division within the party over the basic character of the dominion constitution; it certainly helps to explain some of the problems and responses regarding the Court in the 1880s.

The Conservative leadership still supported the creation of the Supreme Court of Canada. That support was probably essential to the successful founding of the institution. Both parties had worked toward establishing a central court of appeal, and if the measure was Liberal in its final initiation, it was Conservative in its base – Fournier himself admitted

TABLE 1
1875 support in the House of Commons for the Supreme Court

Motion	Conservatives		Liberals		Totals	
	Yeas	Nays	Yeas	Nays	Yeas	Nays
For a six-month hoist	30	25	8	96	38	121
For removal of jurisdiction over property and civil rights	32	23	8	95	40	118
For reduction of justices' salaries	32	20	17	79	49	99
For clause 47	17	34	95	6	112	40
For ratification by the Quebec legislature	17	24	3	82	20	106

that the bill was founded on the extensive work done by the Macdonald government.[20]

One proposal to amend the bill succeeded in 1875. A motion to end appeals to the United Kingdom and to make the Supreme Court the final court of appeal for Canada was adopted, after much acrimonious debate, as clause 47 of the bill. Here was a threat, both explicit and implied, to those constitutional ties to Great Britain so essential to Canada and so dear in the minds of many Canadians. The clause would soon lead to a confrontation between the Canadian and British governments.[21]

The establishment of the Court seems to have been well received by the public. Some questions were raised, particularly regarding the Court's jurisdiction in cases arising under provincial legislation, but the positive benefits were clear. The Canada Law Journal spoke for many: 'It has long been a rule of national policy that, for the security of private rights and the administration of the public laws, there should be a judicial department in every well organised government ... This being so, a supreme constitutional authority becomes a necessity as a department of the public government of the nation; and for this, as a part of its high functions, the Supreme Court of Canada comes into existence.'[22] It was, however, up to the political authorities to support the Court and to the justices to conduct themselves so as to fulfil public expectations.

The selection of the initial personnel was crucial. Given the need to establish the legitimacy of the Court in the public eye and to gain its acceptance in all sectors of the young nation, it was natural that various major groups and regions would be represented and that the existing bench would be a major source of recruitment. Regional representation in bodies of the central government had already become a major criterion. Sir John A. Macdonald established the practice in naming his first cabinet, and Alexander Mackenzie entrenched the procedure. In the case of the Supreme Court, however, flexibility in seeking high-quality jurists who also met necessary regional, ethnic, or religious criteria was severely limited by the small number of posts available.

Of the six seats, two were allocated by law to the province of Quebec, leaving four to be distributed elsewhere. The historic regional attitudes in the country, and especially in Ontario, made it essential to give Ontario at least as many seats as Quebec. This left two seats, at most, to be filled from outside central Canada. There is no evidence that the government gave any serious consideration to appointing a western representative, a fact that is not surprising given the population of the west and the Mackenzie government's strained relations with British Columbia. Instead, the unimaginative (and therefore politically safe) decision was made to appoint one justice from each of the two major maritime provinces. The emphasis on provincial representation was balanced by one other factor – political affiliation – as two Liberals, three Conservatives, and one bipartisan were named to the Court.

About the Ontario appointments there seemed to be little debate. As compensation for accepting the same number of seats as Quebec, there was pressure to give the chief justiceship to an Ontarian. Edward Blake, the brilliant lawyer and forceful Liberal politician, was first offered the post. He declined, accepting the justice portfolio instead, thereby acquiring control over Court appointments.[23] The chief justice of Ontario, William Buell Richards, was an attractive second choice. He had been a moderate Reformer in the provincial assembly (1848–53) and attorney-general of Canada West (1851–3); he had been on the bench for twenty-two years and had served as chief justice of the Court of Queen's Bench since 1868. He was considered 'a man of large common sense and an able Judge,' but had only recently recovered from a serious illness. Less attractive was another motivation behind his promotion. He had been 'at open feud in Court for a long time' with a colleague; the minister of justice sought to end the conflict by separating the two men.[24] Although Richards at age sixty added status and respectability to the Ottawa bench, the appointment of Samuel Henry Strong was probably more important. Just fifty years old, Strong was the youngest and most vigorous of all of the initial members of the Court. At the bar he had demonstrated particular ability in equity and as defence counsel. Having been intimately involved in early discussions regarding the establishment of a supreme court, he was clearly committed to such an institution in principle. After drafting the first Supreme Court bill, Strong was rewarded in 1869 with appointment to the Court of Chancery, followed in 1874 with promotion to the Ontario Supreme Court. He was regarded as 'a scientific lawyer and one of the best Appeal judges we have – but he is blessed with a shocking bad temper.' Over the next twenty-seven years the Supreme Court of Canada would benefit from his considerable abilities, but would also suffer from his several pronounced faults. In the meantime, he was reported in 1875 to be 'extremely anxious' to join the Court in Ottawa.[25]

From New Brunswick came William Johnston Ritchie, who had been a judge for twenty years and provincial chief justice since 1865. In the New Brunswick Supreme Court he had developed a considerable reputation for his knowledge and insight into commercial law. Ritchie's appointment to the Supreme Court of Canada brought several advantages. Apart from his own merits, he had ties to Samuel Tilley, an important Conservative politician, and to a commercial élite committed to progressive economic expansion. Writing in 1870 in response to Macdonald's first Supreme Court bill, Ritchie criticized many of the details but was forthright in his support for the idea of such an institution:

An efficient appellate tribunal as a Court of *dernier ressort*, and whose precedents would be a rule of decision for the Courts of all the Provinces, is without much doubt much required. It should, I think, be so constituted as to secure its being at all times presided over by Judges in whose learning and character the Profession and Public have, from experience, confidence. It should be easy of access – speedy in its action – and, with a view to dispatch and cheapness, simple in its procedure. It should deal only with cases of sufficient magnitude, either in the amount or principle involved, to warrant further investigation and expense; and then, with the substance of the matter in controversy on broad principles of law and justice, to the discouragement of mere formal or technical objections which do not affect its merits.

Although Ritchie's commitment to the Supreme Court of Canada was unquestioned, in New Brunswick he had shown an unfortunate tendency toward lengthy, over-elaborate judgments, some of which were much delayed before being handed down.[26]

For Nova Scotia the choice was less straightforward. A number of names were put forward by interested local parties, but no one individual stood out. The minister of justice is reported to have sent an emissary to Halifax to enquire into the capabilities of the local candidates. The post eventually fell to William Alexander Henry, who, like many other pro-Confederate politicians in Nova Scotia, had been defeated in the 1867 election and had returned to private law practice. Henry was a competent barrister, but no more than that. By 1874 all of the Nova Scotian fathers of Confederation except Henry had achieved some reward through the dominion government. The Mackenzie government rectified that situation early in 1874 by appointing Henry a judge ad hoc to hear Nova Scotia petitions concerning controverted elections; less than two years later he was called to Ottawa. He owed his Supreme Court appointment to his political career, to his pro-Confederation sacrifices, and to his considerable support among members of the local bar and provincial members of Parliament. Henry's lack of judicial experience was a weakness, as was his level of intellectual ability.[27]

The official offers of appointment to these four English Canadians were made on 11 September,[28] but the offers to the two Quebec members were delayed because the second Quebec member had not yet been chosen. One position had already been promised to Télesphore Fournier, who as minister of justice had piloted the Supreme Court bill through the House of Commons. Over the years Fournier had been repeatedly distracted from his legal career by his political interests, but his achievements as a lawyer were such that he had become a leader of the Quebec bar.[29]

The second Quebec position was subject to considerable manoeuvring as the Mackenzie government sought to gain various political advantages. It was cabinet's view that the two ablest legal minds in the province were A.-A. Dorion, chief justice of the Court of Queen's Bench, and Rodolphe Laflamme, a capable lawyer and member of Parliament. It was decided that Laflamme, who was interested in joining the bench, could not be spared from the government and that he should therefore be offered an appointment in such a way that he would not accept. Dorion refused the proferred post, apparently feeling that a puisne justiceship on the Supreme Court would be a decline in status.[30] Several other names were considered, and the position was finally offered to Jean-Thomas Taschereau in the expectation that he would decline. It was felt that he would not want to move to Ottawa; once the post was rejected and a political advantage gained from having offered the position to a Conservative, the government planned to name either Joseph Doutre or Louis Sicotte, both long-time Reformers.[31] Taschereau accepted, however, although by the time he resigned in 1878 many observers must have wondered why. Taschereau was the only original member of the Supreme Court to have undertaken advanced study of the law at the university level, in his case in Paris. When he joined the Court in 1875, he was sixty years old and had been on the bench for ten years, most recently on the Court of Queen's Bench.[32]

The original six-man panel reflected several important characteristics. Five were Canadian-born, a relatively high figure in the light of the immigrant nature of much of English Canada; the sixth, Strong, had arrived from England at age ten. It was of some advantage to the Court that five members had been active politically (Taschereau being the exception). The Canadian élites in this period were small and overlapping; to appoint long-standing members of those élites (Ritchie's grandfather, for example, had been a judge in Nova Scotia) was to ensure the acceptance of the Court and its compatibility with the government. That two provincial chief justices were among the members was important for the Supreme Court's prestige and for the fulfilment of its covert functions. The median age at appointment was fifty-nine. At this stage of the dominion's history, when the various regions were still in the process of accommodating themselves to a federal system, it was probably wise to establish a regional selection criterion. The Mackenzie government should be given credit for its bipartisan appointments, which assured the Court the support of both political parties (although this did not prevent partisan complaints[33]). In general the appointments were well received in the press and by members of the bar, with the exception of W.A. Henry. It was unfortunate that several able people, such as Blake and Dorion, had refused appointment – the intellectual strength of the Court clearly suffered as a result. Such refusals and the consequent weakness of the Court were to be frequent problems throughout the coming years.

Ritchie and Strong brought to the Supreme Court a strongly centralist understanding of the British North America Act. Early in 1875 a case had come before Ritchie in New Brunswick challenging the right of provincial officials, directly or indirectly, to prohibit the manufacture or sale of alcoholic beverages or to limit their use. In his judgment Ritchie adopted a broad definition of the central government's power to regulate trade and commerce and declared the provincial legislation ultra vires:

The power thus given to the Dominion Parliament is general, without limitation or restriction, and therefore must include traffic in articles of merchandize, not only in connection with foreign countries, but also that which is internal between different Provinces of the Dominion, as well as that which is carried on within the limits of an individual Province ... Under the British North America Act, 1867, the Local Legislatures have no powers except those expressly given to them.[34]

The decision is of interest because it reveals a strongly centralist leaning on the part of Ritchie, and because Henry Strong relied on this judgment in a similar case in Ontario before being appointed to the Supreme Court.[35]

With the judicial panel selected, the Supreme Court of Canada could get down to the work of preparing to commence operations. One major obstacle remained, however. Colonial Office concerns over the constitutionality of clause 47 of the Supreme Court bill had caused the bill to be reserved by the governor-general, and it now awaited approval from the queen-in-council.[36] While discussion and consideration of this legal problem continued, the Supreme Court remained in limbo.

This state of suspended animation was frustrating to the prime minister and his colleagues. In the summer of 1875, Alexander Mackenzie had conferred with British officials in Whitehall, and he believed that agreement had been reached regarding the legislation: the Court would be allowed to get under way, but if British law officers agreed that clause 47 was unconstitutional, the Canadian cabinet pledged to modify the clause so that the objections were satisfied. This does not appear to have been the Colonial Office's understanding of the consultations. This disagreement became apparent late in September when the dominion government sought royal assent to the orders-in-council appointing the justices and the registrar. The cabinet put pressure on the Colonial Office and on the administrator in Canada, General O'Grady Haly, to proceed with these initial steps in organizing the Court.[37]

Why was the Canadian government so insistent on immediate establishment of the Supreme Court? First, the cabinet was trying to manoeuvre the Colonial Office into a position where rejection of the Supreme Court bill would be very difficult. Genuinely worried that the legislation might be turned back at Whitehall, the government hoped that by empanelling the Court and by filling the vacated positions on the provincial benches considerable confusion within the dominion judicial system might ensue if the Court were not allowed to stand. Second, the government was experiencing a series of confrontations with British officials, especially the forceful and newly arrived governor-general, Lord Dufferin, over several matters, but particularly over British Columbia's complaints against the central government. The Canadian politicians were becoming increasingly resentful of what they considered to be British interference. Third, the Supreme Court Act allowed for a two-stage establishment of the institution. The governor-in-council could order the appointment of judges and officers to facilitate the organization of the Court, but a second order was required for the Court to exercise its judicial functions. When General Haly delayed the first order, Ottawa officials saw further signs of British interference. Fourth, Edward Blake was creating internal problems for the cabinet. When he became minister of justice in May 1875 he was already convinced that the government had failed to stand up sufficiently to British authorities. By September Blake was prepared to push back against Downing Street and to force the cabinet to do likewise.[38] Blake's argument that numerous important cases awaited appeal to the Supreme Court was simply a ploy, as indicated by the paucity of appeals in the early sessions of the Court. It is true that once the process of appointment began, any delay could throw into chaos the judicial calendars in the various provinces, but that situation was of the government's deliberate making.

Finally, under the Mackenzie government's insistent pressure, General Haly assented to the order-in-council and on 8 October 1875 administered the oath of office to the chief justice and to the registrar.[39] On 8 November the five puisne justices were sworn into office. Arrangements for the Court's functioning were taken in hand. Staff members were appointed, including a capable young registrar, Robert Cassels Jr. Law books were ordered. Temporary accommodations were made available in the Senate wing of the Parliament building, while plans were made to provide permanent quarters elsewhere. Rules and procedures began to be considered.

The governor-general went out of his way to give prestige to the Court. 'I think,' wrote Blake to one of his colleagues, 'the Governor's idea is that we ought to give the occasion [of swearing in the puisne justices] all possible eclat.' Lord Dufferin followed this up by acting as host at a state dinner on 18 November in honour of the Supreme Court members; he called for 'social, moral, and ... material recognition proportionate to their arduous labours, weighty responsibility, and august position.' At least partly at Dufferin's suggestion, the justices adopted the stately scarlet and ermine robes of the English bench.[40]

The early support for and status of the Supreme Court should not be overstated, however. When the minister of justice outlined the physical requirements of the Court, he allocated only four rooms on a permanent basis (a courtroom, a judges' consulting room, an office for the staff, and a room for counsel); a fifth room would be needed for the library until construction of the parliamentary library had been completed. Here was a beggarly institution. No offices were planned for the justices; all the staff were to share just one room; and there was to be no separate permanent library. At first the government planned to build an extension to the West Block in order to house the Court. But when the estimate of $120,000 for construction was presented, the plans were set aside. Instead, the Court continued its 'temporary' use of the Parliament buildings. It occupied rooms around the House of Commons; a converted reading room was used as a courtroom and a few surrounding offices were placed at the disposal of the justices and staff.[41]

The government's refusal to spend much money on the Court was a reflection, among other things, of an emerging tendency to downgrade the institution. Appeal to the Judicial Committee had been maintained, relegating the Supreme Court to subordinate status. The Court's appellate jurisdiction began to be narrowed,[42] and its workload was not expected to be substantial. Blake commented that the registrar's prospective duties would be 'very light.' When J.-T. Taschereau discussed the possibility of resigning because of ill health early in 1876, the minister of justice responded, 'The Council are hopeful that the comparative ease which may be expected in your new position [at the Supreme Court] will act favourably upon your health.'[43] The establishment of a central appeal court was becoming at least as much a matter of status and form as it was of real substance.

Prior to the Court's first official sitting, some essential items of business had to be disposed of. Court attire had to be ordered. One set each of scarlet and black robes, as well as a three-cornered hat, was required for each justice. There was some question as to the exact design – which British court robes were to serve as the model? Would the chief justice's robes differ from the others? When these questions had been answered and each justice had been measured, the orders were sent off to London to be filled by the 'Robe Makers to Her Majesty.'[44] More important than court costume were the rules of the Court. Draft regulations were drawn up by Chief Justice Richards, Justice Strong, and Registrar Cassels and then submitted for consideration and alteration first to Justice Taschereau and then to the other justices. By mid-January 1876 the Supreme Court rules were prepared, and before the end of February the rules of the Exchequer Court were approved, although additions and changes were made thereafter.[45]

One characteristic of these minor decisions stands out. As the Supreme

Court was being established, there was a strong tendency to adopt, copy, or emulate the practices found in Ontario courts. When a court seal was ordered, the seal of the Ontario Court of Queen's Bench served as a model. When a policy was adopted regarding requisitions, the practice of the same court was followed. When regulations were needed regarding the copying of documents for the public, the procedure of the same court was again copied. The rules of the Ontario Court of Appeal were adopted for use in the Supreme Court.[46] These minor examples of Ontario's influence are perhaps illustrative of the way in which Ontario was slowly but steadily shaping the structure of the central government (and other sections of the country) in its own image.[47]

As the rules of practice for the Supreme Court were being drawn up, amendments to the Supreme Court Act were being drafted. In 1876 changes were made in the rules of evidence, in matters concerning the Exchequer Court, and in habeas corpus proceedings. The premier of Ontario requested and received an amendment emphasizing that provincial judges had discretion to refer questions to the Supreme Court. Minor alterations were made to the act in 1877. In 1878, possibly to attract more work for the Court, a government bill increased the number of Court terms from two to four, established a monetary minimum in cases appealable from the maritime provinces, and clarified the rules respecting the right of appeal from various provincial courts; the bill was dropped when it was emasculated by Senate amendments.[48]

Predictably, the early work of the Court was light. The Supreme and Exchequer Court Act was not proclaimed until 10 January 1876. In *Brewster* v *Chapman* (unreported), it was held that the right of appeal to the Supreme Court did not exist in respect of any judgment rendered prior to that date. Therefore, at the first official sitting of the Court, on 17 January, there was no business to deal with and the justices immediately rose. The deputy minister of justice wrote at this time, 'I think the Supreme Court will be a good institution – and work well, & that they will soon have abundance of work.'[49] That abundance of work was not, however, immediately forthcoming. In April the first case was heard by the Court – a reference from the Senate of a private bill. Did this legislation (An Act to incorporate the Brothers of the Christian Schools in Canada) fall within exclusive provincial jurisdiction, under either section 93 (education) or section 92 (11) (incorporation of companies with provincial objects), the senators asked? The four justices present (Taschereau and Henry were absent) considered the problem, although there is no evidence that argument by counsel was heard. Justices Ritchie, Strong, and Fournier found, without giving reasons, that the bill was within an area of exclusive provincial jurisdiction; Chief Justice Richards abstained from concurring in this judgment because he doubted that, in the Supreme Court Act, Parliament had intended that judges should, on reference of a private bill, express their opinion as to the constitutional right of Parliament to pass such a bill.[50]

In June three appeals were heard by a panel of five justices (Henry was again absent). The Court sat for just one week and then rose; it was not to sit again until the following January, when the number of appeals increased. With all members of the Court finally together, eleven cases were heard in the winter term of 1877, and a further twelve were heard in June; the Court sat for a total of seven weeks. By the winter term of 1878, the Court calendar had expanded to include twenty-one appeals, heard in just three weeks. The work of the Court was expanding in quantity, but there were problems. Of the forty-seven appeals heard by the start of the second sitting in June 1878, judgments had been delivered in only thirteen instances – a pace that would soon cause a good deal of concern and one that is difficult to explain.[51]

What work the justices did perform was not done impressively. Their early judgments manifest a diffuseness and prolixity that are disturbing for their apparent commentary on the justices' intellectual discipline. At the same time, however, the judgments are generally reflective of the quality and character of decisions then being written in the lower courts of Canada. R.C.B. Risk's description of the Ontario courts of the time aptly depicts the Supreme Court of Canada:

In Ontario the courts seemed to assume that the common law was composed of rules firmly settled by authority, primarily English authority. It was almost never expressly justified, beyond the justification implicit in its mere existence and the internal authority of courts in a hierarchy ... The process of making decisions seemed usually to be simply finding facts and applying rules. If the law was obscure or uncertain, the court simply had to look harder to find it. This process of finding almost never included any reasoning, even to deduce implications from the rules. The judgments contain virtually no discussions of the functions of courts, especially their responsibility for the common law or interpreting statutes, but a basic and pervasive article of faith was apparent: their function was only to apply the law in an impartial way.[52]

The Court was also showing some early indications of difficulty in adjusting to the bilingual character of its field of jurisdiction. The language of administration was English – even French-speaking personnel corresponded with each other in English.[53] In the Charlevoix by-election case of 1877, Justice Henry issued a pre-trial order to have the record translated into English and forty-five copies printed. Henry had decided that under section 133 of the British North America Act the right existed to use either French or English in any pleading or process before the Supreme Court that issued from the province of Quebec; further, the cost of translation of the papers for the use of the Court could not legally be imposed on the parties to the proceeding. The problem was that the Supreme Court had no means of coping with such a contingency in the short time available. The staff was insufficient for the task and no money was provided to hire special translators. The Department of Justice was at first unwilling to release any additional funds for the purpose; the minister had adopted a policy of keeping 'to the lowest practicable point the expenditures in connection with the Court' – presumably because of the economic recession and in fear of encouraging attacks on the institution. The department refused the registrar's request that an official translator be added to the Court staff. Instead, the hiring of a translator in this special instance was authorized by order-in-council, but in the future the registrar and the reporter would be expected to add translation to their other duties. Perhaps stimulated by this case, early in 1877 the Court set about translating into French the year-old rules of the Exchequer Court. The Supreme Court Reports usually published the various reasons for judgment in their original language (and untranslated); this meant that the Reports were less useful to most of the profession than they might have been.[54]

A large proportion of the cases with which the Supreme Court would deal in the coming years – in fact, for most of its history – were civil or commercial cases involving minor issues of law or of law and fact. Such appeals dominated the work of the Court in both public and private law. A good example of this can be found in *Johnston* v *The Minister and Trustees of St Andrew's Church* (1877), which reached the Supreme Court early in 1877.[55]

James Johnston was an elder of the congregation of St Andrew's Church in Montreal and had been a pew-holder in the church continuously from 1867 to 1872, leasing the pew from the church. In December 1872 the trustees notified Johnston that they would not let him lease a pew for the following year. Johnston responded by an immediate attempt to pay the next year's rental fee in advance; he continued to occupy his pew but was 'molested and disturbed in his use and occupation' of the pew by church elders and other members of the congregation. The trustees finally placed a sign on the pew stating that it was now 'For Strangers'; they took Johnston's books and cushions from the pew and firmly dispossessed him of his seat. Johnston brought suit against the trustees of the church claiming $10,000 damages.

Johnston's suit was dismissed by the Quebec Superior Court. The judgment was upheld in the court of Queen's Bench (appeal side). Nevertheless, the disgruntled church-goer had claimed in excess of $2,000 in damages, an amount large enough to ensure access to the Supreme Court of Canada as of right. In January 1877 a full panel of six justices heard the case. Five months later the decision was handed down, upholding Johnston's appeal 4–2.

The Court majority, led by Justice Ritchie, ruled in Johnston's favour on the ground that having tendered the rent in advance he was, under the by-laws, custom and usage, and the constitution of St Andrew's Church, entitled to a continuance of the pew for the year 1873. The Court allowed 'reasonable but not vindictive damages' in the amount of $300. Each of the four justices in the majority wrote a separate judgment (Fournier in French), covering a total of some forty pages.

Chief Justice Richards and Justice Strong dissented in separate judgments. Strong showed great sensitivity in the first civil-law case to come before the Supreme Court. Unlike Richards, who defined the issue as a leasehold dispute in accordance with common-law doctrine, Strong saw no implicit renewal in the act of pre-payment of rental fees. In his view the trustees of St Andrew's fulfilled the terms of their charter and in doing so caused no actionable tort to Johnston. Strong reached this conclusion after a careful consideration of the civil-law authorities. He concluded that 'as a matter of law it is out of the question to say that a lease having been made for a fixed term of one year, such a lease can be prolonged indefinitely by the proof of any usage or custom.'

The Supreme Court's settlement of an internal dispute between a church and a member of its congregation is a telling example of the trifling issues the Court was to consider in the coming years. That the justices would spend their time and energy writing six different judgments, covering sixty-three pages of the Supreme Court Reports, is striking. Like the Canadian judiciary elsewhere, the justices appear to have been content to do the work that came before them; no matter how unimportant the case, most of the judges tended not to distinguish among the appeals. In this there is already a hint of a passive institution that accepted its subordinate and limited position.

The justices' status and that of the Supreme Court itself were quickly perceived to be lower than was desirable. Lord Dufferin advanced various artificial techniques to redress the problem. He first suggested that 'the title of Lords Justices' be conferred on the Court members; it had already been determined, he pointed out, that the justices should be addressed by the bar as 'my Lords,' and he believed the queen would sanction the broader 'dignity.' This idea was followed several months later by the proposal from the governor-general and the colonial secretary that W.B. Richards be named a knight in the queen's honours list. The British officials felt a title to be appropriate for the chief justice as the senior judicial personage in the dominion and as the deputy of the governor-general whenever the latter was absent. Similarly, care was taken to assure the justices a high place in the table of precedence within the dominion.[56]

But the causes of the Supreme Court's relatively low prestige were much deeper than Dufferin's proposals recognized. Neither the bar nor the government itself had much respect for the young institution. Early indications that the Court was perceived to be of only limited importance have already been noted. Late in 1877, R.G. Haliburton, one of the lawyers for the appellant in *Lenoir v Ritchie* (1878), wrote to the minister of justice suggesting that the government put pressure on the Supreme Court members to agree to hear the case. The government rejected outright Haliburton's request, but the deputy minister of justice's memorandum on the proposal was more equivocal: any intimation to the justices of the government's views at this time was 'rather premature.'[57]

There were several fundamental causes of this low regard for the Court. First, the Supreme Court was an intermediary court that could be completely bypassed by appellants. Second, those who favoured strong provincial rights and those who feared any impairment of ties with the mother country viewed the Court with distrust if not disdain. Third, the Supreme Court of Canada directly confronted a basic, persistent perception held by central politicians. One historian writing about the late 1840s pointed to the 'considerable suspicion of the legal system and profession [that was] a traditional factor in Canadian politics.' Politicians, he continued, distrusted 'a centralized and complex system of justice. A recurring theme in early nineteenth century Canadian experience was the attempt of the legal profession to assert its special right to design the legal system and the challenge of this right by individuals fearful of being exploited by the profession and distrustful of professional expertise.'[58] The way in which the Supreme Court of Canada had been designed and the character of its jurisprudence had seriously violated this image. The Court was thus faced with a pre-existing hostility even before commencing work. It would take a particularly able group of justices to overcome this problem; unfortunately, this was one major area of immediate deficiency.

Both the quality and conduct of the Court's members contributed to the institution's weak image. The commitment of the justices themselves to the institution can be questioned. W.A. Henry absented himself from Ottawa in the spring of 1876 and for three months in the fall of 1877, in the latter instance taking a leave of absence to visit England 'on urgent private business.' S.H. Strong took a six-month leave in the winter of 1877–8. Strong's absence was serious, since it came during a sitting of the Court and caused resentment among members of the bar. In a letter to the editor of the *Canada Law Journal*, one barrister complained,

there are several important cases from Ontario in which judgements are to be given, and others set down to be heard next January, and though we have the utmost confidence in the learned Chief Justice, suitors, or at least their counsel, will not have the same confidence in some other members of the Court, who are not familiar with our [Ontario] laws. And the absence of so able a lawyer as Mr. Strong will weaken the effect of the decisions.

This narrow provincial viewpoint was echoed by Désiré Girouard, a future member of the Supreme Court, who grumbled to Sir John A. Macdonald that Strong had undoubtedly been given leave by the government so as to influence the decision in an upcoming electoral disputes case.[59]

Two other justices were disappointments. J.-T. Taschereau had been a problem for the government since he first came to Ottawa. It had been expected that he would not accept the initial appointment because he would not want to leave his home in Quebec City. In January 1876 he asked for an exemption, on the ground of poor health, from the statutory requirement that he live within five miles of Ottawa; Taschereau intimated that any refusal by the government would force his resignation. The government was unwilling to grant the exemption, but the prospect of such a precipitate resignation so early in the Court's life disturbed the minister of justice. It was decided that if Taschereau wished to resign, he would be offered a pension based on his income on the provincial bench; in the meantime the problem would be treated as a 'profound Cabinet secret.' Negotiations continued by letter over the next several months, while the reluctant justice stayed in Quebec City. Taschereau's request for leave during the June 1876 sitting was refused; since Justice Henry would be absent, Taschereau's presence was mandatory if a quorum was to be obtained. The very thought of the Supreme Court lacking a quorum at its first sitting to hear appeals must have caused trepidation among the government leaders. Taschereau made his way to Ottawa, but obviously none too happily. The prime minister described the result:

The Supreme Court Session passed off all right. They rose on Saturday at 1-30 and Taschereau was off on the train at 2: He tried on Friday Evening to get the Court to sit until 10 pm to enable him to leave at 10-50. Richards refused and Taschereau told him angrily he would be revenged for that. Fournier left on Monday. Strong is very angry and insists on both men doing *some* work. Neither of the Frenchmen opened their mouths in Court from first to last but both *looked* very wise which probably had the same effect on the audience as if they were wise.[60]

This unattractive picture of the Court's first full sitting is complemented by Taschereau's obvious lack of commitment to the institution.

The aversion to Ottawa so pronounced in Justice Taschereau was shared by others. Some, such as Henry Strong, apparently returned to their home towns when they were not required at the Court for extended periods. Advising a prospective member of the Court in 1879 who hesitated to accept because of the need to move to Ottawa, J.R. Gowan (an Ontario County Court judge himself) commented, 'There may be some disadvantages in a residence in Ottawa but then there are advantages[,] obvious ones, also. Moreover judging from the past the judges need not spend a very long time in the year at the Capitol. Do not be in a hurry to move[;] take your time about that. You have a right to consult your personal & domestic convenience in the matter.'[61] Clearly, Taschereau was not the only jurist who found the federal capital unattractive.

The problems with the Quebec justice continued. He maintained a permanent residence only in his home town throughout his three years on the Supreme Court bench. By 1878 complaints began to appear in the legal press regarding Taschereau's violation of the Supreme Court Act's residency requirements. Finally, in the summer of 1878, Taschereau decided to resign. He used ill health as his explanation, but it is clear that his heart had never been in the Ottawa job.[62]

In contrast, Chief Justice Richards' problem was not a lack of interest or of devotion to the Court or to his duties, but genuine ill health, which affected his leadership of the Supreme Court. He was able to deal with the pressures of the position during 1876 when there was not much Court business, but when the number of cases increased in 1877 Richards began seriously to consider retirement. His health so influenced his work that he went abroad in the fall of 1878 in the hope of regaining his strength. Richards was in Europe when Taschereau submitted his resignation. The letter of resignation informed Prime Minister Mackenzie that the Quebec justice would be unable to sit during the fall term of the Court and that his resignation should be dated any time prior to that sitting, some six weeks hence. With Richards absent, Taschereau's replacement could not be sworn into office, and with both Richards and Taschereau absent the Supreme Court would lack a quorum. In the confusion it was necessary to delay the opening of the fall sitting and to summon the chief justice home from overseas to administer the oath of office to the new justice.[63]

Within two months the chief justice too had retired under pressure from the Macdonald government.[64] As the first leader of the Supreme Court of Canada, W.B. Richards had performed well below expectations and short of the essential needs of the nascent institution. He had failed to take active control of the business of the Court, and he was unable to blend the disparate personalities and abilities on the bench into an effective, co-operative unit. Several contemporary accounts credit the chief justice with an able legal mind, breadth of thought, and practical common sense, but his brusqueness of manner and his lack of physical vigour prevented him from taking effective charge of the Court.[65] His shortcomings were especially unfortunate because it was vital to the effectiveness of the Supreme Court as a national body that it establish its right to the respect and approbation of the Canadian people.

Two vacancies thus appeared on the bench. Taschereau was replaced by Henri-Elzéar Taschereau, a nephew. Elzéar Taschereau had been a Bleu member of the legislative assembly from 1861 to 1867 and had been defeated in the 1867 election. He returned to his private law practice, and was appointed in 1871 at age thirty-five to the Quebec Superior Court. Once on the bench, Taschereau found time to develop his interest in criminal law; he wrote a two-volume reference guide to the criminal law in the dominion. The work was a useful compilation of existing statute law and procedure, and the young judge went beyond his basic task by suggesting a number of possible improvements in the law – most notably the assimilation and consolidation of criminal law across the country. Taschereau also demonstrated a strongly centralist interpretation of the British North America Act.[66] Two days before leaving office in 1878 and twenty days after its defeat at the polls, the Mackenzie government named Taschereau to the Supreme Court of Canada.

Richards' resignation necessitated two appointments by the Macdonald government in January 1879. W.J. Ritchie was named chief justice. The selection of Ritchie was safe (he was the senior puisne justice), attractive (he carried the prestige of having been a provincial chief justice), and gave the Court some continuity. The choice also set the pattern, seldom broken, of the promotion of the senior justice when the chief justiceship became vacant.

The opening on the bench at the puisne level was filled by John Wellington Gwynne of the Ontario Court of Common Pleas. He had been trained in chambers in Upper Canada (specializing in equity) and in England in the 1830s before commencing a legal practice of thirty years, mainly in Toronto and Hamilton, including a period as solicitor for the Great Western Railway. In 1869 he was appointed to the Ontario bench. There he gave evidence of his understanding of the British North America Act as a strongly centralist document. Gwynne's promotion to the Supreme Court was well received; he had proved himself in the Ontario court to be conscientious and intelligent, and it was felt that his extensive knowledge of equity jurisprudence would make him particularly useful in dealing with civil-law cases.[67] But he seriously considered rejecting the nomination. Gwynne's comment to a fellow Ontario judge is evidence of the attachment that such men as himself and J.-T. Taschereau felt for the provincial capitals: 'I know not how I shall ever bear leaving Toronto and the associations of kindred and Friends. You may rely upon it [that] I shall defer the evil day as long as possible.'[68] Gwynne's appointment seemed to entrench the regional criterion for selection to the Supreme Court of Canada, but given the political reality of Ontario's strength within the dominion, it was unrealistic to expect that the Macdonald government might have looked elsewhere for a candidate.

With these two new puisne justices, the Supreme Court reached a position of stability in its personnel. It would be over nine years before the next new member was named – the longest such period in the history of the institution. This stability might enable the Court to acquire consistency in its decisions, to entrench an effective procedure, and to create a harmonious, co-operative atmosphere. It remained to be seen whether these results would actually ensue.

2

Early Problems

1879–1892

Unfortunately for the Supreme Court, the unfavourable image of the institution had become entrenched by the end of the 1870s. A wide variety of interests, concentrated in central Canada, expressed fundamental disillusionment with the Court and its role in the dominion. Early in 1879 the *Canada Law Journal* articulated these general views:

The Supreme Court, for years before its organization, was thought to be almost a necessity. There are those who think that, owing to the peculiar circumstances of this Dominion, it cannot be of that great practical use and benefit which its founders expected. There are not wanting some who say that it has been in a measure a failure. It is not, therefore, saying too much when we assert that it is now, and will be for some years to come, on its trial. It has great disadvantages to contend against.[1]

Others were not so willing to allow the Supreme Court to work to overcome its problems. In April 1879 Joseph Keeler, the Conservative member of Parliament for Northumberland East (Ontario) from 1867 to 1874 and 1879 to 1881 and a local entrepreneur, introduced a bill to abolish the Supreme Court and the Exchequer Court. Alexander Mackenzie sought to protect his creation by moving an indefinite suspension of the bill, but Prime Minister Macdonald declined to support this tactic; Mackenzie's motion was defeated by a vote of 120 to 44.[2] Although there was a partisan element in this attack on the Supreme Court, both the vote and the ensuing debate gave evidence of the depth of discontent with the Court. In part, the move to destroy the Court represented the rural community's animosity toward the costs and time involved in litigation and toward the 'lawyer-ridden' character of Canadian society. As well, there was an element of retrenchment and of rural objection to big and expensive government; the justices were too highly paid, and the Court itself, which cost $57,332 in 1878, was too great a drain on the public purse.[3] More basically, the quality of decisions was criticized; the tendency of justices from other regions or trained in other systems of law (civil law, equity law, common law) to overrule expert provincial courts was attacked. After an extended debate on first reading and after a good deal of bickering, the bill was not heard of again.

In hindsight, both the bill and the debate are surprising. That disillusionment with the Supreme Court was so strong as to contemplate abolition of the institution is striking and very revealing. The prime minister's role in the proceedings is worthy of comment. During the debate Macdonald promised that the Court was safe in his hands and that it would continue to exist,[4] yet he countenanced a discussion of the bill in principle by allowing the bill to go to second reading. Given his basic and ongoing support for the Supreme Court and for strong central institutions, there are two obvious explanations for Macdonald's conduct: either he succumbed to the pleasures of a partisan attack on the recently defeated Liberals, or he saw a genuine need to provide some outlet for the rising chorus of complaint against the Court.[5] If the latter was the case, the debate certainly did not serve to clear the air or to dissipate the discontent. The continuing discontent was particularly apparent within the Conservative party. The party had divided badly on several votes in 1875, and Macdonald faced a major internal problem in coping with this split. Indeed, it was likely an important factor in inhibiting the government's attempts to deal with the Supreme Court and the attacks against it in the 1880s.

Much of the vocal support for Keeler's bill in Parliament came from Ontario, and outside the House the reaction to the debate indicated that the opposition to the Supreme Court was real. A Toronto legal journal summarized many of the basic objections, and added: 'The profession, as a whole, have not that confidence in it which should appertain to a court of final resort; for example, there is hardly a lawyer, in this Province at least, who would not, on a question of Ontario law, prefer the opinion of our Court of Appeal, or even of one of our Superior Courts.' A year and a half later, the same journal pointed to the recent decision in *McKay* v

Crysler (1880) as proof of the Supreme Court's deficiencies. A total of nine Ontario jurists (in the Court of Chancery, the Court of Appeal, and Strong and Gwynne in the Supreme Court) had been overruled by three outsiders (Ritchie, Fournier, and Henry) on points of law on which the Ontarians were especially versed. Such rulings 'do not tend to establish confidence in the Court in this Province.'[6]

The narrow provincialism of these views may be disappointing to the modern observer, but they reflected real characteristics of the young and not yet united dominion. Sometime in 1882, Justice H.-E. Taschereau forwarded to Sir John A. Macdonald a memorandum suggesting several changes in the structure of the Supreme Court: 'It is admitted by all those who are in favour of *a* Supreme Court that the present one cannot be continued as it is organized. It is obvious that Ontario will not submit any longer to have the decisions of its own Courts reviewed by Quebec judges, and that Quebec cannot be expected to consent any longer to have its civil law administered by English law judges.'[7] Taschereau was incorrect in viewing the objections simply as a manifestation of English-Canadian antagonism toward French Canadians, although that was a factor. In 1883, for example, the legal journals of Montreal and Toronto became involved in unseemly squabbling about Justice Gwynne's criticism of obiter dicta from the Quebec Court of Queen's Bench.[8]

The objections emanating from Quebec were at times similarly parochial, but in general had much more substance and were more firmly grounded than those from Ontario. Quebec had a distinct system of law and it was difficult to accept that jurists unversed in the civil law should be sitting on Quebec appeals. The seriousness of French-Canadian denunciations became apparent when seven Quebec Liberal members broke party ranks to support the Keeler bill in 1879.[9] Private correspondence confirmed the hostility in the province; one writer informed the prime minister that '"The Supreme Court" is the *most unpopular* institution in Canada' and that the abolition of that and similar Liberal institutions (the Royal Military College was mentioned) would be strongly supported by the electorate.[10] A Montreal legal journal confirmed the widespread dissatisfaction among members of the bar in Quebec; lawyers in the province had long been unwilling to take any case to Ottawa that could possibly be carried to the Judicial Committee. The reason for this, explained *The Legal News*, was that the justices on the Supreme Court had been trained in dissimilar legal systems in the different provinces, and it was generally felt that appeals from Quebec were determined chiefly by the two justices from Quebec.[11]

These complaints were followed up in 1881 by a confidential petition to Sir John A. Macdonald, signed by forty-one Conservative backbenchers, some three-quarters of whom represented Quebec constituencies. The petition pointed to items in the 1881–2 spending estimates – $12,500 to be spent on the Supreme Court building and $925 to be spent on additional personnel. The backbenchers declared that to vote for these items would alienate the electorate and would threaten a rejection of the government at the polls. The petitioners pledged to vote for no increase in Supreme Court expenditure 'so long as the promises made by the Government during the Session of 1880 shall not have been fulfilled in such a manner as to render justice to the Province of Quebec.'[12]

The reference to the parliamentary session of 1880 is important. At that time Joseph Keeler had again introduced his bill to abolish the Supreme Court. During the debate the prime minister had defended the Court and addressed directly the widespread attacks on the institution:

I think we ought not to repeal this Court. We ought not to wipe it out of existence. We ought to face the question, however, and enquire into the cause of the dissatisfaction which is so prevalent. It seems to me there must be a remedy ... the Government desire to address themselves earnestly to this matter, and to make a full and exhaustive enquiry into the best means of making the Court, in every sense, efficient and satisfactory.

This pledge to reform the Supreme Court to meet basic criticisms was sufficient to defeat Keeler's bill in 1880. A motion for a six-month suspension of the bill received bipartisan support in a vote of 148 to 29; the continued opposition came largely from Quebec.[13] However, one year later there was no public evidence that Sir John A. Macdonald was doing anything about the Court other than living up to his nickname, 'Old Tomorrow.'

At the same time, the Quebec members of Parliament pressed ahead with their attack. The sponsorship of Keeler's bill was taken over in 1881 by Auguste Landry, Conservative member for Montmagny (1878–87). In 1881 and 1882, Landry introduced measures to abolish the Court.[14]

It was clear, however, that with strong bipartisan opposition to the outright dissolution of the Court such attacks would accomplish very little. As a result, in 1881 the major solution for Quebec's discontent changed. Critics hoped that a reduction of the Supreme Court's jurisdiction would limit the institution's intrusion into provincial legal affairs. Désiré Girouard was the first to bring forward such a measure: the appellate jurisdiction of the Court was to be abolished in all matters relating to property and civil rights, of a strictly local or private nature, or coming within the exclusive jurisdiction of the provinces. These restrictions were not to apply to constitutional issues or to cases coming from the Exchequer Court.[15] During the debate, Girouard offered to alter the bill so that only the province of Quebec would opt out of the Court's jurisdiction in the proposed areas. A letter to the prime minister the following day indicated that this was a sincere suggestion, an attempt to meet the attitudes of the two founding cultures and legal communities.[16] But opting-out was as unpopular a formula in Ottawa in 1881 as it would be one hundred years later.

Although Girouard's proposal was taken up by Landry and introduced each year from 1883 to 1886, this attempted emasculation of the Supreme Court did not receive broad support. At a meeting of the Montreal bar, leading French- and English-speaking lawyers passed a resolution decrying any reduction in the Court's field of appellate jurisdiction. The legal press in Montreal articulated the feeling that this was too drastic a measure.[17]

The attacks against the Supreme Court represented a basic disagreement about the nature of the Canadian polity. The controversy concerned the philosophical nature of the Canadian constitution, and it was acknowledged as such at the time. A Manitoba member of Parliament emphasized to the House that the debate over the Court had to do with 'whether the Canadian constitution is based on the federative principles or the legislative union principles.'[18]

The opponents of the Supreme Court argued repeatedly and correctly that the institution was intruding into provincial fields of jurisdiction and was imposing centrally made decisions on the various provincial communities. Some things, the critics suggested, were better dealt with at the local level, and the law was one of them. Each province had its own judicial system of long standing and of relative efficiency (although it was true that the maritime provinces lacked appeal courts of their own). The judges in the provinces knew both the provincial law and local conditions far better than did six justices in Ottawa, only two of whom, at the most, were intimately familiar with the provincial community and law appealed from. It seemed obvious to the critics that a better decision would likely be handed down by a five-man Ontario Court of Appeal or a five-man Quebec Court of Queen's Bench than by a hybrid court in Ottawa that was a jack of all trades but master of none.

The centralists argued that the young country needed to be pulled together, to be given unity and a sense of direction that would help Canadians fulfil their great destiny. To achieve this a strong central government was required, and the Supreme Court of Canada was the judicial and legal component of this scheme. George Foster, a Conservative member of Parliament from New Brunswick, referred to this national role for the Court:

My chief reason for being in sympathy with the Supreme Court is that it is a national court, a bond of union for the whole country – that in it we unite the different phases of legal talent and ability – of race, and of creed and of Province; that the whole Dominion brings them together, where we can look upon them as the central fountain of judicial decision for the whole country. So the Provinces are united by another bond, and they are not simply divided and kept apart among themselves.

The Supreme Court was part of 'a bond of greater and closer union.'[19]

From the point of view of most of its political supporters, the Court was an instrument of centralization, and it was natural that the institution would draw the attention and criticism of those opposed to a strong central force in the Canadian constitution. What made the attacks sharper and potentially more harmful was the existence within the Court of real weaknesses.

The challenges to the Court also raised several basic questions regarding the role of the judiciary in the Canadian political system. In the fall of 1879 the Supreme Court upheld the validity of the Dominion Controverted Elections Act. The Court asserted its power of judicial review of federal legislation:

In view of the great diversity of judicial opinion [wrote Chief Justice Ritchie] that has characterized the decisions of the provincial tribunals in some provinces, and the judges in all, while it would seem to justify the wisdom of the Dominion Parliament, in providing for the establishment of a Court of Appeal such as this, where such diversity shall be considered and an authoritative declaration of the law be enunciated, so it enhances the responsibility of those called on in the midst of such conflict of opinion to declare authoritatively the principles by which both federal and local legislation are governed.[20]

Here was a direct challenge to the traditional supremacy of Parliament as well as a reflection of the judges' perceived role in establishing a uniform constitutional jurisprudence for Canada. This assertion of judicial independence stood in contrast to the reference procedure in which the Court acted as an instrument of the political executive.[21] The implications of a unitary judicial system in a federal state and of judicial review were still being worked out. But any tendency on the part of Supreme Court justices to weigh their indepedence confronted some powerful forces. Not only was the British political tradition opposed to any such development, but the judicial culture provided little support. Any ideas of judicial independence quickly weakened, but not before reflecting some of the conflicting ideas present in the political culture and some very real tension in the young dominion. These conflicts and tensions were clearly products of the evolving definition of judicial independence and of Canadian federalism, and contributed to some of the attacks against and doubts about the Court that were emerging.

The strain evident in these various attacks on and defences of the Supreme Court reflects the tension that is always present in a federal state. This was particularly so in Canada; the young dominion was only slowly adapting to the various needs and demands of the country and its regions and peoples, and the existence of a unitary judicial system (led by the Supreme Court of Canada) in a federal state exacerbated these tensions. The attacks were a manifestation of provincialism and of local uncertainties as to the nature and role of the central power. At the same time, however, the defence of the Court and the general, if rather hesitant, agreement that such an institution was desirable and could be useful indicate the yearning of many Canadians for a broader identity beyond provincial borders and the commitment of Canadians to the new dominion. Thus, the attacks on the Court were perhaps a natural function of the country at that particular stage of its development.

This is not to dismiss the disillusionment regarding the Supreme Court. The institution had some very real weaknesses. Unfortunately, little could be done about some of these shortcomings. Litigation was expensive, but it always had been. Ottawa was 'an out-of-the way, and to [the potential justices] uncongenial place' and lacked the intellectual advantages of a larger legal community; but it was unrealistic to suggest that the Supreme Court might be located in any other city. This, of course, did not prevent a spokesman for the Toronto legal profession from urging the clear benefits of moving the Court to that city.

It is moreover, most wholesome for the Judges themselves ... that they should live in a large rather than in a small city, and be subject to the restraining and beneficial influence of a strong public and professional opinion, and surrounded by a large, able and well-trained Bar, and within the precincts, of such a place for example, as Osgoode Hall, replete with the noble traditions of its learned Judges, strong in their integrity and devotion to duty, examples for all time to those who shall occupy judicial positions.[22]

Complaints such as these would simply have to be lived with; some of the other problems could be solved. There were weaknesses in the manner in which the Court arrived at and delivered judgment. It is unclear how often the justices in the early years consulted one another as their reasons for judgment were being formulated. Given the tendency of several justices to absent themselves from Ottawa when not sitting in court or in chambers, consultation or circulation of draft judgments must have been difficult and seems to have been rare. There is evidence, however, that at least some took advantage of the intellectual benefits of interchange of opinions.[23] Conferences were held in the chief justice's office to discuss cases standing for judgment,[24] but how often these meetings occurred and what benefits accrued from them is unknown. It is certain that the justices' tendency to write concurring and dissenting judgments attracted the ire of many in the legal profession. These multiple judgments emphasized the lack of harmony on the bench, weakened the authority of the decision, and sowed the seeds of future litigation by the expression of a diversity of opinion on various points left undetermined by the decision.[25] Edward Blake proposed in Parliament that the procedure of the Judicial Committee be adopted: the justices should deliberate at the earliest possible moment following the case; having reached a general conclusion on the decision, one member of the Court should be assigned to prepare a draft judgment which would be circulated among and amended by the other members of the Court; this, and only this, judgment would then be delivered on behalf of the entire Court.[26] But multiple judgments were traditional in the common law and were essential to its development; in its single opinions the Judicial Committee was exceptional. The justices of the Supreme Court chose to retain the practice of issuing multiple judgments.

It was one thing to hand down the decisions of the Court, but it was quite another to make the reasons for judgment readily available to the courts below and to the legal profession. For the rapid and effective influence of the Supreme Court in Canada, it was essential that its judgments be quickly distributed – any delay meant confusion and uncertainty as to the implications of each new decision. Recognizing this need, the Mackenzie government had included an innovative measure in the Supreme and Exchequer Court Act: publication of the judgments would be the responsibility of the court registrar rather than that of a private publisher. No other court in the dominion (or in Great Britain) published its own judgments; here was a way of assuring that the reasons would reach the profession as soon as possible.

The first volume of the Supreme Court Reports appeared late in 1877; this and succeeding volumes were soon subjected to strong criticism. There were too many errors in typography and editing; citations and style lacked uniformity; the reporter revealed a lack of knowledge of the common law; some of the decisions were in a 'foreign' language; the headnotes were often a poor guide to the essential issues being adjudicated.[27] More serious was the length and obscurity (in reasoning and in style) of many of the judgments. One senior queen's counsel in Quebec charged that 'the length of the reports published is discouraging for any one. To find out the enunciation of a useful principle of law applicable to another case, is almost impossible in these prolix deliverances. When we read a book, there is a summary of matters and an index somewhere to shorten the labour. In these endless reports you have to go through a mass of useless matters before you find out what you want.' He concluded that it was time for private enterprise to take over publication of the Reports.[28] Most frustrating to the legal profession was the delay in publication. The time between the closing of argument in a case and the publication of the reasons for judgment was far too long – the announcement of the decision often took as long as six months, and the publication of the reasons averaged some eighteen months. Delay was particularly pronounced in Quebec cases.[29]

This tardy reporting was disconcerting to the legal profession and to the courts below. New cases were affected by the decisions; solicitors needed to know what advice to offer their clients. The chairman of the Committee on Reporting of the Upper Canada Law Society suggested that in advance of actual publication it was essential to communicate the decisions to the profession. Could not the railway or the telegraph be used to some advantage, he asked, in facilitating communication? No improvement was forthcoming, however, and three years later another Toronto lawyer wrote the justice minister about the delays, adding, 'I am perhaps not sufficiently respectful to the Court but I breathe an atmosphere of discontent that permeates Osgoode Hall.'

The chief justice denied that there were any grounds for complaint,[30] but it was not quite as easy for the Court staff involved with publishing the Supreme Court Reports to avoid responsibility. Some delays were the fault of the printers, but the blame for almost all of the dilatory character of the publishing lay with the justices themselves. When the justices handed down their decisions, not all of them had formally prepared their judgments. Presumably, they had worked out mentally or in rough notes the direction their judgments would take, but that was as far as some went. It was incumbent on the registrar and reporter to prod the often grumpy justices to complete their work in order that the staff could get on with the Reports. At times the prodding had no effect and some cases simply went unreported,[31] but for most the process was merely lengthened considerably. There were several stages in the publishing process, and at each of these a justice could become an obstacle. First, it was necessary to get the justice's notes and have them written up by a secretary; then the notes for each case had to be compiled; the copy was then sent to the printer; a galley proof was struck and proofread; and finally the Reports were printed. The frustration of the registrar and reporter becomes apparent in the letterbooks of the Supreme Court as the staff begs for notes or for return of the printer's copy, or as a justice is persuaded not to alter his reasons after they have been set in type.[32]

The greatest culprit was Henry Strong. Missives went out repeatedly to Strong asking for his notes; staff were sent to his house to bring him books or to pick up papers. The registrar was even forced to use veiled threats: further publication of the Reports would be stopped until the pages were returned to the printers. Nothing seemed to alter the Toronto justice's work habits; he was simply not well organized, and deadlines meant little to him. His habits are illustrated by a footnote in an 1884 case: 'The learned judge [Strong], having mislaid his judgement, directed the reporter to report the case without it.' In April 1888, after ten years of attempting to cope with the problem, the reporter submitted an account of all outstanding cases decided since 1 January 1887 and as yet unreported. Of the total of sixty-two cases, twenty-four were at the printers, three were being prepared in the registrar's office, and ten were unaccounted for. The justices were responsible for the absence of the remaining twenty-five: one judgment of Fournier's was missing, one of Ritchie's, two of Ritchie and Strong's, and twenty-one of Strong's.[33]

Plainly, much of the problem lay within the purview of the justices, and change would have to come from them. But there were some actions that others could take. The government authorized the reporter, beginning in 1881, to furnish to the major law journals his own notes of the decisions. The notes were supplied as a service by the Court, but they were brief, lacked authority, and reflected the reporter's limited legal knowledge. Within a few years the reporter, Georges Duval, began to send his notes only to the *Canada Law Journal* in Toronto, on the assumption that the other legal journals in the dominion could copy the Toronto journal's information. The resulting complaints from other magazines did nothing to enhance the Court's image.[34]

There were a few direct attempts to improve the Supreme Court Reports themselves. The registrar and the Department of Justice kept a closer watch on the problem and on the work of the reporter. A few minor changes in format were made in the hope of pleasing the profession. Most important was the decision late in 1885 to add an assistant reporter, C.H. Masters, to the Court staff. This was the most useful step taken to deal with the problem. Masters quickly proved himself able; he soon took on responsibility for reporting all cases from the English-speaking provinces, while Duval continued to look after those from Quebec. As well, a separate clerk was hired to work for the justices, freeing the reporter from such tasks.[35] The backlog of unreported cases began to diminish.

In the meantime, the circulation of the Reports had shrunk considerably. At first, arrangements had been made with the Law Society of Upper Canada to include in its membership fees a subscription to the Reports; as a result, 900 copies of the first volume went out to Ontario lawyers. By the early 1880s this had risen to 1,200 copies as the Law Society extended the distribution.[36] But the number of subscriptions elsewhere in the dominion was remarkably low. For volume 4 (1880) the regional breakdown of the subscription list was as follows:[37]

Rowell and Hutchinson of Toronto	1,350
(including 1,100 for Law Society of Upper Canada)	
Federal government offices in Ottawa	68
Prince Edward Island	7
Nova Scotia	21
New Brunswick	32
Quebec	85
Ontario	8
Manitoba	0
North West Territories	0
British Columbia	2
United States	7
Total	1,580

For a reports series that ought to have been basic to anyone trying to keep abreast of law in the dominion, this distribution is not very impressive. In 1884 the Law Society of Upper Canada cancelled its agreement to distribute the Reports to all members. This unfortunate (from the point of view of the Court) development led to an immediate 50 per cent reduction in the number of copies printed and a near-doubling of the per-volume cost.[38] The status and authority the Supreme Court Reports commanded diminished to match that of the Court itself.

Throughout the 1880s the personnel of the Court continued to pose problems. In 1886, while sitting in chambers, Justice Henry issued a writ of habeas corpus in the case of a convicted murderer, stating that the British Columbia Supreme Court, including its chief justice, Matthew Begbie, had deliberately approved a false order so as to ensure a conviction. The west coast jurists were furious. When Henry denied that he intended any disparagement, Begbie cried: 'This is to confess himself incompetent to understand the English language.'[39]

This lack of tact was by no means the greatest of William Henry's problems. In 1880, in a letter to the prime minister, Justice Strong launched a virulent attack against his brother judge. The January term had just finished, and in every case 'the deliverances of Mr. Justice Henry were if possible worse than any of his preceding efforts. You cannot without reading them realise the absurdity of these productions. They are long, windy, incoherent, masses of verbiage, interspersed with ungrammatical expressions, slang and the veriest legal platitudes inappropriately applied.' As examples, Strong pointed to the judgments in *Smith* v *Regina*, *Pugsley* v *King*, *Milloy* v *Kerr*, and *Reynolds* v *Barned's Banking Company*.[40] Others of Henry's pronouncements had already been published, he lamented, 'and will stand for all time in the history of our judication as proof of the incompetency of the Supreme Court.' In Strong's opinion, Henry's presence and work at the Court were so destructive that he must be removed from office: 'I do not hesitate to say that nothing but his removal from it can save the unfortunate Court and moreover if that is not effected during the on-coming Session the time will have passed when even that will do. I trust you will see Mr. Justice Gwynne who will I am sure be found to confirm all I say.'[41] On the one hand, it is difficult to say what is most disturbing about Strong's letter to Sir John A. Macdonald: the alleged unfitness of Henry, the admitted incompetence of the Supreme Court itself, or the meanness of such an attack by a colleague. On the other hand, the letter can be seen as evidence of Justice Strong's considerable concern for and commitment to the role of the Court.

Indeed, where S.H. Strong was concerned, the term 'colleague' and the idea of collegiality or of co-operation were clearly inappropriate. Several years after this attack on Henry, Strong privately informed an influential Conservative member of Parliament that Chief Justice Ritchie had laid down 'absurd rules' in a recent order. 'All the majority [of the Court] care for is to make appeals fas[t] as possible & so get rid of work.' The minister of justice, Strong went on, should be urged to correct the situation by altering the Supreme Court Act.[42]

Strong's intemperate behaviour behind the scenes may have been paralleled in the courtroom, but specific instances for the 1880s have not come to light. Chief Justice Ritchie, however, was certainly guilty of inappropriate courtroom behaviour. A writer in the *Manitoba Law Journal*, for example, contrasted Justice Gwynne ('one of the kindest and most courteous of gentlemen') with Ritchie, 'whose proverbial rudeness amounts at time to almost boorishness.' Another commentator pointed to the chief justice's possession of a 'temper quick and ardent.'[43]

The chief justice had clearly failed to mould the individual justices into an effective, harmonious unit. A prominent counsel recalled years later that this was the central weakness of the Supreme Court in the 1880s: 'Originally, Ritchie, Strong, Gwynne, and Henry developed immediate antagonism, and since then there has always been a sad lack of consultation and cooperation.'[44] There remained a strong tendency for the various members of the Court to act independently, a tendency symbolized by the courtroom itself. Gabled windows complemented an arched, partially panelled ceiling. Three double rows of desks for counsel and several rows of benches for the public faced the justices, who sat in front of a carved wooden screen. But the most striking of the room's appointments was 'the bench' itself. There was not, as there is in the modern (post-1946) courtroom, one bench; rather, there were six individual desks for each of the six individual justices. They did not sit together at the Supreme Court; they sat separately.[45]

In their courtroom the six justices dealt with a series of major constitutional cases in these early years of the dominion. Two major factors guided the justices in facing these issues; a lack of precedents from the Judicial Committee of the Privy Council and a British North America Act which, if not always clearly written, at least seemed to demonstrate a desire for a strong central government – an interpretation several of the justices had enunciated before moving to Ottawa. These two factors were soon reflected in the Court's decisions.

In the early years of Confederation both the governor-general and the lieutenant-governor conferred the title of queen's counsel on selected members of the bar of Nova Scotia. A challenge to the legality of such appointments by the lieutenant-governor reached the Supreme Court of Canada in *Lenoir* v *Ritchie* (1880).[46] Counsel for the province argued that in all matters under exclusive jurisdiction of the local legislature, the lieutenant-governor represented the queen and possessed all powers enjoyed by the colonial governor prior to Confederation. The Supreme Court of Canada, however, rejected this claim and unanimously affirmed the judgment of the provincial Supreme Court. It was held that the lieutenant-governor no longer was a direct representative of the queen; Confederation had ended the direct relationship between the provincial governments and the crown and had relocated the royal prerogative powers in the governor-general. 'Nothing can be plainer,' wrote Justice Gwynne, 'than that the several Provinces are subordinated to the Dominion Government, and that the Queen is no party to the laws made by those Local Legislatures.'

Similar reasoning was followed in 1881 in *Mercer* v *Attorney-General of Ontario*.[47] Again it was held that in matters of escheat the provincial government did not represent the queen and that therefore the provincial attorney-general could not appropriate the property escheated to the crown. Confederation had been a manifestation of a desire 'to confer upon the Dominion,' as Justice Gwynne put it, 'a *quasi* national existence – to sow in its constitution the seeds of national power – to give to it a national Parliament ... and to constitute within that national power so constituted and called the 'Dominion of Canada,' certain subordinate bodies called provinces ... of whose legislatures her Majesty does not, as she does of the Dominion ... constitute a component part.' This emphasis on the superior role and position of the central government coloured several of the Court's leading early constitutional judgments.

The constitutional implications of those decisions for the development of provincial autonomy were profound. The denial that the queen was an integral part of the government of the provinces seriously undermined the attempts in the 1880s of Premiers Oliver Mowat and Honoré Mercier to achieve provincial autonomy. In ruling for the subordinate status of the provincial governments, the justices were simply interpreting the terms of the British North America Act strictly and thus giving effect to its inherently centralist principles.

That this was a matter of strict construction rather than a powerful centralist bias is indicated by the justices' handling of the leading case of *Citizens' Insurance Company* v *Parsons* (1881).[48] In this case the justices helped to establish major restrictions on the federal authority over trade and commerce; provincial legislation regulating local business was declared valid. This ruling was affirmed and extended further by the Judicial Committee.[49]

While the Supreme Court of Canada was handing down its interpretation of the British North America Act, the justices' rulings were increasingly superseded or constrained by the binding opinions of the Judicial Committee. Litigants in several major cases, such as *Russell v The Queen* (1882)[50] and *Hodge v The Queen* (1884),[51] avoided the Supreme Court completely by appealling directly to London. Other cases decided in the Court, such as *Mercer, Parsons,* and *Attorney-General of British Columbia v Attorney-General of Canada* (1889),[52] were either overturned by the Judicial Committee or reinterpreted so as to strengthen the position of the provincial governments under the British North America Act.

The response of the justices of the Supreme Court of Canada to this process of judicial reinterpretation in London was exactly what might have been expected in an environment of judicial conservatism. The precedents now existed to guide the Canadian justices in their work; their task was to apply them. Thus the Judicial Committee's ruling in *Mercer* (1883),[53] overturning the Supreme Court of Canada both in that case and implicitly in *Lenoir v Ritchie,* served as the basis of the court's judgment in *St Catharine's Milling and Lumber Company v The Queen* (1887)[54] and in *Liquidators of the Maritime Bank v The Queen* (1890).[55] By this process the queen in right of the province was affirmed as part of the constitution of the provinces, and provincial authority and legislative power were thereby strengthened.

These decisions placed the Supreme Court in an awkward position. Required to follow the binding precedents set by the Judicial Committee, the justices frequently were denied input into a case; *per saltum* appeals avoided any contact with the Supreme Court, moving directly to London from the provincial court of last resort. The Court in Ottawa was thus in a weaker position than an intermediate appellate court; it was bound by decisions which inferior Canadian courts had helped to produce but which all too often lacked the influence of the justices of the Supreme Court of Canada. The ambiguity of this process, as seen from the point of view of the Ottawa justices, undermined their stature and reinforced the tendency to judicial strict construction.

The quality of many Supreme Court constitutional judgments was reasonably good.[56] Relatively clear, straightforward decisions were being handed down as the justices sought to give effect first to the apparent meaning of the British North America Act and later to the interpretation provided by the Judicial Committee. But the competence of the Court was not so apparent elsewhere.

In other areas of law the intellectual quality of the Supreme Court in these years is better revealed. In *The Queen* v *McLeod* (1884)[57] a passenger sued the crown for negligence in management of the Prince Edward Island Railway (operated by the central government). The case was tried before the Exchequer Court, thus in the initial instance involving Supreme Court personnel. On that occasion Justice Henry, sitting alone, found for the plaintiff. Opting to distinguish an apparent Supreme Court precedent in *The Queen* v *McFarlane* (1883),[58] Henry relied in part on his lone dissenting judgment in that case. So much for stare decisis; worse was yet to come.

The Queen v *McLeod* was appealed to the Supreme Court. There it was heard by a panel of five judges, including Henry himself, who was thus placed in the invidious position of being asked to render judgment on his own decision, a situation not unique to this case. Both in *McFarlane* and later in *The Queen* v *Farwell* (1888)[59] Henry heard appeals against one of his own Exchequer Court decisions; understandably, he held for himself in each case, although he was always in dissent. Here is evidence of the problem caused by the small number of judges and the link between the Exchequer Court and the Supreme Court.

In *McLeod*, Henry's decision was reversed. Chief Justice Ritchie held that the railway having been established for public purposes, 'it is subordinate to those principles of public policy which [prevent] the Crown being responsible for the misfeasances, wrongs, negligences, or omissions of duty of the subordinate officers or agents employed in the public service on these public works, and therefore the maxim *respondeat superior* [let the master answer] does not apply in the case of the Crown itself.' Pointing out that the common-law rule *rex non potest peccare* (the king can do no wrong) forbids suits against the crown in tort, the chief justice extended that principle to subordinate agencies. He supplemented this position by repeated appeals to 'constitutional principles,' none of which he identified. Finally, Ritchie took a strict constructionist stance: the statute establishing the railway provided no remedy for relief, so therefore no remedy existed.

This narrow and superficial reasoning was exposed by the impressive dissenting judgment of Télesphore Fournier. Fournier went to the heart of the issue: 'Is it not greatly extending the applicability of the true meaning of this maxim [the king can do no wrong] to apply it to such a case as the present one, when in truth the political power of Her Majesty is not in question, but merely Her Majesty's civil responsibility in a matter of a contract?' The Quebec justice contended that such an extension was inappropriate, and supported his reasoning through an analysis of a wide range of English precedents and legal authorities. Fournier's judgment illustrates the ability of justices from one legal tradition to deal intelligently and effectively with the ideas and approaches of another tradition.

In contrast, Justice Henry's dissent in support of himself fails to establish a reasonable position. Defending his Exchequer Court judgment, Henry admitted that 'in giving the judgement of the Exchequer Court in this case I laid down certain propositions as I thought affecting the positions of the different parties to this suit. I may possibly have laid down some of them a little too strongly – stronger than I intended.' He nevertheless maintained his previous reasoning. Where the government enters into a contract and fails to keep it, the government should be as amenable to the law as a private party. Unfortunately, Henry neglected to rule that a contractual relationship existed in this instance. He would have been on stronger ground had he addressed himself to the negligence of the railway and its responsibility in tort law.

The Queen v *McLeod* thus reflects several of the problems experienced by the Supreme Court bench in these early years. Most of the justices delivered able judgments from time to time, as Fournier did in this instance. The difficulty was that these were occasional. The justices were inconsistent in their willingness to examine a legal issue in a penetrating, well-reasoned manner.

During this period the justices did develop procedures for operating effectively and for carrying out some of the Court's basic judicial functions. Several of the justices, particularly those from English-speaking Canada, actively questioned counsel. Considerable weight was attached to the oral argument of counsel as compared with written facta. And the judges demonstrated a willingness to listen to fresh argument and to adjust their thinking when new precedents were brought to their attention.[60]

The Court's workload increased appreciably. In the years from 1879 to 1892 decisions were rendered on 1,007 cases, an average of 71.9 appeals annually. Of these, 33.8 per cent were upheld by the justices, 52.1 per cent dismissed, 0.2 per cent varied, and 13.1 per cent quashed, settled, or disposed of on preliminary motions (0.8 per cent were references). This was surely a sign that despite all its problems the new institution had become an important cog in the judicial machinery. One indication that public dissatisfaction with the Court was not entirely shared by the legal community is the fact that during the 1880s only fifty-three cases were taken on appeal from the Supreme Court of Canada to the Judicial Committee of the Privy Council; in only twenty-six of these cases did the committee agree to hear the appeal.[61] The Supreme Court was becoming the final court of appeal for the majority of Canadian cases.

The increased workload meant that the number of justices available at the Court presented problems. A quorum was still only one short of the total number of members of the Court, and illnesses or leaves of absence caused delays. H.-E. Taschereau and J.W. Gwynne both received leaves in 1884, at different times. In 1888 it was necessary to summon Justice Taschereau from France so that a quorum could be obtained. In 1889 both Fournier and Ritchie were away on leave.[62] Henry Strong seemed to suffer from ill health throughout the decade, although disillusionment with the Court might also have been a factor in his frequent requests for leave. In 1879, 1880, 1885, and 1890 Strong applied for leave, and received it every time but the first. Several times between 1884 and 1888 Strong actually tendered his resignation. He had stayed on at the prime minister's request, but in 1888 Sir John A. Macdonald finally gave way, writing to the minister of justice: 'I have written Strong. You would grant his pension. He may as well *go*.'[63] Strong did not go, however.

The absences or threatened departures might have been caused in part by the low level of judicial salaries. Several sources point to the difficulty of persuading able lawyers to join the bench and accept a large reduction in their income.[64] The Supreme Court justices' salaries remained unchanged throughout the 1880s ($8,000 for the chief justice and $7,000 for each puisne justice), and they were clearly insufficient. One member of Parliament reported a rumour concerning the financial straits in which the justices found themselves: 'Talking of salaries I may tell you privately that "on dit" here that every Sup. Ct. Judge but Ritchie c.j. has drawn his salary nine months ahead at the Bank. The Bank discounts these notes & when it was said to the manager what a risk he was running his reply was "The Bank counts all that but it wd. be a greater risk to refuse!"'[65] Such financial difficulties could not have made work at the Supreme Court any more enjoyable.

In May 1888 Justice Henry died at the age of seventy-one. During the summer months the justice minister and the prime minister considered possible replacements. In a letter to Macdonald, John Thompson, who had stepped down from the provincial bench in 1885, revealed much regarding the factors that determined appointment to the Supreme Court. The only able man on the Nova Scotia bench, he wrote, was the chief justice. 'He is vastly better than Henry ever was – but that is saying nothing. His good qualities are no doubt known to you. He would be a respectable Judge of the Appeal Court but not a strong one. He has never had the patience or care for detail which are necessary to make a man a sound lawyer unless he has gifts which are not bestowed in his case.'[66] In Thompson's opinion, Wallace Graham was an excellent lawyer, well read, and would make a better judge than the chief justice, but Graham lacked judicial experience, 'which I think is of very great value to a Judge of the highest Appeal Court.' In New Brunswick no one candidate stood out, although several names had been put forward. The selection process was a careful one, and the ministers involved were going out of their way to choose someone who would be a real asset to the Court.

Lacking an obvious nominee from the maritimes, both Thompson and Macdonald, particularly the latter, opted to use the appointment 'to break up the system' of strict regional representation. It was felt that the Ontario bench offered more able candidates than did the maritimes. But the prime minister also had another end in mind: 'We must endeavour to get a good man who will not throw Dominion rights away.'[67] Worried by the constitutional decisions emerging from the Supreme Court and by the challenges to the national government, Macdonald sought to influence the direction of the Court through the appointing process. The press hinted that at least two judges turned down the appointment before Christopher Salmon Patterson of the Ontario Court of Appeal accepted the post.[68]

At the same time that the vacancy was filled, it was rumoured that the government was contemplating having the chief justice step down (if he could be persuaded to do so), to be replaced by John Thompson, the minister of justice. It is true that Thompson toyed with the idea of moving to the Court at this time, but as Henry's replacement. Sir John A. Macdonald, however, had been unwilling to part with his strongest cabinet minister, and the justice minister decided not to press the issue.[69]

In the face of attacks against and problems within the Supreme Court the government proceeded cautiously with reform. In 1880 several minor procedural changes were made, most notably (in response to some complaints) in giving the Court the power to order a new trial.[70] In 1882 a government bill was introduced which attempted to meet Sir John A. Macdonald's 1880 pledge to make substantial changes in the Court.[71] The bill proposed to add to the Supreme Court two judges-in-aid. These junior judges would be selected, on a rotating basis, by the government from a roster consisting of all six members of the Quebec Court of Queen's Bench and all six members of the Quebec Superior Court. At Ottawa the judges-in-aid would sit on civil-law cases, thus making available a minimum of four French-speaking justices trained in the civil law. Unfortunately for the government, the bill was not well received for a variety of reasons – the confusion in the lower courts owing to the loss of personnel; the constant change (and thus instability) of jurists hearing civil-law appeals in Ottawa; and the dangers inherent in permitting judges-in-aid to rule on cases appealed from their own courts. One moderate Conservative member of Parliament from Quebec advised the prime minister privately that, if instituted, the bill would 'render the court more unpopular still, *if possible*.'[72] In response to these objections (including a unanimous resolution from the Montreal bar), the bill was not taken past second reading.

The attacks against the Court in general and the difficulties the bill encountered reinforced Macdonald's inclination to take no action.[73] It would be potentially damaging (to the Court, to the dominion, and to the Conservative party) to open up to debate the subject of the Supreme Court; if the Court was discussed as little as possible, perhaps its profile would be lowered and it could simply get on with its work. The problem with this strategy, of course, was that the Court was forced to continue to work within the structure of the existing act; no positive alterations were to be made by the government.

This is not to suggest that amendments did not continue to be proposed. In 1882 H.-E. Taschereau suggested to the prime minister that appeals from Quebec should cease in all cases except those involving criminal, constitutional, or election law (essentially the proposal of Landry). One year later Justice Gwynne made some detailed suggestions regarding Exchequer Court procedure. In 1880 Henry Strong had forcefully recommended severing the Exchequer Court from the Supreme Court. This was Strong's method of removing William Henry from the Supreme Court (he would become the sole member of the separate Exchequer Court), but it was also a positive proposal for coping with some of the Supreme Court's problems.[74]

That the justices individually could advise the government of the day on minor procedural and broad policy matters relating to the Supreme Court is an indication of the close link between the judiciary and the cabinet. That link was widely perceived to be a source of strength and stability in Canadian society. Government leaders saw the courts as one of a variety of institutions through which political plans for the nation might be achieved.[75] In the Ontario-Manitoba boundary dispute, for example, Prime Minister Macdonald informed the justice minister, 'By skilful steering we can go before the Privy Council with three Courts deciding in our favour: 1. Queen's Bench, Quebec – Reinhart's Case; 2. Queen's Bench, Manitoba; 3. Supreme Court, Canada. This will be of incalculable advantage to us in England.'[76] But if the politicians were making use of the Supreme Court, the justices were making use of the politicians, hoping to influence judicial appointments or the nomination of queen's counsel.[77]

Of more direct benefit was the judges' ability to encourage structural changes in the Supreme Court. Strong's suggestion of separating the Supreme Court and the Exchequer Court was adopted by the government in 1886 and introduced in 1887.[78] Exchequer cases involved considerable time and effort for both the staff and justices of the Supreme Court. When the Exchequer Court sat in Ottawa it was a simple matter to use Supreme Court facilities, but it was not so easy when cases were tried in Halifax, Montreal, or Toronto. Special arrangements were required to make use of local facilities; a rota was established for the justices who had to travel to these various cities. The severance of the two courts relieved the justices and staff of a good deal of laborious work. That the government was willing to sponsor such legislation is a sure sign, along with the cessation of Landry's bills, that political discussion of the Supreme Court was becoming politically safe. Indeed, Edward Blake's 1890 proposal for an expanded use of the reference procedure to offset any sense of partiality in the federal government's use of disallowance is surely a sign that the Supreme Court of Canada was perhaps not merely tolerated but seen as an institution of some impartiality and of some positive function.[79]

Other changes were soon implemented. The Supreme Court registrar was given the authority to sit as a judge in chambers, thus facilitating the hearing of motions and the issuing of various minor orders. Other minor changes were made in 1888 and 1889.[80] One proposal that did not gain approval was Edward Blake's 1882 motion that the printed records in the courts below be accepted for appeals to the Supreme Court, avoiding the costly practice of a separate printing of the records for the Court. The chief justice disagreed, pointing out that the Supreme Court had repeatedly discouraged unnecessary reprinting of records.[81] These various amendments, when they were finally put forward, resulted in positive change for the Court.   .

Another area where change was required was in accommodations. The Court had spent its first five years in rooms in the Parliament buildings. Lacking a permanent home, the institution may have seemed transitory or weak, an image that probably encouraged those who opposed the Supreme Court.

The lack of permanent accommodation was, at least in part, simply a matter of circumstances, although it also reflected government priorities. In 1876, in the midst of an economic recession, the Mackenzie government, already opposed on principle to large-scale government spending, had set aside plans to construct a Supreme Court building. The Macdonald government, after coming to office in the fall of 1878, presumably deferred action because of the attacks against the Court. A proposal for a permanent home would be likely to draw further attention toward the institution, and any scheme that involved spending large sums on behalf of the Court was certain to attract the ire of critics.

The Macdonald government, however, did eventually demonstrate its basic commitment to the enduring presence of the Supreme Court. Early in 1881 plans were drawn up to refurbish a building formerly used as stables and workshops. Located at the southwest corner of the West Block, the building was an attractive two-storey gabled stone structure in the Parliament Hill style of the day. The building's origins were a source of denigration of the Court over the next fifty years and more. Small and unpretentious as the structure was, the Supreme Court was not even given full use of the building. The first floor was designated, despite the protests of the chief justice, as the first home of the national art gallery – a sign of the continuing inferior status of the Court.[82]

The building's outward appearance was altered to make it more ornate, particularly by adding gabled windows to light the second-floor courtroom. The first floor contained offices for the staff and rooms for counsel, as well as the 'Picture Gallery.' On the second floor were rooms for the justices, a judicial conference room, consulting and waiting rooms, and the courtroom. There was no law library for the use of counsel, and Chief Justice Ritchie hoped to use the space occupied by the art gallery for that purpose.[83]

The Supreme Court moved into its first permanent home early in 1882,[84] but it was not long before space limitations and the condition of the building began to cause problems. There were complaints about the unsuitable site, about the 'dreadful' smell that pervaded the building, and about the distance to the parliamentary library.[85] In 1887 a major report was forwarded to the Justice Department and the Public Works Department detailing the weaknesses of the courthouse. The courtroom was too small and the ceiling leaked; there was no room to dispose of chamber business, motions, taxation, bills of costs, and other such items, so that the justices dealt with these matters in their own small offices; the lack of a library necessitated using the walls and windows of the conference room for shelving space, thus causing frequent interruptions by readers to the justices' meetings; storage space for books had been exhausted, and the registrar had been forced to resort to the attic ('reached by a step ladder') to store his Reports; the location of the rooms meant that the justices had no privacy, since the corridor outside their offices was used as a public thoroughfare. The chief justice, the report went on, complained 'of the discomfort, inconvenience and bad ventilation of his room, as well as of the general unsuitable nature and insufficiency of the accommodation provided for the Court and the Judges.'[86]

In 1887 the art gallery was moved out of the building, but most of the space was required for the newly separate Exchequer Court.[87] Two years later, in 1889, plans were formulated for a proposed major extension to the Supreme Court building. When Chief Justice Ritchie was shown the plans, his response was disparaging.

Much as I would assuredly [?] appreciate the improved accommodation I cannot help regretting that money would be spent on the present unsuitable building. It appears to me that the contemplated expenditure with a moderate amount added would be quite sufficient to defray the cost of a Building suitable & proper for holding the sittings of the highest Court in the dominion. I do not think any amount expended on the present building will make it satisfactory.

Given the position and status of the Supreme Court, he argued, surely a suitable building in a proper location would be fitting. He feared that any expenditure on the present courthouse would effectively prevent necessary basic changes.[88] Ritchie's fears proved well founded.

The government, however, had no intention of erecting a new courthouse. The Department of Justice procrastinated. A leading cabinet minister, Sir H.-L. Langevin, minister of public works, informed the deputy minister of justice 'that a new Courthouse will never be built in his day.' Indeed, for years after, rumour in Ottawa had it that Langevin had been the major opponent of a new building, all because the Supreme Court had found against the minister in a 1877 controverted elections case, declaring the Commons seat vacant and requiring Langevin to pay all court costs. Such spite is not entirely unbelievable, but the minister's opposition was supported by others. The deputy minister of justice, for example, advised his minister that a new building would not be 'justified.'[89] Instead, the old building, improved, would have to make do.

In 1890 a construction contract was let for $10,765, a figure which, by the completion of the contract, had grown to $30,457.[90] This paid for a major addition to the existing structure. A basement (which the original section lacked), two additional storeys, and an attic were constructed, almost doubling the size of the courthouse. Extending north toward the river, the new section was seventy-one feet long and forty-seven feet wide. On the outside it was finished in a style corresponding in material and detail to the existing structure. The judges' rooms were moved into the new section, and several old offices were knocked down to make room for a law library. When combined with the private entrance that the justices insisted upon, the new arrangement afforded privacy and a suitable facility for the growing number of law books and reports. Several other rooms were refurbished, and stairs replaced the ladder to the attic.[91]

The addition and the internal alterations ended most of the complaints about the building. Ritchie's basic criticism remained unresolved: the courthouse did not represent the high status that the Supreme Court deserved. But given the opinion of the public and the political leaders at this time, the physical representation of the Supreme Court of Canada was probably an accurate reflection of its position in the Canadian political structure.

3

The Strong Court
1892–1902

The structure and practice of the Supreme Court of Canada have always been such that the chief justice has not had the power to impose his authority on his fellow justices; instead, the chief justice's leadership on the Court has been dependent on the force of his personality. Only one chief justice has ever truly dominated the Supreme Court of Canada – Sir Henry Strong. But his dominance was not leadership. Strong's irascible and argumentative temperament facilitated his control over the Court and created problems among his colleagues and with members of the bar. Despite Strong's overweening hand, however, there were several (sometimes subtle) signs that the Court was improving.

After several years of stability in the Court's personnel, the 1890s proved to be a period of change and controversy. Chief Justice Ritchie, in his seventy-ninth year, had been suffering from ill health and had applied for an extended leave of absence; his previous vigour had begun to ebb and the quality of his judgments had been publicly perceived to be slipping.[1] In September 1892 Chief Justice Ritchie died, followed ten months later by the most recent recruit, C.S. Patterson.

The Conservative government now had a chief justiceship and two vacancies to fill. Rumours and suggestions abounded regarding the chief justiceship. It was frequently mentioned, with approval, that Sir John Thompson himself (who did not become prime minister until December 1892) was attracted by the post. But it was difficult for Thompson to abandon a party and a government that lacked an alternative leader. Thompson's appointment to the Court would have pleased several commentators who argued that promotion by seniority should not be allowed to become an entrenched practice. Others pointed to the Supreme Court's weak image and hoped that an appointment from outside the Court might be used to bolster the institution's stature and to strengthen its position.[2] One of the chief Conservative advisers in legal matters, Senator J.R. Gowan, was particularly opposed to the automatic promotion of the most senior puisne justice, S.H. Strong. Soon after Ritchie's death, Gowan wrote to Thompson:

I suppose Strong will be looking for the place [of chief justice]. He at one time expressed anxiety to retire. It might be expedient to allow him to leave, with a better retiring allowance. If he could be *trusted to come down* at the proper time – I mean when his ability for work was on the down grade, but like the Archbishop of Gil Blas, – he might not be easy to convince in that direction –

I do not myself see that the public interests could suffer, if the appointment of a new Chief was postponed for a season. Gwynne and Patterson are great workers any way.

Two weeks later, the senator returned to the same theme. 'The Supreme Court needs badly no doubt a general accession of working men, but unless Strong has turned over a new leaf his appointment as CJ would not help much I think. I have no faith in the man in any way. Why not leave things as they are for a time.'[3] Gowan was a former county court judge of excellent reputation, and his assessment of the Supreme Court and some of its members carried weight. In particular, his emphasis on the weakness of the work ethic at the Court stands out.

Gowan's advice was not followed, however. One week after assuming the office of prime minister, Thompson promoted Henry Strong to be the Court's third chief justice. Over the following decade it became apparent that the selection was a poor one. No one could question Strong's intellectual capacity or his interest in the civil law and the French language, but some of his personality characteristics were decidedly abrasive. Gowan's concern regarding the new chief justice's industriousness was only part of the problem.[4]

Two vacancies remained to be filled. With Ritchie gone there was no longer a maritimer on the Court, and it is not surprising that Thompson, a Nova Scotian, moved to fill that void. Robert Sedgewick had had a long-standing association with the prime minister as a Nova Scotia Conservative, as a Halifax lawyer, and as deputy minister of justice in Ottawa from 1888 to 1893. Raised in Nova Scotia, Sedgewick commenced a successful legal practice there in 1873. A specialist in equity law, he held a lectureship in this field at the Dalhousie law school. A supporter of the Conservative party (and of John Thompson in particular), Sedgewick had been active in municipal, provincial, and federal politics. In 1885 he became recorder for Halifax, and shortly thereafter began to solicit from the new minister of justice a position on the Nova Scotia Supreme Court. Instead, Thompson brought him to Ottawa to be deputy minister of justice. In that position Sedgewick became familiar with the Canadian Supreme Court through his administrative duties and through his appearance as counsel before the Court.[5] Aged forty-four at his appointment, Sedgewick, it was hoped, would bring new vigour to the bench. Now three of the four common-law justices were specialists in equity.

The vacancy created by Patterson's death went to a maritimer despite growing rumblings from the west about lack of representation. George King, the son of a local shipbuilder, had been born and raised in Saint John, New Brunswick. In 1865 he joined a law practice in his native city and soon began to turn his attention to political affairs. As a Conservative member of the provincial assembly from 1867 to 1878, King joined the provincial cabinet in 1869, serving as attorney-general (1870–8) and premier (1872–8). Defeated in the federal election of 1878, he was appointed two years later to the Supreme Court of New Brunswick. On the bench he earned an excellent reputation for the soundness and quality of his judgments. King was mentioned as a possible appointment to Ottawa as early as 1888, and thus his promotion in 1893 came as no surprise – indeed, he had carefully let the prime minister, with whom he was on friendly terms, know that he was not averse to joining the Supreme Court. King was a specialist in commercial law as well as criminal law. Sir Henry Strong, a man not easily given to the distribution of compliments, praised King's ability: 'He was a great lawyer, especially in the department of commercial law. He was probably the best commercial lawyer in the Dominion, especially familiar with shipping law and commercial law generally in its larger sense.'[6]

Despite this infusion of new blood, the government remained concerned about the personnel of the Supreme Court. Age and infirmity were becoming apparent. Every one of the four standing members of the Court took at least one leave of absence during the 1890s; some took several. Though the justices were not remarkably old (except for Gwynne, who turned eighty in the spring of 1894) they were definitely slowing down. This was, of course, in an age when retirement at a prescribed age was still uncommon.[7] The Thompson government approached the matter indirectly, using the carrot rather than the stick. A motion was introduced into the House of Commons, and passed despite Liberal opposition, to allow any justice of the Supreme Court of Canada who had reached age seventy and served in the judiciary at least fifteen years (including at least five at the Supreme Court) to retire with a lifetime pension equal to 100 per cent of his salary.[8] The effect of the resolution was to make Gwynne eligible for the special pension immediately; Fournier would become eligible within two months, and Strong within fourteen months.

This alone, however, was not enough to stir these justices. Early 1895 the new minister of justice, Sir Charles Hibbert Tupper, began to apply the stick. The chief justice (with whom Tupper had already spoken) was informed that both Gwynne and Fournier would be asked to retire, possibly at full salary. Tupper added, 'Writing to you in strict confidence I am prepared, I may say, in the event of a refusal to bring in a Bill next session, which would enable the Government to prevent [the] possibility of the present state of things, to the great injury of commerce and of justice.' At the same time the justice minister instructed the Supreme Court registrar to supply information as to the age, attendance record, and cases delayed by absences of the two oldest justices.[9]

The search for ammunition against Gwynne and Fournier was fairly successful. During the six Court sittings of 1893 and 1894, Gwynne had been absent owing to illness on twenty days as well as on leave for five and a half months (including a further half of one sitting). These absences had necessitated adjournment of the Supreme Court for lack of a quorum on four separate occasions, for a total of eleven sitting days. Fournier had not been absent, except for a leave of absence covering one full term.[10] In these responses, the registrar answered the questions posed but went no further. The chief justice, although not called upon to respond, went out of his way to approve of and co-operate with the justice minister's actions, thus abetting a direct violation of the supposed institutional independence of the judiciary. Fournier, Strong pointed out, had been absent in 1891-2 and in 1894, both times on official leave. Moreover, the Quebec jurist, who was clearly 'in very bad health' and was reportedly suffering from Bright's disease, was unlikely to be able to withstand the heavy work of the upcoming session. Strong testified as to Fournier's value to the

Court: 'He is very amiable and courteous and is popular with his colleagues ... I miss him very much as he has an excellent knowledge of his own law, that of Lower Canada in which he had great experience.'[11] Justice Gwynne, however, was a different story. Strong was not concerned about the number of Gwynne's absences and the adjournments caused by them; apart from attacks of gout, Strong reported, Gwynne's health and level of activity were good for his age. It was Gwynne's personality that was impaired:

What I complain of is the quality of his work – his extreme senile irritability and constant attacks upon myself even in Court. Further he has refused to attend conferences and his method of doing his work, is to write his judgements without any consultation and then call on the other judges to agree with him, shewing much wrath if they venture to differ. I am afraid he and I cannot get on together and if he will not or cannot be made to give way I am afraid I must.[12]

Given this picture of an aged, quarrelsome Court, it is no wonder that the Conservative governments of the day sought to alter the personnel.

Strong felt that Tupper's means of forcing retirement would not work.[13] Rather than holding out the mere possibility of a 100 per cent pension (which the chief justice estimated would not be strong enough temptation for either justice), he recommended that they be forced off the bench outright. 'I do not think it would be unreasonable that a law should be passed compelling retirement at 80. Although the Statute does not say so it is implied that a judge will take his retirement when from age he becomes incapacitated and no man is fit for judicial work after 80. The same may be said of a man who is disabled by chronic illness.'[14] With this carte blanche from the chief justice, the minister of justice was free to proceed. Tupper immediately communicated with both Fournier and Gwynne. The Quebec justice was clearly amenable to retirement. He lasted through the winter sitting of 1895, even though he was operating at reduced capacity,[15] and was given a leave of absence until September on the understanding that he would resign at that time. Seriously ill (he died in May 1896), Fournier had little choice but to retire. Money was clearly the one factor that made the decision difficult. In September Fournier sent a pathetic note from his home, asking that his salary be extended one more month. The government refused.[16]

The Quebec vacancy on the Supreme Court bench was reportedly first offered to A.R. Angers, who had recently resigned from the cabinet in protest over the handling of the Manitoba schools question. The Conservatives' traditional strength in Quebec was weakening, and an attempt to regain the public loyalty of one of the more important Quebec leaders made political sense. Angers, however, though he would have made a respectable appointee, was not to be enticed.[17]

The government then turned to the long-time Conservative member of Parliament, Désiré Girouard. Born in 1836, he had received his formal legal education at McGill University, where he had worked with an outstanding corporate lawyer and future prime minister, J.J.C. Abbott. After being called to the bar in 1860, Girouard established his practice in Montreal. He also demonstrated an interest in legal scholarship; he published a number of articles, particularly on marriage law, bankruptcy, and bills of exchange, and he was a founding editor and a major contributor to the *Revue Critique de Législation et de Jurisprudence du Canada* (1871–4). Girouard wrote two books on the law, one on bankruptcy in 1865 and one on bills of exchange in 1890.[18] In the 1870s he turned to politics to supplement his legal activities and served as a Conservative representative for Montreal in the House of Commons from 1878 to 1895. In Parliament he attacked the Supreme Court in its early years. How he was able to rationalize joining an institution that he had so opposed is unknown. Since those early attacks, he had rejected offers of appointment to lower courts, and had stood out in the House for his impartial handling of the hearings in the McGreevy–Langevin scandal in 1891.[19] Girouard brought to the Supreme Court a good legal reputation and a wide knowledge of the law, particularly in the commercial sphere, but he had no judicial experience.[20]

Retiring and replacing Justice Gwynne was not easy. In February the justice minister wrote to Gwynne as he had to Fournier. The Ontario justice apparently agreed to step down. Seven months later Tupper asked Gwynne to continue work for the time being because the Ontario members of cabinet had been unable to supply a suitable nominee to the Court. A few days later it was clear that at least two names had been put forward – Judges Rose and Ferguson of Ontario – and that the latter had been offered and had declined the promotion. Tupper once again asked Gwynne to stay on at the Supreme Court. The minister of justice did attempt to deal with some of the immediate problems raised by Chief Justice Strong's presence. Gwynne was asked to attend the judicial conferences so that newspaper comment would cease. 'It will not be long before you have relief,' continued Tupper, 'and meanwhile I pray you do all you can to pour oil on the trouble[d] water.'[21]

The manoeuvrings that took place during 1895 show the Conservative government of Sir Mackenzie Bowell in a new light. Some positive and forceful steps were taken in attempts to improve (as the government viewed it) the Supreme Court of Canada. General accounts of political affairs in that year portray the cabinet as so caught up in its own internal divisions and in the quandary of how to deal with the Manitoba schools question that it had no time or energy for dealing with other, minor problems. These incidents reveal activist elements within the cabinet, in this case led by Sir C.H. Tupper. Quebec-based personnel within the Conservative Party were obviously willing and able to co-operate with his initiatives, while Ontario-based leaders were not. The failure of the justice minister's activities relating to the Ontario post on the bench reveals further the serious divisions in the government (which would soon erupt in open revolt) and the debilitating effects of those divisions on the government's ability to govern.

The attempts to force retirement, the repeated absences of several justices, and the problems caused by Chief Justice Strong's personality naturally resulted in instability on the Court. Equally unfortunate was the entrenchment of the public's generally negative perception of the institution. A Toronto law journal commented in 1896 that 'this Court has long lacked the confidence of the Bar, both in the English-speaking provinces and in Quebec, and the present state of affairs will minimize what confidence still exists.'[22]

The Laurier government, which took office in the summer of 1896, was much more cautious in its dealings with Supreme Court personnel than the Bowell government had been. In 1898, when a vacancy on the bench occurred, effective action was quickly taken. On the death of Robert Cassels, the first registrar and an influential figure in helping the Court achieve what stability and stature it had, Edward Cameron was promptly named to the post.[23] But without a death or a voluntary retirement on the bench itself, the Laurier government was not about to risk any political strength in trying to force retirements.

The new government was active, however, in lining up its nominees for prospective vacancies. David Mills, a prominent member of the Liberal party, was promised Gwynne's post whenever it became available. As several years passed and the seat remained occupied, the government became frustrated; Mills quoted the prime minister as saying, 'He [Gwynne] must retire. We will impeach him if he does not.'[24] But this was bluster. The cabinet was willing to use such posts to reward friends, but not to create enemies. Justice Gwynne apparently was still willing to consider retirement, and his health was somewhat poor, necessitating a leave of absence in the spring of 1896. Nevertheless, the government was unwilling to pursue the matter or to make retirement financially more attractive to the Ontario justice. Laurier wrote late in 1900, '[Gwynne] is now nearly ninety years of age, & really his usefulness is gone through physical weakness.' Because of Gwynne's age and his physical frailty the government expected that death or voluntary retirement would soon remove the justice.[25] Until then no action would be taken.

At the same time the retirement of the chief justice began to be discussed. Strong had been chief justice for five years and had recently been appointed to the Judicial Committee of the Privy Council; the government hoped that with this newly enhanced stature Strong would be willing to retire from the Supreme Court at the convenience of the government. The cabinet wanted Edward Blake to be the new chief justice. Offers of appointment were made in the fall of 1896 and of 1897, but the eminent Canadian counsel was unwilling to accept.[26] Blake's refusal was unfortunate, for the Supreme Court would have benefited from Strong's retirement.

The chief justice was continuing to create a number of problems both in and for the Court. He 'overshadowed everybody' on the bench, as one contemporary observer put it,[27] but he dominated without leading. His temper was quick and at times uncontrolled. A legal journal recounted one confrontation brought on by Strong's irascibility. An Ottawa barrister was arguing a habeas corpus case which the justices were not inclined to hear:

... the lawyer remarked that the Statute imposed certain duties upon Supreme Court judges which they could not endeavor to shirk. 'I am not going to sit here and listen to language of that sort,' remarked Mr. Justice Strong in a rather angry tone. 'What is that, Mr. Strong?' queried the lawyer, who had not apparently heard his lordship's remark. 'Mr. Strong:' roared the judge, now thoroughly enraged. 'Is that the way to address a judge of the Supreme Court? I leave the bench.' And with these words he left for the library. The lawyer tried to go on, but as there had only been five judges sitting, there was no quorum. At last *Mr.* Strong was sent for, and when he took his seat the lawyer apologized for his *faux pas*.[28]

A London, Ontario, barrister also complained of Strong's courtroom behaviour. The lawyer had been so incensed by Strong's handling of *The King* v *Love* (1901) that an unemotional interview with the minister of justice was impossible. Instead, he made a written complaint, asserting that the 'conduct of the Chief Justice, silently acquiesced in by the rest of the Court, was brutally despotic.' Not content with Canadian channels, the lawyer informed the colonial secretary at Westminister about Strong's behaviour, but of course nothing came of it.[29]

Strong's intemperate behaviour was further illustrated in a 1901 incident in which an Ottawa lawyer laid assault charges against the chief justice. He alleged that Strong had used violent language in court and had later accosted and assaulted the barrister in the hallway outside the courtroom. (The fact that the lawyer was currently leading a campaign to compel the justices to wear wigs may have had something to do with the altercation.) The chief justice denied the allegations, and when the story appeared in the press urged the government to prosecute the newspaper for criminal libel.[30] The government chose to ignore the affair. Whether or not the assault actually occurred, the incident is indicative of the problems Strong's behaviour created.

Potentially more damaging, both for the government and for the court, was an 1898 cause célèbre. Sir Henry had long been known for his intolerant attitude toward the unskilled workers employed at the Supreme Court. The messengers and ushers in particular had frequently suffered from his sharp tongue, and on several occasions he had registered official complaints with the registrar and the justice department, sometimes resulting in a dismissal. One worker, who was lame and partially blind by the late 1890s, drew Strong's repeated ire; presumably it was this messenger who was involved in the following incident. In the fall of 1898, while sitting on the case of *Chicoutimi* v *Price*, the chief justice asked counsel for the names of judges who had heard the case in the courts below. As counsel was answering, Justice Taschereau called Strong's attention to the conduct of one of the court officers; the chief justice reacted by stating, in a voice loud enough to be heard in the courtroom, that the worker was evidently incapable and ought to be dismissed. Not having heard Taschereau's comment, those in attendance in court assumed that Sir Henry's criticism referred to the judge in the court below.[31] Any such statement would, of course, have been completely inappropriate. That Strong's comment was given credence was in turn a reflection of the existing image of the chief justice. He was already well known for his intemperate, crotchety behaviour and his injudicious conduct. The incident was made more serious because the case was on appeal from Quebec; it was assumed that the attack was being made by an arrogant English-speaking judge against a French-Canadian jurist. The

French-speaking lawyers reacted quickly and forcefully. The Quebec bar voiced its anger and called for the censure and retirement of the chief justice. The incident prompted other similar complaints. Ottawa counsel, for example, joined in the chorus of protest. As the Ottawa *Citizen* reported,

Yesterday morning it leaked out in the court house that some of them [Ottawa lawyers] had great grievances to utter against the treatment they received from Chief Justice Strong while arguing their cases before the court. They say that as a rule they were treated by the chief justice in anything but a polite manner, and this week more than ever. While pleading a case one of the lawyers referred to the opinion of a certain judge of this district, whereupon the chief justice, it appears, remarked that he was only a local judge, and when the opinions of three other judges were given, the chief justice is reported as having said that it would be better for them to leave the bench.[32]

Such conduct was intolerable on the bench, and the stature of the Supreme Court was not so great that such revelations would do no harm.

Unfortunately, this incident in the fall of 1898 came on the heels of another episode in May of that year. The details are complicated, but the essence of the affair was that the timing of the hearing of cases at the Court had unexpectedly speeded up and counsel in Toronto and Chatham, Ontario, were given less than twenty-four hours' warning that their presence was required in Ottawa; counsel's inability to reach Ottawa in time and the chief justice's stringent application of procedural rules resulted in the dismissal of the appeal and the rejection of a motion to rehear the case. The appeal was lost unheard, and the public and the Ontario bar were scandalized. Injustice had been done; the essential purpose of the Supreme Court had been ignored by insistence on a rigid interpretation of procedural rules and 'because a Judge loses his temper.' The justices, it was pointed out, should consider the obligations of counsel occasionally rather than simply their own convenience.[33]

The bar showed its anger much more effectively than did the newspapers. Resolutions attacking the Court's conduct were passed and forwarded to the minister of justice; lawyers communicated directly with the minister, and a movement began within the Ontario bar, led by the highly respected B.B. Osler, to persuade the government to retire both Strong and Gwynne and to rejuvenate the Supreme Court. The minister, David Mills, summoned Justice H.-E. Taschereau before him to discuss the case; that the interview was with Taschereau rather than with Strong himself is an indication that at least part of the responsibility for the incident lay with the chief justice and that the government considered that the affair could not be easily remedied simply by approaching Strong. Mills was upset, and threatened the Court with legislative action:

[I] pointed out to him [Taschereau] that unless the Supreme Court took a proper view of their duty towards clients and counsel, it would be absolutely necessary to legislate upon the subject, to prevent the miscarriage of justice by proceedings so arbitrary and so capricious as those adopted in the case of Hall vs. Moore. Judge Taschereau deprecates legislation, and says he hopes we may be able to adopt some rule that would have the effect of meeting the convenience of counsel, and doing justice to litigants, without Parliament intervening to coerce the court against the abuse of this power.[34]

Effective leadership of the Court was, at least at times, passing from Strong's hands.

The reaction against Sir Henry Strong in the summer and fall of 1898 revealed an existing and long-standing discontent. The specific incidents that occurred in that year merely provided an opportunity for the bar to express its vexation with the chief justice. But the calls for new blood and for a more effective Court were becoming a constant refrain.

It was not merely Strong's bad temper that caused problems for the Court; at times he acted in a petty manner and against the best interests of justice. In the case of *Stephens v McArthur*, for example, argument was heard in January 1890, but judgment was not handed down until November. Since the case involved questions affecting the validity of every chattel mortgage and bill of sale issued in the prairies, lawyers in the west were naturally eager to learn the reasons for judgment. The Law Society of Manitoba telegraphed to the Supreme Court for a copy of the judgments, which it planned to have printed immediately in the *Western Law Times*. Henry Strong, who wrote the majority judgment, refused to allow it to be copied until it had been printed in the Supreme Court Reports.[35] What purpose could be served by such a refusal is unknown. To decline to make available its judgment was directly contrary to the function and purpose of the Supreme Court of Canada. Strong did great disservice to the efficient functioning of the law and to the Court. Perhaps the real reason for his refusal to release the judgment was that it was not yet written, since this was so typical of his work habits; if true, it would have been far better for him to have said so.

The need for a replacement for Strong was becoming increasingly apparent. The Ontario justice had long suffered from bouts of illness, which may have caused him to proffer his resignation in 1887. Through the 1890s he soldiered on, but found it necessary to absent himself from the Court because of illness in 1892, 1893 (six months' leave), 1897 (six months' leave), 1898, 1900, 1901 (two months' leave), and 1902 (three months' leave). His health problems were varied. In 1897 Strong's doctor 'certified that he greatly needed rest and change; that he had no organic trouble; but that his nervous system was seriously out of order – that in fact it has been more or less for years.' To Edward Blake, such a vague ailment was not sufficient justification for these extended absences:

I cannot conceive that it is for the interest of Canadian suitors, or accordant with the spirit of the law, that the head of the Supreme Court should, when not incapacitated by illness, be absent from his Court. It seems that the Chief Justice absented himself during the whole of the last Sittings, and is absenting himself during the whole of these [Fall 1897] Sittings, under leave, though perfectly well. It is supposed by some that this leave was granted with reference to his appointment to the Judicial Committee; but, surely, Canadian suitors have a right to the benefit of the services of the head of the Court in the Supreme Court of Canada.

Later, Sir Henry was reported to be suffering from 'Rheumatic Gout,' from insomnia, and from injuries received in an accident involving a runaway horse.[36]

Whatever the medical cause, Blake was quite right in saying that the Supreme Court was severely weakened when its chief was repeatedly absent. His comings and goings and the uncertainties caused by his sporadic disposition to resign must have created a great deal of instability and unrest within the Court. Strong did not get along with Justice Gwynne; he informed the new Liberal minister of justice that one reason retirement was attractive was Gwynne's continued presence. There is, however, some evidence of friendship between the chief justice and Justice Girouard.[37]

Even when he was on the job, physical frailties hindered Strong in his work. He was still the major cause of delay in publishing the Supreme Court Reports; an 1892 account indicated that in fifteen judgments delay was caused by the justices, and in all but one of these it was Strong who was at fault. In 1893 Sir Henry persuaded the Department of Justice to hire a temporary stenographer to help him catch up with his work. The new employee soon became a permanent secretary to the chief justice, but before long Strong needed even more assistance. By 1901 Strong was objecting to dictating his reasons for judgment to the secretary, because he now found it impossible to draft his decisions if anyone else was in the room; could he instead have a phonograph for dictation purposes, since his rheumatism made writing quite painful?[38]

According to one minister of justice, Strong had considerable difficulty in judging personalities. The chief justice had commented on the abilities of several maritime justices; in the minister's opinion, 'Strong however knows very little of the men — probably never saw any of them and must be very defective in his judgement of men for he has been known to praise our Judge James who is simply a dangerous fool.'[39] Such weakness in assessing the competency of others must have seriously impaired Sir Henry's effectiveness in dealing with his fellow justices and with counsel, and helps to explain the various contretemps in which he frequently found himself.

It is unfortunate that the Laurier government did not act to replace the chief justice. Strong was apparently willing to leave, and at the government's convenience, provided a larger income could be secured from some source – for example, from sitting on the Judicial Committee of the Privy Council. The chief justice suggested Elzéar Taschereau as his successor, but in 1897 the government was obviously not enamoured of the idea of promoting the senior puisne justice. When Edward Blake declined appointment, the government apparently looked no further, and asked Sir Henry to remain as chief justice until a successor could be found.[40]

Such an arrangement could not go on forever. For one thing, Justice Taschereau was losing his patience. Frequently required to assume the workload and responsibilities of a chief justice, he received no recompense, tangible or otherwise. In 1897 he requested extra pay while he was acting chief justice, and was unsuccessful. Four years later he was more forceful; he asked that next time Strong went away, someone else on the Court – Gwynne, for instance – be named to shoulder the extra duties.

A Court not presided over by its Chief, it has well been said, is a disabled court. May I be allowed to take this opportunity to submit to your consideration, should in the future the Chief Justice be unfortunately again prevented from sitting, that, as it has been my lot to so often replace him for years past, it would be fair that Mr.

Justice Gwynne, as the next senior, should in his turn be asked by you to do so. Extra unremunerated duties should, when possible, be divided among us.[41]

This growing pressure from the bench to take action was reflected politically. Early in 1901, when Strong sought another six months' leave of absence, the cabinet initially rejected the request as not 'in the public interest'; later a two-month leave was granted. Questions were asked in the House.[42]

Finally, late in 1902, after several years of rumours that his departure was imminent, Sir Henry Strong took his leave of the Supreme Court of Canada. An active, effective, and influential minister of justice, Charles Fitzpatrick, had apparently found the appropriate incentive: Sir Henry would receive remuneration in addition to his pension through his appointment as chairman of the commission to revise and consolidate the public statutes of Canada.

Since 1901 the government had been actively considering various prospective replacements for Strong. What was needed, wrote the prime minister, was a 'man who could give to the Court a prestige and authority which, unfortunately, it has not.' Edward Blake's name was brought forward again, as were those of Chief Justice Armour and Chancellor Boyd, both of Ontario.[43] But in the end, Elzéar Taschereau, as the senior puisne justice, received the honour.

The details of the attempts to retire some of the Supreme Court members make clear how important money was. The point was made repeatedly that a justice could be eased out only if the financial blow of his reduced income could be cushioned. That John Gwynne never did retire, preferring to remain in office at full salary until he died early in 1902 (at age eighty-seven), is illustrative of the problem. Supreme Court salaries, on which pensions were based, had not altered since the founding of the institution. By the 1890s, public opinion was beginning to hold that judicial salaries in the dominion were no longer adequate. One legal journal published a table indicating that throughout the self-governing colonies of the British Empire only two (Tasmania and Natal) paid their chief justice and puisne justices less than the dominion; the Australian colony of Victoria offered salaries more than twice as large.[44] The general price index had declined during the last three decades of the nineteenth century, so that the purchasing power of the justices' fixed income actually improved slightly. By 1900, however, prices had begun to rise and the justices' income gradually fell behind.[45] It is possible that lawyers' incomes were rising in the 1880s and 1890s; this would help to explain some of the problems in recruiting men to the bench. Weak pension benefits, in particular the lack of protection for a justice's widow, were also a problem.[46] Yet the governments of the day were either unwilling or politically unable to do anything about such issues.

The annual costs of the Supreme Court had been steadily rising, from $54,530 in 1880, to $60,840 in 1890, to $66,087 in 1900. The staff had slowly increased; by the turn of the century there were eleven employees (six more than in 1880) – a registrar, a reporter, an assistant reporter, a librarian, two clerks in the registrar's office, one secretary for the justices, one caretaker, and three messengers.[47] Expenses associated with the Court came under careful scrutiny by the opposition (no matter which party) and were frequently the subject of partisan complaint. In 1900 the minister of justice made it clear that the objections to an expensive Supreme Court were still influential in the House. 'The difficulty in connection with the Supreme Court,' David Mills confided privately to a fellow cabinet member, 'is that I find our friends ready to kick at every suggestion of any additional expense, maintaining that it costs altogether too much for what it does.'[48]

The Supreme Court seemed to be caught in a vicious circle. Its weak reputation persuaded many that little money should be spent on it. Any attempts to improve the institution were met by that objection. Yet the Court's perceived failure to improve was a justification for refusal to implement any innovative changes that might increase its budget.

One example of the inhibiting effect of this attitude will suffice. The Court had long been troubled by the small number of justices. The availability of only one justice beyond the number needed for a quorum gave the Court too little flexibility. Given the personal and health problems that regularly appeared among men of the justices' age group, the potential for conflict of interest necessitating withdrawal, and the growing tendency to use the justices for extra-Supreme Court functions, it was often difficult, if not impossible, to raise a quorum. The obvious answer to this was to appoint one or more additional justices, a proposition made even more attractive by the increasing demand in western Canada for representation on the Supreme Court bench. But at no time in this period does any government appear to have considered seriously any such proposal. To suggest an increase in the number of puisne justices would be to risk public debate about the costs and value of the Supreme Court as an institution. No government was willing to accept the risk.

Instead, both the Liberal and Conservative governments of the day sought to deal with the problem of too small a bench 'on the cheap.' It has already been seen that in 1882 the Macdonald government tentatively put forward and then withdrew a proposal to co-opt justices from lower courts in Quebec. In 1888 the same government suggested that the quorum be defined as four justices in cases of temporary absence or incapacitation; this bill was withdrawn when the immediate problem at the Court was solved.[49] A similar solution came from Justice Taschereau in 1892 but was quickly quashed by Strong on the ground that Ontarians would object to a court that might be composed of 'two French judges and two from other Provinces,'[50] evidence that provincialism was still strong in sections of the country. One year later Sir Henry Strong made a proposal of his own to deal with the problem: when necessary the Exchequer Court judge could be permitted to sit on the Supreme Court as a judge ad hoc. The chief justice, on his own authority, approached the judge of the Exchequer Court to gain his approval,[51] but nothing further came of the idea.

Finally, early in 1896 the Conservative government submitted a bill stipulating that any four of the justices could constitute a quorum and could hold court where the parties consented to be heard by such a court. The measure passed through the Senate and the House of Commons without debate and became law.[52] But this did not seem to solve the problem, and further solutions continued to be proposed.

In 1896 the Laurier government introduced a bill to appoint ad hoc judges from the provincial superior courts when necessary. The bill passed through the Senate, but was withdrawn before debate in the House of Commons. Reaction in the legal journals was definitely mixed, and the government anticipated some problems in gaining the approval of the House.[53] Six years later the government put forward a new bill to name assistant judges to the Supreme Court when necessary, but this too was withdrawn.[54] The cautiousness of the Laurier government regarding retirement and new appointments was paralleled by its reticence in dealing with the general problems faced by the court regarding personnel.

A minor factor that exacerbated the problem of an insufficient number of justices was the first appointment of a member of the Supreme Court to extrajudicial duties. In 1896 George King was named to an Anglo-American arbitration commission to settle Canadian claims for damages caused by American seizures of west coast sealing vessels in the Bering Sea. Though the duties took King away from the Court only for a short time, the appointment was both a sign of things to come and a commentary on the Supreme Court. In the coming years members of the Court would be called upon to perform various political and quasi-judicial functions outside their assigned Court responsibilities. That the members of the Supreme Court of Canada were now being included among the possible appointees for such tasks is a sign of a slowly growing respect for some of its members and thus for the Court itself.

There were other indications of enhanced status, many artificially imposed by the government in attempts to bolster the Supreme Court's image. In 1881 and 1893, following the practice established with W.B. Richards, the incumbent chief justice was knighted. This was indeed a plum to be sought after, as revealed by Justice Taschereau's comments while holidaying in India. 'Je n'ai pas besoin de vous dire que, sous tous les rapports,' he informed Prime Minister Laurier, 'la position des Juges de cette Cour [Supreme] devrait être entourer de tout le prestige possible et mise sur un pied qui la feront ambitionnier par les plus hautes sommites [sic] de la profession.' This was the original intention of Sir John A. Macdonald, Taschereau assured the new government leader, and could now be accomplished by recommending to the queen that the puisne justices 'devraient être knighted'; the chief justice ought to be made KCMG, and the puisne justices given the lesser KB.[55]

While knighthoods were not handed out as readily as some might have wished, the Conservative government of Sir Mackenzie Bowell did alter the title of the chief justice. Henceforth the head of the Supreme Court of Canada would be known as the chief justice of Canada, 'as a distinguishing mark.'[56] The change underlined Ottawa's feeling that the Court ought to occupy the central position in the judicial system of the entire dominion.

A more substantial change in the prestige of the Supreme Court members was associated with the Judicial Committee of the Privy Council. The idea of colonial representation on the committee had been discussed for several years prior to the passage of the Judicial Committee Amendment Act in 1895. By that legislation it became possible for the monarch to summon a limited number of colonial justices to her imperial Privy Council; the justices sat on the Judicial Committee. In 1897 the first three jurists from the self-governing colonies joined the committee; the chief justice of Canada was the Canadian representative. Sir Henry Strong was delighted with the honour,[57] and took it seriously enough to contemplate resignation from the Supreme Court and a move to England to take up full-time duties there. It soon became clear that the latter step was impracticable, because no salary was attached to the appointment. Indeed, money became a significant barrier to Strong's fulfilling his committee duties. In 1897 and 1898 the Canadian government gave the chief justice an allowance of $1,000 to cover travelling expenses to London. Strong, however, found the sum inadequate, and was forced to spend an additional $1,000 of his own each year.[58] The chief justice's pleas for more money fell on the sympathetic ears of the solicitor-general, Charles Fitzpatrick, who in arguing Strong's case reflected the Anglo-Canadian tradition of a mutually supportive judiciary and government.

With reference to the application for travelling allowance to the Chief Justice, I would like to draw your attention to the fact that in England the highest judicial officer in the realm, the Lord Chancellor, has always been a member of the Cabinet and delivers up his seals of office when his party goes out of power. Sir William Anson speaks of him as 'a necessary party to the innermost councils of the Crown'. We have no such officer, it is true, in Canada, but occasions arise with every Government when it is most important to obtain the advice and assistance of the most skilled judicial officer in the country. This makes it very advisable that the utmost good feeling should exist between the Government and the Chief Justice of the Supreme Court so that his services may be obtained when required. I am sure that you will agree with me that valuable assistance of a confidential nature can be rendered by the Chief Justice which would fully justify the granting of a liberal provision for his expenses in attending the sittings of Her Majesty's Privy Council in England.[59]

Fitzpatrick demonstrated a similarly political perception of the chief justice's position when he himself occupied the post not many years later. In the meantime, Strong attended the committee from 1897 to 1900, and remained a member until his death in 1909.

The selection of the chief justice of Canada for membership on the Judicial Committee was intended as a compliment, as a recognition of the pre-eminence of the position. There was, from time to time, discussion of naming particularly prominent provincial chief justices, but this never occurred. The honour was reserved for the members of the highest court in the land.

Another position of status and prestige was that of deputy governor-general. In the temporary absence of the governor-general, the chief justice of the Supreme Court (or in his absence the senior puisne justice) took on some of the essential or formal duties associated with the head of state. Oaths of office were administered, bills were given royal assent, and Parliament was opened by the deputy on occasion. In 1898 H.-E.

Taschereau took advantage of the swearing-in of the Earl of Minto as governor-general to complain that the task had fallen to the senior puisne justice because the chief justice was absent (again). Two years later Taschereau, in his capacity as deputy governor-general, forwarded to the colonial secretary a complaint about the position of the puisne justices within the table of precedence in Canada. The Quebec justice's repeated complaints in this matter over the next few years show how important such visible signs of status were to many people.[60]

The Supreme Court staff also were given public recognition. Some were named queen's counsel or were given special invitations to state dinners and functions. The registrar, after some manoeuvring, was raised to the rank of deputy head within the civil service. Both Taschereau and Fitzpatrick were active in pushing this promotion; the former argued that 'such a distinction conferred by the Executive Power upon the first officer of the Court would reflect upon the Court itself and add to its prestige and dignity.'[61]

All of these honours were awarded at the government's discretion and largely reflected the perceived need to underline the Supreme Court's position as an institution rather than to reward meritorious service. One other sign of recognition, however, acknowledged the higher status and visibility of the court. In the fall of 1893 the Colonial Office inquired whether a member of the Court would be available to conduct an investigation in Jamaica into charges against the local attorney-general. Chief Justice Strong was asked to undertake the commission; when he found it necessary to refuse, Chief Justice James Macdonald of Nova Scotia was chosen.[62] In 1902 the chief justice of Canada was chosen as the president of a three-man board of arbitration to settle a minor claim between the Republic of San Salvador and the United States. Sir Henry Strong travelled to Washington to hear arguments and sided with the American commissioner in his award. The chief justice once again gave evidence of his none-too-diplomatic personality. The *New York Times* reported that a 'stormy sequel' to the award had occurred; the Salvadorian representative on the commission 'said he had been offensively treated by his fellow members. He declared he had not received the respect due to him. Sir Henry Strong, Chief Justice of Canada, who is President of the commission, told Dr. Pacas in plain language that he was under a misapprehension and made a scathing criticism of the Salvadorian member's course.'[63]

The wide variety of non-judicial tasks performed by members of the Supreme Court demonstrated the institution's close involvement in the political life of the nation. The justices' occasional service as commissioners or as deputy governor-general was paralleled from time to time by more direct association with government affairs. Chief Justice Strong's ties with the minister of justice, Sir Charles Hibbert Tupper, offer one example. In January 1896, in the midst of tense political negotiations in Ottawa, Chief Justice Strong had to plead with Tupper not to publish a letter in which the chief justice had lavishly praised Tupper's performance. Three months later Strong became closely involved in the restructuring of the Conservative cabinet. Both through Tupper and directly to prospective cabinet members, the chief justice offered advice as to who should represent Ontario and what policy should be adopted regarding the contentious Manitoba schools question.[64] Strong obviously did not regard his activities as incorrect, but his concern that his letter to Tupper not be published indicates, perhaps for the first time, a sense that public standards of judicial behaviour were beginning to change: the public would not wish to be presented with evidence of overt connections between the chief judicial officer and cabinet ministers at the height of a partisan political controversy. But that sense did not stop him from maintaining close relationships behind the scenes.

A further indication of the line now beginning to be drawn between partisan involvement and a broad political role for the judiciary comes from the activities of Elzéar Taschereau. The Quebec justice had a long-standing interest in the criminal law. In 1875–6 he had published a two-volume study of Canadian criminal law, followed by a revised edition in 1888, well after he joined the Supreme Court. Judging from contemporary book reviews, the volumes were well received:

The work before us is a valuable compendium of criminal law. It contains a mass of information collected with the greatest care from a number of sources, English, American and original ... Whenever the author has found it necessary to express his own views on any point, or to criticise enactments or authorities, he lays down his propositions with clearness, and treats them in a way which shows him to be master of his subject. The country is under a great debt of gratitude to Mr. Justice Taschereau for his most successful effort to clear up difficulties in this most important branch of the law.[65]

As an acknowledged authority on criminal law, Taschereau approached the minister of justice in 1889 to offer his services in drawing up a draft criminal code for submission to Parliament. Taschereau's offer was not accepted, though the government soon set about drafting the country's first criminal code, which passed Parliament in 1892.[66] After passage (and therefore after any amendments could be immediately made), the Quebec justice publicly attacked the legislation. Saying that he now questioned the desirability of a criminal code, Taschereau proceeded to complain that the new code omitted various crimes; it was poorly written; and it was not comprehensive enough. The letter, addressed to the attorney-general, was made public, according to Taschereau, because the Chief Justice of England had followed a similar procedure in 1879.[67]

This public criticism of government policy met with little disapproval. Most journals ignored the issue of a jurist publicly dealing with a matter of government. Only the *Canada Law Journal* condemned Taschereau for acting publicly and for not offering his suggestions earlier and in private. The *Toronto World* pointed out that the deputy minister of justice, Robert Sedgewick, was directly responsible for drafting the legislation and was now joining the Supreme Court; how would relations be between Taschereau and his new brother justice?[68] There is no evidence that the Quebec justice's actions harmed either himself or the Supreme Court. The Liberals made weak attempts in the House of Commons to use the issue to embarrass the government, but the prime minister effectively dismissed what was potentially a damaging letter: '[T]he views of the learned judge are contrary to the professional opinion of both Houses of Parliament, and utterly condemned by nearly every judge of the United Kingdom who has expressed an opinion on the subject.'[69] Clearly there was no public or political perception that such activities by a judge were improper. Taschereau was dealing with matters on which he had acknowledged expertise. That his role in the affair was a public one and involved government policy was accepted and acceptable. Having presented his case, the Quebec justice quickly turned to revising his now outdated book on the criminal law; a new edition was published by the summer of 1893.[70]

Perhaps Taschereau's reactions to the new code can be partially explained by his frustration that his expertise in criminal law was being little used at the Supreme Court. In various statutes between 1876 and 1892, the Supreme Court of Canada's jurisdiction in criminal matters was increasingly restricted: 'There shall be no appeal from a judgement in any case of proceedings for or upon a writ of *habeas corpus, certiorari* or prohibition arising out of a criminal charge ... and, there shall be no appeal in a criminal case except as provided in the Criminal Code.'[71] Sections 742 and 743 of the 1892 Criminal Code restricted appeals to the

Supreme Court from decisions of the provincial appeal courts to those criminal cases in which there had been not only an affirmation of a conviction but also a dissent among the judges in the court of appeal.[72]

These restrictions appeared to fly in the face of other plans to have the Supreme Court of Canada play a prominent role in criminal law. It was the clear intention of at least some fathers of Confederation that the Supreme Court should render the criminal law of the new nation uniform throughout Canada. If the Court was to hear criminal appeals, the law would be interpreted nationally, rather than by several provincial judges issuing different decisions on the same matter. John A. Macdonald had drawn attention to the importance of a national criminal law when he defended the terms of union in 1865.[73] He viewed the multiplicity of state criminal jurisdictions in the United States as a source of disunity and injustice, and wanted to ensure against a similar development in Canada. This potential national role for the Court in criminal law was underlined by the Macdonald government in 1887 and 1888 when criminal appeals to the Judicial Committee were terminated.[74]

This apparent contradiction in the role of the Supreme Court of Canada regarding criminal law continued until the 1960s. The restricted access to the Court made it virtually impossible for the justices to fulfil their national responsibility in criminal law. As late as 1967 one writer observed that appeals to the Supreme Court of Canada were so restricted that in the majority of cases the final court of appeal on questions of law was the provincial court of appeal.[75] As a result a large body of criminal law developed at the provincial appeal court level that was beyond the reach of the Supreme Court of Canada. There was a clear intention to enact a uniform and relatively comprehensive national criminal code, and the parallel movement to deprive the Supreme Court of an influential role in this area is perplexing.[76]

A number of basic problems remained with the Supreme Court throughout the 1890s. The Supreme Court Reports continued to be the subject of numerous complaints. The selection of reported cases was criticized, as were the style and length of dissenting judgments. Most frequent were objections regarding the tardiness of publication.[77] In 1895 the original reporter, Georges Duval, retired. The new team of C.H. Masters, reporter, and L.H. Coutlée, assistant reporter (for Quebec cases), improved the efficiency of the reporting process. The Justice Department agreed that cases could be reported without waiting for a judgment from any dilatory justice. The result was that in volume 25 (1895), in six instances the decision of a justice was reported but with no reasons given; two unanimous decisions were reported, but with no reasons given; two unanimous decisions were summarized from the oral reasons for judgment; and in four cases the result alone was given, with no reasons and no indication of the justices' votes. While this speeded up the reporting process, the quality of the reporting was questionable; recording a decision without any findings on the points of law involved rendered the report useless to the profession.

Nevertheless, the Reports were improving. In 1891 a Toronto legal journal urged the Upper Canada Law Society to re-establish members' automatic subscription to the Supreme Court Reports, a proposal that was adopted a few years later. More extensive circulation was highly desirable, and would help to solve a new problem that was arising: an overrun of almost one thousand copies of each volume had begun to accumulate at the courthouse, creating serious storage difficulties.[78]

Another problem area for the Supreme Court was the library. In the early years provision of funds for a law library had been delayed because there was little room for a library until the 1891 building addition has been completed. Prior to that time counsel in attendance at Court had had recourse to the parliamentary library. Although there was a small judges' library, presumably the justices also had to use the parliamentary library from time to time. What books there were at the courthouse were cared for by an employee who doubled as caretaker for the building. When questioned in the House about the government's policy regarding a law library, Sir John A. Macdonald replied, 'I do not know that the Government have seriously considered their policy on the subject.'[79] In the late 1880s the original librarian-caretaker was replaced temporarily by the registrar of the newly independent Exchequer Court. By the end of the 1880s the limited library facilities had been opened to counsel, who made considerable use of the holdings. So busy was the library during the Supreme Court terms that the hours were extended until 10:00 P.M.; when a catalogue was first being prepared in 1889, a major hindrance was that barristers 'were using the books day and night during the recent terms.'[80] Thus, although government policy was undeveloped, the need and demand for a full law library clearly existed.

Approximately coincident with the opening of the new extension of the courthouse in 1892, a search for a librarian 'well educated (professionally if possible), having at least some knowledge of French' was undertaken.

In the fall of 1892 H.H. Bligh, a legal scholar with two books to his credit as well as extensive legal experience, was named to the post. By selecting an individual as accomplished as Bligh, the government seemed to be making a solid commitment to maintaining and enlarging what was by then a 14,000-volume library.[81] Moves were made to fill several weaknesses in the holdings. Efforts were made to acquire a more extensive and complete series of American reports, both state and federal. Arrangements were made with an American book supplier in Boston. Particular attention was paid to enlarging the civil-law and French-language holdings.[82] In 1894 Prime Minister Thompson made plain his government's desire for a good library: 'The Supreme Court Library, of course, inasmuch as it is a resort for barristers from all the provinces of Canada, ought to be a first-rate library. It is very far from being so, good as it is, and it will take a grant of $30,000 or $40,000 to make it anything as good as the best state libraries in the United States. As it is now, it ranks less than a third among the libraries of Canada.'[83] But neither Thompson's nor succeeding governments were ever able to carry out this policy successfully. Requests for funds were scaled down to avoid heavy attack in Parliament, and even then faced frequent criticism.

The workload of the Supreme Court continued to grow during the 1890s. For the period 1893–1902 875 cases were dealt with by the court; the annual average of 87.5 cases was up appreciably from the period of Sir W.J. Ritchie's leadership (71.9 per cent). In the cases the justices manifested a stronger tendency to affirm lower court decisions: 55.3 per cent were confirmed and 31.8 per cent were overturned (most of the remainder were disposed of on preliminary motions). Perhaps the tendency to reject appeals helps to explain the smaller number of appeals carried from the Supreme Court of Canada to London (43 in the 1890s, or 4.8 per cent of all Supreme Court decisions).[84] That figure could also be taken to reflect a growing satisfaction with or confidence in the judgments of the Court.

The feeling was growing at the Court that too many appeals were going to Ottawa. In response to one suggestion that intermediate stages of appeal be reduced and access to the final domestic court of appeal made speedier, Chief Justice Strong responded that such a step would be inadvisable: 'There has been a great abuse of the right of appeal to the Supreme Court. Many appeals, especially in cases in which judgments had been given against municipal corporations and joint stock companies sued by poor men have appeared vexatious and oppressive and have been spoken of from the Bench in terms of condemnation both by Mr. Justice Taschereau and myself.'[85] Such appeals abused the Court and undermined its function and hoped-for stature.

It is unclear how much co-operation and intellectual exchange occurred among the justices. Judicial conferences were certainly held, but their frequency is unknown; and because Justice Gwynne refused to participate, the effectiveness of the conferences must have been impaired. Two letters in the Girouard Papers suggest that other forms of intellectual exchange must have been stimulating and productive. First, draft judgments were circulated and discussed by at least some of the justices. Early in 1896 Gwynne complemented Girouard on 'your admirable judgement' in *St Louis* v *The Queen*.

It has given me much pleasure and edification so much so that I have revived [revised ?] my former views and have written a few lines in concurrence with you. I have seen Taschereau J. and he wishes you to leave out all reference to him as now he will adopt your judgement when you change it so as to omit all reference to him. I return you yours with many thanks and think you had better see Taschereau and alter your judgement so as to be the judgement of the court.

Second, private discussions took place between individual justices. This is obvious from the letter quoted above and from an 1897 note from Gwynne giving his excuse for being absent from a meeting of the justices: 'Let me see you if you can after conference,' he continued. 'You know my views in all cases.'[86] Co-operation and intellectual exchange seem to have been part of the judicial process at the Supreme Court. But this could accomplish only so much. In *St Louis* v *The Queen*, Gwynne concurred with Girouard (and took two pages to say so); Taschereau submitted a separate judgment. The degree of co-operation can be exaggerated; the legal profession had the impression that 'full and free consultation and exchange of opinion between the judges' did not, at this time, occur.[87]

One series of cases brought the Supreme Court of Canada directly into the political limelight. In 1890 and 1891 the Manitoba legislature passed several acts terminating public financial support for denominational schools and effectively ending the official status of the French language. Appeal of the language legislation did not reach the Supreme Court until 1979,[88] but the schools legislation quickly became a major political issue in the tense atmosphere of rising cultural conflict in the first half of the 1890s.

Sir John A. Macdonald rejected requests to disallow the legislation, preferring to avoid the issue by leaving it to the courts. In the same way some had advocated in 1889 the use of the courts (through reference to the Supreme Court) to rule on the validity of the contentious Jesuit Estates Act.[89] In the politicians' attempts to avoid dealing with such potentially damaging issues or to devolve onto someone else at least part of the political blame or responsibility, it was perhaps inevitable that the courts would become involved.

In 1891 the case of *Barrett v the City of Winnipeg*,[90] which involved the Manitoba Public Schools Act of 1890, reached the Supreme Court of Canada. The act had been upheld by Justice A.C. Killam and by the full Court of Queen's Bench, but at least some western observers anticipated an unfavourable response to the legislation from the Ottawa-based Court. The *Western Law Times* noted that almost every case ('nearly ninety per cent') from Manitoba was overruled by the Supreme Court: 'If reports are to be credited, our school case is to suffer a like fate. Fortunately we still have the Privy Council to rely upon.' This expectation was confirmed when the Supreme Court handed down a unanimous judgment (5–0, with Gwynne absent) allowing the appeal. The same journal suggested that the two French-Canadian jurists had been swayed simply by their Roman Catholicism; as for the others,

The judgment of Chief Justice Ritchie impresses us rather as an argument in favour of Separate Schools than a judicial finding. Mr Justice Patterson's is far more satisfactory as a judicial opinion, but it is undeniably apologetic in tone, and conveys the idea that it was arrived at after a consideration of matters somewhat extraneous to the statutes which do, or do not, confer the privilege in dispute. We would not be at all surprised to see the finding of the Supreme Court reversed by the Judicial Committee. If Mr. Justice Strong had delivered a separate judgment we feel sure it would have been of much assistance in determining the grave interests at issue in this matter.

The opinions of Ritchie and Patterson were directly compared on specific points with a view to determining the intellectual merits of the Supreme Court decision.[91] When the Judicial Committee reversed the Supreme Court ruling and restored the decision of the Manitoba court, the *Western Law Times* gloated: 'We were not at all surprised to find the Supreme Court itself over-ruled, and in truth such an event is nothing new to that body, the confidence of the public in which as an exponent of constitutional questions has long been on the wane, and it is difficult after this last reversal to say what weight that Court will in future carry in such questions, if any.'[92]

But this was not the end of the issue. Discussion soon commenced regarding the right of denominational schools supporters to appeal to the governor-general-in-council for remedial action under section 93 (3) and (4) of the British North America Act. The federal government referred to the Supreme Court the question of the validity of such appeals and of the government's power to take remedial action. Here, as in the case of *Barrett v the City of Winnipeg*, the government was using the judicial system in an attempt to avoid a difficult and contentious decision.[93] Conveniently, the Supreme Court held, 3–2, that the federal government was relieved of all responsibility to act further in the Manitoba schools question. Though such an opinion was what most western spokesmen wanted, there was still considerable discontent on the prairies over the Court's handling of the reference. Counsel appeared for the province of Manitoba but declined to argue the case; Chief Justice Strong appointed a leading Toronto barrister, Christopher Robinson, to present a case on behalf of Manitoba. The *Western Law Times* was furious, contending that since the province had counsel present Strong had no power to name an additional representative and that the province had a right to determine its own conduct of its case (that is, a right not to argue the case). Strong, however, refused to listen to such complaints, saying that the reference process must not be weakened by such conduct.[94]

Strong's leadership in this and other cases was effective. But the Reports reflect a chief justice who sometimes was intellectually lazy and frequently irresponsible. In *Fraser v Drew* (1900), for example, he used one of his favourite techniques – handing down an oral judgment that was never followed by a written version. He thus avoided the work of writing out the judgment and the rigorous task of developing a rationale for the decision. Strong informed the parties, 'We are all of the opinion that the appeal must be dismissed with costs. If some English decisions favour the appellant's case, the weight of Canadian and American decisions are the other way. We decide this appeal on the principle that the question of fact was left to and dealt with by the jury in such a manner that we cannot interfere with their findings.'[95] Strong made no attempt to reconcile the divergent authorities to explain why he found the English decisions less weighty, and counsel and lower court judges received no guidance or explanation of the law.

In another case, *the Ontario Mining Company v Seybold* (1901), this same laziness was demonstrated. Chief Justice Strong, orally and for the four-man majority, stated that 'for the reasons given by the learned Chancellor in this case, and more particularly for the reasons given by the Judicial Committee of the Privy Council in *St. Catharines Milling Co. v. The Queen*, by which we are bound, and which governs the decision in this case, the appeal must be dismissed.' This is the majority judgment in toto; no further reasons were given. This contrasts with the dissenting judgment of Justice Gwynne. In a twenty-page opinion, he effectively analysed the legal issues at hand and argued strongly that the *St Catharines* precedent was not applicable. Rather than dealing with Gwynne's points and explaining the disagreements, Strong ignored the dissent. It is also disturbing that the chief justice carried the majority of his colleagues with him, not just in the decision but in the failure to explain their thinking.[96] Strong's personality, his intellect, and the problems he created dominated the Supreme Court of Canada in this period.

By the turn of the century, the Supreme Court of Canada was twenty-five years old. It had acquired experience and procedures that helped it to fulfil its purposes and responsibilities, but many problems still existed. That of personnel has already been discussed at length. The Court's reputation remained poor; the editor of the *Canada Law Journal* wrote privately that the Supreme Court 'is held in Contempt by the profession.' Though it is fair to say that reputations, once acquired, are hard to shake off, the justices were partly to blame for the Court's problems. Some incidents, particularly those involving Chief Justice Strong, have survived to help explain some of the Supreme Court's disrepute. The justices' manner of hearing cases also drew criticism. Donald McMaster, a respected Montreal lawyer, noted: 'The hearings are not always models of judicial investigation, and there is too much disposition to plunge into general dissertation before Counsel has opportunity to explain what the particular case is and what the Judges below thought about it.' This tendency of the judges to interrupt counsel's argument was 'so frequent, and [of] such a character,' added a law journal, 'that unless the counsel engaged has unusual courage, determination and skill, his argument may never be fairly presented to the Court.' The justices often conversed on the bench 'in a tone loud enough to be heard at the back of the court room, on subjects entirely foreign to the arguments.' The chief justice's objection to the reading of passages from authorities and reports or of excerpts from the evidence also drew criticism. This rule was felt to be particularly hard on Quebec counsel who perceived the need to inform the common-law justices as to the nature and meaning of the French-language sources. The *Canadian Law Times* concluded, 'All these matters are most unpleasant to the counsel engaged before the Court, and tend to shake public confidence in the Court. It has unfortunately become such a common subject of conversation when the Court is sitting that it is impossible not to notice.'[97]

In 1902 the legislative and public attacks on the Supreme Court were renewed. L.-P. Demers, Liberal member of Parliament for St Jean d'Iberville and a distinguished legal figure in Quebec, introduced a bill to end the Court's jurisdiction over provincial law. The proposal was not heard of again after first reading. In the same session a member recalled the early attacks on the Court and judged there had been no improvement over the succeeding twenty years. In 1903 Demers introduced his bill again; after some debate it was defeated.[98] Public discussion of the Court's problems was taking place in both the press and legal journals. The *Canada Law Journal* in 1902 chastised the government for its lack of action in redressing the weaknesses apparent in the Supreme Court. News of further conflict among the justices had just become public, and this time, it was pointed out, Chief Justice Strong had not even been present.

The spirit of discord and misrule which has been a characteristic of this court is somewhat remarkable where many of its members are models of courtesy and kindness. Every one knows perfectly well where the blame lies for this miserable condition of things. The attention of the Government has been called to it time and again, and the Government, of course, must be held responsible. It is idle to say that nothing can be done. Something must be done. The court cannot be a success, but must be a discredit to the country, until some change is made which will supply or remove any discordant element, and cause its business to be conducted with proper regard to the respect due to itself, as well as to the feelings and rights of those whose duty calls them to assist in its deliberations.

The journal echoed the complaints of the 1880s. How could an adjudication ever be considered satisfactory when one or two justices from a province were overruling the judgments at the provincial level of up to five 'men of at least equal attainments, and having special knowledge of the law affecting their various provinces'? The journal concluded by demanding a reorganization of the personnel '[i]f the Court is to be continued (the wisdom of which may be questioned).'[99] The signs were clear. The Supreme Court of Canada had not yet been able to place itself in a position where it was well accepted as a basic, necessary, and valued component of the Canadian political system.

It was unfair, however, to say that the Court had not improved during its first twenty-five years. If, for example, its stature was not as great as some might wish, the Court and some of its members were much more highly regarded. In 1898 the *Canada Law Journal* sent a photograph of the Supreme Court justices as a New Year's greeting to its subscribers. In 1902 the *Canadian Law Review* featured a series of photographs of the individual justices.[100] Both of these initiatives were signs of a growing interest in and respect for the Court. The personnel of the Court had been improving in quality; the scholarly publications of Taschereau and Girouard, as well as of the staff, are proof of increased intellectual activity. Strong's membership on the Judicial Committee exposed him to new jurists and to a complex set of different legal problems. Justice Taschereau's 1901 visit to Washington to study the American Supreme Court is another indication of a more inquiring intellectual atmosphere.[101]

4

The Court in Decline

1902–1918

During the first decade of the twentieth century, particularly in the early years, the Supreme Court of Canada experienced the heaviest turnover in the personnel on the bench in the history of the institution. Within less than two years (1901–3) five vacancies occurred. In May 1901 George King died, followed in January 1902 by John Gwynne. Late in 1902 Chief Justice Strong retired, and in 1903 two of the new appointees died. The instability caused by this turnover in personnel had serious consequences for the Court.

In the ten years between 1901 and 1911, the Laurier government had the greatest opportunity of any administration in Canadian history to shape the character and direction of the Supreme Court to the extent that it could be influenced by the quality of members of the bench. Sir Wilfrid Laurier and his ministers of justice appointed ten new puisne justices and two chief justices. Yet the early results were disappointing. The government's selection criteria seemed mainly to reflect a mixture of such considerations as merit, political patronage, and the interests of the government rather than the Court.

The tone of the appointments was set with the first. Some four and a half months after the death of Justice King, Sir Louis Davies was named to the Court. Replacing a maritimer, Davies was the only member in the history of the Court to come from Prince Edward Island. Born in 1845 on the Island and educated there, he had received his legal training at the Inner Temple in London. Davies was admitted to the provincial bar in

1867 but soon turned to politics. He was a member of the provincial assembly from 1872 to 1879, and quickly became an influential leader, serving as premier and attorney-general from 1876 to 1879. Defeated provincially in 1879, Davies served in the House of Commons (1882–1901) and as a member of the Laurier cabinet (1896–1901). In addition to his political activities, Davies was the president of a printing company and of a local bank. He lacked wide experience in the law. He had been a member of the bar only five years before assuming electoral office; his practice had been limited, and of course he had no judicial experience. In 1892 the Conservative minister of justice had privately commented in scathing fashion on Davies' legal knowledge: 'Mills is well read, Laurier far from it and Davies a mere gabbler of phrases which he has picked up in a very inferior practice.' It is true that Davies had earned his appointment to the Supreme Court solely through his service to the Liberal party and government.[1]

Davies' nomination was not well received by the legal profession. The *Canada Law Journal*, for example, hoped that the new justice would add strength to the Supreme Court, but doubted that he would: 'That this has been an unsatisfactory tribunal in many ways, and much so of late years, is well known to the profession, and is much to be deplored. The attention of the Government should be directed to making this Court, what it is not, the strongest and best thought of Court in the Dominion. There are of course great difficulties in the way, but we doubt if it can be said that due effort has been made in the direction indicated.' If Davies' appointment was an indication of the government's efforts to improve the Court, then the government was not trying very hard. A month later the same journal argued that the quality of the Canadian judiciary had been declining lately, and if the government did not act soon to stop the deterioration, perhaps the country would be better off with a direct electoral system of selecting judges.[2]

This discontent and the government's willingness to make weak appointments to the Supreme Court were both confirmed less than five months later with the elevation of David Mills to replace Justice Gwynne. Mills had had a varied and impressive career. After earning a law degree at the University of Michigan, he taught school for several years. From 1867 to 1896 he was a member of Parliament and an influential Ontario member of the Liberal party, serving as minister of the interior in the Mackenzie cabinet and as minister of justice (sitting in the Senate) in the Laurier government. Mills also had newspaper and commercial experience, but his legal experience was at least as limited as Davies'. Although he received his law degree in 1855, Mills did not begin to practise law until the 1880s. Only in 1883 did he gain admission to the Ontario bar; thereafter his legal practice, which was in London, Ontario, was limited. His interest in the law was theoretical or scholarly, and in 1888 Mills was appointed professor of constitutional and international law at the University of Toronto. Later he lectured on medical jurisprudence in the university's medical faculty. Mills's practical legal experience was concentrated in constitutional law.[3]

David Mills owed his judicial appointment to his political career. He had faithfully served his party in the House of Commons for twenty-nine years, and on his electoral defeat in 1896 expected and sought his reward as a natural consequence of that service. As a result of the representations he made at that time, Mills was promised the first Ontario vacancy to occur on the Supreme Court. There is no evidence that consideration was given to his appointment to a lower court. He accepted both his nomination to the Senate and his post as justice minister apparently in order to protect this pledge of appointment.[4] As the minister directly responsible for the Supreme Court, Mills found himself in a conflict of interest, caught between what was best for the Court and his own aspirations to the bench.

Mills repeatedly had to beat back other applicants for the prospective vacancy and to turn aside various attempts to have him accept a lesser post. This task became the more necessary when rumours of his imminent appointment to the Court became public and were subjected to considerable criticism.[5] In 1900, for example, the prime minister tentatively suggested the elevation of Justice McMahon of Ontario to the Supreme Court. Mills would have none of it. McMahon could have a provincial chief justiceship, but he could not move to the Supreme Court of Canada. After all, McMahon had become a Liberal only in 1873 and had joined the bench long ago. 'I don't think that after 34 years' public service to my own pecuniary detriment that I should prefer one who has made no sacrifice at all, especially when he is already on the Bench,' declared Mills. He also warded off attempts to appoint him as an ad hoc justice: 'It was not what was proposed to me, and I will not take it.'[6]

Finally, with Gwynne's death early in January 1902, Mills's path was open, and he took it. But he could not avoid considerable public criticism. The attacks were based on several grounds. At age seventy, it was felt, he could not be expected to retain his vigour and health for long. The legal profession was distressed at Mills's almost complete lack of practical legal experience. Both the public and the bar were upset at the patronage nature of the appointment. The *Canada Law Journal* pointed to the existing weaknesses of the Supreme Court and to the real difficulties of forming a satisfactory Court in the dominion.

But certainly the task can never be accomplished by the present laissez faire policy, or by the appointment of men because they have a political 'pull,' or by appointing those who for some reason it is desirable to shelve ... As a writer in the lay press has recently expressed it: 'To treat the bench as a mere place of reward for political service, and appoint men to it whose only claims are those of political services, is little short of a crime.'[7]

These were fair criticisms. The concerned public was beginning to articulate new standards regarding the bench. Judicial appointments that were perceived to be based merely on political service were no longer acceptable.[8] The quality of the Supreme Court bench had in some respects reached bottom. Of the six justices, only two (Strong and Taschereau) had had previous judicial experience, and they were both growing old. The remaining four (Sedgewick, Girouard, Davies, and Mills) had come directly from the bar, and only Girouard had had an active practice at the time of his appointment. The last three appointees to the Court had come directly from Parliament. 'The composition of the tribunal has never been regarded by lawyers as satisfactory,' commented the *Canadian Law Times*, 'but there can be no doubt that it is less so now than at any former period in its existence.'[9]

Perhaps in response to such criticism, the Laurier government over the next few years took steps to improve the character of appointments to the Court. Immediately upon the retirement of Sir Henry Strong, John Douglas Armour was elevated to the Supreme Court. The new justice had had a distinguished legal and judicial career: twenty-four years at the bar; a member of the Ontario Court of Queen's Bench from 1877 to 1901 and chief justice from 1887 to 1901; chief justice of Ontario and of the Court of Appeal from 1901 to 1902. Armour was one of the few provincial chief justices after 1875 who agreed to leave his high position for a puisne justiceship in Ottawa.[10]

At the same time, it was necessary to appoint a new chief justice. There is no evidence extant of any debate within the government over this problem; once again the senior puisne justice was promoted. Elzéar Taschereau had been at the Court for twenty-four years, and was one of the few justices to give substantial evidence of an ongoing interest in legal scholarship outside the requirements of his position. He had published two further editions of his work on criminal law, and in 1895 he had become dean of the faculty of law at the University of Ottawa.[11] More than that, however, the continuing opposition to the Court emanating from Quebec and the political problems the Liberal party was beginning to experience there made the appointment of the first French-Canadian chief justice an attractive move. Taschereau's elevation met with general approval. A Toronto legal journal, for example, remarked, 'Sir Henri Taschereau is persona grata to the Bar, and is deemed the best lawyer in a weak Court, which will now, however, be strengthened by the addition of Mr. Justice Armour.'[12] In contrast to the two earlier appointments to the Supreme Court, the two in November 1902 were based on solid grounds and had potential advantages for the institution.

In 1903 the Laurier government detracted from the immediate advantages of a good judicial appointment by naming Justice Armour, aged seventy-two and in failing health, as one of the two Canadian commissioners on the Alaska Boundary Commission. This political use of a member of the Court was unfortunate, but it is clear that the government was less concerned with the Supreme Court itself than with the national interest as defined by the cabinet. Armour sailed for England in May, having participated in only two Court terms, and died overseas shortly after briefs to the commission commenced. His death, coming so soon after the death of Justice Mills in May, was a real blow to the Court, and the cabinet had now to search out two more new members.

With Armour absent overseas, Mills's sudden death necessitated naming a new member of the Court almost immediately if the spring sitting was to be held. The replacement was in several respects a good choice. Wallace Nesbitt had practised law for some twenty years, first in Hamilton and then in Toronto. At the relatively young age of forty-five he was prepared to abandon a lucrative practice for the bench. Though lacking judicial experience, Nesbitt had an outstanding reputation as counsel, and his nomination to the Supreme Court was widely acclaimed. What was remarkable about the appointment was that he was a known Conservative supporter, and his selection was surprising given the highly partisan nature of most of the Laurier government's appointments.[13]

In choosing the replacement for Justice Armour, the government sought to respond to the rising pressure from the west for representation on the Supreme Court bench. Demands for such an appointment had become more insistent in the 1890s. When no western jurists were promoted either then or when the vacancies were filled in 1901–2, western pressure increased. Western lawyers met to pass resolutions; western members of Parliament raised the matter in the House. In response, the government was able to persuade another provincial chief justice to replace Armour,[14] and Manitoba Chief Justice Albert Clements Killam was appointed to the Supreme Court in 1903.

The selection of a westerner was dictated by the Court's need for judicial experience and for greater prestige as well as by western appeals for recognition. Killam was chosen not simply because he was a westerner but also because he was an able jurist of long experience. He had practised law for eight years in Toronto and Winnipeg, and had served briefly as a Conservative member of the Manitoba legislature. In 1885 Killam had been appointed to the Court of Queen's Bench, one of the first Manitobans to be named to the local bench. In 1899 he had become chief justice of that court. As a jurist, Killam had earned an excellent reputation both for his manner and for the quality of his judgments. His lectures to Manitoba law students on equity jurisprudence were highly regarded. Killam was only fifty-three years old, and could be expected to have an extended impact on the Supreme Court.[15]

On the one hand, it seems that Killam's appointment to the Court may have been planned in advance, for in the winter of 1903 he was called to Ottawa for discussions with Clifford Sifton and the minister of justice. On the other hand, there were rumours that both Chief Justice Charles Moss of Ontario and A.B. Aylesworth had rejected the post.[16] In any event, Killam joined the Supreme Court less than a month after Armour's death. Commentators in both the east and the west viewed Killam's appointment as 'a recognition of the growing importance of the west' and of the man's own abilities.[17] Perhaps surprisingly, Ontario journals did not seem upset by the apparent loss of one of their province's positions on the court, possibly because of Killam's ties to Ontario.

With the appointment of J.D. Armour, W. Nesbitt, and A.C. Killam to the Supreme Court, it seemed that the Laurier government was turning its back on the practise of patronage appointments. But it was not so. After just eighteen months on the Supreme Court, Justice Killam was persuaded to resign and to accept nomination as head of the Board of Railway Commissioners for Canada. The board had been established in 1903 to take over the various regulatory powers of the government regarding railways. A quasi-judicial body and one designed, among other things, to answer western grievances concerning freight rates and handling, the board would gain much credibility from the appointment of such a man as

Killam.[18] However, for Killam to accept the new post and for the government to select him was a strong blow to the Supreme Court. This was the only occasion on which a member of the Court stepped down in order to assume another government position. The resignation occurred in a period of turnover in Court personnel and when the prestige of the Supreme Court and the respect for it as a judicial institution were low. The Laurier government had seemed in 1903 to have the best interests of the Court at heart; in 1905 the truth appeared to be otherwise. Moving a judge to another governmental body caused the Supreme Court to be lumped together with the slowly rising number of government boards and commissions. Rather than being seen as an institution apart, enjoying special status at the peak of the national judicial structure, the Court was shown to be what it really was in this period: a political body subject to the partisan political manoeuvrings of the government.

In that same year, 1905, the Supreme Court witnessed one of the few premature resignations in its history, further compounding its instability. For 'reasons purely private,' Wallace Nesbitt informed the government of his wish to resign less than two years after he had joined the Court. Nesbitt does not seem to have been suffering from poor health; a position on the bench simply turned out not to be the sort of career he wanted.[19] Four of the Laurier government's first five appointees to the Court had now left within two years of joining.

The post vacated by Justice Killam reverted to Ontario. John Idington of the Ontario High Court of Justice was promoted to the Supreme Court. After joining the bar in 1864, Idington established his practice in Stratford, where his became one of the leading law firms in western Ontario. In 1879 he became crown attorney for Perth County. Over some forty years at the bar he was known for his industry and for his knowledge of criminal and municipal law. In 1904 Idington was appointed to the Ontario bench, and less than a year later was called to Ottawa. He thus joined the Supreme Court with almost no judicial experience. In Ottawa he was known as the teller of occasional jokes, and bore 'the reputation of being the wit of the Court.'[20]

Idington's appointment was a surprise both in Ontario and the west. Those in Ontario had expected someone with greater judicial experience to be named; those in the west had anticipated the appointment of someone from the bench of British Columbia or Manitoba. One law journal stated that the selection of Idington was an indication of how difficult it was to persuade jurists to accept 'promotion (so called)' to Ottawa. This explained why only one current member of the Supreme

Court (Taschereau) had had substantial judicial experience before moving to the federal Court. One solution, the editorial continued, was to raise the salaries of the justices.[21]

In the meantime there was a second vacancy to fill. In the fall of 1905 Wallace Nesbitt was replaced by Justice James Maclennan. A specialist in equity law, the new justice had had twenty-one years' experience at the bar, most of it in Toronto in partnership with Oliver Mowat. After unsuccessful attempts at a political career, Maclennan joined the Ontario Court of Appeal in 1888 and remained there until 1905.[22]

It seemed as though the changes on the Supreme Court bench would never stop. In 1906 there were two further vacancies. Chief Justice Sir Elzéar Taschereau was in only his seventieth year, but he had been on the bench for over forty-four years, most of them at the Supreme Court. In 1904 he had been appointed to the imperial Privy Council (and thus to the Judicial Committee thereof), according to Taschereau, on the 'condition … that I should vacate the Chief Justiceship.' Without a substitute selected, however, the government was in no rush to hold him to his pledge. In 1905 Taschereau let it be known that he would not be averse to retiring. Such hints escalated into a 'repeatedly expressed desire' as his health worsened.[23] Taschereau's energy had declined. He had in the past few years seemed as much concerned with status as with the real purposes of the Court. Early in May 1906 he stepped down. Just three months later the senior puisne justice, Robert Sedgewick, died after a year-long illness.[24]

In searching for a successor to the chief justice, the government actively canvassed outside candidates. Once again the Laurier cabinet approached Edward Blake. Offering him the post, the prime minister indicated his awareness of the Court's weakness and of the potential of strong appointments as a means of dealing with the problem: 'You are aware, no doubt, that our Supreme Court does not at this moment command that respect and confidence so essential to the proper discharge of the high functions with which it is entrusted. It would be needless to seek causes for this unfortunate condition of things. At the same time, the feeling is universal that nothing would so strengthen the Court, as your acceptance of its presidency as Chief Justice.' Blake was already seventy-one years of age and in poor health; realizing the heavy demands that would be made on him if he were to make a real effort to redress the Court's image, he rejected the offer.[25]

In the meantime the minister of justice, Charles Fitzpatrick, had his eye on the post. Rumours suggested that he was considering the move as early as 1904, but the prime minister opposed his appointment on the ground that it would hurt the cabinet: 'I still hope [Fitzpatrick] may be induced to give up his intentions. Fitz knows my views on this subject. I have done all I could to dissuade him from it, and more I cannot do.'[26] But in the end Laurier capitulated, and for the only time in its history the chief justiceship of the Supreme Court of Canada was filled from outside the judiciary.

The son of a Quebec lumber merchant, Charles Fitzpatrick had been educated at Laval University. At different periods he had been crown prosecutor in the Quebec District, but he had acquired far greater experience as defence counsel in criminal cases. Among his more notable clients had been Louis Riel (1885), Thomas McGreevy (1891), and Honoré Mercier (1893), whose cases all involved political matters. For a time Fitzpatrick had put his growing legal experience to use as a professor of criminal law at Laval. He entered politics in 1890, first as a Liberal member of the Quebec legislature (1890–6) and then as a member of Parliament (1896–1906). With the election of the Liberal party in 1896 he was appointed solicitor-general, at that time a position outside the cabinet. Fitzpatrick had been unusually active as solicitor-general, taking a leading role, for example, in dealing with the Supreme Court. In 1902 he was promoted to the influential position of minister of justice. Fitzpatrick was the first English Canadian from Quebec to join the court and the first English-speaking Catholic. Exactly why he chose to leave the government in 1906, at fifty-two years of age, is unclear. Unlike other cabinet ministers who joined the Supreme Court, Fitzpatrick never gave up his involvement in politics.[27]

In contrast to the appointments of Davies and Mills, there was no public reaction against Fitzpatrick's nomination to the Court despite his prominent political career.[28] Though his actual legal experience was somewhat narrow and dated, his role as defence counsel in notable cases had created a public perception of a successful legal career. The concerned public did not, apparently, object to the naming of politicians to the bench; the emphasis was now on legal experience, and it was precisely in that area that Davies and Mills had been weak.

The other vacancy on the Court was filled by the most famous justice in the history of the institution, Lyman Poore Duff.[29] Called to the bar in Ontario in 1893, he practised briefly there before moving to the west coast, where he established a solid practice in Victoria. Duff was active in the Liberal cause in British Columbia, and first rose to national prominence in 1903 as junior counsel for Canada before the Alaska Boundary Commission, of which the current minister of justice had been a member. In the following year (1904) Duff joined the Supreme Court of British Columbia, where he acquired two years' experience before the move to Ottawa. Despite his short legal and judicial career and his relatively young age (forty-one), Duff's appointment was greeted with strong approval. It is clear that his name had already become well known across the dominion and that his reputation was good.

> In choosing a western instead of an eastern man to fill the vacancy at Ottawa caused by the death of Mr. Justice Sedgewick, we think no mistake has been made. If there must be representation of the various provinces or groups of provinces upon the Bench of the Dominion Court, it is time for the western group to have its turn; and if it be contended that for material to make up the highest Court in the country, distinguished jurists should be chosen irrespective of locality ... there is reason to believe that in the new Judge of the Supreme Court a rara avis has been secured for the Ottawa cage ... Mr. Justice Duff in his two years on the provincial Bench has gained a reputation both for learning and sound sense, and we look to see him increase it in his new surroundings.[30]

The appointment pleased many because it seemed to meet the standards for judicial appointment. With the 'reassignment' of a post from the maritimes to the west, the territorial distribution of seats was firmly realigned. The maritimes would never again have more than one justice on the Supreme Court, and the west would never have less than one. The Court was young in judicial experience: Girouard had been on the bench for eleven years (all at the Supreme Court), Idington for two (one in Ottawa), Maclennan for seventeen (one in Ottawa), Duff for two, and Fitzpatrick, the leader, not at all. There were not many national courts of appeal around the world that had such junior justices, and this judicial inexperience was a reflection of the Laurier government's system and criteria for appointment.

Two and a half years later, the justice with the longest judicial experience left the Supreme Court. James Maclennan chose to retire just one month short of his seventy-sixth birthday. He had recently completed twenty years on the bench, and opted to take his pension (at full salary).[31] The vacancy was first offered to Featherstone Osler, senior puisne justice of the Ontario Court of Appeal. The leading law journal of the day regarded such an offer as natural and proper, implying that the senior puisne justice in the provincial appellate court was the candidate ex officio best suited and most favoured by the profession.[32] Osler, who was now close to retirement, rejected the offer, as he had in 1888.

The new member of the Supreme Court was Francis Alexander Anglin. The son of a politician, Anglin followed his father's path in supporting the twin causes of the Liberal Party and Irish Catholics. He had been in practice in Toronto for sixteen years, specializing in corporate and civil work, and because of his Liberal connections he handled a large amount of work for the crown. Anglin's interest in the law had led him to write several articles and a book on trusts and trustees, which was well received.[33] After petitioning and manoeuvring for a position on the bench over a period of some seven years, Anglin was named in 1904 to the High Court of Ontario, Exchequer Division. His conduct there earned the approbation of the legal profession, and early in 1909, at the age of forty-three, he joined the Supreme Court of Canada.[34]

The last appointment of the Laurier government was made after the death of Désiré Girouard in March 1911. The senior puisne justice died at the age of seventy-five from injuries received in a sleighing accident in Ottawa. His replacement was Louis-Philippe Brodeur. Called to the bar of Quebec in 1884, Brodeur found time outside his law practice in Montreal (with Honoré Mercier) to dabble in politics. Occasional newspaper articles led to a deeper involvement, and he campaigned successfully for election to Parliament in 1891; he was a Liberal member until 1911. For three years he was Speaker of the House of Commons (1901–4), and between 1904 and 1911 he held three different minor portfolios in the cabinet. A close friend of Sir Wilfrid and Lady Laurier, Brodeur was a popular individual, but he had shown no great skill in politics or in law.[35]

By the standards of the day, the government had made several good appointments to the Supreme Court, notably Armour, Killam, Duff, and Anglin. But these were spoiled by the use of Court vacancies to reward partisan followers, too often with weak credentials in their legal knowledge and experience. With inconsistent government support, the Supreme Court had little hope of improving its reputation or quality. All of the appointees had given political service to their party before joining the Supreme Court. But those who had worked in non-elected roles, such as Duff, Idington, and Anglin, had been active lawyers prior to joining the bench, and they tended to make good judges. Those who had served in elected capacities, such as Davies, Fitzpatrick, and Brodeur, had not, in the years immediately preceding appointment, had much time for the law; they were not up-to-date, had given no evidence of a commitment to the law, and did not seem to have as well-developed a legal cast of mind; as justices of the Supreme Court of Canada they did not make as useful a contribution to the law as did those judges who had come from a full-time legal career.

Given the political nature of the appointments and the actively partisan background of many of the personnel, it is not surprising that in the first two decades of the twentieth century the Supreme Court justices became more heavily and directly involved in national politics. Reference cases, though by no means frequent, were of such a character as to make the Court particularly vulnerable to political involvement and partisan attack. In 1903 two questions involving the redistribution of parliamentary seats were referred to the Court, in part because of the insistence of the opposition Conservative party.[36] In 1912 the Court was forced to express its opinion regarding the emotional issue of the *ne temere* decree, involving the power of the provincial legislature to put into legislation a papal decree dealing with mixed marriages. When the justices divided evenly along denominational lines (three Roman Catholics versus three Protestants) as to whether Protestant clergy in Quebec could officiate at the marriages of Roman Catholics, the impartiality of the Court was brought into question – though not many observers thought to challenge the inappropriateness of the reference system that had placed the justices in that invidious position.[37] In 1902, in a different reference, the government found itself caught in a complex web spun by its own political machinations. While still minister of justice, David Mills had advised the cabinet on a legal matter. Sir Louis Davies, also still in the government, had disagreed with Mills's view and had insisted upon a reference of the issue to the Supreme Court, carrying a majority of the cabinet with him. By the time the reference had been prepared for argument, both Mills and Davies were on the bench. The deputy minister of justice, E.L. Newcombe, moved to have Mills excluded from the panel, allegedly because he disagreed with the point of view most favourable to the government, and to replace him with Davies, who was known to support the opposite view. This 'attempt to pack the Court' was 'all wrong,' argued Mills. 'You see this proposal of your deputy is an attempt to exclude only those whom he thinks adverse to his opinion. This is not consistent with his duty. No member of the Government who advised this reference against its Law Officer should sit.'[38] The outcome of this reference was not reported, but it serves to reveal some of the dangers of the reference system and the dangers of the Supreme Court's being too closely connected with the government.

The close ties between the Court and the government were known, and attempts were made to exploit them. As in 1877, counsel continued from time to time to ask the department of justice to exert pressure on the Court to hear a motion, or speed up judgment, or give some other consideration.[39] There is no evidence that any pressure was actually exerted by the department. Sometimes the ties were simply reflected in shared political gossip or in social interchange.[40] It was the natural tendency of the justices who came from active political positions to maintain their lifelong interest in partisan political affairs. A few months after joining the Court, David Mills received a letter full of political news from an old associate; he responded, 'I thank you for your letter of the 5th inst. as I feel that I have entered stagnant waters since I have gone out of public life, and the interest awakened by an occasional letter from an old friend is the only ripple upon its surface.'[41] After long political careers, the absence of the stimulation and challenge of politics left a gap that some sought to fill by giving advice to active politicians on how to handle various problems. This was true of Sir Louis Davies and particularly of Sir Charles Fitzpatrick.[42]

Fitzpatrick's involvement was extensive, but his public role had a non-partisan appearance. Any activities regarding policy advice or partisan affairs took place behind the scenes, unknown to the public. In 1906 the newly appointed chief justice carefully declined to sit on contested election cases, but such scruples seemed to be short-lived. Less than three months after joining the Court, Fitzpatrick wrote the prime minister asking 'as [a] personal favour' that the vacancy at the Court created by Justice Sedgewick's death be filled by Judge Cannon of Quebec. One of the chief justice's ties to the government was a $5,000 personal debt to Sir Wilfrid Laurier.[43] Nor did Fitzpatrick limit himself to dealings with his late Liberal colleagues. Shortly after the Conservative victory in 1911, involving the defeat of a reciprocity treaty with the United States, the chief justice was approached by Elihu Root, a former American secretary of state and currently a senator, to give a speech in New York explaining the rejection of reciprocity and emphasizing Canada's ongoing friendship with its American neighbour. This the chief justice did, with the approval of Robert Borden, the new prime minister. Soon Fitzpatick was recommending legislation and offering specific political advice on handling Senate appointments, on responding to the Manitoba schools issue, and especially on affairs in Quebec (where the Conservative party was noticeably weak). In his native province Fitzpatrick stepped into a sensitive local situation in mid-1913 by dispensing patronage in the Quebec City region; and while chief justice he acted as Borden's personal agent to the provincial Conservative party.[44] By the time the war commenced, the chief justice had become an important adviser to the government, particularly on matters relating to minority rights and to

Quebec. In 1916, at the request of the prime minister and T.C. Casgrain, the leading French-Canadian cabinet minister, Fitzpatrick drew up a memorandum offering advice on the disallowance of the most recent schools legislation in Manitoba and on the larger problem of French-language rights in the dominion. He spoke out publicly in defence of French as an official language. As racial tension mounted in 1916 and 1917, the chief justice did his best to keep the government in touch with the concerns and resentments of his Quebec compatriots. He spoke at military recruitment meetings in his native province. He even went so far as to pass on to the minister of justice some private notes of judgment that touched on federal legislation.[45] It is not surprising that in the fall of 1918 Sir Charles Fitzpatrick left the Supreme Court of Canada to become the lieutenant-governor of Quebec.

It is possible to defend the political involvement of Fitzpatrick and others as being in the broader national interest. But it is important to realize that such ties to the political arena simply maintained Canadian governments' view that the Court and its members were political instruments to be used whenever and however it was necessary or desirable to do so.

Much of the evidence makes clear that the close connections between the government and the Supreme Court were encouraged by many of the justices. Neither they nor the politicians viewed the judges' activities as incorrect or inappropriate. Indeed, as Fitzpatrick himself made clear in 1900, the judiciary continued to be perceived in the long-standing British tradition of working closely and co-operatively with the government.[46] Lyman Duff, for example, not long after joining the Court, was prepared, after consulting with government members, to visit British Columbia on behalf of the government to help to deal with a political problem there in the provincial Supreme Court. As well, his abilities and his Liberal interests were well enough recognized that his name was considered in a proposed cabinet shuffle in 1907.[47] While activities such as Duff's took place behind the scenes, those of others did not. Chief Justice Taschereau seemed bent on repeating his 1893 direct intrusion into the political arena. That earlier intrusion had involved a policy matter on which the justice had some expertise; in 1904 that was far from the case. In London to sit on the Judicial Committee, the chief justice spoke out publicly on the Dundonald affair;[48] according to newspaper reports, Taschereau criticized British press accounts as 'being loaded up by Ottawa Tory sources' and advised that the imperial government would be wise to recall Lord Dundonald before the end of the week. Taschereau's conduct was the subject of debate in the Canadian House of Commons. Within two days the chief justice had left for Canada, apparently summoned home by an embarrassed cabinet (though the government denied it).[49] Such open involvement in partisan matters was becoming less acceptable.

Another non-judicial activity was the justices' participation in various boards and commissions. The growing tendency to employ members of the judiciary as arbitrators and commissioners was a matter of considerable controversy and complaint among the legal fraternity at the time. Sir Henry Strong (retired) and E.R. Cameron, the registrar, were both appointed members of the statute-revising commission from 1902 to 1906; in 1905 these same two were asked to prepare a revised and amended Criminal Code.[50] In 1903 John Armour was named to the Alaska Boundary Commission. In 1907 Chief Justice Fitzpatrick was appointed to the Pecuniary Claims Arbitration Commission of Great Britain and the United States; he was actively involved until 1912 in negotiations and hearings dealing with the settlement of outstanding Canadian-American disputes. The experience gained in this post led to the chief justice's appointment to the International Claims Commission involving the United States and France, and in 1915 to the International Peace Commission as the Canadian representative.[51]

More sensitive, because of the partisan and emotional character of the issues involved, was Lyman Duff's acceptance of two special tasks from the Borden government. In 1916 a serious scandal was brewing, allegedly involving the illegal letting of munitions contracts, the minister of militia and defence, Sir Sam Hughes, and the use of contracts to benefit the officials of the Shell Commission.[52] The charges were laid by the Liberal party, now in opposition, which sensed an opportunity to deliver a mortal wound to a weak and vulnerable Conservative government. To investigate these allegations and to relieve the political pressure, Sir Robert Borden appointed a two-man royal commission, the junior member of which was Justice Duff. Although the prime minister's desire to exploit the prestige and supposed neutrality of the judiciary is understandable, Duff's decision to become involved in such an obviously partisan wrangle exposed himself and the Supreme Court to the risk of political attack and diminished reputation.

Less than a year after Duff had finished this task, the government called on him to become the sole central appeal judge. The Military Service Act of 1917 had imposed conscription on adult Canadian males. Both the legislation and the principle of compulsory military service were highly contentious, involving powerful currents of ethnic animosity. Under the act individuals were allowed to apply for exemptions, and an extensive administrative staff was set up to review the applications – local tribunals, appeal tribunals, and finally a central appeal court. The amount of work demanded of Duff in this post was considerable; the entire system dealt with nearly four hundred thousand applications for exemption. The nature of the appeals exposed the justice to pleas for special consideration – Sir Wilfrid Laurier, for example, requested favoured treatment for several persons. The work was laborious and emotionally draining, as indicated by Duff's later recollection: 'After the last war, he could not bear the thought of having the conscription records placed anywhere where the public could reach them. The papers of the local tribunals and appeal bodies in Quebec were full of hatred and bitterness and would have been a living menace to national unity. He had, therefore ... burned them and he was glad to say no real record of conscription existed.'[53] By the end of the war Duff was suffering from nervous exhaustion, and took a leave of absence for recuperation.[54]

There can be no doubt that Justice Duff accepted these onerous assignments out of a sense of public duty. He was being criticized for agreeing to act on the Shell Commission, he knew, but in the face of changing public standards for judicial behaviour Duff declined to alter his own view of the judicial role. In writing the prime minister, Duff made it clear that he had no regrets about his non-judicial activities: 'I have a perfectly clear conscience on the score. it is possible to carry the notion of judicial retirement from the world to the point of the ridiculous, and I have no doubt I should have done wrong had I not acted upon your request [to join the royal commission].'[55] This sense of commitment to the national interest in wartime, as well as Justice Duff's position above the domestic field of partisan political conflict, led to the frequent rumours in 1917 that he was being seriously considered as cabinet material, even as the head of a new Union government. How much Duff himself encouraged such speculation is unclear, but it is true that through his willing involvement in non-judicial tasks outside the Supreme Court he had allowed his name to be associated with national political affairs. In the special political circumstances that existed in the summer of 1917, it was natural that he would attract attention from those looking for a new type of national leader.[56] Justice Duff's sincere national commitment is revealed by his refusal to accept any honorarium, either as royal commissioner or as central appeal judge; it was against the provisions of the Supreme Court Act, he argued, to accept any payment beyond his regular salary plus expenses, and no amount of government pleading could change his mind.[57] This was one decision by which other justices did not feel bound.

The individual justices were active outside the Court in supporting the state, and so was the Court itself. In the summer of 1918, for example, the Court dealt with a case involving several urgent issues of great national importance, not all of which were legal in character. *In Re Gray* (1918) concerned an application for habeas corpus and had been referred to the full Court by Justice Anglin in chambers.[58] George Edwin Gray, a young, unmarried homesteader and farmer in northern Ontario, had lost his exemption from conscription in April 1918 when an order-in-council cancelled exemptions granted by the Military Service Act of 1917. His claim for exemption had been disallowed by the local tribunal but allowed by the appeal tribunal; an appeal of this ruling had been taken to the central appeal judge by the military authorities but had not yet been heard. Without waiting for the appeal to be heard and on the ground that the statutory exemption had now been removed by the order-in-council, the military authorities ordered Gray to report for duty and, when he refused to do so, seized him and held him in custody. Gray then applied for a writ of habeas corpus on the ground that Parliament's delegation of its legislative powers to the cabinet, under the War Measures Act of 1914, was ultra vires and that the order-in-council of 1918 was therefore invalid.

The case involved several important issues. A major section of the War Measures Act was being challenged, potentially invalidating scores of orders and regulations issued by the cabinet under that authority. More immediately, much of the military conscription could be brought to a halt and the statutory exemptions reinstated. This threat was made even more real by an almost precisely similar case in which the Supreme Court of Alberta had found the 1918 order-in-council ultra vires.[59]

With these issues at stake, the Supreme Court of Canada moved quickly into action. The deputy minister of justice, E.L. Newcombe, arranged with the chief justice and the staff for a special session of the Court to be called to hear the case. Newcombe then went before Anglin in chambers and suggested that the application be referred to the whole Court in order to obtain an authoritative ruling binding on lower courts, and assured Anglin of the prior approval of the chief justice. The extraordinary session was held on 18 July 1918, all six justices sitting.

The decision upheld the power of the legislature to delegate its legislative powers (Idington and Brodeur dissenting). In their reasons, the justices were obviously impressed with the import of the issue in question and with the win-the-war attitude pervasive at the time. In refusing to undermine the War Measures Act, the chief justice commented:

'Our legislators were no doubt impressed in the hour of peril with the conviction that the safety of the country is the supreme law against which no other law can prevail. It is our clear duty to give effect to their patriotic intention.' Justice Duff also demonstrated his emotional commitment to the war effort:

[T]his Act of Parliament supervened upon a decision which was the most significant, indeed the most revolutionary decision in the history of the country, namely – that an Expeditionary Force of Canadian soldiers should take part in the war with Germany as actual combatants on the Continent of Europe; a decision which would entail, as everybody recognized, measures of great magnitude; requiring as a condition of swift and effective action, that extraordinary powers be possessed by the executive.

As explanations of the wartime mood and decisions these statements contained much accuracy, but as legal judgments they were weak.

In *In Re Gray*, the Supreme Court demonstrated its important role as an instrument of the state. A hearing was needed, and needed quickly; it was willingly arranged. Judgment was handed down just one day later, on 19 July. Special care was taken to make the reasons quickly available. Anglin's judgment appeared in the Toronto *Globe*; the chief justice sent a draft copy of his decision to the *Canada Law Journal* before a final revision of the judgment had been completed. The Court was eager to have the reasons published officially as soon as possible.[60] The judges' vulnerability to the emotional wartime environment may have led them to issue too sweeping a judgment. Peter Hogg has commented:

In effect the War Measures Act transferred to the federal cabinet virtually the whole legislative authority of the Parliament for the duration of the war. The court held that even a delegation as sweeping as this one was valid. However, the four opinions each contained indications that the power of delegation was not absolute, and that an 'abdication', 'abandonment' or 'surrender' of the Parliament's powers would be invalid. But since none of the majority judges regarded the War Measures Act as an unconstitutional abdication, abandonment or surrender, it is not easy to imagine the kind of delegation which would be unconstitutional.[61]

Judicial power was thus an integral part of the system through which the war was prosecuted.

The close ties between the judiciary and the political executive had the potential for influencing judicial decisions handed down by the Supreme

Court of Canada. *In Re Gray* makes clear the potential for indirect influence. Another case reveals just how loosely defined the standards of behaviour were and, in the existing judicial culture, how vulnerable the Court was to direct interference. There is strong evidence that in 1911 Mackenzie King, then minister of labour, directly interfered in the judicial process in a case that was important to him emotionally because it affected the reputation of his grandfather. While *Morang and Company* v *LeSueur* (1911) was before the Supreme Court, King and his cousin 'made a direct attempt [wrote one of the justices involved] to influence the decision of the members of the Court by communicating facts which afterwards came out in another litigation.' As deplorable as this interference was, the justices' decision to say nothing of 'the offence' was equally unfortunate. There seems to have been a tacit acceptance by the Court of political interference.[62]

Nevertheless, the Court's work carried on. The number of appeals continued to rise, and the Court became much more efficient in its handling of cases. In the fall of 1903, for example, fifty-six appeals had been inscribed for hearing: ten from Ontario, thirteen from Quebec, eighteen from the maritimes, and fifteen from the west – a healthy balance among the various regions. By the time the Court adjourned in mid-December, argument had been heard and judgment given in all but eleven cases. Of the eleven, eight stood for judgment and only three had been deferred for hearing in the next term. This was, as a law journal pointed out, 'a thoroughly satisfactory state of affairs.' By 1913 the total number of appeals had risen to 176, the largest number to date, including thirty-four from British Columbia and twenty-eight from the prairies. By the fall session alone of 1918, the number of cases inscribed had reached seventy-four, a number the chief justice found 'alarming.'[63]

And the Court sought to become even more proficient. In 1907 a new rule was adopted limiting the number of counsel to be heard for each side (two) and the amount of time for argument (three hours).[64] This rule ought not to be seen as evidence of a declining emphasis on oral presentation, but rather as an attempt to gain the potential advantages of brevity and succinctness. Particularly under the influence of Charles Fitzpatrick, genuine attempts were made to deal more effectively with French-language and civil-law appeals. The library was notably improved, and in 1908 a French-language stenographer was appointed to the Court staff.

The internal environment at the Supreme Court also seemed to be improving. Personality conflicts had declined, owing particularly to the departure of Sir Henry Strong. The more co-operative atmosphere was the product of the efforts of many justices; the recently resigned Wallace Nesbitt, for example, gave an informal dinner at the Rideau Club to welcome Lyman Duff to the Court.[65] Sir Charles Fitzpatrick, however, appears to deserve much of the credit in advancing a more collegial spirit. He thoughtfully solicited some recognition, such as a knighthood, for his senior puisne justice, Désiré Girouard, as Girouard neared the end of his career. When conflicts occurred at judicial conferences, as they inevitably did, quarrels were not prolonged. After one such confrontation, Justice Brodeur quickly apologized and pledged that he would always be disposed to co-operate 'à ce résultat afin que nous pouissions rechercher efficacement une solution équitable des problèmes qui nous soul sommes [?] & afin que nous pouissions remplir d'une manière [?] satisfaisante nos fonctions qui sont d'une responsibilité si terrible.'[66] An atmosphere now existed in which a justice sought quickly to express his regrets and his willingness to work with his colleagues in the future.

The practice of circulating draft judgments for comments was maintained during this period and perhaps even increased. Fitzpatrick, at least at times, consulted not only his fellow justices, but also some of the Court staff, including his secretary and the registrar. According to a 1914 report in *Maclean's Magazine*, judicial conferences were held at various times as well as at a regular meeting on Saturday afternoons.[67]

The intellectual environment at the Supreme Court remained active. More articles and digests were being published, and staff members had begun to write commentaries (never unfavourable) regarding some of the Court's decisions.[68] But the quality of the intellectual environment, particularly among the justices, should not be exaggerated. Mills, after all, had referred to the Court as 'stagnant waters.' More indicative of the intellectual level of the Court, perhaps, is the conservative nature of some of the decisions. The Supreme Court justices of the early twentieth century were even more thorough than their predecessors in searching for precedents as a sure and secure way through the tangle of legal problems. In fact, the Court at this time handed down the strongest judgment it would ever render in support of stare decisis. In the leading case of *Stuart v Bank of Montreal* (1909) four justices (Fitzpatrick, Duff, Davies, and Anglin, Idington dissenting) adopted a formalistic approach to the issues and chose to be bound by a previous decision despite available grounds for distinguishing that decision and despite testimony from the appellant indicating that no injustice had been done her. Nevertheless, the Court, led by Justices Duff and Anglin, adopted the precedent explicitly on grounds of stare decisis. Justice Duff underlined the influence of the predominantly British judicial culture and of the Supreme Court's subordinate position:

Some question is raised, whether or not we are entitled to disregard a previous decision of this court laying down a substantive rule of law. This court is, of course, not a court of final resort in the sense which the House of Lords is because our decisions are reviewable by the Privy Council; but only in very exceptional circumstances would the Court of Exchequer Chamber or the Lords Justices, sitting in appeal ... have felt themselves at liberty to depart from one of their own previous decisions. That is also the principle upon which the Court of Appeal now acts ... and the Court of Appeal, in any province where the basis of the law is the common law of England, would act upon the same view.[69]

Here is solid evidence of the jurisprudential constraints placed on the judges' approach to the law by the Supreme Court of Canada's position as an intermediate appellate body. The justices felt themselves to be simply unable to develop the law in significant new directions; any such initiative lay with the senior appellate body. In the meantime, precedents would be binding for the Canadian judges. The advantage of such a line of reasoning was the stability and security that it gave to the law.

In 1908, in *Iredale* v *Loudon*, the ends to which such rigidity could lead were demonstrated.[70] A majority of the Court held that by adverse possession title had been acquired to the second floor of a Toronto building; but at the same time a different majority held that the owner of the second floor, James Iredale, had acquired no proprietary right in the supports to the building (and in particular the support to the second floor). Iredale's request for an injunction to prevent the owners of the rest of the building from tearing down their portion of the building was rejected. The practical absurdity of such a ruling left the Supreme Court open to ridicule.

Another example of the narrowness of the justices' thinking is the case of *Cameron* v *Cuddy* (1914).[71] The two parties were disputing a timber contract in British Columbia. One side claimed that there had been a major shortfall from the amount of timber contracted for, but through a technical defect arbitration had failed. Both parties admitted that a shortfall existed, but the lower court declined to take that into account and ordered full payment of the purchase price. The Supreme Court upheld this ruling, finding that the point at issue was one of procedure rather than of substance, thus perpetuating a clear injustice. The Judicial Committee pointed out to the Canadian courts that it had been their responsibility to step in and adjust the arbitration process so that the parties involved might gain their rights. Instead, the provincial court and ultimately the Supreme Court had taken a very restricted view of the judicial function and a narrow interpretation of the law involved.

In the area of civil liberties the Supreme Court justices in this period combined the safety of stare decisis with an unquestioning acceptance of long-standing racist attitudes in Canada by upholding the power of the state to pass discriminatory legislation aimed at particular racial groups. In 1902 the Judicial Committee upheld on jurisdictional grounds a British Columbia statute disqualifying Canadians of Chinese, Japanese, and North American Indian descent from voting.[72] The 1914 case of *Quong-Wing v The King* tested Saskatchewan legislation prohibiting the employment of white female labour in places of business or amusement kept or managed by 'Chinamen.'[73] In the face of an applicable precedent and in a racist Canadian environment, it would have been unrealistic to have expected the Canadian Supreme Court to do other than confirm the legislation.

Four justices (Fitzpatrick, Davies, Duff, and Anglin) refused to distinguish the case from earlier decisions and opted to uphold the state's right to violate Quong-Wing's basic civil liberties. In three separate judgments the majority refused to discuss any such principles, insisting instead on a simple jurisdictional test of the legislation. The chief justice opined that this statute was no different from any other factory or employment legislation: 'There are many factory Acts passed by provincial legislatures to fix the age of employment and to provide for proper accommodation for workmen and the convenience of the sexes which are intended to safeguard the bodily health, but also the morals of Canadian workers, and I fail to understand the difference in principle between that legislation and this.' The intellectual depth of this argument was matched by Davies (with whom Anglin concurred) and Duff. Davies concluded that since the provincial legislature had authority to legislate as to civil rights, the statute must be valid; it was as simple as that. Provincial powers in the field were absolute and unqualified ('plenary'). It was not for the Supreme Court to employ any other criteria in assessing the use of those powers. Duff, the westerner, tried to argue that the special circumstances of the western population required such protective legislation:

In the sparsely inhabited Western provinces of this country the presence of Orientals in comparatively considerable numbers not infrequently raises questions for public discussion and treatment, and, sometimes in an acute degree, which in more thickly populated countries would excite little or no general interest. One can without difficulty figure to one's self the considerations which may have influenced the Saskatchewan Legislature in dealing with the practice of white girls taking employment in such circumstances as are within the contemplation of this Act; considerations, for example, touching the interests of immigrant European women, and considerations touching the effect of such a practice upon the local relations between Europeans and Orientals.

Such rationalizations accurately reflected popular Canadian attitudes. But the justices' refusal to view the issue as anything other than one of the distribution of powers is striking, as is their inability to rise above popular attitudes.

Only Justice Idington, in dissent, stood out against his colleagues, finding the legislation an abrogation of a naturalized citizen's rights. He condemned the statute as 'but a piece of the mode of thought that begot and maintained slavery,' but his arguments swayed neither his fellow justices nor the majority of Canadians. The Supreme Court of Canada thus became part of a system maintaining legalized racial discrimination in Canada.

Finally, the Court also dealt with areas of law that involved various aspects of the process of industrialization, which by the turn of the century was already well advanced. The administrative state was rising in the early twentieth century as one means by which economic expansion could be facilitated and directed.[74] The first governmental regulatory agency to serve this function was the Board of Railway Commissioners, to which Albert Killam had been transferred in 1905 as chief commissioner. The board's mandate was to enforce government railway regulations and to assist railway expansion and efficiency. Though the Supreme Court over the next several decades generally upheld the board's regulatory authority, the justices did not easily accommodate the wishes of the quasi-judicial board. In a 1909 case,[75] for example, the Court affirmed a board order for the erection and maintenance of fences by the Canadian Northern Railway along rail lines which passed through lands that were settled or improved but not yet enclosed. The board's authority was upheld, but the justices accompanied their decision with warnings that the board's powers would be closely scrutinized by the Court; as Chief Justice Fitzpatrick wrote, 'each individual case is to be considered before an order is made.' In restraining the regulatory agency, the Court acted to control economic development to a degree.

This is even more apparent in cases where industrialization and economic growth invaded private property rights.[76] Jennifer Nedelsky points to *Canada Paper Company* v *Brown* (1922)[77] as a useful example of this. A.J. Brown brought suit to restrain the pulp and paper company's local sulphite plant from emitting 'nauseous and offensive odors and fumes.' In decisions that were not particularly well reasoned, the justices unanimously held that the constraint on Brown's ability to enjoy his private property was sufficiently extensive and distinct to warrant granting a perpetual injunction against the Canada Paper Company. Justice Idington, for example, weighed Brown's occupation of his ancestral summer home, which had been in his family for over one hundred years, with the company's pollution of the air 'for mere commercial reasons'; in such a contest, the rights of private property took precedence. The justices chose to believe that the injunction would not necessarily lead to the cessation of the company's operations in the area. But Duff warned that in every case the Court would compare the common good of the community with individual claims – where sufficient harm to the former would be done by such an injunction, it would not be granted. While an awareness of the need for a balanced perspective existed, the Supreme Court was nevertheless active in restraining corporations and economic development in the interest of private property rights. Given this traditional common-law approach, it is not surprising that business and political leaders sought to restrict the juridiction of Canadian courts in such matters.[78]

Nor was the Supreme Court of Canada willing to break new ground in the interests of industrial workers. Led by Justice Girouard, the Court reversed decisions in provincial appeal courts which had held employers negligent in the case of industrial accidents. It was not enough to find that employers had failed to create a safe workplace, held the Court; the employer's negligence must also be proven to be the cause of the worker's injury. For proof, substantial evidence was needed, not 'mere conjecture.' In the absence of such evidence, a strict construction of the law would be applied.[79] It would not be through the Supreme Court of Canada that the law would be adjusted to meet the new circumstances of the workplace.

The judicial conservatism of the Supreme Court justices is attributable to a number of factors. One was the judicial inexperience of the justices. There was inconsistency in some rulings and a general reticence in others. The justices were learning on the job, and the quality of their decisions suffered. Lyman Duff, for example, was slow to join in a full share of the Court's intellectual work. As his biographer relates:

Duff, however, did not plunge into the work of the court as he did into Ottawa society. There was in him a certain diffidence about taking an active part in the deliberations of his fellow judges, an understandable reaction from a relatively young westerner suddenly finding himself a member of the highest court in the land. He did not, as Anglin did after his appointment in 1909, start writing judgements in important cases at once, choosing rather to side with one or another of his colleagues. Not until he had been on the court for two months did he write a judgement, and even then it was an uncharacteristically short one. And not until he had been four months on the court did he write his first judgement to express the views of the court as a whole. In fact, Duff used this whole prewar period to develop his judicial talents.[80]

By these calculations, Duff spent his first eight years on the Court developing his judicial abilities to the level of which he was capable. During those eight years he was not yet at his best. Such learning, ideally, should be done in the courts below; the highest court in the land ought to consist of experienced, skilled jurists.

The judicial conservatism of the Court was apparent not just in the reasoning in specific cases but also in the overall tendencies toward various dispositions of appeals. For the period 1903–13 (for which the complete statistics for all cases are available), the Supreme Court of Canada affirmed lower-court decisions in fully 60.2 per cent of all decisions, reversing just 24.2 per cent.[81] Could it be that, unsure of their own abilities and knowledge and aware of the lack of respect for the Supreme Court, its justices subconsciously tended not to challenge decisions from senior provincial courts—either to avoid being challenged themselves or to reach for acceptance among members of the legal community?

As part of his work on the Statute Revising Commission, the registrar, E.R. Cameron, undertook to revise the Supreme Court Act. Less than two months after his appointment to the commission late in 1902, Cameron on his own authority decided that something more drastic was needed than a simple collation of recent amendments concerning the Supreme Court Act. He wrote to the minister of justice:

I may say that I am re-drafting the Supreme Court Act, as I find it impossible to do justice to the subject, as it appears to me, in any other way. As soon as it is type-written I would like to go over it with you, before having it finally printed. There will be so many alterations in many of the sections that you may think it advisable that the Bill, as revised and approved by the Commission with all the amendments considered necessary and advisable, should be passed at the next session of the House.[82]

The registrar decided to take advantage of his opportunity to amend the legislation with a view to removing various anomalies or problems in the Supreme Court's jurisdiction, as indicated by various rulings on practice over the past several decades.

The initiative and the first decision to proceed with the revision came from the administrative head of the Court, operating under the cloaking authority of the Statute Revising Commission. But the registrar was completely open about the work being undertaken. Cameron quickly involved the minister to whom he was responsible (bypassing the deputy minister) and gained at least the tacit approval of Fitzpatrick. Over the next year the various changes were ironed out and approved, at least tentatively, by both the commission and the Justice Department. In 1904 the proposed amendments were circulated, on authority of the minister, to the bar associations and the provincial attorneys-general. As well, a copy of a memorandum outlining the proposals reached the *Canadian Law Review*, which reprinted it for the benefit of the profession as a whole.[83] Cameron's explanations of the various changes were detailed and precise, citing the rulings where problems had arisen and giving the intent of the alterations. Reactions and suggestions to these changes were solicited and received before the final draft was drawn up. At the end of this legislative drafting process the minister chose not to submit separately to Parliament the new Supreme Court Act; instead, it was adopted simply through the general authority of the legislation approving the revised statutes.

The basic thrust of the amendments was reinforced by a new set of rules drawn up in 1907 largely by Cameron and Chief Justice Fitzpatrick. The overall aim of all these changes was twofold: to clarify the jurisdiction of the Supreme Court and to increase its efficiency. In the ten years from 1893 to 1903, there had been a considerable rise in the number of motions to quash for want of jurisdiction. The Reports noted fifty such successful motions in the period, and even more had been unsuccessful.[84] With greater precision and clarity in the phrasing of the act and with the response to specific rulings, it was hoped that the amount of time spent by the Court on jurisdiction would decrease considerably. The new rules reinforced this by directing that every appeal required, at an early stage, an order from a judge of the Supreme Court in chambers confirming jurisdiction. This new procedure would make heavy use of the registrar (who in 1887 had been given the authority to act as judge in chambers) and aimed at saving the Court time and effort and saving the appellants large sums spent in what might turn out to be improper appeals.[85] The increased efficiency that would accrue from this change was reinforced by a move to end what were regarded as frivolous appeals. From the beginning, appeals from Quebec had been limited generally to cases where the amount in controversy was at least $2,000, but no such limits were applied to the other provinces or territories. In 1897 legislation limited appeal from Ontario generally to cases where the amount in controversy was at least $1,000. In 1902 legislation was adopted for the Yukon Territory requiring a minimum sum in controversy of $2,000.[86] Cases involving minor sums continued to be appealed from elsewhere, however. In 1900, in a Nova Scotia appeal concerning goods worth $80, Justice Taschereau quoted an earlier complaint by Chief Justice Strong concerning the easy access of unimportant cases, and added: 'The Maritime Provinces enjoy the costly privilege of bringing appeals to this court upon such paltry amounts ... That such appeals should be possible is a blot upon the administration of justice. I hope the bar from the Maritime Provinces will assist in obtaining the necessary legislation to put an end to that state of things.'[87] In keeping with the legislative tendency and the justices' pleas, Cameron took the initiative in proposing monetary minima for appeals from every province and territory. The original suggestion of $500 was reduced eventually to $250 and was applied to appeals from British Columbia and the maritimes.[88]

The use of monetary criteria to determine access to the Supreme Court of Canada came under serious attack in later years. It should be noted, however, that no such criticisms were voiced in the period when the new limitations were adopted. When comments were made, they concerned the level of the monetary limit, but not the philosophy behind a limit of this character. Some in the maritimes, including members of the Nova Scotia bar, sought a lower sum; there was some pressure from Ontario for a higher sum.[89] Monetary criteria reflected accurately the Canadian climate of opinion.

One other change was discussed regarding the court's basic structure. This was the recurrent issue of expanding the number of justices on the Supreme Court bench, either through creating a seventh permanent position or by the occasional naming of ad hoc members. Illnesses and leaves of absence continued to cause problems – as, for example, in 1906, when Chief Justice Taschereau was granted a leave of absence and all but one of the appeals from Quebec were delayed until a second civil-law justice could be present. Taschereau himself called for the naming of ad hoc justices or a reduction of the quorum to four. In 1910, after only a year on the Supreme Court, Frank Anglin submitted, without consulting any of his colleagues, a draft bill allowing appointment of ad hoc justices.[90] The government took no action.

Finally, in 1918, after almost forty years of off-and-on discussion, the government guided through Parliament a measure allowing the appointment of ad hoc justices, to be chosen either from the Exchequer Court or from provincial superior courts. Late in the winter term of 1918 the Supreme Court had been forced to suspend sittings, since Duff was unavailable owing to his duties as central appeal judge and Davies was ill. The legislation permitted the chief justice to ask the senior judge of the Exchequer Court to sit as judge ad hoc; if the latter was unavailable, the chief justice could then ask a provincial chief justice to designate a superior court justice from that province to sit in Ottawa temporarily. Perhaps surprisingly, there was no requirement that a justice from Quebec should be replaced by a civil-law jurist.[91] The legislation was immediately put into effect, and over the next ten years it worked well. And yet it was a temporary solution. Before the year was out the prime minister was contemplating the expansion of the Court to seven members.[92]

Their perceived status remained important to the incumbent justices. The adverse image of the Court itself rendered the justices quite sensitive and vulnerable personally.[93] Several of them reacted by placing disproportionate emphasis on visible signs of status. The issue of the justices' position in the Canadian table of precedence was raised once again by both Taschereau and Davies.[94] As usual, knighthoods were awarded to the new chief justices – to Taschereau in 1903 (KB) and to Fitzpatrick in 1907 (KCMG). The latter had caused a fuss over the honour. Originally the Colonial Office had arranged for him to receive a knight bachelorhood, but through the prime minister and the governor-general protests were lodged and a rejection of the lesser title was threatened until the more prestigious honour was agreed upon.[95] In 1901 the Canadian cabinet had refused to accept as administrator, in the absence of the governor-general, the general officer commanding in Halifax; the cabinet suggested instead the appointment of the chief justice of Canada.

This change was agreed to by the governments involved, but it resulted in several problems. Sir Henry Strong pointed out that when performing these additional duties the general officer commanding had always received a per diem allowance equal to one-quarter of the governor general's salary; on principle, he claimed, the same payment should be made to the chief justice when acting in a similar capacity.[96] A few years later, Sir Elzéar Taschereau chose to make a public issue out of his claim that the title 'Excellency' was due him when he was acting as administrator. Taschereau took it as a deliberate slight to Canadians that the title had been dropped when Strong first assumed the office, and he pressed hard in asserting his right to the title – a right that was eventually acknowledged by the Colonial Office and by a reluctant Sir Joseph Pope, Canadian clerk of the Privy Council. Sir Joseph was similarly none too gracious in meeting the demands of Strong and Fitzpatrick to be known as 'chief justice of Canada.'[97]

In 1904 Chief Justice Taschereau was named to the imperial Privy Council, and he attended the summer sittings of the Judicial Committee five times (1904, 1906–8, 1910). Fitzpatrick, however, could not be appointed to the committee immediately. Two was the maximum number of Canadians allowed, and although Sir Henry Strong never attended after 1900, he declined to resign. By 1909, however, Fitzpatrick was named both to the imperial Privy Council (a position he wanted badly) and to the Permanent Court of Arbitration at the Hague as one of the British members. The chief justice enjoyed this latter position so much that he went to particular lengths to arrange his reappointment in 1913.[98]

Problems with the Supreme Court Reports continued. There were delays in printing and in publishing the reasons for judgment,[99] though the difficulties were much less serious than in the 1880s. An attempt was made to solve the printing problems by shifting the work in 1905 to a private publishing firm. Delays caused by the justices were less frequent, but they still existed. The registrar explained that

the whole trouble arises from the fact that *all* the reasons for judgment of the Judges are not handed down when judgment is pronounced. It is sometimes weeks afterwards before I have the complete number in my hands. The result of my discussion with Mr. Newcombe [deputy minister of justice] was that there is only one way of improving the situation and that is either by direction of the Justice Department or an amendment of the Supreme Court Act requiring that the reasons should be handed down at the same time as the judgments.[100]

In the registrar's opinion, the problem was not in the system of distribution or publication, but rather in the justices' practices.

One explanation of the justices' failure to prepare reasons for judgment immediately may have been that of efficiency: if the case was not reported, no reasons need ever be prepared. The procedure of delaying preparation of judgments was thus a time-saving measure. But when the case was significant enough to report, reasons ought to have been published, and such was not always the case. One example is *The King* v *Stewart* (1902). A panel of four (Gwynne having died) handed down a 3–1 decision dismissing the appeal and the cross-appeal. No reasons were given by the majority (Strong, Sedgewick, and Girouard); Taschereau wrote a detailed explanation of his dissent. Similarly, in *McKee* v *Philip* (1916) no report of the case was apparently planned until Justice Duff complained to the Justice Department. The deputy minister, who had been one of the counsel in the case (acting in a private capacity), pushed the registrar to have the case reported. The result was decidedly less than satisfactory: the four judges in the majority each provided a few very brief, general comments, totalling three pages in length, while Duff in dissent explained his reasoning for fourteen pages. Readers of the Reports were thus left with little explanation as to why these cases were decided the way they were. The deputy minister expressed his frustration: 'We have a similar case which occurred recently of the King v. Stewart, where the government has gone to great expense in bringing questions affecting the contracts before the court of appeal and in which although the appeal has been dismissed we have succeeded in obtaining only the reasons of the dissenting judge.'[101] Such reporting was obviously less helpful to the profession than it might have been. It is apparent that in the reporting of cases both leadership and clear criteria were lacking.

These complaints fitted in with criticism of two other tendencies reflected in the Reports. One was the ongoing debate as to the usefulness of dissenting judgments. The second was the frequent attack against the multiplicity of judgments. O.M. Biggar, a leading member of the Ontario bar, analysed volume 45 of the Reports in this latter regard. For the twenty-four appeals reported in that volume, there appeared a total of eighty-nine written opinions, including seventeen in dissent and seventy-two in favour of the majority. Although thirteen of the judgments had been unanimous, in only two of those cases had there been just a single judgment. Of the twenty-four appeals reported, two had one judgment, three had two judgments, four had three judgments, eight had four judgments, five had five judgments, and two had a full six judgments.

The justices' inability to concur with one another and their adoption of a variety of grounds had a bewildering effect: 'The result, as will appear by a most cursory glance at some of the headnotes, is a confusion out of which the editor is with difficulty able to drag some semblance of principle.'[102] Collegiality among the justices was not yet strong enough to affect the number of judgments written. As well, the justices exhibited little sense of moderation or control over the extent to which multiple judgments were issued.

There was one other area of complaint regarding the Supreme Court Reports, and that was the selection of cases to be reported and the actual process of reporting. Any justice could ask that a case be reported, but for the most part the decision-making was handled by the chief justice and the reporter. At times the Department of Justice would become involved, either when consulted by the registrar or when requesting (not always successfully) that a particular case be reported. As for the process of reporting, a suggestion was made in 1917 by the deputy minister that a transcript of notes of oral argument should be taken by the reporters to help them prepare their notes to the case; this is another indication that oral argument was taking on an increasingly important role.[103]

The staff continued to be active. The greatest area of improvement within its responsibilities was the library. E.R. Cameron solicited additional funds, lobbied for political support among influential cabinet members, and made detailed arrangements for acquisitions to improve the holdings. He addressed himself particularly to the major gaps in works on the civil law, which had been the subject of complaint from a Quebec lawyer: 'The lack of standard French legal works had been the subject of complaint ever since I knew the Supreme Court.' Cameron consulted with two leading Montreal counsel, Eugène Lafleur and Pierre Mignault, and drew up a list of some 5,500 volumes needed.[104] The requested sum of $25,000 was not directly provided, but the library expenditures were allowed to increase markedly; from around $4,000 at the turn of the century, purchases rose to around $10,000 annually before the end of the first decade. The consequent increase in the size of the holdings led to serious accommodation problems and to an expansion of the library staff.

Indeed, the entire Court staff was growing. By 1918 the Court employed sixteen people (plus two on military duty overseas): a registrar, two reporters, four librarians, seven secretaries and clerks, and four messengers. Salaries rose for both staff and justices. After years of complaint, the level of remuneration was raised in 1906 to $10,000 for the chief justice and $9,000 for each puisne justice. This pleased many, though some thought it was still not enough to attract the very best members of the bar. In 1903 pensions had been placed on a more generous footing, but only for the lifetime of the judge;[105] no benefits were available for a justice's widow.

The long-standing tendency to undermine the Supreme Court's authority and to challenge its position in the nation continued during the period from 1902 to 1918. In 1911 rumours circulated that the Court might be divided in some way, perhaps along geographical lines – one court for the west, and one for central and eastern Canada. That such a suggestion could be taken seriously is an indication of the ongoing disillusionment with the Supreme Court. In 1915 Sir Wilfrid Laurier, by then leader of the opposition, supported a political doctrine that would have undercut the essence of the Supreme Court's judicial position as originally intended. Laurier objected to an amendment to the Supreme Court Act on the ground that any such change would 'violate the principle which should be inviolate – that provincial laws shall be interpreted by provincial courts and federal laws by federal courts.' Here once again was the basic challenge offered in the early 1880s: would this be a centralizing court, designed to provide a unified, coherent jurisprudence in all areas of law for the entire country, or would the Supreme Court of Canada deal simply with the much more limited field of federal law? The question was raised again in 1917 when a bill was introduced in the Senate to remove disputes involving property and civil rights or merely local or private matters of provincial jurisdiction.[106] Just as the tensions involving Confederation itself would not fade away, so too the debate over the role of the Supreme Court of Canada was to continue – both because of the weakness of the Court and because of its role as a symbol of centralization.

Over the first two decades of the twentieth century the Supreme Court of Canada had shown few signs of improvement. Indeed, if appeals taken to the Judicial Committee are an indication of lack of respect for the Court, this period was probably the weakest in the Court's history. In the period 1903–13 (for which the complete statistics are available) 14.5 per cent of all decisions were taken to London, a dramatic increase from the period under Sir Henry Strong's leadership, when only 5.1 per cent of decisions went to the Judicial Committee.[107] Those disturbed by the increased tendency to allow the Court to be used as a political instrument in the hands of the government would likely agree that this period was one of decline for the Court. In general, public assessments of the Supreme Court pointed to its weaknesses. An American observer in 1916 noted the lack of respect for the Court and the selection of less-than-the-best judicial candidates:

And to one accustomed to appreciate the regard in which the highest Court in the United States is held both at home and abroad, it is puzzling that a people so clear headed and progressive as those of the Canadian Dominion, should not realize that its conditions require and demand as the keystone of its national arch a Court possessing its highest esteem and confidence, strengthened by its best and brightest legal intellects and honoured by its country.[108]

Among the various explanations for the Court's failure to become 'the keystone' of the national political structure, one answer stood out at this time because it was a relatively new explanation and because it was beginning to be offered fairly frequently. The Supreme Court of Canada 'is supreme only in name,' said the Ottawa *Citizen*. The Court's judgments could be appealed to and overruled by the Judicial Committee of the Privy Council; was this consistent with Canadians' perceptions of themselves and of their country?

It is surely rather a strain on Canada's national self-respect to be thus placed. Canada must depend upon the opinion of an exterior court, so far as law and the interpretation of it are concerned. Her power to decide for herself is not complete. So long as this is the case, it is hardly consistent to talk of 'Imperial partnership,' or of the possession of local autonomy. It may have been necessary for a colony in its earlier stages, but for Canada in the year 1913 one may well doubt its need or its tolerance.[109]

The nationalism arising from the First World War and increasingly articulated in the 1920s would serve to extend and deepen such feelings.

The Supreme Court itself did not share the perceived failure of the institution. For the Ottawa justices the Court already was a key national institution. As stated in a 1904 decision, the Supreme Court of Canada

was established, as far as possible, to be a guide to provincial courts in questions likely to arise throughout the Dominion. We think it was the intention of the framers of the Act creating this court that a tribunal should be established to speak with authority for the Dominion as a whole and, as far as possible, to establish a uniform jurisprudence, especially within matters falling within section 91 of the B.N.A. Act, where the legislation is for the Dominion as a whole, or, as I have said, where purely provincial legislation may be of general interest throughout the Dominion.[110]

The power and influence implied in this ideal had yet to be realized.

5

An Instrument of Politics

1918–1933

In the fall of 1918 Sir Charles Fitzpatrick resigned as chief justice of Canada. The resignation was unexpected. In 1915 Fitzpatrick had taken leave on doctor's orders. In the spring of 1918 he again took leave because of poor health. By the fall his health was used as the official explanation for his retirement; he described himself as having a 'permanent infirmity disabling me from the due execution of my office of Chief Justice of Canada.'[1] But this was not the real reason for Fitzpatrick's departure.

Fitzpatrick had begun to lose some interest in his judicial functions, but at the same time a political problem increasingly attracted his attention. The conscription crisis of 1917–18 was playing havoc with Canadian unity. French Canadians felt alienated from the federal system and from the central government, which by December 1917 had become the almost exclusive preserve of English-speaking Canadians. Two manifestations of this alienation occurred early in 1918: a motion was put forward in the Quebec legislative assembly offering to withdraw Quebec from Confederation, and violent anti-conscription riots took place. Fitzpatrick's retirement must be viewed in the light of the problems of national unity and of his own lifelong commitment to politics as a representative of the people of Quebec. There can be no doubt of his increasing involvement in politics in 1916–18, nor of his genuine concern about the alienation of French Canadians. The lieutenant-governorship of Quebec was about to become vacant, and the chief justice felt that by accepting that post he could aid the cause of national unity. 'I want to help you and my people,' he wrote the prime minister, 'and for that purpose I will make the sacrifice of my position.' The intent was sincere, but the method of ameliorating the problem was embarassingly naïve. C.J. Doherty, the minister of justice and the leading Quebec Conservative, was very doubtful of the wisdom of the move and had to be persuaded – an indication of Fitzpatrick's commitment to the task.[2] Finally, all was agreed and arranged. On 21 October 1918 the fifth chief justice in the history of the Court stepped down from office to become lieutenant-governor of Quebec.

While the rationale for Fitzpatrick's departure is admirable from some points of view, it served to reinforce the Supreme Court's ties to the broader political system. In this it was a fitting climax to the most actively political era in the history of the Court. Indeed, even after retiring Fitzpatrick continued to involve the court in partisan political wrangling.

Since members of the Supreme Court had begun to attend the meetings of the Judicial Committee of the Privy Council in 1897, the annual estimates had contained a sum intended to defray expenses of travelling to and staying in London. By 1913 the allowance was $2,500 annually. In that year Fitzpatrick put in no claim for the money because he did not attend the Judicial Committee sittings. In 1914 he did claim the money, though (despite the prime minister's statement to the contrary) there is no evidence that Fitzpatrick actually attended any hearings of the Judicial Committee in that year. In 1915 and 1916 the description of the allowance was changed slightly in the estimates; instead of being called a travelling allowance, it was simply referred to as an allowance 'to cover expenses in connection with Judicial Committee of the Privy Council.' The chief justice promptly claimed and was paid the full $2,500 each year, though because he stayed in Canada he presumably had no actual expenses 'in connection with' the committee. In 1917 the description of the allowance was again altered slightly so that attendance was explicitly required, and consequently Fitzpatrick made no claim for the money.[3]

No public notice was taken of this until May 1918 when a Conservative Unionist member of Parliament from eastern Ontario, J.W. Edwards, accused the chief justice of 'deliberately stealing from the treasury of the country and putting the money in ... [his] own pockets.' The Ottawa press followed up on the question and quoted Fitzpatrick as saying that he took the money only when he went to London. The prime minister, however, read to the House a statement from Fitzpatrick outlining the terms of each allowance voted and when he had claimed the money. A week later the issue was raised again, this time by W.F. Nickle, Conservative Unionist member for Kingston. The government was asked for its policy and intentions regarding the payments. The government replied that the payments had been made legally and, despite the chief justice's offer to return the money, the government did not intend to try to recover the funds. As part of this response, a lengthy letter from Fitzpatrick to the prime minister was read to the House, justifying his acceptance of the funds as within the letter of the law.[4] There the matter rested for almost a year.

In March 1919 Edwards returned to the fray. He moved in the House of Commons that Fitzpatrick should repay the $5,000 paid him in 1915 and 1916. A lengthy debate ensued; the motion was 'talked out,' and adjournment of the House occurred before a vote could be taken. Five days later a brief letter from the now lieutenant-governor of Quebec was read to the House. In view of the government's explicit statement that his conduct in the matter had been legal and that he had acted in good faith, and in view of the misunderstanding on the part of some members of the House as to what they had voted for, the $5,000 was returned.[5] There the matter ended.

It was a sordid little affair. Fitzpatrick had acted legally, but his conduct was hardly ethical. He had demeaned the position of chief justice, and he had jeopardized the entire procedure by which members of the Supreme Court were encouraged to participate in the Judicial Committee.[6]

With serious national and international problems at hand, the government of Sir Robert Borden had little time to deliberate over the selection of Fitzpatrick's replacement as head of the Supreme Court. Publicly it was anticipated that either Lyman Duff or Frank Anglin, more likely the former, would be given the post; no public support existed for John Idington, a more senior puisne justice.[7] There is little evidence as to how seriously the government canvassed these or other potential candidates, but none of those named was selected. Instead, Sir Louis Davies was named chief justice of Canada. Seventy-three years old, he was the most senior puisne justice, having served for seventeen years on the Ottawa bench. Though he had been in poor health, Davies wanted the post. He telegraphed Borden on 1 September applying for the promotion and listing his credentials. When he received a noncommittal reply, he telegraphed again, adding that if promoted he would resign at the end of three years when twenty years' service on the bench had been completed (and his pension rights strengthened). The prime minister decided to take Davies' name forward to cabinet, but its agreement was not easily won. Borden commented in his diary, 'Much discussion [in council] as to appointments to the Supreme Court. I carried Davies by a narrow majority.'[8] Davies was not a strong selection. He had not stood out during his years on the Court, he was old, and he had demonstrated no leadership abilities.

The vacancy on the Supreme Court at the puisne level had to be filled from the province of Quebec. According to rumours in the press, consideration was given to appointing C.J. Doherty (the minister of justice) or Eugène Lafleur, a leading Montreal lawyer; it is also likely that Justice L.P. Pelletier of the Quebec Court of Appeal turned down the appointment.[9] The man finally selected was Pierre Basile Mignault, and his appointment was as strong as Davies' was weak.

Born in Massachusetts where his French-Canadian father practised medicine, Mignault had moved to Montreal for his higher education. By 1918 he had practised law for forty years in Montreal and had become a leader of the provincial bar. His stature had been recognized by his being hired by the crown to appear in important cases, such as the 1912 marriage reference, and by his appointment in 1914 to the International Joint Commission. Most impressive, however, were Mignault's scholarly achievements. His list of publications was outstanding. He was a man dedicated to a study and analysis of the law, before, during, and after his tenure on the Supreme Court. His greatest work was a nine-volume study of the Quebec civil law, which began to appear in 1895, was completed in 1916, and remains an essential reference work today. Mignault held a chair in civil law at McGill from 1912 to 1918. His was a good appointment, combining a first-rate scholarly mind with extended and practical legal experience. At the time of his joining the Court, he was sixty-four years old and lacked any judicial experience.[10]

Following these appointments, the personnel of the Supreme Court remained constant for the next five years. That semblance of stability is somewhat misleading, however; discussion of Sir Louis Davies' projected retirement was frequent and public from 1922 onward.

The first justice to leave the Court in the 1920s was Louis Brodeur. By the fall of 1923 he was only sixty-one years old, but his health was poor and his arthritis made it difficult for him to write his judgments. There was little opposition to his retirement, but the new prime minister, W.L. Mackenzie King, did not want the justice to leave unrewarded. King considered himself to be particularly close to Brodeur; in his diary he referred to the jurist as being 'like a brother or a father.' The prime minister arranged for Brodeur to replace Sir Charles Fitzpatrick as the new lieutenant-governor of Quebec.[11] Four months later the vacancy at the Court was filled by Arthur Cyrille Albert Malouin of the Quebec Superior Court.[12]

The appointment of Albert Malouin was probably the least thoughtful in the history of the Supreme Court of Canada. It was not that he was a weak judge; rather, he did not regard the move as a 'promotion.' Malouin simply did not wish to serve. Another member of the Court described the new justice's attitude and the process of appointment:

Our latest recruit, Mr. Justice Malouin, tells me that the first suggestion he heard of his appointment was a telephone message from the Minister of Justice informing him that the Order-in-Council had been passed, though not yet signed by the Governor. He was not at all anxious to come. He has been for years an invalid, and was rescued from a lingering diabetic end by insulin. The true inwardness of the thing is, as I am informed by two friends high in the politics of Quebec, that the Minister of Justice [Sir Lomer Gouin] is coming himself at the earliest possible opportunity. Moreover, I am also told that it was the disposition shewn by the Prime Minister to act upon the recommendations of the Minister of Marine [Ernest Lapointe] rather than his own, with regard to this very appointment, which was the immediate occasion of Gouin's resignation. Gouin's nominee was [Thibaudeau] Rinfret, of Montreal, and in the alternative [Louis] St. Laurent, whom you know, either of which would have been a most suitable appointment ... Malouin makes no secret of the fact that his health does not permit him to exert himself.[13]

That the government would choose to appoint a seriously ill man, without his approval, is disturbing. The impression is gained that Malouin was named to create an obstacle to the demands of Sir Lomer Gouin, rather than to secure a strong candidate for the court.

At this time a struggle was taking place within the Quebec wing of the federal Liberal party between 'conservative,' big business interests (led by Gouin) and 'liberal' forces (led by Lapointe).[14] The Supreme Court was caught in the middle of this contest. Further evidence of the political nature of the decision-making is seen in a letter from Malouin's wife. A month before her husband heard of his appointment Madame Malouin wrote, not to solicit the post for her husband, but rather to object to the possible naming of a Conservative to the Court. Emphasizing her Liberal background – as a daughter of Senator Louis Lavergne and a long-time friend of the Lauriers – she complained of rumours circulating that Ferdinand Roy, the law partner of the Liberal premier of Quebec and a pro-conscription Conservative, would be named to the Supreme Court. It was unthinkable that such a man should be appointed to 'one of the most envied position[s] in the Dominion of Canada – there are splendid men in Montreal and Quebec good liberals – true friends good lawyers, who would be delighted to accept the position – why should a nasty Conservative – get the best position a liberal government can give? – Just think of it – my blood is boiling –'[15] The partisan character of such wrangling is not surprising, but it is important to emphasize that these partisan criteria were active and were hindering the selection of the best possible candidates for the Supreme Court. Rumour had it that St Laurent, Roy, and Rinfret were being considered for the post.[16] Instead, an unwilling Malouin was selected out of the blue – only to resign eight months later.

On 1 May 1924 Sir Louis Davies died, just before his seventy-ninth birthday. He had genuinely intended to retire in 1921, but was inhibited from doing so by a disagreement over the amount of his pension. The disagreement had dragged on without resolution. Lately his health had been poor and he had not been active on the bench. The minister of justice reported that Davies by the end of 1923 was 'no longer in a position to perform his duties.' The prime minister privately accused Davies of 'holding on to office too long,' something that was as much the government's fault as the chief justice's.[17]

The willingness of Davies to retire encouraged the government to plan for his successor. Indeed, as early as September 1923 consideration was given to a major injection of new blood into the Supreme Court by combining Davies' resignation with that of Brodeur, thus providing two openings. This is the explanation for the offer of the chief justiceship in December 1923 and again in January 1924 to Eugène Lafleur.[18] After Davies' death, Lafleur was approached again. Mackenzie King described the cabinet meeting and his interview with the Montreal lawyer:

Attended meeting of Council at noon discussed appmt. of Chief Justice and got Council to agree to Lafleur being offered the position anew, the Maritime province men agreeing to let their chance for nominee pass if Lafleur would accept. Quebec to wait re her further nomination. Ont. to let chance go by – I sent for Mr. Lafleur at 5 & talked with him in my office, the tears came into his eyes as I spoke to him of the confidence of the Govt. & the bar in his ability & of our desire to have him fill the position to strengthen the bench & uphold Br[itish]. conception of Justice – he spoke of not being indifferent to a desire to be of public service, but of getting on in years, that what the Supreme Court needed was younger men. I agreed except as regards the Chief Justice who must be of authority & experienced in his profession. I spoke of his going to Imp. Privy Council to take part with Law Lords there. He promised to reconsider, but did not give me any assurance. The Imp. p.c. may be the means of securing him.

The prime minister asked the governor-general, Lord Byng, to see Lafleur and urge him to accept.[19]

Despite repeated rejections, the post was kept open in the hope that Lafleur would change his mind. Pressures were exerted over the summer and one last effort was made early in September 1924. The prime minister emphasized the Court's requirement of a highly regarded leader.

I need not tell you of the need which exists in Canada today to place at the head of our judiciary one whose pre-eminence in his profession would gain for the Supreme Court the place it should hold in the respect of the bench and the bar not only of our own country but also of the British Isles. Nor need I assure you of the unanimity with which members of the profession, and all classes in Canada would welcome your appointment ...

You are the one man in Canada who can meet what today is our country's most imperative need, and it is on this ground that I feel justified not only in urging upon you the acceptance of the post, but of going as far as may be possible in the meeting of your wishes to have you accept it.

Again, Lafleur declined, saying that he was too old: 'I have long thought that what the Court needs most is to be rejuvenated, and it is not by appointing men who are nearing the 70 mark that you will really strengthen it.' [20] The government had to admit defeat. The fall term was approaching and the appointment of a chief justice could no longer be delayed.

The attempts to place Eugène Lafleur at the head of the Supreme Court of Canada in 1924 are interesting in several respects. One striking element in all of the discussions and correspondence extant is the overwhelming agreement among officials, candidates, and observers that the Ottawa bench was badly in need of improvement.[21] Another important feature of the 1924 movement was the high quality of the man chosen to help lead the Supreme Court out of the wilderness. By 1924 Lafleur had enjoyed almost forty-two years at the bar and was quite likely the most eminent counsel in all of Canada. He had published frequently on legal matters and had lectured at the McGill law school. He had appeared frequently before the Supreme Court and the Judicial Committee, and his international reputation was such that he was invited to chair an arbitration commission to settle a Mexico–United States border dispute. In earlier years his Protestantism allegedly stood in the way of his elevation to the bench.[22] One is struck by the wide-ranging support for Lafleur's appointment.[23] Interested Canadians genuinely wanted a strong Supreme Court; once in a while they were even willing to do something about it.

The chief justiceship remained to be filled. Many names were suggested, names such as Sir Robert Borden, Justice W.R. Riddell of Ontario, Chief Justice Sir W. Mulock of Ontario, and E.L. Newcombe, deputy minister of justice. Mulock would have accepted the post to round off his career, but he was too old (eighty years of age). Newcombe was backed by the powerful minister of justice, Ernest Lapointe, but the prime minister rejected the suggestion: 'I opposed strongly because of his being a Tory thro' life. It wd. make our friends very much annoyed, & there are plenty of good men in our own ranks.'[24] Other outsiders were not seriously considered.

The choice in fact centred on the three most senior justices already on the Supreme Court – John Idington, Lyman Duff, and Frank Anglin. Idington was never a strong contender. His age was against him; the prime minister referred in his diary to the justice as '86 & senile.' He was actually only eighty-three years old, but his retirement was considered to be imminent.[25] Idington's position as senior puisne justice was by no means sufficient to overcome this weakness at a time when the government was intent on rejuvenating the Court.

Lyman Duff had all the credentials necessary for a chief justice of Canada. He was regarded by most of the legal profession across the dominion as the most able jurist on the Supreme Court. His merit had been recognized in 1919 by his appointment to the Judicial Committee of the Privy Council, the only Canadian puisne justice ever to be so honoured. He had also accepted an official connection, as Visitor, with the Harvard Law School, a further sign of his rising international reputation. As well, Duff wanted the chief justiceship and apparently co-operated with lobbying attempts to promote his candidacy.[26]

Unfortunately, in the eyes of the King government the British Columbia justice had two fatal flaws. First, he had co-operated with the Conservative and Union governments in 1917–18 and, as central appeal judge, he had been directly associated with the politically explosive issue of conscription. Some commentators, including a biased Arthur Meighen, leader of the Conservative party, felt 'that Quebec's opposition was entirely responsible for [Duff's] not getting [the promotion].'[27] Second, and probably more important, Duff had a drinking problem, and perhaps had even become an alcoholic. All of the specific evidence of his heavy drinking comes from the early 1920s, and it may be that his resort to alcohol was a by-product of his nervous exhaustion at the end of the war.

In the summer of 1918, Sir Charles Fitzpatrick wrote: 'I hear that Duff has broken down under the strain. Do you know where he is?' This problem was compounded when Duff was passed over for the chief justiceship in the fall of 1918; he allowed his disappointment to show. [28] Whatever the cause, there can be no doubt as to the result and the effect in 1924. The governor-general expressed a hope that Duff would not be appointed, saying that the justice had been intoxicated both at the opening of Parliament and at a state dinner. Douglas Abbott recalled appearing as junior counsel in a case around this time. The argument was to be presented one afternoon before a panel including Duff; the chief justice informed counsel that since Duff could not be present the hearing would have to be postponed until the next term. Duff, it turned out, had been at a country club the night before and had imbibed too freely – he was absent from the Court for over a week. [29] These and other examples disturbed the abstemious prime minister greatly. He tried to investigate the problem; in the end he came to the conclusion that such a man ought not to be chief justice.

Frank Anglin was junior to Duff in seniority and, though he had his supporters, he lacked the reputation for outstanding ability that Duff enjoyed. Anglin was, however, a better-than-average member of the Court, spoke French well, and had a reputation as a writer of literate judgments. He had carefully maintained his Liberal credentials, refusing to accept extrajudicial tasks from the Union government and maintaining useful social connections with Mackenzie King. [30] The prime minister himself described the process of elimination by which Anglin was selected:

I have tried very hard to secure Lafleur as Chief Justice, but in vain. It leaves the choice between Duff & Anglin, the former is probably the abler but is dissipated, gets off on sprees for weeks at a time. Was intoxicated at last opening of prlt. & at Sir Louis Davies' funeral. I regard him too as a bit of a sycophant where the tories are concerned & more or less the favourite with the big interests. Anglin is narrow, has not a pleasant manner, is very vain, but industrious steady and honest, a true liberal at heart. Both are personal friends. I imagine the bar as a whole prefer Duff, some do not know his habits. I think I am doing the right thing in appointing Anglin ... While I wish we could have secured Lafleur & I do not altogether like appointing Anglin because of the feeling of the bar against him, I nevertheless think in the interests of justice and the dignity of the bench, his appointment is preferable to any other all circumstances considered. [31]

The appointment of Frank Anglin as the seventh chief justice of Canada caused internal problems at the Supreme Court. The government had been aware of the potential for such conflict; an outside appointment had appealed, according to one cabinet minister, because of 'the difficulty which we are all aware exists as to the competition for the place [of chief justice] among the present Judges.' Lyman Duff was deeply hurt at being passed over and so resented Anglin's elevation to the post that he seriously considered resigning. Though some attempts were made to soothe Duff's feelings, rumours that Anglin had written to the Justice Department advising against Duff's elevation likely made remote any prospect of reconciliation. From this point on relations between the two were frosty.[32]

Anglin's promotion and Malouin's retirement left the government with two vacancies. Sir Louis Davies' death had left the Court without a representative from the maritimes, and it was to be expected that one of the new appointments would be from that region. The choice was Edmund Leslie Newcombe, the long-time deputy minister of justice. Called to the bar in 1883, he practised law first in Kentville and then in Halifax, where he earned a good reputation, particularly as a trial lawyer. In 1892 he was appointed lecturer in marine insurance at Dalhousie. In 1893 he accepted the post of deputy minister of justice, just vacated by his fellow Nova Scotian, Robert Sedgewick. Newcombe served in this post for a little over thirty-one years, becoming one of the most influential members of the civil service in that period. As deputy minister he acquired extensive experience in the drafting and interpretation of statutes, in constitutional law, and in litigation before the Supreme Court and the Judicial Committee. Although much of his work as deputy minister had been administrative, Newcombe had nevertheless been able to retain many ties to his original profession. He had even found time to appear, in a private capacity, as counsel before the Supreme Court and the Judicial Committee from time to time.[33] He was sixty-five years old when he joined the Court.

Newcombe's appointment was supported by the leading cabinet ministers from the maritimes and by his immediate superior, Ernest Lapointe, who had pushed for Newcombe's consideration as chief justice. The deputy minister had expected to receive the senior post, and there was some concern about the impact of his disappointment. Always careful to assess the political advantages in any appointment, the prime minister had ruled out Newcombe as chief justice on the ground of his life-long affiliation with the Conservative party. However, given the broad support for him within the Cabinet, Mackenzie King was prepared to agree to the deputy minister's assuming the puisne justiceship; the prime minister even saw political benefits in it: 'Our [Liberal] friends will not like it, but it will please the Tories & will offset not appointing Duff. It will, too, be a good apptmt.' By and large the appointment was well received, although the prime minister's old mentor and current chief justice of Ontario, Sir William Mulock, penned a scathing denunciation of Newcombe's fitness for the position, emphasizing his weak legal experience and his dogmatic nature; the 'Supreme Court requires strengthening, not weakening.'[34]

The second vacancy went, by law, to a member of the Quebec bar. Here too there does not seem to have been much debate. Thibaudeau Rinfret had been strongly recommended for the position when Justice Malouin was chosen. Now, eight months later, with internal party conflict more subdued, it was possible to revert to the much more able candidate. A member of the bar since 1901, Rinfret had early joined a Montreal law firm with strong ties to the Liberal party. There his legal career flourished, and he accepted appointment as professor of comparative law and the law of public utilities at McGill University. He busied himself as well with Liberal affairs and was twice defeated as a Liberal candidate. Though Rinfret had real ability, his brother's influential position in the Liberal party and his own Liberal credentials were undoubtedly helpful in gaining his appointment first to the Superior Court in Montreal in 1922 and then to the Supreme Court. On the Superior Court, Rinfret had earned a reputation for ability and hard work. The prime minister reflected in his diary that the new justice was 'a young promising man ... [who] will strengthen the bench materially.' At age forty-five Rinfret would provide some useful energy to a court the average age of whose members was now over sixty-five.[35]

Though the government's decisions regarding appointments had been and would continue to be much influenced by partisan political considerations, it is fair to point out that the political leaders of the day genuinely sought an overall improvement in the quality of the Supreme Court of Canada. This was reflected in two amendments made to the Supreme Court Act in 1927. The one, a long time in the making, finally increased the number of permanent members of the Court to seven. The second established compulsory retirement at age seventy-five and applied the provision not just to future members but to all current members of the Supreme Court, one of whom, John Idington, was eighty-six years old by the time the legislation became law.[36]

The Mackenzie King government was convinced that age had become a negative factor for some members of the Supreme Court in the 1920s. Sir Louis Davies, in his seventy-ninth year, had been felt to be incapable of performing his duties and simply to be waiting for an appropriate pension. At the same time, Idington had been described by the prime minister as 'senile.' Action concerning statutory compulsory retirement was delayed by the general elections of 1925 and 1926 and by the special circumstances of the minority governments of 1925–6. There is little doubt, however, that the Liberal government was coming to support some such policy at least by 1924. Justice Idington's ill health and consequent extended absences simply hastened legislation and gave the measure both substance and a sense of urgency. Idington had been absent for the entire spring 1925 term and for all but one day in each of the two succeeding terms. In 1925 he missed a total of fifty-eight days, in 1926 thirty-eight days, and in the first term of 1927 twenty-two days. What was worse, he failed first to request a leave of absence. In February 1926 the minister of justice asked him to resign.[37] Idington's reply is not extant, but he obviously refused, necessitating the legislation of the following year.

The entire affair was unfortunate. The attachment of a sick old man to his office (and to his full salary), despite his obvious incapacity even to attend Court sittings, is pathetic. It is surprising that there is not more evidence of public outcry at the presence of such an ineffective judge on the court. Idington's behaviour was, however, influential in gaining bipartisan support for the compulsory retirement of Supreme Court justices.

The other amendment affecting the personnel of the Court was at least as necessary as that regarding retirement. Within a few years of the Court's creation, it had become clear that in view of the frailties of old age, an excess of one justice above quorum did not give the Court sufficient flexibility in meeting its duties. By the turn of the century the growing tendency to appoint some of the justices to other posts outside the Court simply put greater pressure on the members. Various solutions to this basic problem had been posed over the years, the most popular being either a reduction in the quorum or the provision of extra justices on a temporary basis. Both solutions had been tried at different times; in 1918 legislation had been passed allowing the use of ad hoc justices. By 1927 the need for additional Court members had been fully proved; since 1918 twelve different ad hoc justices had served on at least 125 cases.[38] In some respects the use of different temporary justices had worked well. Justice Mignault, for example, pointed to the intellectual advantages of the interchange that this system facilitated.[39] But the instability of the system was a crucial weakness, and there was little debate when the amendment was introduced to increase the number of justices by one. Indeed, the only question that is difficult to answer was why the increase had not been authorized earlier. Perhaps the delay was caused by financial considerations. The federal government had always been somewhat niggardly in matters concerning the Supreme Court, and there was the fear that any dramatic increase in expenditure would attract attention and criticism to a vulnerable institution. The old adage 'let sleeping dogs lie' had likely worked to the disadvantage of the Supreme Court by inhibiting discussion and change.

With the forced retirement of John Idington and the addition of a sixth puisne justice, the King government once again had two vacancies to fill. It was certain that one of these would go to a man from the prairie provinces. During the debates in the House of Commons one argument put forward for creating the additional seat on the bench was the difficulty in providing representation for the west. As well, Mackenzie King was still busy undermining prairie support for farmers' and progressive parties and attracting errant Liberals back into the fold. Various local Liberals appealed to their federal leaders to give the prairies representation on the Supreme Court. Lyman Duff's presence on the Court was no longer adequate; the prairies wanted their own man. Some, forgetting Killam's brief interlude on the Court, argued that the prairies had never been represented. In 1924 one influential Ontario Liberal informed the prime minister of western demands: 'I met a number of Western men among others Dunning and Judge Martin and they are strong for another man from the West in the Supreme Court. They pointed out that Nova Scotia had McLean in the Exq. Ct. When I said that the East was entitled to a man and the number was fixed. They all seemed to be so strong about it that I [thought I] would write you and prepare you, but you probably have [heard] it long ago.'[40] But in 1924 neither of the two vacancies could be used to meet prairie demands – one was Quebec's by law and the other was the maritimes' by tradition. Western representatives had little sympathy for east-coast claims, but Mackenzie King was too astute a politician to risk alienating the maritimes, particularly at a time when eastern sensitivities were more than usually acute.[41]

The King government did nothing to discourage western claims. In the context of 1924 it was simply not possible to meet them. Rumours, however, continued to circulate that Idington's Ontario seat would be transferred to the prairies. Though several names were put forward in the period from 1924 to 1927, one name dominated discussions, and it was no surprise when John Henderson Lamont was appointed to the Supreme Court two days after Idington retired. He had practised law in Toronto for four years before moving west in 1899, setting up practice in Prince Albert and soon becoming crown prosecutor. Before long he found himself heavily involved in the local affairs of the Liberal party, becoming a member of Parliament (1904–5) and a member of the provincial assembly (1905–7). As attorney-general he was a member of the first provincial cabinet. Two years later, at the age of forty-one, Lamont left politics and joined the Saskatchewan Court of Queen's Bench, transferring in 1918 to the provincial Court of Appeal. By the spring of 1927 he had acquired over nineteen years' experience on the bench, though his practice of law had been limited. He was sixty-one years old when he was appointed to the Supreme Court.[42] On the provincial bench he had acquired a reputation as an excellent jurist, but his Liberal credentials were important. While other candidates were attacked for their weak party loyalty, Lamont's claims could be championed by the party faithful. The prime minister's Ontario informant wrote, 'If you should think of it [appointing a westerner] I believe Judge Lamont of the Court of Appeal in Saskatchewan is the strongest man out there and besides he is one of ourselves, was Attorney General in Premier Scott's Cabinet. As far as I could find out he was the man they [prairie Liberals] wanted and I am of the opinion he would be a good man in the Supreme Court.'[43] So it was that a seat on the Supreme Court bench was permanently allotted to the prairies.

The other vacancy went to an Ontario representative, since with Idington's departure only one Ontario justice remained on the Court. Several names were mentioned for the post, and Justice John Orde of the Ontario Supreme Court, Appeal Division, felt that he had been promised the position as early as the summer of 1924.[44] Possibly this was true, but three years later circumstances had changed. The son of Robert Smith, one of the other candidates, had been elected to the House of Commons in 1926, and he exerted pressure on behalf of his father. This influence, combined with Robert Smith's obvious abilities, was sufficient to lead to his selection as the newest member of the Supreme Court of Canada. Called to the bar in 1885, he had practised law in Cornwall, Ontario, for many years, acting also as a director and secretary-treasurer of the Montreal and Cornwall Navigation Company. He was also active in local Liberal party affairs and sat as a member of Parliament from 1908 to 1911. In 1922, when a judgeship became vacant in Ontario, one of the cabinet ministers chiefly concerned with patronage prepared a memorandum 'regarding three of our friends whose names have been most constantly pressed upon us by a large number of Liberals in different parts of the Province.'At the top of this list stood the name of Robert Smith, whose toils as a Liberal were detailed and who was described as 'a lawyer of excellent standing with a varied town and country practice and experience in the Courts.' In 1922 Smith was appointed to the High Court Division, Supreme Court of Ontario. Less than a year later he was transferred to the Second Appellate Division of the same court, and early in 1924, at the request of the chief justice, he was promoted to the First Appellate Division. No less a legal mind than Newton Rowell privately recommended Smith's elevation to the Supreme Court in 1927: 'If Mr. Justice Smith would accept the position I do not think a better appointment could be made from Ontario. He is very highly regarded both by the bench and the bar. He has been a great success as a judge and his appointment would give universal satisfaction.'[45] In Smith the Supreme Court of Canada acquired a man with extensive legal experience (over thirty-six years at the bar). Though he had been on the bench for less than five years, his abilities had quickly attracted attention and promotion. He was sixty-seven years of age, too old to qualify for a pension by the time he reached seventy-five. But Smith wanted the promotion to Ottawa very much, and after a brief attempt to negotiate a special pension agreement he accepted a vague government pledge to look after him when the time came.[46]

Two points can be made about these appointments and the selection process. First, though it is clear that meaningful prior activity on behalf of the government party was an essential factor, the government at the same time sought out highly qualified candidates, by the standards of the day. The partisan element in the selection process was clearly not a barrier to merit; the private praise given to such appointments as Rinfret, Lamont, and Smith makes this obvious. Second, though religious affiliation was declining as a factor in the increasingly secularized society of twentieth-century Canada, it was still there. Since the appointment of Frank Anglin in 1909, the Court had contained an even number of Protestants and Roman Catholics. Although Roman Catholics made up almost 39 per cent of the country's population, almost all were concentrated in the province of Quebec; outside that province less than 4 per cent of the population was Roman Catholic. On those grounds it was possible to argue that Protestants were underrepresented, and such reasoning was advanced from time to time.[47] There is no evidence as to what effect such pressure had on the selection process.

In the fall of 1929 P.B. Mignault became the second member of the Supreme Court to be forced into retirement owing to the new age limit. The example of John Idington made a strong case for compulsory retirement; Mignault demonstrated the weakness of setting an arbitrary date. At seventy-five he was still active and pulling his weight in the Court. Throughout the 1930s he continued to publish useful scholarly articles. However, particularly in the early stages of the new regulation, it would have been difficult for the government to make an exception in Mignault's case – there is, in fact, no evidence that such an exception was either requested or considered.[48]

Given his scholarly interests and training, it is not surprising that Justice Mignault had emerged at the Supreme Court as the first great defender of the civil law. Prior to this period no firm pattern had emerged for handling civil-law cases; some common-law justices, particularly Henry Strong, proved to be quite adaptable and sympathetic to the different perspectives and tradition involved, while other such justices (Gwynne and Henry, for example) tended to adhere to a common-law treatment of the cases.[49] None of the early Quebec members of the Supreme Court were militant upholders of the civil law. Taschereau, Fournier, Girouard, and Brodeur were vigilant on behalf of the civil-law tradition, but appear not to have seen any great threat to that tradition from a close working proximity to common-law influence.

The presence of only two Quebec justices on the Court meant that they were always in a numerical minority on any panel in these years. But in the absence of any perceived threat to the Civil Code, the justices were not noticeably defensive and showed no strong signs of deliberately working together. When Désiré Girouard first arrived at the Court, for example, his Quebec colleague was frequently absent; without any prior judicial experience, Girouard was left to write either the majority or the unanimous judgment in the ten reported civil-law cases heard in 1896–7. During their ten years on the bench together, Girouard and Taschereau frequently went their separate ways, even in majority. Taschereau dissented from the majority, of which Girouard was a part, five times; Girouard dissented from Taschereau's majority judgment four times; Girouard frequently wrote a separate judgment when in the majority with Taschereau. On only one occasion did the two justices dissent together in a civil-law case.[50]

This trend continued with the accession of Charles Fitzpatrick. In his five years that overlapped with Girouard's tenure, twenty-two civil-law cases were reported. In six of these one of the Quebec justices was absent;

in six more appeals they were on opposite sides in the decision. In only ten cases did they stand together in the majority, and never in dissent. In many cases, however, Fitzpatrick revealed a disturbing tendency toward an inappropriate reliance on precedent for some of the issues involved, particularly in his defence of the sanctity of private property.[51]

The appointment of Mignault to the Supreme Court in 1918 brought the foremost authority on the civil law to the Ottawa bench. It was not long before the new justice criticized members of the Quebec bar and judiciary for relying on principles of English common law instead of the Civil Code. Pointing to the fate of civil codes in South Africa and Louisiana, he warned that the intrusion of common law would subvert the distinctive character of the Quebec civil law tradition.[52] With a learned and articulate defender of that tradition now in an influential position and with an increasing sensitivity in Quebec to English-Canadian ascendancy, it is not surprising that a new response to civil law cases began to emerge.[53]

In two early cases Mignault's influence on the construction of the Civil Code was apparent. In the first, *Desrosiers* v *The King* (1920),[54] Brodeur and Mignault were in the majority led by Justice Anglin. The Court ruled that English decisions should not be cited as authorities in cases from the province of Quebec that did not depend upon doctrines derived from English law. In the second case, *Curley* v *Latreille* (1920),[55] the majority (including Mignault but excluding Brodeur) ruled that English decisions could be of value in deciding Quebec cases under certain circumstances. The justices held that English decisions could be used in civil-law cases only when it had been ascertained that the principles upon which the subject matter dealt were the same and were given a like scope in their application. Even here, however, the Court ruled that English precedents could not be used as binding authorities but as *rationes scriptae*. Mignault expressed his admiration of Anglin's grasp of the civil law in this case, and lectured the Quebec lower court and Justice Brodeur on the limited place of precedent in civil-law cases.[56]

Mignault's presence on the Court at this time did much to enforce the status of the Civil Code. Anglin's consistent backing was crucial; without the support of a common-law justice, Brodeur and Mignault could never have prevailed in civil-law cases.

Justice Rinfret arrived in 1924; now Mignault had an effective co-defender of the Civil Code, a position Rinfret maintained for the next thirty years, long after Mignault's retirement. The two Quebec justices participated in all fifty-nine reported civil-law cases that came to the Court during their tenure together. They were in the majority in all but two of the judgments.[57] Of the fifty-nine judgments, Rinfret wrote twenty-two opinions for the Court or for the majority; Mignault wrote fifteen. On only three occasions did Rinfret dissent from Mignault on a civil-law case; Mignault never dissented from Rinfret.[58] Again their common-law supporter was Chief Justice Anglin, who tended to join with Mignault in other areas of law as well. Justice Duff showed a marked uninterest in civil-law cases. He rarely wrote an opinion in such cases; he gave the leading judgment only twice in this period (1925–9) and dissented four times.

Mignault's legacy at the Supreme Court was a new sensitivity to the civil law. Quebec justices had begun to work together consistently and were able to command the support and respect of their common-law colleagues. This was a pattern Rinfret maintained in the following years.

The government allowed a full term of the Court to pass after Mignault's departure before naming his replacement. Without two Quebec justices present, tradition required that civil-law cases be postponed. Both the chief justice and the solicitor-general, Lucien Cannon, urged the minister of justice to fill the vacancy quickly, but the minister, Ernest Lapointe, would not be hurried. From England his telegraphed response indicated his commitment to making an effective appointment and to strengthening the nation's courts:

Appointment most important essential Supreme Court being made exceptionally strong STOP Would prefer leave it until I return STOP Chief Justice [of the provincial] Appeal Court unable working might be persuaded retiring both appointments could be made together possibly facilitating matters STOP Please tell Anglin help us in making delay unobjectionable STOP vacancy occurring while I am away surely sufficient excuse for postponement.[59]

Finally, in January 1930, after the post had allegedly been turned down by Louis St Laurent and possibly by Justice Philippe Demers,[60] Lawrence Arthur Dumoulin Cannon was named to the Supreme Court of Canada.

The son of a Quebec Superior Court justice, Arthur Cannon had taken up legal practice in Quebec City in 1899. Among his law partners over the years were such leading figures as Sir Charles Fitzpatrick and L.A. Taschereau, the premier of Quebec. Cannon was a leading member of the city council, from 1908 to 1916, and followed his brother into the provincial assembly when he served from 1916 to 1923. By the 1920s Cannon had become a leader of the Quebec bar. He joined the Quebec Court of King's Bench, Appeal Division, in 1927, and less than three years later was promoted to the Supreme Court.[61] His judicial experience was limited, but he had practised before the bar for some twenty-eight years. He also had excellent political connections: he had married the daughter of Sir Charles Fitzpatrick and his brother was the solicitor-general of Canada.

Individual members of the Court continued to carry out non-judicial functions. Purely formal duties, such as acting as administrator in the absence of the governor-general, occasionally fell to the chief justice or a senior colleague. These are of little note except that they provide an example of the ongoing tension between Duff and Anglin.

In 1932, Chief Justice Anglin was out of the country, and the governor-general authorized Lyman Duff to act as deputy in Ottawa during a vice-regal tour of the western provinces. The chief justice returned earlier than anticipated and took serious umbrage at Duff's acting in a position Anglin thought should be his own. The government received a formal letter of protest from Anglin challenging (mistakenly) Duff's standing and the governor-general's right to appoint anyone other than himself.[62] The pettiness of the problem underlines Anglin's sense of competition (or perhaps jealousy) regarding Duff and the chief justice's genuine thirst for status and the symbols of power. Mackenzie King perceived vanity to be an important if unfortunate motivating force behind many of Anglin's activities as chief justice.[63]

Appointments to royal commissions added to the justices' duties. In 1919 Prime Minister Borden sought to name two Court members, Davies and Anglin, to conduct an inquiry into the 1918 military police raid on the Jesuit seminary in Guelph, Ontario. Both wisely declined the appointment and thus avoided being drawn into a bitter ethnic and religious controversy centring on conscription. Davies explained, 'After reading the discussion in the House of Commons which led up to the promise of the enquiry being made I concluded that this enquiry would almost certainly develop into a politico religious controversy which I felt it was undesirable the Chief Justice of Canada should be mixed up with.'[64] This sense of separation between the judiciary and political controversies was not yet fully shared by the other justices.

Less sensitive commissions continued to be readily accepted. Sir Charles Fitzpatrick, E.L. Newcombe, and the registrar were all members of the 1923–7 Statute Revising Commission. Lyman Duff clearly felt it was his obligation as a public servant to accept such tasks. As a result, in 1926 he became chairman of the commission to apportion church properties between the assenting and dissenting congregations of the newly formed United Church of Canada. In 1931 Duff was named chairman of the Royal Commission into Railways and Transportation in Canada. So exhausting was this work that when the commission's report was finally submitted in 1932 Duff collapsed, suffering a 'complete nervous breakdown,' and it was expected that he would 'not likely ever sit on the bench again.'[65] Though he recovered, his illness illustrates the potential demands of such work and how much the Court was affected by being deprived of various justices' labour, often for extended periods. Nevertheless, as Duff himself would have argued, such public service was of value to the country.

As well, the Supreme Court justices continued to offer political and legal advice to the political executive. Some of this was solicited. Justice Mignault, for example, was asked to investigate and prepare a memorandum on an article of the Boundary Waters Treaty. In 1923 the attorney-general of Ontario solicited Lyman Duff's views regarding a proposed piece of legislation. On another occasion Prime Minister Borden sought the chief justice's advice concerning the vacant lieutenant-governorship of his native province.[66] In none of these instances did the justice involved object to the request; each time the justices co-operated with the politicians.

On other occasions the initiative lay with the justices, particularly in matters pertaining to their legal expertise. Justice Rinfret recommended changes in the Code of Civil Procedure to the premier of Quebec. Amendments were also made to the Supreme Court Act or the Judges Act. Several minor changes were passed in this period – in 1920, for example, the minimum amount in controversy required in a *de plano* appeal was standardized across the country at $2,000 – and in many of these the justices were closely involved.

What is interesting about this practice is the justices' easy direct access to the political executive or to the legislative process. In the era after the Second World War, such direct contact became much less common; with the growing sense of separation between the judiciary and the executive or legislative functions, justices in recent decades communicated such suggestions only through an intermediary, the registrar. But in the 1920s there were no qualms about direct contact. The justices, usually jointly but on occasions individually, put forward almost annually various proposals for Supreme Court reform, sometimes as general suggestions and other times in polished legislative drafts.[67] This direct contact between the justices and the executive is further evidence that there was only limited separation between the judiciary and other elements of the national government. It is also apparent that this situation was as much due to actions and attitudes of the members of the Court as it was to the politicians.

One substantial legislative change regarding the Supreme Court affected salaries. In 1920 the salary of the chief justice was raised to $15,000, and the salary of a puisne justice was raised to $12,000. By the late 1920s pressure again began to mount for further increases. Canada paid its Supreme Court members less than almost every other comparable common-law jurisdiction in the world.[68] Public spokesmen pointed to the importance of an attractive salary level in persuading able legal minds to accept appointment to the Court. There was little disagreement on this point; none the less, no further increases were authorized until after the Second World War.

By 1930 the annual Supreme Court budget was a little over $150,000; the staff now consisted of twenty-one people.[69] The character of the staff was changing somewhat, partly as a result of changes in the civil service and partly as a result of the Court's growing workload. During the 1920s, as retirements and resignations occurred, older employees who had exhibited scholarly interests and a devotion to the law were replaced by bureaucrats. Many of the senior staff were lawyers who happened to be civil servants; now the staff was dominated by civil servants who happened to work at the Court. The result was a loss of scholarly enthusiasm on the one hand and increased efficiency on the other. Men like Edward Cameron, Charles Masters, and even the young T.L. McEvoy departed at the end of the decade, taking with them a devotion to the law which had been a special feature of the first five decades of the Court's life.

Despite its subordinate position to the Judicial Committee of the Privy Council, the Supreme Court played an influential role as constitutional umpire in Canada. This role was manifested in two major ways: the development of a significant jurisprudential position under the leadership of Lyman Duff, and an increased emphasis on the reference system.

Following a precedent set by the Judicial Committee Act, 1833, the framers of the Supreme Court Act, 1875, had included section 52, which empowered the governor-in-council to refer to the Court 'any matters whatsoever as he may think fit' in order to ascertain the opinions of the learned judges. The justices could at any time be called upon to give their opinions on often abstract legal problems lacking the normal adversarial, circumstantial, and factual context of regular cases. These references were outside the judicial norm and were disliked by many of the justices. In the *McCarthy Act Reference* (1885) the members of both the Supreme Court and the Judicial Committee declined to give reasons for their conclusion that a federal statute regulating the liquor trade was ultra vires; without reasons it was difficult for legislative planners to ascertain the probable limits of federal power.[70] As a result of the judicial reluctance to make the system useful, and as a reflection of the Court's stature, few references were sent to the Court in the early years.

In 1891 political leaders, pushed by Edward Blake, amended the Supreme Court Act to correct defects in the system. Provision was made for the representation of different interests before the justices in a hearing; the right of appeal to the Judicial Committee was made explicit; and, most important, the justices were required to give reasons for judgment. The government rejected proposals by Blake to limit references to questions involving the federal power to disallow provincial legislation or the federal appellate power regarding education. Instead, the government authorized references on the constitutionality of any provincial or federal statute or 'any other matter.'[71]

Nevertheless, the justices continued to balk at the reference system, and there were only a small number of references prior to the end of the First World War.[72] In 1894 Elzéar Taschereau challenged the constitutional authority of the Parliament of Canada to make the Supreme Court a court of first instance and an advisory board to the federal executive.[73] The Judicial Committee refused to comment on 'hypothetical questions' in a 1903 reference, adding: 'It would be extremely unwise for any judicial tribunal to attempt to exhaust all imaginable or hypothetical circumstances which might have a bearing on concrete cases.'[74]

Finally, in 1910 the Laurier government referred a question to the Supreme Court on the validity of references.[75] A full panel held 5–1 (Idington dissenting), that it was within the power of the governor-in-council to refer cases to the Court, but the range of opinions in the decision revealed the justices' uncertainty on the issue. Justice Idington wrote the only judgment to confront directly one of the basic issues involved: by adding an advisory role to the court's duties the government was seriously affecting the nature of the judicial function of the Supreme Court by imposing a political function. The only common thread running through all six judgments was that reference decisions were opinions only and were not to be taken as judicial judgments or as binding on any courts. This may have comforted the justices, but in reality all lower courts throughout Canada have viewed reference judgments as judicially authoritative.[76]

Political interest in the reference process continued to grow. Between 1902 and 1910 eight issues were referred to the Court under the auspices of the Laurier government. A procedure similar in some respects to the reference system was also instituted in this period. The Railway Act, 1903, empowered the Board of Railway Commissioners to 'state a case in writing, for the opinion of the Supreme Court of Canada upon any question which in the opinion of the Board is a question of law' – a power the board quickly took advantage of.[77] The usefulness of the Court to the political and administrative process was obviously increasing. This use of the Supreme Court illustrates the desire for increased efficiency. Referring a question to the law officers of the crown would provide legal guidance, but reference to the Court would provide an opinion that would effectively be binding; the state could then act within those legal parameters.

While the governments of Sir Robert Borden and Arthur Meighen (1911–21) used the reference system infrequently (only three references were reported during those years), they built on the idea of direct access to the Court by government agencies. The Board of Commerce Act, 1919, empowered the board to refer questions of law 'in a stated case' to the Supreme Court, which it soon did.[78]

By the 1920s the perception of the Court's usefulness as a political instrument was well entrenched. An amendment to the Supreme Court Act in 1922 specifically permitted appeals of provincial references to reach the Supreme Court from the provincial courts of appeal. One provincial reference was heard, and for the first time members of the public sought to use the reference process through a petition to the government.[79] But it was left particularly to that consummate politician, Mackenzie King, to make extensive use of the politically advantageous reference system. Avoiding issues of federal-provincial dispute by referral to the Court was an attractive political solution to potentially contentious and politically costly wrangling. Time or the Court's opinion or both might alter the circumstances so that an acceptable answer to the issue would be more apparent. In 1927, for example, at the dominion–provincial conference, questions on jurisdiction over civil aviation and over water-power on navigable waterways were referred, and it was debated whether other problems ought to be dealt with similarly.[80] In all, fourteen references went to the Court from the King administration during these years.

The advantages of the reference tactic were made clear in the water-powers question. First, delay was gained. The issue was a difficult one for the King government, which was being pushed by several different governments and interest groups. Reference to the court temporarily removed the issue from the political arena and postponed disagreeable debate with the premiers of Ontario and Quebec, and at the same time enabled the government to avoid taking a specific stand on the question.[81] Second, the government initiating the reference had the authority and ability to structure the questions posed to the Court in such a way as to direct the responses. In the case of the water-powers reference the bench, both during argument and in the judgment, pointed to the unsatisfactory and manipulative character of the questions presented. Writing for a unanimous Court, Justice Duff felt constrained to remind those involved of the advisory nature of the opinions handed down, and added, 'when a concrete case is presented for the practical application of the principles discussed, it may be found necessary, under the light derived from a survey of the facts, to modify the statement of such views as are herein expressed.'[82] Apart from its obvious legal disadvantages, the reference procedure was expensive[83] and inflexible; while the reference was underway, debate was constrained and finding a political solution to the issue was difficult.

The impact of this political use of the Supreme Court had been made even more apparent a few years earlier. In 1921 an appeal called into question the constitutionality of the Canada Temperance Act in Alberta. Justice Duff recounted the political interference in the case:

The temperance people were making a row about it, and the Minister of Justice [C.J. Doherty], being anxious to ascertain the probable result of the appeal then pending, sent for two members of the Court, Anglin and Mignault, and obtained from them information as to their own opinions and the opinions of their colleagues and the probable result of the appeal, and as a consequence legislation [11-12 Geo. v, c. 20] curing the defect was introduced before our judgment was delivered. Doherty felt safe in that case, because he and the two judges mentioned were educated at the same Jesuit college in Montreal, wth, as you may imagine, very close reciprocal affiliations.

Within two weeks of the argument's having been heard (and well before a decision was rendered), the minister introduced the curative legislation in Parliament. The majority of the Court held that this remedy was retroactively effective; only Justice Idington argued that such action by Parliament 'cannot retrospectively affect the civil rights of [the] appellant.'[84]

The reference system drew the Court directly into constitutional law, as did many ordinary cases. By the 1920s the Court had developed an extensive constitutional jurisprudence, particularly under the forceful leadership of Lyman Duff. Both in Ottawa and in London, as a member of the Judicial Committee (after 1918), Duff was in an influential position.[85]

By this time the Judicial Committee had articulated a strongly decentralist perception of the British North America Act. Duff's view, even before he joined the committee, meshed easily with this constitutional jurisprudence, and his concern for the 'federal character of the Union' fell on sympathetic ears.[86] His own appreciation of the constitution and of the Judicial Committee was made apparent in a letter written in 1925:

The B.N.A. Act endows the Dominion with very great powers indeed, and in the early days the Supreme Court of Canada was so impressed with the sweeping character of the language employed in defining the powers of the Dominion that it proceeded to give a series of decisions, the effect of which, if they had stood, would have been to take away from the provinces all but the slightest trace of political autonomy. What the Privy Council did was to protect the Constitution of Canada from this kind of judicial assault, and it has not gone beyond this. You and I, and everybody else who knows anything about the subject, know that according to the original design of the B.N.A. Act, great communities like Ontario and Quebec were intended to possess individually a high degree of self-government ... Now the Canadian courts, if left to themselves, it is not too much to say, had they stood, would have thrown our constitutional law into a state of chaos which would have required, before the exit of the nineteenth century, an entire revision of the whole position, but this was averted by the Privy Council.[87]

With such views Duff easily reinforced the constitutional jurisprudence of the Judicial Committee. That committee, he felt, had employed great 'statesmanship' in interpreting the British North America Act, and Duff hoped that it would be 'many a long year' before appeals to London were terminated.[88]

It is no exaggeration to say that until very recently Lyman Duff was the dominant force in constitutional matters on the Supreme Court of Canada.[89] During the Duff years the Supreme Court heard close to two hundred constitutional cases. And while Duff and his colleagues were obliged to follow the constitutional jurisprudence set down by the Judicial Committee, they were not simply subservient to the jurisprudence. Indeed, in several matters the Duff-led Court drew implications from Judicial Committee decisions; but those new implications tended in the basic provincial directions established by the Judicial Committee. Among these new directions, Duff and the Court contributed significantly to the interpretation of the federal power to regulate trade and commerce, but only after reaffirming the Judicial Committee judgments on peace, order, and good government.

Lyman Duff plainly shared the Judicial Committee's fear of the unchecked use of the federal power in matters relating to peace, order, and good government. In the *Insurance Reference* (1913),[90] for example, Duff led the Court majority in defeating the federal government's attempt to set national standards for the insurance industry. While acknowledging the national importance of insurance, the justices feared the long-term implications of granting such power to the federal Parliament. For Duff, the Court was obliged to prevent the thin edge of the wedge from intruding into provincial matters. If the Court condoned the use of the federal power in this case, Duff argued, there would be no end to its use in other related matters in the future. He concluded, 'The Act before us illustrates the extremes to which people may be carried when acting upon the theory that because a given matter is large and of great public importance it is for that reason a matter which is not substantially local in each of the provinces.' Duff's judgment in this case illustrates the extent to which he was in sympathy with the constitutional philosophy of Lord Watson as expressed in the *Local Prohibition* case (1896), which gave formal judicial status to the 'autonomy of the provinces.'[91]

Lord Watson's judgment in *Local Prohibition* did not end the controversy over the scope of the federal general power. During Duff's tenure on the Supreme Court, the Judicial Committee – principally under Viscount Haldane – went further in restricting the power of the federal Parliament. In *In re Board of Commerce Act* (1922),[92] the committee ruled that the federal Parliament would not intrude on the 'quasi-sovereign authority' of the provinces over matters relating to 'property and civil rights'. The Parliament of Canada could invade provincial territory, Haldane wrote, only 'in highly exceptional circumstances' such as war or famine. The committee ruled that since the matter of fair prices did not meet the test, the acts of the federal Parliament were ultra vires.

For its part, the Supreme Court had deadlocked in this case: three justices (Davies, Anglin, and Mignault) voted to uphold the federal statute, while Duff, Idington, and Brodeur voted against the legislation.[93] Duff's judgment shows that he was as adamantly opposed to easy federal intrusion into provincial areas of jurisdiction as were Watson and Haldane. He feared that if the federal Parliament was permitted control over the 'scarcity of necessaries of life, the high cost of them, the evils of excessive profit taking,' then there would be no saying where this would end; it could conceivably lead to 'nationalization of certain industries and even compulsory allotment of labour.' Duff's position was a judicial domino theory applied to construction of the British North America Act. 'In truth if this legislation can be sustained under the residuary clause,' he wrote, 'it is not easy to put a limit to the extent to which Parliament through the instrumentality of commissions ... may from time to time in the vicissitudes of national trade, times of high prices, times of stagnation and low prices and so on, supersede the authority of the provincial legislatures.' In order to prevent such a scenario from becoming reality, the federal Parliament must be stopped at the very beginning of the process.

The Judicial Committee was obviously impressed with Duff's line of reasoning when it ruled against the federal act. It is plain from Duff's judgment that he was not binding himself unduly by a narrow or unwilling acceptance of Watson's jurisprudence in *Local Prohibition*. Duff emerges in *Board of Commerce* as a jurist with his own views on the development of Canadian constitutional jurisprudence. That those lines happened to be strongly in favour of the provincial legislatures and hence compatible with the line of jurisprudence developed by the Judicial Committee was, for him, additionally persuasive. The *Board of Commerce* case shows that at least one justice of the Supreme Court of Canada influenced the Judicial Committee in important constitutional matters.[94]

The number of overall cases coming before the Supreme Court in these years appears to have remained steady.[95] The judicial conservatism of the Court and its members continued to predominate. The best example in this period can be found in the famous *Persons* case, in which on reference the Supreme Court ruled unanimously that women were not 'qualified persons' eligible for appointment to the Senate. The restricted views by the five justices, the narrowness of the definitions involved, and the unexpressed but apparent insistence of the justices that change be instituted through legislatures rather than courts stand out in the reasoning of the justices. This is particularly true when the opinions are contrasted with the opinion of the Judicial Committee, which reversed the Court's judgment.

The Court adopted a strict constructionist view of the issue. There can be no doubt that the term 'person' as used in 1867 in the British North America Act referred to men, since only men qualified for public office at that time. The Court was asked to interpret the terms of the act in the light of modern conditions. The justices could have looked at the act with a view to seeing whether women were formally excluded from assuming a role in the government of the country, but they chose not to do so. Chief Justice

Anglin explicitly rejected as irrelevant the social and political implications of the issue. The justices, in short, failed to view the British North America Act as a living constitutional document; they interpreted the act as an ordinary statute and restricted its terms to the context of 1867. The members of the Court effectively froze the terms of the British North America Act to a specific period of history. In so doing, the Court retreated from its common-law tradition of applying constitutional statutes in the light of recent developments.

The Judicial Committee dismissed the Supreme Court's opinion with a pointed observation: 'Their Lordships do not conceive it to be the duty of this Board ... to cut down the provisions of the Act by a narrow and technical construction, but rather to give it a large and liberal interpretation.' It is difficult to imagine a clearer rejection of the Supreme Court's strict constructionism in constitutional matters.

Chief Justice Anglin, writing for himself and Justices Mignault, Lamont, and Smith, relied on the common-law disqualification of women to hold office. Justice Duff chose narrower grounds, limiting himself to the terms of the British North America Act. Their reasons indicate a desire to reaffirm the status quo. Stability and order were to be upheld by the courts; it was for the legislature to initiate change. This deliberate eschewing of judge-made law is an accurate reflection of the Court's long-standing perception of the judicial function; nevertheless, in the context of the late 1920s, as the *Ottawa Evening Journal* pointed out, the decision made not only the law but the Supreme Court appear an ass.[96] For this the government must accept some responsibility. Rather than deal with the problem directly, it chose to allow the issue to be resolved by the court. The reference system encouraged a perception that the courts were a proper venue for dealing with political problems. This led to an expanding role for the courts where essentially political problems were seen to be justiciable.

The evidence is sparse as to how the justices handled these cases once argument had been heard. Under Chief Justice Davies there was some exchange of draft judgments among the judges and there seem to have been judicial conferences.[97] But the impression remains that Davies was not over-efficient in co-ordinating judicial reasoning, nor very concerned with improving the intellectual quality of the decisions.

Frank Anglin took a more active role as leader of the Court. He tried to encourage the writing of single majority judgments – something for which the Canadian Bar Association was pushing – and for a time he was successful. However, a chief justice's powers in such matters are limited to persuasion, and soon the force of individual personalities led the Court away from the practice.[98] Sometimes one justice would offer to write a draft judgment for the majority. This draft was then circulated, discussed, and altered if necessary. More often, and in cases where initial agreement was not apparent, individual drafts were exchanged, stimulating argument and reconsideration. Discussions were held by mail, in private meetings, and at conferences the frequency of which is unclear.[99]

The reporting of decisions seemed to improve, although the Supreme Court Reports continued to suffer from some weaknesses. The citation policy, for example, omitted references to private reports series if a public series was available; thus, the citation of the Dominion Law Reports was less frequent than it should have been, making the Supreme Court Reports less useful to the profession.[100] In addition, the Supreme Court Reports failed to report a number of cases some observers thought were of note; in 1924, for example, the Dominion Law Reports reported seventeen cases that did not appear in the Supreme Court Reports. But despite these omissions the quality of the Supreme Court Reports was reasonably good. Most of the early problems had been solved; in particular, justices were less slow in drafting their reasons for judgment. By now the normal time between the handing down of the decision and the submission of formal reasons was only four weeks,[101] facilitating a much more rapid communication of the information to the profession.

The improvement in the Supreme Court Reports was reflected in a growing circulation. In 1920 the government took over publication from a private publisher and made the Reports available on a mass subscription basis at a heavily subsidized rate. The registrar visited provincial bar associations to solicit subscriptions. By 1922 every provincial bar association in the country had contracted to provide each member with a subscription. The decisions of the leading court in the land now reached every practising lawyer in Canada. The print run soared, and issues quickly went out of print. By the late 1920s the average print run was 6,500 copies, of which 5,500 circulated on a subscription basis to members of various Canadian bar associations.[102]

The growth in circulation was part of a broader expansion planned by the registrar, E.R. Cameron. Cameron saw the Supreme Court as the apex of the Canadian judicial system, a position that created for the Court a unifying and co-ordinating role, a task of drawing the country together into one great nation. Just as the justices handed down decisions binding on the whole country, the Court staff could perform a service by producing an all-Canada reports series. In 1923 the reports of the

Supreme Court and the Exchequer Court were combined in a new series, the Canada Law Reports. Informing the profession of the change, Cameron commented, 'It is believed that this wide distribution of the Reports will further the aim of the Fathers of Confederation in providing by the British North America Act for the establishment of Dominion Courts, to institute thereby a legitimate centralizing agency for the promotion of National Unity.'[103] The new series was the first step in the registrar's plan to centralize the publication of all provincial law reports under the editorship of the staff of the Ottawa courts. In the years 1926–9 Cameron travelled to several provincial bar associations and the annual conventions of the Canadian Bar Association advocating the proposal, but the idea never gained sufficient support to be adopted.[104]

The Supreme Court staff was infused with and acting upon a sense of the potential power and influence of the central level of the federal political structure. This sense of national mission or purpose affected the Supreme Court as a whole. Discussion increased in these years regarding the possible termination of appeals to the Judicial Committee. This was partly the result of Canadian opposition to colonialism and of Canadians' pride in their own self-sufficiency; it was also a result of decisions handed down in London in 1925 and 1926, striking down long-standing Canadian legislation, and in 1927, rejecting Canadian territorial claims to Labrador. Abolition of appeals was proposed in Parliament, in various meetings, and in private correspondence.[105] Many still disagreed with any such suggestion, however, and even the favourable discussions were almost always negative toward the Judicial Committee rather than complimentary toward the Supreme Court. The unfavourable discussions were frequently strongly condemnatory of the Supreme Court.[106]

The national role of the Court was also reflected in the activities of Chief Justice Anglin. As a means of fostering goodwill between the bench and the bar, attracting the attention of those in high political places, and underlining the Court's position at the top of the Canadian judicial structure, Anglin gave a series of dinners in Ottawa. He invited the governor-general, lieutenant-governors, the provincial premiers and attorneys-general, federal cabinet ministers and members of the Privy Council, several members of the diplomatic corps, the provincial chief justices, leading civil servants, leading members of the bar, and, of course, the puisne justices of the Supreme Court.[107] Anglin's effort to raise the profile of the court was probably a product of his own desire for status, but in magnifying his own position he also emphasized the position and role of the Supreme Court.

6

Toward Centre Stage

1933–1949

The early years of the Great Depression witnessed considerable ill health and personal problems among the justices of the Supreme Court of Canada. In December 1931 E.L. Newcombe died, and in the following year all other members of the Court (with the exception of Arthur Cannon) were unwell. The leader of the opposition recorded the general public concern: 'Had a pleasant talk with Aimé Geoffrion, K.C. he discussed the great weakness of the Supreme Court, Duff ill, Anglin ill, Rinfret overdone & ill, Lamont & Smith not too well or up to much – 4 vacancies probable, – difficult to fill.'[1] A genuine problem existed. Most serious was the ill health of Chief Justice Anglin. Early in 1929 he applied for a leave of absence in the hope that a prolonged rest in the Caribbean would restore him to vigour, but the cure was unsuccessful. In the fall Prime Minister King found the chief justice 'to be failing, to have lost all his brightness, has little to say for himself.' In each of the next four years Anglin found it necessary to apply for further leaves. On the first three occasions the government acceded to his requests, but by early 1933 some other response was called for.[2] Mackenzie King, as leader of the opposition, was quite disturbed by the chief justice's condition: 'C.J. Anglin ... called here this afternoon. He could not speak & I felt he was going to pass away when he took a seat. He will not last long ... Saw Judge Anglin about resigning [;] advised him to do so, he can hardly speak ... It is quite sad to see a man give up his life work. Anglin is only 68 [67], – a fine intellect, but too vain. I shall be surprised if he lasts long.'[3]

Should a man in such physical condition have been on the bench at all, much less have been serving as the head of the highest court in the country? Rumours of Anglin's impending resignation had been circulating publicly for the past two years, and the government decided that now was the time for decisive action. The chief justice was threatened with an investigation into his capacity to hold the position.[4] Early in February he tendered his resignation to take effect on the last day of the month; three days after that he was dead.

The government of R.B. Bennett was now faced with the problem of selecting a new head of the Supreme Court of Canada. There is no evidence that anyone other than Lyman Duff was seriously considered for the post, but Bennett did have some qualms. Duff had been seriously ill in 1928 and had undergone abdominal surgery for cancer in 1931. In 1932, following his strenuous work on the Transportation Commission, he had suffered a severe nervous breakdown. Each of these illnesses threatened his life and his ability to remain on the bench. His capacity for recovery was impaired by his alcoholism. Late in 1932 Duff seemed to have rebounded, and order and companionship had been brought to his domestic life by his sister.[5] Bennett discussed the problems of the Court with Duff and voiced his misgivings about the justice's future role there. Duff responded by offering to resign if doing so would facilitate government policy regarding the Supreme Court. Still Bennett hesitated. Finally, in mid-March he confirmed the elevation of Duff.[6] Once decided, Bennett threw his full support behind the new chief justice, naming Duff a knight (KCMG) in 1934.

The selection of the new chief justice was a popular one. His elevation had been widely predicted and met with considerable approval. Several newspapers and magazines compared Duff to the most 'distinguished judicial luminaries in the world,' while others judged him to have the best legal mind in the modern history of Canada.[7]

With the leadership of the Court finally stabilized, two vacancies had to be filled. Newcombe's death in 1931 had left the Court with no representative from the maritimes. The position had tended to rotate among the three eastern provinces, particularly between Nova Scotia and New Brunswick. It is therefore not surprising, given that no one from the latter province had been on the Court since 1901, that both the prime minister and members of the local bar turned to that province for a candidate. For the last several years Bennett had called for an improvement in the quality of judicial appointments. Over a month after Newcombe's death, the prime minister wrote a thoughtful letter to the premier of New Brunswick explaining the difficulties of finding an able candidate from his native province. 'To be perfectly frank with you,' he wrote,

we have no one in New Brunswick fitted by training and experience to become a member of the Court of last resort, in this Dominion. We certainly have several that are as good as some members that now sit on the Bench ... I really find myself in a most difficult position. When you think that New Brunswick has been represented in the Supreme Court of Canada by Chief Justice Ritchie and Mr. Justice King, you can readily understand how hesitant I am to become a party to appointments that will make the contrast so apparent.

There were no outstanding barristers in the province, Bennett decided; an unidentified judge was rejected as too old. Judge Oswald Smith Crocket also had a serious weakness. 'I have a very high opinion of Mr. Justice Crocket. He is a friend of mine. We sat in the House together. But the truth is, for eighteen years he has been a Trial Judge, and to suddenly transfer him to the Court of last resort in Canada, and expect him within a reasonable time to acquire the habit of an Appellate Judge, is asking a very great deal.'[8]

The prime minister pondered the problem for eight more months (at least tentatively offering the post first to the unnamed older judge) before finally (and presumably reluctantly) asking Justice Crocket to join the Court. Crocket had been born and raised in New Brunswick, the son of the chief superintendent of education. He was called to the bar in 1891, and thereafter supplemented a none-too-extensive legal practice by court and sports reporting for local newspapers. By 1896 he was active in local politics, transferring his allegiance to the Conservative party in 1898 and eventually sitting in the House of Commons (1904–13). Crocket had never seemed particularly interested in the law; he had left much of the work of his practice to his partner in Fredericton. Nevertheless, he accepted his due reward from the Conservative government in 1913, joining the Supreme Court of New Brunswick, King's Bench division. Three years later he accepted the additional post of sole judge of the provincial Court of Divorce and Matrimonial Causes. In these two judicial capacities Crocket remained until his move to Ottawa in 1932.[9]

Crocket was not a strong candidate. His experience at the bar was limited, and his years as a trial judge, as Bennett recognized, had not developed in him the mental attitudes and perspectives required of an appellate judge. At age sixty-four it was probably a little late to expect

Crocket to acquire a different judicial training, particularly with his reputation for inflexibility and a steadfast commitment to the security of traditional methods and approaches.[10] His judicial limitations probably were a major factor in Chief Justice Duff's patronizing and disdainful attitude toward him.[11]

One term after Crocket's appointment, another vacancy was created by Anglin's resignation. The minister of justice selected a native of his own constituency as the replacement. Frank Joseph Hughes had been called to the bar in 1911. The law firm Hughes helped to establish in Toronto soon began to specialize in insurance law, particularly in motor-vehicle litigation, though the firm also had a wide general practice. Although he did a good deal of trial work, Hughes became best known as appeal counsel. The young lawyer also had experience as assistant crown attorney in York County. At age forty-nine Hughes brought vigour and a first-class legal ability to the Supreme Court. Hughes was a Catholic, and his appointment upheld the tradition of allotting one of the common-law seats to a member of that church.[12]

Hughes's appointment was arguably a good one. His lack of judicial experience was compensated for by his considerable work as appeal counsel. Unfortunately, after accepting the position, the Toronto lawyer soon found that it was not at all to his liking. He suffered a heart attack in 1933, and the move to Ottawa had a serious effect on his family. After a year in the new environment, he decided to leave, explaining: 'I have found it quite impossible to adjust myself and my family in a home outside of Toronto, in which I have lived so long.' In August 1934 he tendered his resignation, but stayed on through the fall sittings until early 1935.[13]

Hughes's departure created a problem for the government. There was already one vacancy on the Court; Justice Smith had retired in December 1933 and his seat had remained empty throughout 1934. The nature of the government's trouble in filling the post is unclear, since no documentation is extant. The rumour that Hugh Guthrie, minister of justice, was interested in the post seems unlikely. Finally, in January 1935, Henry Hague Davis was named to the position. Davis, the son of a Brockville, Ontario, merchant, had been called to the bar in 1911. Davis's legal practice included corporate law and criminal defence work. In 1933, after over twenty years in practice, Davis went to the Ontario Court of Appeal. On the Ontario bench he developed a reputation for a perceptive, discriminating mind and for judgments that were 'lucid and convincing.' He came to the Supreme Court at the age of forty-nine with two years' judicial experience. His appointment was so highly regarded that one law journal predicted Davis would eventually become chief justice.[14]

In July 1935 Guthrie selected a second resident of his constituency to join the Supreme Court of Canada. Patrick Kerwin, after being called to the bar in 1911, had formed a partnership in Guelph with Donald and Hugh Guthrie. Donald Guthrie died in 1915 and Hugh Guthrie was in the House of Commons continuously throughout this period, so that much of the work fell to Kerwin, giving him experience in a varied general practice. In the fall of 1932 his partner appointed him as a trial judge of the Ontario Supreme Court. He gained three years' judicial experience there before his promotion to Ottawa at age forty-five. Kerwin's appointment seemed to confirm two tendencies: he had no major political claims to the post, and, as a Catholic, he further entrenched the tradition begun by Anglin and maintained by Hughes.[15]

The Bennett government had now appointed four new members of the Supreme Court and promoted one other member to the position of chief justice. The government had been surprisingly slow in naming replacements; there was no acceptable excuse for leaving Robert Smith's seat vacant for almost fourteen months. But at the same time the government showed an impressive thoughtfulness regarding the process. Even though those selected were not all outstanding jurists, the Bennett government had tried to do the best it could for the Court. The traditions of regional and religious distribution of seats were not challenged, despite the lack of strong candidates in the maritimes. Except in the case of Crocket, politics – that is, reward for political service – played a more limited role in the choice of the new justices. This was not a pattern to which the incoming King government would adhere.

Justice Lamont's health began to deteriorate in the fall of 1935, apparently owing to heart disease. He was granted leave in November and died four months later. Lamont had had a history of ill health, and the vacancy came as no surprise; recommendations for the post were being received in Ottawa for two months prior to Lamont's death. It was taken for granted by all concerned that the new justice would come from the prairies. Several members of the provincial benches received strong and influential support, but one barrister, A.B. Hudson, had the backing of T.A. Crerar, the federal minister of the interior, and of the president of the Manitoba Liberal Association. Strong claims were also made that Manitoba deserved a representative on the Supreme Court.[16] It took the government only two weeks after the vacancy was created to select Hudson as the replacement.

Albert Blelloch Hudson had lengthy political experience. He was called to the Manitoba bar in 1899. The details of his private law practice are unclear, but it must have been extensive; he became a member of the bars of Alberta and Saskatchewan in 1906. In 1914 he turned to politics. He was elected to the provincial legislature as a Liberal and served as attorney-general from 1915 to 1917. Hudson left the provincial political scene in 1920 and was elected as a Liberal-Progressive in the federal general election of 1921. Over the next four years he was influential in maintaining links between the Liberal and Progressive members of the minority Parliament; at least twice he rejected offers to enter the King cabinet. In 1925 Hudson returned to his private law practice, and remained án important force in Manitoba Liberal circles. He did not actively solicit appointment to the Supreme Court, but he did let it be known that he was available. He joined the Court at age sixty, with no judicial experience.[17] He was probably not the strongest candidate available for the post, but his political ties were strong enough to overcome his liabilities.

Hudson's appointment was favourably received, especially in the west, where he was considered a solid and respected spokesman for the prairies. That perception became important in the next few years when the Court judged legislation passed by the Alberta government. His genuine concern for the Supreme Court of Canada had been demonstrated in 1923–4 when he and others had tried hard to have Eugène Lafleur appointed to the Court as a means of strengthening the institution.[18] Finally, Hudson knew his way around the corridors of power in Ottawa and in the Liberal party – and in some respects that was beneficial for the Court.

With Hudson's membership, the Court evinced a healthy range of age and experience. Lyman Duff, aged seventy-one, had thirty-two years' experience in the judiciary, thirty years of which had been on the Supreme Court. At the other end of the scale, Justice Kerwin was the youngest at forty-six, and Justice Hudson had no judicial experience. The average age of the Court members was fifty-eight, and the average amount of time spent on the bench was twelve years. The maritimes had one representative, Quebec two, Ontario two, the prairies one, and British Columbia one. Three justices were Roman Catholic, two were Presbyterian, and two were Anglican.

The one member of this Court who was not active was Arthur Cannon. Though he was only fifty-nine, his health had begun to deteriorate, necessitating leaves of absence in 1936, 1937, and 1939. During this last leave the Quebec jurist died. Six weeks later a replacement was named. Though he was not the government's first choice for the position, Robert Taschereau was a prominent representative of Quebec's ruling élite. Related to four previous members of the Court, he was the son of the long-time premier of Quebec, L.-A. Taschereau. Robert Taschereau had been called to the bar in 1920. He joined his father's large law firm in Quebec City, where he acquired a broad legal experience. He taught criminal law at Laval University (1929–40) and civil law at the University of Ottawa (1935–40). Taschereau also turned to politics, and sat as a Liberal in the Quebec legislative assembly from 1930 to 1939. At the age of forty-three, he joined the Supreme Court with no judicial experience.[19] His appointment was surprising; the strength of his ties to the ruling élite and to the Liberal party could not hide the fact that there was nothing outstanding about his career in law to this point.

In 1943 Justice Crocket retired at the age of seventy-five. His place was taken by one of the most outstanding legal minds ever to come out of the maritimes. Ivan Cleveland Rand read law in a leading Moncton office before proceeding to Harvard Law School, from which he graduated cum laude. Rand then joined the bar of New Brunswick in 1912 and entered private legal practice, first briefly in Moncton and then in Medicine Hat, Alberta. In 1920 he returned to Moncton and turned to politics. Late in 1924 he was appointed attorney-general in the provincial Liberal government; subsequently he was defeated in one by-election, successful in another, and defeated in a general election, all within the space of nine months. In 1926 Rand left his private law practice and joined the Canadian National Railway, first as Atlantic regional counsel and then as commission counsel. He moved to Ottawa in 1943, just before his fifty-ninth birthday.[20]

There was little debate within the government as to the appointment of Rand.[21] The new justice brought to the Court a wide range of experience, with highly developed knowledge in corporate, labour, and administrative law. This and the quality of his intellect more than compensated for his lack of judicial experience. Rand's appointment brought to three the number of justices named to the Supreme Court since the King government's return to office who had come directly from the bar and who also had given service to the Liberal party.

In the meantime, Chief Justice Sir Lyman Duff had reached retirement age. In fact, he had passed the point of mandatory retirement in January 1940. The government waived compulsory retirement and extended Duff's term for three years. The reasons for the only retirement waiver in the history of the Court are unclear, except that it reflected Duff's standing and reputation. The prime minister recounted one of the government's considerations: 'Discussed with Lapointe position of the Supreme Court, Duff's time being up in January. Four of the judges are anything but well.

Court very weak. He could think of no one suitable being appointed Chief Justice – from B.C., or to take Duff's place on the Supreme Court Bench. I agreed to having Duff's term extended a year if he were agreeable.' To move for the extension well in advance of the time required must have given the Court additional stability. While this extension gained all-party support in 1939, the same was not true early in 1943 when the government sought to add a further year to Duff's term. Opposition members pointed to the chief justice's age and lack of vigour – he was now seventy-eight – and both directly and indirectly to his chairing of the politically contentious 1942 royal commission on the dispatch of Canadian troops to Hong Kong. This time the extension of his term was resisted by the opposition and others.[22]

The government held the chief justice in high esteem; the prime minister considered appointing him the first Canadian-born governor-general in 1940. Duff continued to lead the Supreme Court as effectively as always, but by 1943 he was feeling his age. To a friend he wrote that he was experiencing 'the sort of lethargy which seems to come over me in fits, and when I feel as if I were utterly drained of energy and capacity for the simplest sort of action.'[23] The chief justice was allowed to retire in January 1944.

In his speech to the Court at the end of his career, Duff summed up his years on the bench. Though his personal influence had been considerable, it was limited by the Court's definition of the judicial function. The Supreme Court of Canada was 'engaged ... in administering and applying in practice rules of law founded on the principles' of the common law and the civil law.[24] The crucial words were 'administering and applying.' No mention was made of developing those rules or principles, or of altering them to changing circumstances, or of using his own considerable intellectual talents to mature the law. Duff had seen his task as administering and applying the rules and principles of others.

The selection of a successor was not difficult. Thibaudeau Rinfret, the senior puisne justice, had been at the Court since 1924, and his French-Canadian background made him an attractive candidate to a government that was trying to subdue ethnic tensions and animosity in the midst of war. It was rumoured that J.L. Ralston, minister of national defence, wanted the post, but King was unwilling to disrupt his cabinet and was attracted by the idea of appointing someone from Quebec. King commented on his choice:

Though he is not strong I do not see how Rinfret could be passed by at this time. It was more or less understood since Duff's term was extended that it would not prevent Rinfret succeeding him. I shall be surprised if Rinfret lasts any length of time, once he has this additional responsibility ...

My own feeling is that Rinfret is a little on in years [sixty-four years old] for the appointment and is not very strong ... However I think it is due to the P[rovince of].Q[uebec]. to have a Chief Justice, and to Rinfret himself for having stood aside for Duff in the last couple of years.[25]

A few months after Duff's retirement, a second vacancy was created when Henry Davis died at the age of fifty-eight. By tradition these vacancies would be filled by representatives of the west and of Ontario. The government delayed the new appointments until the fall of 1944. First named was Roy Lindsay Kellock of Ontario, who had been called to the bar twenty-four years earlier. Kellock had been a member of a major Toronto law firm and had an excellent reputation as litigation counsel. He was appointed to the Ontario Court of Appeal late in 1942, where he remained until his elevation to Ottawa in 1944 at age fifty.[26]

There was some competition for the western vacancy. The contest was among the three provinces without a spokesman on the current Court. Since British Columbia had been represented by Duff for almost forty consecutive years, its claims to the seat were not strongly voiced. No resident of Alberta had ever been a member of the Supreme Court of Canada. In making this point, one western senator cited Alberta's rich natural resources, its development projects, and its increasing population, arguing that it was potentially one of the country's most prosperous provinces and it deserved representation. The status attached to a place on the Supreme Court bench is reflected in the senator's comment that he expected the prime minister to respond favourably, 'knowing that your sense of equity will incline you to correct a situation which puts Alberta in a condition of inferiority among the other provinces.'[27]

But Alberta lacked a strong influence in cabinet or in the Liberal party caucus to counter the impact of the Saskatchewan Liberal members of Parliament led by the powerful minister of agriculture, James G. Gardiner. The issue was discussed at a meeting of Saskatchewan MPs, and Gardiner made it clear that he felt his province's claims were persuasive. Justice Lamont was from Saskatchewan, but when he died, 'for reasons which do not need to be discussed now that appointment was transferred elsewhere [Manitoba]. I think that every consideration should be given to the possibility of having one of the present vacancies filled from Saskatchewan.'[28] Most frequently suggested were T.C. Davis (of the provincial

Court of Appeal), W.M. Martin (chief justice of the same court), and the recently defeated provincial attorney-general, J.W. Estey. In the end, Estey was chosen.

A maritimer by birth, James Wilfred Estey had been trained in law at Harvard. In 1915 he moved to Saskatoon, where he became a lecturer in economics and law at the University of Saskatchewan (1915–25), was called to the bar (1917), and entered private practice. Estey was involved in several law firms and partnerships, and developed a special expertise in litigation. From 1915 to 1921 he was assistant to the local crown prosecutor, and from 1921 to 1929 acted as the local agent for the provincial attorney-general. He was elected as a Liberal to the provincial legislature in 1934, where he sat for the next ten years; he served as minister of education (1934–41) and attorney-general (1939–44) until he and his government were defeated in June 1944. He was available to take on some new task when the call came from Ottawa three months later.[29] Though there is no doubt as to the intellectual qualifications of Estey, his appointment is a further indication of the King government's criteria for selection: no preference for judicial experience, considerable weight to service to the Liberal party, some minimum level of ability, and influential friends.

One final appointment to the Supreme Court was made by the King government. Justice Hudson died early in 1947, and once again there was debate as to which western province should provide the new justice. On this occasion most of the support seemed to be for someone from British Columbia, but it seemed difficult to find a qualified person who would accept the appointment. Prime Minister King commented on the problem in his diary:

Ilsley [the Minister of Justice] was anxious to appoint Mr. Locke, of Vancouver, B.C., as a Justice of the Supreme Court. I urged that another effort be made to secure Colonel [Brigadier Sherwood] Lett. There is real difficulty in obtaining qualified men for the Supreme Court Bench. A choice had to be made from one of the four western provinces. Several of those who have been invited to come to the Supreme Court have declined.

Brigadier Lett turned down the proferred appointment, as, apparently, did others.[30] One is presented with the disturbing picture of the country's Supreme Court, at a time when it was about to be placed on a new and higher level of responsibility and stature, being unable to attract the most desirable candidates (as judged by the government).

One of the difficulties in attracting new members to the Court was the justices' remuneration. Salary levels had not risen since 1920. In 1932 the justices' salaries were subjected to a special 10 per cent additional income tax, and again during the Second World War the high general taxation rates fell heavily on the justices' income. A further problem was the absence of pensions for widows; when a justice died, his pension rights (or annuity) died with him. The salary and pension questions were constantly raised by the legal profession during this period, especially through the Canadian Bar Association. Some judges from other courts, including Justices Cannon and Lamont, registered their complaints against the level of remuneration and taxation by allowing their taxes to fall in arrears.[31] Progress in dealing with these problems was finally made toward the end of the war. In 1944 provisions, though by no means generous, were made regarding annuity payments to widows. Salaries were increased in 1946 to $20,000 for the chief justice and $16,000 for each puisne justice, and then in 1949 to $25,000 and $20,000 respectively. While these levels of remuneration would have been attractive to lawyers located outside the country's major economic centres, such as James Estey, they were apparently well below the expectations of leading members of the bar in the big cities.[32] But there were still problems in attracting new justices. One western member of Parliament pointed out, for example, that many western Canadians found the prospect of moving to Ottawa unappealing;[33] this was not a problem unique to western Canadians or to this period.

The post on the Supreme Court eventually went to Charles Holland Locke. The son of a county court judge, he was the last member of the Court to receive his basic legal training in law offices rather than in a university setting. Called to the Manitoba bar in 1910, he began practice in Winnipeg. In 1928 Locke joined a law firm in Vancouver. There he became a leader of the provincial bar and acquired a reputation for considerable ability. His appointment to the Supreme Court at age fifty confirmed the government's lack of interest in judicial experience, but was an exception to the strong tendency to reward past political service to the party in power – Locke had been active in the Progressive Conservative party.[34]

This does not mean that party service had been abandoned as a major criterion of selection. Mackenzie King was reluctant to appoint Charles Locke to the Court, and in fact two other men were being considered for appointment as a reward for cabinet service. In 1948 King toyed with the idea of offering the chief justiceship (which was not vacant) to Louis St Laurent as recompense for having stayed on in politics. In 1947 and again in 1948, serious consideration was given to allowing J.L. Ilsley to retire to the Court. Ilsley had performed major service in the cabinet since 1935, and was very interested in spending his remaining public years on the bench. To make room for Ilsley, King contemplated expanding the number of justices at the Court or shifting Justice Rand back to New Brunswick as chief justice (or even back into private practice).[35] That the prime minister could have considered removing one of the best judicial minds on the Court to make room for a political colleague is revealing. The Supreme Court of Canada was still viewed as an institution open to partisan political exploitation on the same level (and no higher, except perhaps in status) as the array of government agencies and boards that now proliferated.

This tendency to partisan use of judicial appointments (not only to the Supreme Court) caused a good deal of concern in this period. Protest against it was, of course, an old refrain within the legal profession. To his credit, R.B. Bennett had repeatedly spoken out against such a selection process,[36] and during his time in office political service was not a major criterion for appointment to the Supreme Court. With the return of the practice under Mackenzie King protests increased, especially in the 1940s, though with little apparent impact.[37] If the position of the judiciary within the political structure was changing, it was not doing so very quickly.

Not surprisingly, the justices' involvement in nonjudicial tasks continued. In 1934 Chief Justice Duff agreed to act as sole commissioner of a federal royal commission to inquire into allegations regarding the manner in which former Prime Minister Arthur Meighen had discharged his duties as commissioner of the Ontario Hydro-Electric Power Commission. The federal inquiry was cancelled when the Ontario government appointed a parallel royal commission, but his acceptance of the assignment does point to Duff's continued willingness to allow himself to become involved in partisan issues. In the fall of 1935 Justice Davis acted as the sole commissioner to investigate the longshoremen's industrial dispute on the Vancouver waterfront. In 1937 Justice Rinfret was named to the famous Royal Commission on Dominion-Provincial Relations. Ill health combined with the extra duties forced Rinfret to resign the appointment within three months.[38] A year later Justice Davis was again persuaded to lead a one-man royal commission to investigate what is known as the Bren-gun scandal. Members of the Conservative party had charged that the contract to manufacture the gun had been improperly handled by the government. Davis, a member of the Court, was placed in the uncomfortable position of having to assess government policy and to weigh partisan charges.

A similar task cropped up in 1942. Again members of the Conservative party alleged that the government had made serious errors in judgment and management in dispatching Canadian troops to Hong Kong shortly before Japanese forces had captured the colony. Once again the King government called on a member of the Supreme Court, Chief Justice Duff, to conduct a one-man commission of investigation. The chief justice claimed to have been pressured into the assignment; 'I dislike intensely going on with the government job,' he wrote to Justice Davis, 'but it was put to me in such a way that I could not refuse.' Duff's report, which generally absolved the government of all charges, aroused considerable reaction among elements within the Conservative party. His biographer makes it clear that the chief justice did not conduct this inquiry in a thorough, balanced, or impartial manner. When the chief justice's extension of term was debated in the House a few months later, his handling of this partisan affair was one of the grounds on which he was attacked.[39] Duff's role in this commission, predictably, brought him (and with him the Supreme Court) into the direct firing line between the Conservative and Liberal parties. Once again the Court and its members could be seen as a political instrument to be used without apparent constraints in partisan controversies.

The use of the justices for such purposes as the Hong Kong inquiry had obvious advantages for the prime minister. He needed a commissioner whom the public trusted, and 'no one,' King recorded, 'would give the same sense of security, of impartiality and of wisdom, in a matter of this kind as the chief justice of Canada.' He needed to make use of Duff's image of neutrality; if that image suffered as a result, for King that was a matter for the future – the problems of the present were more important. Partisan political problems were also considered more vital than the character and stature of the Supreme Court of Canada. The prime minister's priorities and the place of the Court in the political system were made apparent when he instructed Duff: 'I really felt it might be a help rather than a burden to him if he would get an ad hoc Judge to act in the courts and forget about the courts for a time, and just interest himself in that [Hong Kong] question which was one of importance to the British Government as well as to our own. One which was an important war matter.'[40]

The war and the solution of an immediate political crisis were top priorities; the Supreme Court ranked so low that its own leader was told to forget about it for a while. From a political point of view and in terms of the immediate national interest King may have been correct in his priorities, but the Court was exploited so frequently that it was often seen as a subordinate institution.

Three years later, in 1945, Justice Kellock was named to head a royal commission on the Halifax vE-day riots. In contrast with this rather innocuous assignment was the 1946 royal commission on espionage. Early in February two Supreme Court justices, Taschereau and Kellock, were appointed to investigate espionage in Canada as a response to the revelations of a Russian defector, Igor Gouzenko. The commission worked in secrecy, and no public announcement of its existence was made until nine days after it had commenced work. All of its hearings were held in camera. Various persons appeared before the commissioners to give evidence, including many who were implicated in some of the charges and some who had been arrested without charges being laid. The commission operated in a quasi-judicial manner, but violated judicial norms and individual civil liberties. Much of the evidence heard was unsubstantiated and would not have stood up in a court of law; persons arbitrarily detained were kept in solitary confinement and were denied the right of habeas corpus and access to counsel. These practices were justified as being in the national interest, and are a reflection of the growing cold-war atmosphere.[41] It had been the government's decision to give the commission the power to detain persons and refuse them the right to counsel. That two members of the highest court in the land could easily and repeatedly violate civil rights and judicial norms is as appalling as it is indefensible.

Royal commissions were not the only way in which Supreme Court justices were used for non-judicial purposes. In 1932 Justice Rinfret was appointed to a government committee respecting the administration of the Pension Act within the civil service. In 1947 Justice Rand was the Canadian representative on the United Nations' Special Committee of Observation in Palestine. Two years later Justice Kellock was named to head an inquiry into the fire that destroyed the *Noronic*.

More common than these assorted tasks were labour arbitrations assigned to the Court. In 1941 Justice Kerwin was named chairman of two conciliation boards dealing with Canadian railway employees. Ivan Rand's arbitration of the 1945 Ford strike led to his compromise (now known as 'the Rand Formula'), obligating non-union workers to pay union fees without joining the union, a practice that became standard in North America.

The period was marked by little intrusion by the justices into the policy-making process of government. It is true Chief Justice Duff seemed to have no compunctions about recommending various acquaintances for judicial appointments.[42] Duff also took advantage of his position and his experience during the First World War to warn the prime minister in 1941 about the potentially disastrous result of conscription. Mackenzie King did not need much persuading in this regard; in 1944, when the cabinet was in the midst of a tense debate over the adoption of compulsory overseas military service, the prime minister wrote, 'I said every member of Cabinet should talk with ex-Chief Justice Duff about what he felt about enforcing conscription in the last war and what he thought it might lead to in this.'[43] It is possible that advice was offered more frequently than this and that the evidence is simply not extant. But even without such advisory activity, the justices' wide-ranging duties, outside their official Court responsibilities, are significant in their extent and number.[44]

These non-judicial activities undoubtedly impaired the Supreme Court in fulfilling its judicial functions, at least by taking justices (and staff) away from their Court work and exposing the Court to additional public criticism. However, the service of the Court and its members to the country should be recognized and appreciated. For various reasons and at various times minor and major extrajudicial duties were carried out in the service of the country. In this sense the Supreme Court of Canada was becoming a useful institution within the Canadian political system, and some of these activities helped to enhance the Court's prestige. But was political activity appropriate for a supreme court in a federal system?

One of the problems the Supreme Court faced in this period was not new but was becoming more noticeable: regional discontent. The western provinces, having finally gained a second seat on the Court in 1927, struggled not so much over retention of the two seats as over their distribution. Because Sir Lyman Duff held one of the seats for a long period, during his tenure only one western seat was available for new appointments. Alberta especially felt its lack of representation on the bench. In 1933 the Calgary Bar Association passed a resolution calling for the elevation of any one of Alberta's judges;[45] in 1936, 1944, and 1947 similar missives reached Ottawa; Justice Frank Ford was a favourite candidate. In any case, it remained difficult to persuade prospective judicial candidates to move east to Ottawa.[46]

Complaints regarding distribution had always been largely about status. A seat on the Supreme Court of Canada was viewed as a reflection of a province's stature and importance within the dominion. Lack of representation could develop into a feeling of alienation, a sense that the

Supreme Court was removed or aloof. The editor of the *Manitoba Bar News* suggested in 1930 that the Supreme Court go on circuit to various provincial capitals once a year.[47] This proposal was followed up in more detail a few years later by a leading Edmonton solicitor, P.G. Thomson, in a letter to the minister of justice, Hugh Guthrie:

Presumably your intimate knowledge of matters legal and judicial is largely centred round Toronto and Ottawa and for that reason you may not appreciate as thoroughly as we do out here the disadvantage, upon occasions, of being so far removed from the Judicial centre of the Dominion. To the ordinary litigant here as well as his solicitor, 'East is East and West is West,' particularly in matters judicial and often where an appeal to the Supreme Court at Ottawa would be advisable the expense as well as the time involved so far as the Western lawyer is concerned is prohibitive.

The Supreme Court was so far away that an appeal of a western case would require a western lawyer to be away from his office for at least three weeks. Thus, it was 'almost compulsory' to employ eastern counsel. To an eastern lawyer the case was simply 'another Western brief but to the Western lawyer it means bread and butter through the loss of a substantial fee.'

As a solution, Thomson proposed that the Supreme Court hold sittings once a year in each of the four western provinces. Other judicial or quasi-judicial bodies went on circuit – the Exchequer Court, the Board of Railway Commissioners, and royal commissions – so why not the Supreme Court?

The benefits would be considerable, Thomson argued. Apart from improving the financial lot of western lawyers in the midst of the depression and acting as a mental stimulant to the western bench and bar, appeals that were barred solely because of expense would now be facilitated. Better still, 'the mingling and comingling of East and West would all make for a better understanding' across the nation. Finally, in the west where so many residents were of non-British background, it was necessary,

especially in these times not only to tell them but to show them what is meant by British Justice and the spectacle of the highest Court in the land sitting in all its dignity out in the West in order to enable the poorest subject in the Dominion to obtain redress would be one to conjure with and would bring home to these people in a way nothing else could the advantages of living in this country and the benefits to be derived if they become good citizens as well as the disadvantages should they fail to do so.

Such a change in the Court's procedure would be 'a landmark in the progress of the Dominion which will long survive and point the way to greater things.'[48]

The minister, after consulting law officers and members of the Supreme Court, rejected Thomson's proposal for a number of reasons. First, if the Court 'were to become a peripatetic institution,' the existing system of rotating justices among cases in order to give them time to deliberate and write would be 'quite impracticable.' Second, the system would be expensive, especially since the maritime provinces were certain to demand equal treatment. Third, the chief justice or the senior puisne justices would be unavailable to perform their duties as deputies to the governor-general. Fourth, the members of the Court would not have access to the libraries of the Supreme Court. Finally,

it is not *prima facie* likely that the spectacle of seeing the Judges of the Supreme Court of Canada moving, bag and baggage, from one Provincial capital or centre to another with all the attendant inconveniences would be calculated to enhance the dignity and prestige of the Court. Nor is there any evidence of any considerable popular demand in the Provinces for such a change in the settled mode of conducting the business of the Court.[49]

The presence of the Supreme Court in provincial capitals might tend to overshadow provincial superior courts and reduce their authority and prestige without enhancing its own. It had long been British practice that the highest appellate tribunal be fixed and stationary at the national capital.

Despite the firmness of Guthrie's rejection, Thomson replied in detail to each of the minister's arguments. The Edmonton solicitor also sought to provide Ottawa with a positive reason for the reform. Provincial autonomy had gone too far, he contended; Ottawa ought to be more active in trying to bind the country together. 'Were the Supreme Court to move around as suggested it would be a practical example of that unity we all speak of but seldom practice and bring home, to the West in particular, in a way that nothing else would the realisation [that] we are in fact as well as in name a solid united Nation.'[50]

Thomson set out to refute Guthrie's charge that there was no popular support for the reform. In the early summer of 1934 the benchers of the

Alberta Law Society were sent a copy of his letter to the minister, and Thomson asked Guthrie's permission to circulate copies of the correspondence among other interested parties. The minister eventually agreed, providing that the material not be published in newspapers or periodicals. In April 1935 the Alberta legislature passed a resolution in support of Thomson's reforms.[51] Nothing more was heard of these proposals. They were not realistic and did not coincide with the incoming King government's ideas of the awesome and majestic power that ought to characterize the Supreme Court. Nevertheless, Thomson's suggestions served to point up important weaknesses in the Court. In the days before efficient air travel, the Supreme Court of Canada was not readily accessible to many appellants and solicitors. As well, the Court was perceived as aloof and lacking in an understanding of the law and the environment outside central Canada. But while the complaints about the court may have been well founded, they ignored its original and ongoing purpose: the institution was designed not to cater to regional differences but to reduce those differences and to articulate a common body of law for the entire country.

The timing of the complaints is important. They were voiced before many of Bennett's New Deal reforms were struck down, before the Alberta Social Credit legislation was found ultra vires in 1938, and before discontent broke out in the early 1940s regarding the high rate of reversals of Manitoba Court of Appeal decisions at the hands of the Supreme Court.[52]

All of these developments in the late 1930s and early 1940s could have encouraged regional discontent in the west regarding the Supreme Court, had that discontent not already existed.

The workload of the Supreme Court of Canada was declining in the 1930s and 1940s, presumably owing largely to the limitation of *de plano* appeals to amounts over $2,000. Tables 2 and 3 detail this decline and the distribution of the appeals by type of law. Except in the category of references, there seems to be no reason to question the representative character of these statistics of all cases heard, not just those reported.

Most of the justices went about their work in a typically private fashion. There can be little doubt that a good deal of correspondence and exchange of views occurred, but most justices, presumably because of concern for confidentiality, did not retain any records of their discussions. Fortunately, the papers of Chief Justice Duff provide some glimpses into the process of judgment.

TABLE 2
Volume of cases* at ten-year intervals

Type	1910	1920	1930	1940
Reference	1	1	3	–
Civil	83	114	74	64
Criminal	–	3	6	4
TOTAL	84	118	83	68

*Reported and unreported

TABLE 3
Volume of cases,* 1944–8

Type	1944	1945	1946	1947	1948
Reference	–	–	1	1	1
Civil	55	39	52	50	59
Criminal	6	5	3	10	12
Habeas corpus	–	1	–	–	–
TOTAL	61	45	56	61	72

Source: PAC, RG13, A5, vol. 2073, no. 156794
*Reported and unreported

Duff plainly took seriously his responsibilities as head of the Supreme Court. Illness, resignation, and political assignments repeatedly kept justices away from the Court during the 1930s, necessitating the use of ad hoc replacements. Duff went out of his way to welcome these temporary members and to make good use of their talents, encouraging them to rewrite draft judgments and to participate fully in the decision-making process. At the same time he kept a careful watching-brief on these justices and on the Court itself. The frequently changing composition of the Court, he explained privately in 1935, 'necessitates, especially on my part, a very severe scrutiny of every one of the appeals and really makes it impossible for me to indulge myself in extraneous arrangements [commitments].'[53]

The various Court members seemed to get along fairly well with one another. The tension of Duff's relations with Anglin was no longer a problem. Indeed, with the accession of Henry Davis to the Court, the chief justice had acquired a good friend and close collaborator. But Duff, who could be quite testy at times, did not get along well with Oswald Crocket. The chief justice had little respect for Crocket's ability or knowledge, and patronized him. One anecdote survives to illustrate the relationship: after considering one appeal, Crocket (hoping to please Duff) approached Duff with the news that Crocket had decided to adopt the chief justice's views in the case and to enter a concurrence; in that case, snapped Duff, he would change his decision.[54]

It is not clear whether there was a standard procedure for dealing with cases once argument had been heard. Certainly there were exchanges of draft judgments and of opinion thereon; some of these exchanges occurred surprisingly close – sometimes less than a week – to the actual handing-down of the judgment. On other occasions formal or informal conferences provided the opportunity required to refine some reasons and discard others, but Duff was unable to convince his colleagues that regular conferences would be beneficial.[55] These exchanges of information were, of course, no guarantee of higher-quality judgments. Justice Davis, for example, commented that 'Cannon suggested that I should accept his view of the Quebec law because it was a Quebec case but I told him frankly that I did not concur in that view of [the] disposition of Quebec cases.'[56] Any hope that exchanges of draft judgments would lead to greater agreement (and thus to fewer multiple judgments in a case) was futile. In *Chapdelaine* v *The King* (1935), the five-man panel unanimously upheld the appeal and ordered a new trial. Justice Hughes wrote the leading judgment (nine pages long); Justice St Germain ad hoc added a second opinion (two pages long); and Chief Justice Duff contributed a four-page judgment concurring with the two justices and which he privately admitted 'adds nothing of substance to what you [St Germain] and Hughes have already said.' Justice Cannon concurred with Duff, but took one page to elaborate on a minor point. Only Justice Crocket was content with a simple concurrence.[57] The tendency toward writing unnecessary multiple judgments, to which Duff was a major contributor, smacks of a lack of intellectual discipline and rigour.

One important trend in the type of cases handled by the Supreme Court was the continuing increase in number and importance of reference cases. In 1934, for example, three references were sent forward by the Bennett government. In one the jurisdiction of the Tariff Board was found to be restricted; in two others dominion legislation (the Companies Act and the Companies' Creditors Arrangement Act) was upheld as intra vires.[58] These last two opinions, combined with recent judgments in the Judicial Committee of the Privy Council, encouraged Prime Minister Bennett to introduce early in 1935 what is known as 'the Bennett New Deal.'[59] Aimed at dealing with some of the social and economic problems of the depression, the legislation covered such issues as unemployment insurance, minimum wages, commodity marketing boards, and agricultural credit. The constitutional validity of much of this legislation was doubtful. The opposition Liberal party, confident of victory in the approaching general election, opted not to challenge the New Deal in Parliament for fear that by doing so they would appear to be anti-reform; instead, the courts would be allowed to assess, and presumably to strike down, the statutes.[60] In this way any adverse public reaction would be directed at the courts rather than at the politicians.

Within two weeks of taking office in October 1935, the Liberal cabinet referred to the Supreme Court some eight statutes of the outgoing government. Counsel was the same for all the references: for the attorney-general of Canada, Newton W. Rowell and Louis St Laurent; for the attorney-general of Quebec, Aimé Geoffrion; for Ontario and British Columbia, the provincial attorneys-general in person. Other counsel represented the attorneys-general of New Brunswick, Manitoba, Alberta, and Saskatchewan. The proceedings were a major political event, with the Supreme Court of Canada the centre of attention. The excitement and sense of occasion were evident. The chief justice, for example, commented privately just days before the hearings began: 'Things are warming up around the court in anticipation of the references.'[61]

Though the references were important in focusing public attention on the Court, they exposed in the most dramatic fashion the potential for political exploitation in the reference system. To ask the Supreme Court to rule on the entire legislative package of a recent government was to require the Court to perform more a political than a judicial function. As one writer put it, 'in a New Deal type situation the reference device singularly lends itself to imposing upon the courts a role approximating that of a political decision maker. Almost inevitably, in such a situation, the courts must weight factors of political policy along with legal factors before rendering their decisions.' To judge a government's policies was a task for the electorate, not the Supreme Court. The potentially dangerous, partisan political elements of the process were revealed in several ways. R.B. Bennett, for example, attempted to defend the legislation by supplying the justices, through an intermediary, with additional information outside the courtroom. The intermediary reported 'that the atmosphere of the Court was saturated with politics' and that the justices were talking of little else.[62]

The references were heard, as required by statute, by a full panel of six justices (one seat being vacant). But when the justices rendered their opinions four months later, the results were not fully satisfactory to any of the interested parties. Viewed as a package, the opinions of the Court did not indicate whether a new constitutional direction had been taken. In two instances the federal legislation was found intra vires, in two instances ultra vires, and in one instance partially intra vires; on the last three statutes the Court divided evenly. Of the individual justices, Sir Lyman Duff was particularly active, writing opinions in every reference – twice for the entire Court and twice for the majority; only once did Duff find himself in dissent. The chief justice was strongly supported by Henry Davis, both in conference and in court. Both justices showed a marked tendency to uphold or extend the powers of the central government. Duff seemed more willing to take into account contemporary social and economic circumstances, and his decisions stand in contrast to his earlier constitutional jurisprudence and to that of the Judicial Committee. Justice Cannon demonstrated an equally strong inclination to maintain provincial powers. Any suspicion that the Court was taking a centralist direction was dispelled after the references were dealt with by the Judicial Committee in London. The Supreme Court was upheld in every instance but one, in which the holding was varied somewhat; in the case of the three statutes on which the Canadian justices had divided evenly, the committee awarded a solid victory to those defending provincial jurisdiction.

In immediate terms any import on the law from these decisions was limited. The references had, however, emphasized the potential constitutional role of the Court – so much so that when candidates for the vacant seat were being discussed, one ex-cabinet minister told Prime Minister King, 'It is clear that the Court from now on will be called upon to deal with constitutional questions more and more and it would be desirable to have on the Court those whose natural views would be inclined to view sympathetically the standpoint of our people.'[63] The references had also attracted public attention to the Supreme Court, and this in itself was unusual enough to be significant. It was no coincidence that an article about the Court soon appeared in Maclean's Magazine (1 April 1936). The writer exclaimed 'The Supreme Court of Canada! Truly a term to conjure with. The highest tribunal in our country. It awes one. Even the shoddy little [Supreme Court] building cannot rob the institution of that peculiar reverence one automatically feels.'

This public attention came at an important time. The handling of the references gave prominence to the Court and substance to its national role. The stature of the Court was further enhanced two years later, in 1938, when the federal government referred three prominent pieces of Alberta legislation.

In 1937, under considerable pressure from his Social Credit party, Premier William Aberhart had pushed through the legislature a series of bills to give effect to social credit theory. Three acts were quickly disallowed by the Ottawa government on the grounds that they were invalid and would seriously disrupt the financial system. Three other bills were reserved by the lieutenant-governor – the Bank Taxation Bill, the Credit of Alberta Regulation Bill, and the Accurate News and Information Bill (the so-called Press Bill) – after passage by a special session of the legislature. An atmosphere of direct confrontation between Alberta and the central government had been created. With some relief the senior politicians involved reached a compromise: the federal powers of disallowance and reservation would be tested by a reference to the Supreme Court, accompanied by a reference of the three reserved bills.[64]

Again, a six-man panel (Rinfret being absent) heard the arguments of counsel. This time, however, the atmosphere was not as charged as it had been in 1936. In the reference regarding disallowance and reservation, only two provincial attorneys-general (from Alberta and British Columbia) were represented by counsel, and only the former was heard. Perhaps this lack of provincial challenge can be explained by the relatively straightforward nature of the issue. The justices found unanimously that the federal powers were unimpaired in law, constitutional practice or usage being deemed irrelevant, and that they were subject only to minor limitations.[65]

The reserved bills were struck down unanimously by the justices. On the grounds that they were themselves ultra vires and/or that they were dependent upon another act that was ultra vires, the banking and credit acts were found to be invalid. Similarly, the Press Bill was struck down; in that instance the reasoning was more varied, but there was agreement that it depended on an act which was itself ultra vires. Beyond that, Duff (writing for himself and Davis) argued that the 'right of public discussion' could be interfered with only at the national level; Cannon agreed, adding that the bill tended to nullify 'political rights.' Kerwin (writing for himself and Crocket) and Hudson declined entirely to discuss the civil-liberties aspect of the issue.[66] The Court was maintaining its conservative tradition with respect to questions of civil liberties. The weakness of the Court's 'defence' of freedom of public discussion was recognized by the chief justice himself:

[W]e concluded the Press Bill to be ultra vires because the effective operation of its essential provisions necessarily depended upon the validity of the Social Credit Act which we held to be beyond the powers of the provinces. You will see that I went beyond this in applying the principles, partly expressed and partly implicit, in Haldane's judgment in the Great West Saddlery case and the principle upon which the limitation of Dominion powers under Trade and Commerce has mainly been based as explained in Bank of Toronto v. Lambe, and held that the capacity of the Province to restrict public discussion on public affairs must necessarily find some limitation by reference to the admitted fact that the parliamentary institutions of the Dominion necessarily pre-suppose for their effective working such public discussion. Davis and I, however, express no opinion on the point whether the Alberta bill offends against this principle. The application of the principle in particular cases, if they arise, might be a very difficult and delicate job. We thought, however, that the statement of the principle would be of some value for two reasons: first, it would probably appeal to moderately sensible people as indicating a restraint which provincial legislatures ought to impose upon themselves; and, second, it might fortify the Dominion in respect of disallowance if any flagrant case arose.[67]

Despite (or perhaps because of) the weakness of this aspect of the decision, the Supreme Court's opinions in these references were roundly applauded. The *Canadian Bar Review* spoke of 'the widespread satisfaction and acclaim' with which the news was received across the country, and suggested that the favourable public reception of the Court's opinions 'furnishe[d] material support' for the developing movement to abolish appeals to the Judicial Committee. The *Vancouver Province* headlined its editorial, 'A Common Sense Judgment,' and the Montreal *Star* stated that the justices had done the people of Alberta a favour.[68]

During the Second World War the reference process continued, and several federal statutes, federal regulations, and Alberta statutes were tested before the Court. Although one of the Alberta acts was upheld in 1943, in general justices tended to support or extend the jurisdiction of the central government. For example, it was held that federal courts had jurisdiction in criminal matters over American military personnel stationed in Canada.[69]

A number of observers were disturbed by the failure of the central government to test, by way of a reference, the validity of the contentious Padlock Law passed by the Quebec legislature in 1937. That legislation seemed to involve a clear violation of civil liberties and to be invalid. Yet the federal cabinet chose neither to disallow the statute nor to refer it to the Supreme Court, much to the disgust of some liberal spokesmen who expected even-handed treatment of doubtful provincial legislation whether from Alberta or from central Canada. Such criticisms were naïve. The reference procedure was a political instrument to be used in a calculated fashion; in the Quebec case the political disadvantages of reference far outweighed any advantages.[70] Laymen easily forgot that the Supreme Court was a passive institution; until an issue was brought before them, the justices could say nothing about it.

The years following the Press Bill opinion underlined the Supreme Court's reluctance to come out strongly in defence of civil liberties. In 1939 Justice Rinfret, writing for the majority of the Court, upheld the right of a tavern-keeper to refuse service to non-whites: 'Any merchant is free to deal as he may choose with any individual member of the public. It is not a question of motives or reasons for deciding to deal or not to deal; he is free to do either.' Only Justice Davis dissented.[71]

Some seven years later a civil-liberties issue arose in the 1946 reference of federal orders-in-council (issued under the authority of the War Measures Act) facilitating the deportation to Japan of Japanese-born residents of Canada or Canadian-born citizens of Japanese extraction. A further order-in-council authorized the establishment of a commission to inquire into 'the activities, loyalty and the extent of co-operation with the Government of Canada during the war of Japanese nationals and naturalized persons of the Japanese race in Canada.' Major portions of the orders were upheld by the seven-man panel of justices, which thereby implicitly condoned government treatment of Japanese Canadians during the war.[72]

The Court as a whole felt bound by Supreme Court and Judicial Committee precedents upholding the unrestricted right of Parliament to take action deemed 'necessary for the security, defence, peace, order and welfare of Canada.' The fact that there were five judgments in this case reveals the Court's uncertainty about the legality of various parts of the orders. For example, a few of the justices, led by Rand, recoiled at the provision in one of the orders which required the deportation of wives and children (Canadian nationals) of husbands and fathers who were Japanese aliens resident in Canada or Canadians of Japanese extraction who had requested repatriation. Justice Rand was offended at the prospects of a natural-born Canadian of Japanese ancestry being forcibly deported; such a person deported to Japan could not claim Japanese citizenship and would in law retain his Canadian citizenship. In separate judgments, Justices Hudson, Kellock, and Estey agreed with Rand that the deportations were illegal. Most of the orders, however, were upheld by the Court.

Between 1933 and 1949 the broader non-judicial functions of both the Court and its members expanded. Constitutional controversies had focused national attention on the institution. The chief justice was well known and highly respected. All in all, the stature and prestige of the Supreme Court were rising, as reflected in the changes in the institution's jurisdiction and even in its accommodation. The *Financial Post* carried this front-page editorial on the Court on 4 May 1946:

Parliament and our Supreme Court are our two key institutions. The value and strength of our Supreme Court, the contribution which it makes to our national stability and unity, depends on the reputation for integrity, skill and wisdom which it wins for itself.

Canada's national stature has done a lot of growing in recent decades. The Supreme Court ought to make sure [that] growth of its stature keeps pace.

The Supreme Court's place in men's minds, its value to the strength and development of this nation, depends solely on the skill, patience and objectivity with which its members hear each and all of the cases before them; on the depth and quality of human understanding reflected in their judgments.[73]

There is no question that the institution was perceived to be potentially important. What was in doubt, as intimated by the *Post*, was whether the Court *by itself* could realize that potential. The immediate answer seemed to be that it would be given considerable assistance in that respect by the political leaders of the nation.

The Supreme Court of Canada building, 1939, Ernest Cormier, architect

The old Supreme Court building, at the foot of Parliament Hill, used by the Court between 1876 and 1946. The building was demolished in the 1950s to make room for a parking lot.

Sir William Buell Richards, chief justice
1875–9

Sir William Henry Strong, member of
the Court from 1875, chief justice
1892–1902

Henri Elzéar Taschereau, member of the Court from 1875, chief justice 1902–6

Pierre Basile Mignault, member of the Court 1918–29

Sir Lyman Poore Duff, member of the Court from 1906, chief justice 1933–44

Ivan Cleveland Rand, member of the Court 1943–59

Bora Laskin, member of the Court from 1970, chief justice 1973–84

Brian Dickson, member of the Court from 1973, chief justice 1984 to present

7

Supreme at Last

1949

The years immediately following the Second World War witnessed a number of significant changes in the Supreme Court of Canada. The construction and occupation of a massive new courthouse was paralleled in law by the termination of appeals to the Judicial Committee of the Privy Council. Now truly supreme in Canada, the Court's new prestige was mirrored in an expansion of its membership to enable it to fulfil more effectively its new national functions.

In 1882, it will be recalled, the Supreme Court had finally moved into its own quarters. Though refurbished at that time and expanded in 1890, the courthouse, on the northeast corner of Bank and Wellington streets, had soon proved inadequate. The registrar complained in 1897 that

nothing has been done to the Building. The walls in the new part, in which are situated the Judges' Chambers and officers' rooms, have never been whitewashed or the cracks made from the settling of the building, filled in. I think I am not using language at all too strong, when I say that the present condition of the building is filthy and quite unfit for the purpose for which it is used. Even the walls of the Court room are water stained, dirty and cracked, and some of the Judges' rooms look as if they were positively going to pieces so large and numerous are the cracks.[1]

Over the next ten years complaints of this sort were echoed repeatedly by members and officers of the Court and by members of the bar.

Fire was a major concern. The building had no fire walls and was constructed partially of flammable materials. Gas lighting was used until 1898, when it was replaced by electricity. A number of sheds had been built against the back of the building, and there were assorted piles of lumber near or against the courthouse. Inadequate storage space inside the building resulted in dangerous stacking of materials, and, of course, the library was crowded and its contents highly flammable.[2]

The crowded library was a second problem. By the turn of the century some 20,000 volumes had been acquired and 1,000 new volumes were being added annually. Already every foot of shelf space in the libary room itself was being utilized, and further shelving had been placed in four other rooms to accommodate the books. The resulting inefficiency was clearly frustrating to librarians, to library users, and to those whose offices were used to store books.[3]

Sanitary conditions were a third concern. Much of the furniture was moth-eaten, and the pests had begun to spread elsewhere in the building. In some of the justices' rooms, reported the registrar in 1900, 'moths have so destroyed the chairs that a person's fist can be shoved through the covering at many points and the material which has been used in the upholstering is alive with these insects. The result is that the judges' robes have been in some cases ruined.' The conditions that bred such an infestation were described in a 1904 letter from the registrar: 'The rooms are so badly ventilated that every morning the Judges require to open their windows for an hour or two, whatever the temperature or condition of the atmosphere may be outside, before it is possible to occupy them. The corridors and the rooms are constantly filled with bad odours, particularly in the morning, evidencing an unsanitary condition of the plumbing.'[4] Our present awareness of the potential harmful effects of such poor conditions suggests that over time the courthouse environment may have had a seriously deleterious impact on the health and mental alertness of both staff and justices.

The presence of the Exchequer Court was another problem. The Supreme Court facilities were shared by the Exchequer Court. The latter Court was perceived as inferior to the Supreme Court, and there was conflict over the two courts' use of the crowded facilities. Exchequer Court judges could use the courtroom and other facilities only when they were not being used by the Supreme Court. One result of this shared usage was occasional friction.[5]

Repeated attempts were made to persuade the Laurier government to take action. A new building was the obvious solution; at the least, major improvements to the existing building were needed. Two ministers of justice (Mills and Fitzpatrick) took up the cause of a new building. Fitzpatrick persuaded the minister of public works to visit the existing structure with him, and both seemed to agree that a new building was needed. Fitzpatrick informed the House of Commons that 'we agree that no improvements of any value could be made and that the whole building would have to be reconstructed.' The leader of the opposition concurred, saying that 'to spend any money on the present building is in my opinion a waste of money.'[6]

In 1906, however, the government agreed to pay only for minor renovations. Improvements were made to the washrooms and the plumbing, new shelving and lighting were provided for the library, and a number of chairs were repaired. In the same year a one-storey extension to the library was built, adding some additional 2,500 square feet.[7]

Not surprisingly, the renovations did little to solve the basic problems. A reporter for *Maclean's Magazine* was surprised by 'the unexpected humbleness' of the courthouse, suggesting on a visit in 1914 that its unpretentious appearance and its location at the foot of Parliament Hill resembled 'to a certain extent the lodge at the gate of some great man's estate.' Complaints continued to be received about the building's quality and about the failure to provide the Court with a new home.[8] By the 1920s the quarters had again become cramped. The physical structure was deteriorating – the floors were warped and the walls had not been painted for a long time. In 1925 and 1927 further minor alterations were made to the building, improving the lawyers' consulting rooms and providing additional office space in the attic. The concerns regarding the hazard of fire remained, and although fire escapes were added in 1930, the library was still considered to be in serious danger.[9]

Perhaps the most telling description of the courthouse's inadequacy was given by Arthur Cannon immediately after his appointment to the Supreme Court in 1930. Returning home from his first visit to his new office, Justice Cannon wrote:

Now that I am back to my room in Quebec I feel more vividly the difference with the small quarters you showed me on Wednesday. I fear that I will not be able to work comfortably in that hole. Evidently the Government when they increased to seven the number of justices of the Supreme Court forgot to provide accommodation for the seventh judge. I think we should draw the attention of the authorities to this abnormal situation.

I must find room for one safe, thirty book shelves, one revolving library, besides the desk and chairs.

If no suitable quarters are available in the building, perhaps the Registrar of the Court could make arrangements for an office near the Court House. This might involve personal inconvenience, but would be better than trying to do my work in inadequate quarters.[10]

During the tenure of the Bennett government, the Public Works Department went so far as to consider possible sites and costs for a new building, but no substantive proposals resulted.[11] Not until the King government returned to office in the fall of 1935 did any real progress take place.

Approximately coincident with the government's reference of the New Deal legislation to the Court, building and health inspectors were instructed to examine and report on the state of the courthouse. Before the year was out a devastating report had been submitted regarding conditions in the building. The inspectors documented fire hazards, rotting floors, deteriorating library books, and cramped quarters. Most shocking, however, was the assessment of the sanitary conditions and the occupational environment. Almost every room was badly lighted and poorly ventilated; there were signs of rodent and insect infestation; washroom facilities were bad for men, appalling for women ('The toilet for the women consists of one bowl placed in a dark corner underneath the stairway. It should be condemned forthwith.') The 'worst features' of the building were the justices' offices:

Practically all of these rooms have insufficient air space and are very badly lighted, the windows being placed in such a position as to render it almost impossible for the Judges to work without artificial lighting most of the time. If a desk is placed in a position where a sufficient amount of lighting is available, the occupant is placed in a draught, which is injurious to health. All of the rooms occupied by the Judges are thoroughly inadequate and injurious to the health of the occupants.

The inspectors recommended that the courthouse 'should be condemned as being injurious to the health of the occupants and totally inadequate for the purpose for which it is used.'[12]

With broad support across party lines and in the press, the government responded quickly. Early in 1936 the minister of justice formally requested cabinet approval for a new building to house the Supreme Court. The prime minister threw his support behind the project, and Parliament passed an appropriation facilitating preliminary planning of a structure projected to cost between $1 million and $2 million.[13]

As has been seen, the courthouse had been in shocking condition for several decades. That action was finally taken in the late 1930s was the result of a combination of several circumstances. First, the role of the Supreme Court was changing. In late 1935 it had been asked to pass judgment on the principal components of the legislative package of the outgoing Conservative government, a previously unheard-of intrusion into the political arena. In addition, discussion of termination of appeals to the Judicial Committee was increasing. Second, the United States Supreme Court in the fall of 1935 moved into its prestigious new headquarters on Capitol Hill, and the contrast with the Canadian Court's circumstances was marked and commented upon. Third, and more important, the new prime minister was interested in the redevelopment of Ottawa as a federal capital. He personally hired a French planner, Jacques Gréber, whose views coincided with the prime minister's on creating an aura of grandeur in Ottawa; erection of a Supreme Court building would give Mackenzie King an opportunity to put some of his ideas into effect.[14]

It is not surprising that the prime minister became directly involved in the overall plans for a new courthouse. In June 1936, accompanied by seven cabinet members, he conducted a tour of proposed sites, walking west from Parliament Hill along the cliff overlooking the Ottawa River. Within two days the government architect received instructions from King to draw up plans for a new three-building complex. The central building would be the executive centre of government, housing the Privy Council, External Affairs, and the Department of the Secretary of State. On either side (and thus in a junior or peripheral position) would be a judicial building (for the Supreme Court and the Exchequer Court) and a building to accommodate various commissions (Civil Service, Tariff, and Radio Broadcasting). Only the judicial building was to be erected immediately.[15] The overall plan was a reflection of the court's new-found central yet subsidiary position within the Canadian polity.

It was now necessary to engage an architect to draw up plans for the buildings. Although the Royal Architectural Institute of Canada lobbied for a nationwide competition to select an architect and a design, the government rejected the idea, preferring at first to use architects in the Public Works Department.[16] Later, probably under the influence of Gréber and in keeping with the grandiose plans for national capitol development, it was decided to hire a private architect. The minister of public works selected Ernest Cormier of Montreal for the lucrative and prestigious task.

Cormier was one of Canada's first architects of international training and stature. His initial training was as a civil engineer at the Montreal École Polytechnique. In 1908 he commenced six years of study in Paris at l'École des Beaux-Arts (where Gréber also had studied), and won a British scholarship for two years' study in Rome. After working in Paris for a few years Cormier returned to Canada in 1919. In Montreal he joined the faculty of McGill University and later taught at l'Ecole Polytechnique. His private practice flourished. By 1937 he had designed a number of important and impressive structures: the Montreal Palais de Justice (1922), churches in Montreal (1924) and Rhode Island (1926), and the main building at the University of Montreal. In 1931 he built his own home, a masterpiece of art deco style on Pine Avenue in Montreal. Cormier designed not only the house's structure and interior detail but also its furnishings. The Montreal architect later erected further major works: the National Printing Bureau in Hull, Quebec, the Laval Seminary in Quebec City, and several churches, hospitals and schools in various North American centres. In 1947 Cormier was selected as one of ten architects to serve on the planning board overseeing the design of the United Nations building in New York City, and he designed the main entrance doors, Canada's gift to the building.[17]

Sometime in 1937 Cormier set to work on the Supreme Court project. He consulted with the chief justice and registrars of the Supreme and Exchequer Courts and with representatives of the bar. Sir Lyman Duff, while emphasizing that the American example far exceeded Canadian needs, urged that a visit be paid to the new Supreme Court Building in Washington, and he himself did so. The chief justice hoped to combine in the new accommodation both the limited needs of the Court and an expression of its new stature. Cormier, on the other hand, had a somewhat more aesthetically pleasing building in mind. Both men agreed that the building ought to be impressive, pointing particularly to the desirability of an imposing foyer. Duff insisted on a small, intimate courtroom on practical grounds of acoustics and need. He failed, however, in his attempt to gain exclusive use of the new building – the Exchequer Court would continue to share the accommodations. The representatives of the bar were concerned about facilities for counsel and access to and user accommodation within the library.[18]

By early 1938 Cormier had prepared his initial designs, which were finalized by the fall of that year. The building had already grown in size and therefore in projected cost. Visually the new edifice would be powerful, dominating, even intimidating. It was set well back from the public thoroughfare it faced, as though well removed from the mundane concerns of society. In shape and style, the building was very powerful. The size of the marble and granite blocks, the entrance steps, and the doors proclaimed the building's latent strength. On entering the building a visitor found himself in a huge foyer (108 feet long, 56 feet wide, and 40 feet high); its scale and elaborate materials reduced the visitor to a level of virtual inconsequence – clearly it was the institution that was important, not the individual. From the foyer the visitor's attention was drawn toward the courtroom, which occupied the central position in the building. The courtroom itself was somewhat disappointing for its failure to focus attention on the bench; despite its rich black walnut walls, the courtroom does not seem to follow through on the building's statement of the Supreme Court's significance.

The Supreme Court building, particularly its roof, was designed to reflect both the style of existing parliamentary and government buildings (but with cleaner lines) and the Court's new stature. In the amount of accommodation and the improved environment and in its modern fire-prevention techniques, the new structure solved the problems that had existed in the old building. But it seems unfortunate that in order to underline the Court's new role and prestige it was necessary to be so overpowering, so intimidating, so removed. The answer to the complaints of later observers about the Supreme Court's lack of public exposure may lie here – it seems to have been deliberately designed as a characteristic of the institution; aloofness was confused with stature.

Public perceptions of the building mirrored its awesome character. It was variously described as 'breathtaking,' 'an architectural spectacle,' and 'a truly humbling experience.' A stenographer working there in 1940 commented that the structure was so grand that every time she came to work she felt as though she was on her way to meet an Egyptian emperor.[19]

The contract for construction of the building had been let in the fall of 1938. By May 1939 work was far enough advanced that the foundation stone was laid by Queen Elizabeth during her visit to Canada with King George VI. Completion of the building in 1941 was approved by the government on condition that space be assigned to the burgeoning war-related Ottawa bureaucracy for the duration of the conflict. Thus it was that the Supreme Court building for its first four years was occupied not by the judiciary but by employees of National War Services, National Revenue, and National Defence.[20]

In January 1946 the Supreme Court of Canada finally moved into its new quarters, although three years later various war-services agencies still occupied third-floor offices. As befitted the occasion, the official opening of the new courthouse was marked by a ceremony patterned after the 1882 opening by Queen Victoria of the Royal Courts of Justice.

But the Supreme Court building was still not complete. First, the building was largely unfurnished, and the old furniture had been brought over from the old courthouse. Ernest Cormier applied in 1945 for authority to design new furnishings. Not until 1947 was he able to begin repairing damage, improving lighting, and designing furniture suitable to the building. Second, it quickly became clear that the library was poorly located and designed. Access to it from the courtroom was difficult and caused a good deal of inconvenience. It was decided to move the library to the third floor, thus making use of space originally designed for storage.[21] The result was a spacious and relatively convenient – if not aesthetically pleasing – library. By 1949 the Supreme Court of Canada was housed in its new structure, an impressive reflection of its national position and role.

For the first seventy-five years of its history the Supreme Court of Canada was not truly supreme. It was possible to appeal decisions of the Court to the Judicial Committee of the Privy Council, which meant that the Supreme Court could be overruled by the British law lords; similarly, the Canadian Court was bound to accept and apply precedents established by the Judicial Committee. In fact, appeals could go directly from provincial superior courts to the Judicial Committee without ever being heard by the Supreme Court. All of these factors seriously undermined the stature and authority of the Court.

This weakness was apparent as early as 1875, and particularly alarmed the Liberal member of Parliament for Hamilton, Ontario, Aemilius Irving. Irving had proposed an amendment to the Supreme Court Act preventing appeals going directly from provincial courts to England; the proposal was defeated. He then put forward a second amendment, which made the Supreme Court of Canada the final court of appeal and prohibited any appeal of its decisions to any court in the United Kingdom. This provision was adopted after considerable debate, and became clause 47 of the act. The clause caused problems for the imperial authorities, who held that a colonial legislature had no power to terminate any British subject's right to appeal to the foot of the throne. Finally, after much negotiation between Canadian and British officials, clause 47 was interpreted as not applying to that right.[22] Any hope of making the Supreme Court truly supreme was thus dashed by British officials.

In 1887 the Canadian legislature returned to the issue by terminating appeals to England in criminal cases. The bill terminating appeal was not reserved or disapproved of by British officials, and remained on the books until it was challenged in 1926. With this one exception in the criminal field, the inferior role of the Supreme Court was not challenged further in the nineteenth century.

The Judicial Committee attempted to restrict Canadian use of the overseas appeal procedure. As early as 1877, in *Johnston* v *St Andrews*, their lordships held that where small amounts of money were in dispute and no general principle was involved, leave to appeal to the committee from the Supreme Court would be refused. Similarly, in 1883, in both *Canada Central Railway Company* v *Murray* and *Prince* v *Gagnon*, leave to appeal was refused on the ground that appeal would be permitted only 'where the case is of gravity involving matter of public interest or some important question of law, or affecting property of considerable amount, or where the case is otherwise of some public importance or of a very substantial character.'[23] In petty matters or on minor points the decision of the Supreme Court of Canada would be final.

The presence of the Supreme Court, however, did have a substantial impact on appeals to the Judicial Committee. Once the Court was established there was a noticeable drop in the number of *per saltum* appeals (those which bypassed the Supreme Court) in the 1880s, especially from Quebec (see table 4). At the same time, 48 per cent of the appeals from the Supreme Court were upheld in London.

The total number of appeals to the Judicial Committee held steady in the 1880s and began to increase in the 1890s. Canadian officials therefore decided to work within this appeal procedure to improve it or make it more acceptable or useful to Canadians. By 1888 the Macdonald government had begun to consider the appointment of Canadians to the Judicial Committee.

At this time Canadians were seeking to play a greater role within the British Empire in general – as seen, for example, in Canadian support for the Imperial Federation movement and the British Empire League. This Canadian support for the empire can be interpreted as a manifestation of Canadian nationalism, as a means by which Canadians could play an important role on the world stage through a gradual assumption of a share of the leadership of the empire.[24] The minister of justice explicitly pointed

TABLE 4

Appeals from Canada to the JCPC by number and per cent upheld

Jurisdiction appealed from	1870–80	1881–9	1890–9	1900–9	1910–19	1920–9	1930–9	1940–9	1950–5
SCC	2 (–)	21 (48)	16 (50)	35 (43)	48 (48)	52 (31)	41 (37)	24 (25)	14 (43)
PEI	–	–	–	–	–	–	2 (–)	–	–
NS	3 (100)	5 (60)	5 (60)	2 (–)	1 (–)	4 (25)	–	–	–
NB	2 (100)	1 (–)	1 (–)	–	–	3 (–)	–	–	–
PQ	48 (36)	22 (45)	21 (29)	27 (37)	12 (42)	22 (50)	9 (22)	1 (100)	–
ONT.	1 (100)	4 (–)	10 (30)	26 (35)	31 (48)	18 (33)	16 (38)	7 (29)	–
MAN.	–	1 (–)	3 (33)	1 (–)	7 (43)	4 (25)	1 (–)	–	–
NWT	–	–	–	–	–	–	–	1 (100)	–
SASK.	–	–	–	–	3 (33)	3 (–)	–	2 (–)	–
ALTA.	–	–	–	–	5 (40)	4 (50)	4 (25)	1 (100)	2 (–)
BC	–	–	6 (50)	7 (71)	26 (46)	13 (38)	9 (33)	1 (100)	3 (100)
Other	–	–	–	–	–	2 (–)	2 (50)	–	–
TOTAL	56	54	62	98	133	125	84	36	19
% avoiding SCC	96.4	61.1	74.2	64.3	63.9	58.4	51.2	33.3	26.3

Source: SCC subject file no. 66

to Canadian membership on the committee as a means of thwarting those who advocated 'the judicial independence of Canada.'[25] Instead, the measure would enable Canadians to share in the formulation of imperial law.

The Conservative governments of the 1890s certainly pushed for Canadian representation on the Judicial Committee.[26] There was considerable discussion of the proposal in Canadian legal journals, particularly because, for some proponents, the reform was connected with criticism of the Judicial Committee's recent constitutional decisions (especially *Hodge* v *the Queen*, 1883). Publications such as the *Legal News* and the *Canada Law Journal* sought to defend the committee and to question the need for change, while the *Canadian Law Times* and *Saturday Night* challenged the committee's lack of knowledge of and contact with the colonies. In 1895 the British government adopted the reform, and within two years senior justices from Australia, South Africa, and Canada had joined the committee.

From that date forward until 1954 at least one Canadian was always a member of the Judicial Committee. Every chief justice of Canada in the period was appointed to the committee, though sometimes after a few years' delay. In addition, one puisne justice, Duff, was named to the Committee. No Canadian outside the Supreme Court of Canada was ever named to the committee, although the Laurier government contemplated nominating Edward Blake.[27] Appointment of a justice to the Judicial Committee became a means by which the Canadian government reinforced the Supreme Court's position at the apex of the national judicial structure.

It is not clear how significant the reform was. Several of the Canadian members attended only occasionally – for example, Strong, Fitzpatrick, and Davies. During the 1920s and 1930s Anglin and Duff took turns on the Committee, each attending in alternate years. Moreover, Canadian participation on the committee was limited to the summer months when the Supreme Court was in recess. Though the reported cases considerably understate the justices' total work when in London, they nevertheless give an indication of the rather limited number of important cases in which this appointment involved the various justices. Sir Henry Strong sat on twenty-eight reported appeals, Sir Elzéar Taschereau on twenty, Fitzpatrick on nine, Davies on three, Duff on forty-four, Anglin on nine, and Rinfret on thirteen. Only four of the justices ever wrote a reported opinion for the committee (which handed down only one opinion in each case). Strong wrote eight, Taschereau one, Duff eight, and Anglin two; the others wrote none.[28] Though the exposure of the Supreme Court leaders to some of the great legal minds of Britain and to a wide variety of legal problems and traditions could only have been beneficial intellectually, its importance and extent can easily be exaggerated. Canadian membership on the committee was only significant as a means of tightening the legal and judicial structure of the empire and of making the Judicial Committee's authority more acceptable to Canadians.

The appointment of Canadians did not end debate over the Judicial Committee. In 1901–2 an imperial conference was held to discuss establishment of an imperial Court of Final Appeal, combining the jurisdictions of the House of Lords and the Judicial Committee. The idea was discussed again from time to time (for example, at the 1911 imperial conference), but nothing came of the proposal. Canadians continued to debate, largely in the legal press, the problems associated with appeal to an overseas judicial body: high costs, inappropriate procedural requirements, unnecessary delay.

The Laurier government accurately reflected Canadian ambivalence regarding appeals to London. In 1906 the prime minister asked both the minister of justice and the chief justice to read over the 1875–6 correspondence regarding the limitation of appeals; the government probably was considering a move to terminate appeals to the Judicial Committee. The following year the government discussed informally a proposal to facilitate appeals from the Supreme Court: if appeals from the Court became a matter of right rather than of royal prerogative, then special leave would not be required to appeal each case.[29]

This ambivalence was also demonstrated in public debate. Supporters of the Judicial Committee pointed to the high calibre of its personnel and to its neutrality on emotive Canadian issues. Detractors argued that the committee did not understand Canadian needs or conditions and made poor decisions, and that until the Supreme Court became truly supreme it could not command the authority and respect normally due a country's highest court. The answer offered to this last criticism was that until the calibre of the Supreme Court was equal to that of the committee, it was silly to speak of altering the imperial system of appeals. As one Ontario lawyer put it,

There is no sense in giving up something that is the greatest boon any country can have, an unequalled appellate court, unless we can adequately fill its place. The Supreme Court of Canada seems never to have occupied, in our mind the place it should properly fill ... those that ask that all these [legal] matters shall be finally settled in Canada ought to turn their attention to providing an adequate equivalent for the brilliant court they wish to supersede.[30]

He was right, but for the most part Canadians seemed quite capable of separating the twin issues of the Supreme Court's quality and of overseas appeals.

In the first two decades of the twentieth century, Canadian appeals to the Judicial Committee increased noticeably, though the proportion of *per saltum* appeals from provincial courts levelled off at about 64 per cent (see table 4). Part of the reason for this increase was that the committee was becoming more lenient in granting leave to appeal. Earlier cases had established the grounds on which leave to appeal would be denied; a corollary to those grounds became apparent in 1903–4. In two separate cases, *Clergue* v *Murray* (1903) and *Canadian Pacific Railway* v *Blain* (1904), the committee restated the barriers to appeal from the Supreme Court, but in doing so seemed to encourage *per saltum* appeals. According to the committee, once an appellant had exhausted avenues of appeal within the appropriate province, he could appeal either to His Majesty in Council or to the Supreme Court: 'But where a man elects to go to the Supreme Court, having his choice whether he will go there or not, this Board will not give him assistance [to appeal to the Committee] except under special circumstances.' The Judicial Committee was laying down rules whereby appeal to London was being presented, perhaps even encouraged, as an alternative to the Supreme Court. In 1913 the chief justice complained of the problem to Lord Haldane, who agreed that at times leave 'has been too freely given' and promised a stricter regime – a promise he fulfilled.[31] But as the numbers indicate, appeal to the Judicial Committee remained a vital aspect of the Canadian legal and judicial system (see table 5).

As a result of Canadian experiences during the First World War, nationalism increased noticeably in the dominion during the last years of the war and during the 1920s. One of the manifestations of this increasing pride in Canada was growing discussion of and support for the termination of appeals to the Judicial Committee. As Canada came to be seen by many of its people as self-governing and independent, the judicial tie to Great Britain came to be viewed as a sign of inferiority, a colonial fetter. Concomitant with the 1926 imperial declaration of equality among the dominions and the United Kingdom, it was argued, should be an end to the colonial character of our judicial structure. Chief Justice Anglin sent Prime Minister King a memorandum reflecting many of these sentiments. 'My "Canadianism,"' Anglin wrote, 'leads me to the opinion that we should finally settle our litigation in this country. If we are competent to make our own laws, we are, or should be, capable of interpreting and administering them.' At the very least, the Supreme Court of Canada ought to be the only route by which appeals could go overseas; but it

TABLE 5
Appeals from the Supreme Court of Canada to the JCPC 1876–1913

Year	Total no. of appeals from scc	Leave denied	scc judgment affirmed	scc judgment reversed or varied	Appeals pending or not prosecuted	Per cent of scc judgments appealed
1876–9	3	3	–	–	–	2.8
1880–9	53	27	9	9	8	7.8
1890–9	43	25	7	8	3	4.8
1900–9	94	50	21	19	4	9.7
1910–13*	72	19	19	18	16	19.5

Source: scc subject file no. 66
* Information for the years after 1913 is unavailable.

would be best to terminate all appeals to London, and if that demanded an 'improved' Supreme Court, it was up to the government to take steps to improve it.[32]

The sense of Canadianism was strengthened in 1926 when the Judicial Committee struck down a federal statute barring appeals in criminal matters. That decision, following a 1925 decision striking down the federal Industrial Disputes Investigation Act, 1907, and the 1927 award of the Labrador interior to the Dominion of Newfoundland, caused Canadian frustrations to mount. In none of these disputes had the Supreme Court of Canada had an opportunity for adjudication. Growing Canadian self-esteem was also reflected in the beginning of a decline in the number of appeals carried to London and a decline in the proportion of cases appealed directly from provincial courts (table 4).

Nevertheless, despite the doubts as to the appropriateness of appeals to England and the rising sense of Canadian self-sufficiency, there was also a recognition of the negative consequences of termination of appeals. The Judicial Committee of the Privy Council was an able court, containing some of the best legal minds in the common-law system; the same could not be said for the Supreme Court of Canada. Even as ardent an advocate of judicial independence as C.H. Cahan, a Montreal lawyer and a Conservative member of Parliament, admitted in 1927 that the time for termination had not yet come. The Supreme Court must first be prepared.

We must ... perfect the machinery of our own courts of justice. We must give to our own Supreme court a higher standing, and create greater confidence in its decisions on the part of the people of this country before we can abrogate the right of appeal to the Privy Council ... I confess that the people have not sufficient confidence in our own Supreme Court to-day to abrogate entirely ... appeals to the Privy Council.[33]

Though Canadian independence seemed to demand termination of appeals, a realistic appraisal of the quality and stature of the Supreme Court demanded a delay. Yet even that did not fully brake the movement for termination.

In the negotiations leading to the Statute of Westminster of 1931, both the King and Bennett governments opted not to push for a formal end to appeals to the Judicial Committee. Nevertheless, with the passage of that statute Canada gained the authority to terminate appeals in the future. In 1933 the Bennett government re-enacted section 1025 of the Criminal Code formally ending appeals to London in criminal cases, the same section that had been struck down in the 1926 decision. Two years later, in *British Coal Corporation* v *The King* (1935), that statute was upheld by the Judicial Committee.[34]

But criminal appeals had never been more than a minor element in Canadian appeals to the Privy Council. The broader movement for judicial independence remained. Aided both by the depression of the 1930s and by the difficulty of appealing overseas during the Second World War, the number of appeals to London and the proportion of *per saltum* appeals continued to decline. By the 1940s the total number of appeals had fallen to just thirty-six for the decade, only a third of which had come directly from the provinces (table 4). Was this a sign of rising Canadian respect for the Supreme Court? Certainly the number and character of appeals were changing more quickly than the regulations themselves.

The value of the Judicial Committee was beginning to be questioned. The rising number of influential centralists of the 1930s and early 1940s could point easily to the committee's emphasis on the decentralist character of the Canadian constitution. In a seminal article, F.R. Scott challenged the anti-repealers' argument that the Judicial Committee was essential as the defender of minority rights in Canada. By examining various linguistic and schools controversies before the Supreme Court and the Judicial Committee, Scott was able to demonstrate that minority groups had received treatment in the Supreme Court equal to and perhaps better than what they would have received in London. 'What the Privy Council had done in our constitution is to safeguard, not minority rights, but provincial rights,' Scott concluded. 'It is submitted that the belief in the Privy Council as a safeguard for minority rights is a popular myth, devoid of any foundation in fact. If so, a principal ground for maintaining the appeal disappears.'[35] In an Ottawa environment where increasingly centralized power was seen as the answer to the country's political problems and needs,[36] such arguments operated powerfully among the influential in favour of termination of appeals.

During the 1930s and 1940s the subject continued to be debated – in Parliament, in private letters, at legal conventions, in schools. The most prominent reason for termination was the developing sense of Canadian self-worth. As Ernest Lapointe, the former Liberal minister of justice, put it in 1932, 'Je ne puis trouver une seule raison justifiant le Canada d'être le seul pays au monde de son rang, sa population et son intelligence, à confesser son incompétence à décider lui-même ses conflits judiciares.'[37] Gradually, proponents of such a viewpoint came to argue that the colonial character of the Canadian appeal system was the explanation for the Supreme Court's mediocre quality. It would not do to await the improvement of the Court because it would never mature until it was freed from the colonial yoke. Abrogation of appeals to England would not only reflect Canadian national independence but would lead to the emergence of a first-class appellate court of last resort. Neither the opponents nor the proponents of termination of appeals defended the Supreme Court of Canada or used it as a positive factor in the debate.

In 1937 the demands for termination increased after the Judicial Committee reversed some of the Supreme Court opinions on Bennett's New Deal legislation. The issue was brought directly before the House of Commons at that time by C.H. Cahan. He returned the following year and again in 1939 with a bill to abolish appeals to London. The bill met with considerable support in Parliament, but Canadians were still not ready for the change. The minister of justice, Ernest Lapointe, counselled delay in 1938. The following year he moved to suspend consideration of the bill while it was referred to the Supreme Court to test Parliament's jurisdiction.

In June 1939 counsel representing the attorneys-general of Canada and six provinces (Quebec, Saskatchewan, and Alberta being absent) met before a six-man panel of the Court to argue the issue. Seven months later the justices handed down their decision. Led by Chief Justice Duff, a majority of four held that the legislation was intra vires, Justices Crocket and Davis dissenting. All six members of the Court wrote reasons for judgment.

The only justice to reject entirely the termination bill was Justice Crocket. He pointed out that the bill affected the relationship between the provinces and the crown. Quebec, for example, in its Code of Civil Procedure, had assured access to the Judicial Committee from the final judgments of the Court of King's Bench in all cases involving $12,000 or more. Ontario and the other provinces enjoyed similar, if less explicit, access to the foot of the throne. The proposed bill to terminate appeals by making the Supreme Court of Canada the ultimate judicial tribunal for all Canadian cases entailed a major rupture of the lines of royal prerogative. It also meant an implicit repeal of the Quebec and Ontario statutes and the other orders-in-council granting appeal to the Judicial Committee.

Striking as it did at the very heart of the relationship between the crown and its subjects, the bill (despite its seemingly simple objectives) effected the most profound alteration in the Canadian constitutional process, short of formal amendment, prior to the Constitution Act, 1982. Justice Crocket was the only member of the Court sensitive to these developments. From the strictly legal point of view, Crocket asserted that the bill 'would amount to an attempt on the part of the Parliament of Canada to arrogate to itself the complete control of the administration of justice in all the Provinces ... in so far as the finality of judgments in civil as well as in criminal cases [was] concerned.'[38] To Crocket's mind the subject matter of the bill fell within the provincial authority over property and civil rights and the administration of justice in the province. The federal residuary power under section 91 of the British North America Act simply could not be construed so as to grant such authority to Parliament.

Justice Crocket was on firm legal ground when he challenged the source of federal authority to terminate *per saltum* appeals from the provinces to the Judicial Committee. He could not accept the proposition that by 'the simple expedient of amending the *Supreme Court of Canada Act*' the Parliament of Canada could bring about a major realignment of the judicial process in Canada.

The majority, led by Chief Justice Duff, took a different tack and in doing so avoided the full force of Crocket's objections. For the majority the issue was settled principally on the authority of the Statute of Westminster. The hurdle that was present in 1926 (in *Nadan* v *The King*) preventing termination in criminal cases was removed by the statute. Duff's reasoning on the meaning of the constitutional provisions empowering the Parliament of Canada to make provision 'for the constitution, maintenance, and organization of a general court of appeal for Canada' is weak when contrasted with the objections of Crocket. Duff failed to address the essential issue: how do those terms of the British North America Act acquire, under the Statute of Westminster, the authority to transform a *general* court of appeal into a *final* court of appeal with the correlative power to terminate a long-enjoyed process of royal prerogative? The chief justice appeared content to rest his case on the ambit or scope of the authority vested in Parliament under peace, order, and good government, hardly an unchallengeable foundation.

It was clear that the Supreme Court's opinion would have to be appealed to the Judicial Committee in order to remove any doubts. But the Second World War intervened, inhibiting appeal overseas. Throughout the war only fourteen Canadian cases were reported in London on appeal. The 1940 Supreme Court opinion on termination of appeals did not reach the Judicial Committee until the fall of 1946.

There can be no doubt that the British government attached great importance to this appeal, for the highest judicial officers in Britain were empanelled to sit on the board. For this occasion the board was made up of seven members: in addition to Lord Jowitt as lord chancellor, Viscount Simon, Lord Macmillan, and Lord Wright, Lord Greene (master of the rolls), Lord Simmonds, and the lord chief justice (Lord Goddard) were present. It would be difficult to imagine a gathering in one place of more judicial stature than that assembled in the Privy Council chambers on those late October days in 1946. The Judicial Committee heard arguments in the appeal for a full six days, an extraordinary event in itself. Counsel were heard for the attorneys-general of Canada and of New Brunswick, Ontario, Quebec, British Columbia, Manitoba, and Saskatchewan. The last two provinces joined with the federal government in supporting the bill; the other four provinces opposed it.[39]

The Judicial Committee viewed the issues involved as being of 'transcendent constitutional importance' and disposed of them one by one. The first issue settled was the authority of Parliament to transform the Supreme Court of Canada into a final and ultimate court of appeal under section 101 of the British North America Act. The board had little trouble agreeing that Parliament had such authority, especially in light of the statute of Westminster. 'No other solution,' the Lord Chancellor concluded, 'is consonant with the status of a self-governing Dominion.'

The committee had more trouble validating that portion of the bill which proposed to end the provincial right of appeal to the Privy Council. The members of the board found themselves in sympathy with the reasons for judgment of Sir Lyman Duff. They adopted the essentials of Duff's line of argument and claimed that section 101 of the British North America Act 'intended to endow Parliament with power to effect high political objects concerning the self-government of the Dominion.' These words, taken directly from Duff's judgment, might not meet the demands of the more rigorous legal mind, but they were the stuff of which Judicial Committee judgments were made when the niceties of the law tended to impede their 'judicial statesmanship.' The board concluded that the terms of the British North America Act authorizing the establishment of a 'General Court of Appeal for Canada' ought, in the light of the Statute of Westminster, to be read more expansively so as to encompass the notions of 'ultimate' and 'final.' The Judicial Committee concluded that it would be an anomaly to permit two avenues of final appeal, one to the Supreme Court and the other to the Privy Council; the result would be a lack of uniformity at the highest levels of law.

But the heart of the Judicial Committee's opinion is in the conviction that the power of establishing a final, ultimate court of appeal was an aspect of self-government, especially since 1931. The lord chancellor concluded, 'It is ... a prime element in the self-government of the Dominion that it should be able to secure through its own courts of justice that the law should be one and the same for all its citizens.' This, of course, makes eminent good sense in a unitary state like Great Britain, but does it make sense in a federal system? Counsel for the provincial attorneys-general pleaded strenuously against the bill in the name of provincial autonomy. They also wished to retain their pre-Confederation right of appeal to the foot of the throne. But the Judicial Committee found the termination bill intra vires under section 101 of the British North America Act.

By January 1947 the way was clear to pass legislation formally declaring the Supreme Court of Canada the final court of appeal. But the government continued to hesitate, a good indication that public opinion was still ambivalent. A private member's bill put forward in the spring of 1947 failed to hurry the government. Most of the provinces were opposed to unilateral action by the federal government making a court, which that government exclusively controlled, the final and ultimate judicial body in Canada on all questions, including constitutional matters. In the context of federal-provincial relations in the immediate post-war years, the federal Government was clearly unwilling to antagonize the provinces over such an issue as the judicial system.

Beginning in the fall of 1945, negotiations were conducted and proposals circulated concerning fiscal and economic planning in Canada. Federal-provincial conferences were held in 1945 and 1946 to discuss proposed social security and taxation schemes. Provincial co-operation was being sought by Ottawa, particularly in the field of taxation, where the federal government supported 'tax rental' agreements. These agreements were still being negotiated in 1947, and this likely affected the federal government's decision to delay provoking the provincial governments.[40] The federal government signalled this delay in the fall of 1947 by arranging the appointment of Chief Justice Rinfret to the imperial Privy Council and thus to the Judicial Committee.

In addition, the federal government was having difficulty making up its own mind on the issue. In the first three months of 1948 the problem was debated in Liberal caucus and in cabinet. While the minister of justice, J.L. Ilsley, supported termination and presented draft legislation to that effect, others were less certain. The wily old prime minister, Mackenzie King, feared alienating anglophile Conservatives who were supporting the Liberal party, recalling Sir Wilfrid Laurier's advice about pro-British feeling among Canadians. Other cabinet members indicated that such a bill would jeopardize Liberal support in their region. Louis St Laurent reported that Quebec Liberal members of Parliament would vote for abrogation of all appeals except in constitutional cases involving a federal-provincial dispute. As discussion continued it became apparent that the cabinet was divided. Mackenzie King's solution, typically, was to defer the issue: the matter would be put to the upcoming Liberal convention in August 1948.

I then put forward the idea that we were having a Liberal Convention in August, among other reasons, to frame a programme for the Liberal Party; by that time I said the Provincial elections will be over and I saw no reasons why the Party should not insert in its programme the abolition of appeals if that was in accord with the view of Liberals throughout the country. That would serve for purposes of election, any good that taking up the matter earlier would render.[41]

The political advantages of delay were clear.

Following the adoption of a convention resolution favouring complete termination,[42] the Liberal government, now led by Louis St Laurent, indicated its intention to adhere to the pledge by introducing legislation early in the next session of Parliament. Following the re-election of the government in June 1949, the legislation was reintroduced and finally passed. The statute provided that the Supreme Court of Canada 'shall have, hold and exercise exclusive ultimate appellate civil and criminal jurisdiction' in Canada and that its judgments 'shall, in all cases, be final and conclusive.' In case there was any doubt about the meaning of this clause, an additional section specifically denied that the royal prerogative or any United Kingdom statute permitted appeals to any overseas tribunal.[43]

What effect this change would have on the Supreme Court remained to be seen. Certainly the Department of Justice was ambivalent. Late in 1948 an internal memorandum listed the pros and cons of abolition of appeals. Among the advantages cited was an old standby: appeal to the Judicial Committee 'is regarded as a mark of inferiority which affects the respect held for the Supreme Court, the calibre of men who will accept appointment to that Court, and the quality of the judgements of the persons who do accept such appointments.' That, however, was countered by the argument 'that the very fact that the Supreme Court judgements are subject to an appeal has the effect of causing the judges to put forth a greater effort to be right.'[44] Time would soon show that appeal to the Judicial Committee had had an important impact on the quality and character of the Supreme Court's work. Placed in a position of inferiority, the Supreme Court justices had quickly accepted the binding precedents from above and had adopted the common-law concept that if new directions were to be enunciated they would come from the highest court. This deference and subordination helped to entrench a conservatism in the jurisprudence of the Supreme Court of Canada. It would take more than simple termination of appeals to alter the Court's approach to the law.

The new legislation did, however, make the Supreme Court of Canada a more prominent and influential institution in the national legal system and political structure. Its new status brought the Court into the line of fire more frequently than in the past. The St Laurent government foresaw this, at least in part, and attempted to deal with the problem in advance.

As many contemporary observers pointed out, it was inappropriate to terminate appeals overseas without adjusting the structure of the new court of last resort. The Liberal governments of the late 1940s agreed with this, and at least as early as February 1948 serious consideration began to be given to possible changes to the Supreme Court. The now retired Sir Lyman Duff was interviewed regarding several proposals, and the deputy minister of justice (F.P. Varcoe) and an Edmonton lawyer (G.H. Steer) organized a meeting in Ottawa to discuss policies and problems related to the Supreme Court. Leading lawyers from all ten provinces were invited, and provincial law societies and the Canadian Bar Association were asked to make representations.[45]

Notes from the meeting reflect the general concerns of persons in close touch with the Supreme Court. It was agreed that the bench ought to be expanded to nine members, but Varcoe's suggestion that the additional two justices be appointed '" at large" without reference to geography' was not adopted by the lawyers present. Five men would continue to constitute a quorum, but the lawyers recommended that no even-numbered panels should sit. The salaries of the justices would have to be raised substantially; $25,000 was suggested as an appropriate remuneration for puisne justices. A majority of the lawyers felt that the Court should continue to sit only in Ottawa rather than go on circuit. As well, a majority held that although stare decisis ought to obtain, the legislation should not mention the subject – though both the federal Conservative party and the Canadian Bar Association were calling for statutory entrenchment of stare decisis with respect to Judicial Committee precedents.

Two further points urged by the deputy minister were apparently not adopted by the lawyers, though that does not necessarily reflect disagreement. First, Varcoe sought to control and streamline the argument of counsel and the decision-making of the Court. Each point of fact or law ought to be fully discussed and authorities analysed as to their relevance ('and not merely referred to for future reference by the judges'). It was hoped that this would reduce the number of authorities referred to and improve the general quality of argument in court. The justices would endeavour to reach a decision at a conference immediately following argument, 'as is always done in the Privy Council.' The overall effect of this, Varcoe anticipated, would be the handing down of judgments more quickly and an improvement in the quality of argument (because 'counsel lacking in experience and capacity would give way to more competent men'). Second, the deputy minister sought to enhance the Court's image:

Some consideration might be given to the problem of developing the good name and reputation of the Court with the public generally. The Canadian Bar Association might even establish a special permanent committee to work on this from year to year. The Canadian Club and service clubs might be persuaded to run a few luncheons along this line commencing say in October. Periodical Press might be willing to publish some articles. The Canadian Bar Association might seek some way to encourage the publication of a book relating to the history of the court and its functions along the lines of the numerous works published in the United States with reference to their Supreme Court.[46]

These plans never reached fruition. The meeting and the recommendations produced were soon lost in a sea of other commentaries and schemes, but they do indicate a genuine sense of concern for the future and quality of the Supreme Court. Coming as it did both from leading members of the bar and from the civil servant responsible for the Court, the initiative is an important sign of the immediate – and, one hopes, long-range – impact of the termination of overseas appeals.

These meetings and the resultant proposals ignored, either deliberately or otherwise, the central concern regarding the Supreme Court. The final arbiter of all legal questions, including all constitutional issues and matters of both federal and provincial law, would now be controlled by just one level of government in Canada. The members of the Court were selected and appointed exclusively by the federal government; they were required to reside in the national capital; and the structure and jurisdiction of the Court were under the exclusive legislative control of the federal Parliament. An 'impartial umpire,' a court that both deserved and commanded the trust and respect of all parties must not only be impartial but must be seen to be impartial. In the case of the Supreme Court of Canada it was difficult to perceive the institution as other than 'an Ottawa court.'[47] Ever since the proposals for termination of overseas appeals took substance after 1946, this had been a central problem for the Supreme Court of Canada. Suggestions were made at the time and would continue to be made almost every year thereafter to deal with the issue, but no acceptable solution was found.

One suggestion put forward in 1949 was that the Supreme Court be brought within the British North America Act, giving the Court greater status and removing it from the legislative control of Parliament. This could be done by expanding section 101 of the act effectively to include the Supreme Court Act. The Barristers' Society of New Brunswick, for example, resolved that a constitutional amendment should be passed providing that no changes in 'the constitution, maintenance or organization' of the Court could be made by Parliament without the approval of a majority of provincial legislatures. The Law Society of British Columbia passed a similar resolution.[48] Constitutionally enshrining the Court was an idea that posed many problems. Over the years, as social needs and circumstances changed, it had been necessary to amend the Supreme Court Act frequently.[49] Judging from past experience, some legislature had to have authority over at least some aspects of the structure and jurisdiction of the Court.

Another alternative involved radical restructuring of the Court. Apart from infrequent suggestions that a new Canadian court be created to take on the Judicial Committee's functions, there were proposals for changes to the existing Supreme Court, such as division into two branches, one for common law and one for civil law. The government took seriously a plan for a new court to deal solely with constitutional cases, comprising four Supreme Court justices and four ad hoc members; when Sir Lyman Duff commented unfavourably on the scheme, however, the impractical proposal was dropped.[50]

A less drastic change involved altering the method of selection of the justices. One idea was that the Senate, whose members represented the regions of the country, could be asked to approve nominations to the Court. Given the role of the Senate in the Canadian political structure and given the principle of responsible government, this plan was not useful; it was merely a thoughtless copying of the United States practice. The House of Commons also considered a suggestion that four of the Court's puisne justices be selected from among those proposed by each lieutenant-governor-in-council; each province would be required to propose at least three candidates, and one of the four justices would have to be chosen from among the candidates put forward by the lieutenant-governor-in-council of Quebec.[51] This idea too was rejected.

What tampering there was with the membership was far more modest: the number of justices was increased to nine. In part this was a reflection on the ad hoc replacements. Despite the addition of a seventh permanent member to the Court in 1927, ad hoc justices had been used frequently throughout the following two decades. This did not make for an effective bench. In Sir Lyman Duff's long experience, '*ad hoc* judges are not a success for the reason that they rarely adopt an attitude of full responsibility'; they detracted from 'the quality of solidarity' so essential to an appellate court. As well, a larger bench was felt to be essential because of the increased caseload the Court could now expect and because the change would allow civil-law cases to be heard by a panel the majority of which had been trained in that legal tradition.[52] The legislation added two new puisne justices to the Supreme Court, one of whom was required to come from the bar of Quebec.

Some other changes were made to the Court at the same time. Judicial salaries were raised in 1949; the chief justice would now receive $25,000 annually and his colleagues $20,000. The jurisdiction of the Court was also altered. The wording of several clauses in the Supreme Court Act was tidied up and the Court's authority to grant leave to appeal from judgments of the highest court of final resort in a province was expanded to cover an area where appeal had previously lain only to the Judicial Committee. As well, the Court was now enabled to grant leave to appeal *in forma pauperis.*[53] In short, in keeping with the Court's new role, potential appellants now enjoyed expanded access to the Supreme Court of Canada.

By the end of 1949, the highest court in the Dominion of Canada had acquired a new lease on life. In new and impressive accommodations, the Supreme Court of Canada exercised a broad jurisdiction over the law of the land and its rulings were truly supreme. This new position had been acquired not because of the Court's own merits but because of national developments. Like the First World War, the Second World War had given a further stimulus to Canadian nationalism, or at least to a Canadian sense of self-worth. The new position of the Supreme Court should be regarded as one aspect of a series of changes in these post-war years – the Canadian Citizenship Act (1946), the accession of Newfoundland to Confederation (1949), the passage of a procedure for amending within Canada sections of the British North America Act (1949), and the selection of a Canadian-born governor-general (1952). The Supreme Court of Canada was simply one of several beneficiaries of these developments. It was up to the Court to take advantage of its new stature so as to earn the respect and trust of Canadians.

8

A Decade of Adjustment
1950–1962

When the newly paramount Supreme Court of Canada met for the first time early in 1950, nothing marked the occasion as special. It was typical of much of the institution's history and reflective of its continuing subsidiary status that the event would be allowed to pass without formal recognition. Chief Justice Rinfret had hoped to draw public attention to the Court's new position through another formal opening of the building, or a reception, or a dinner. But the government claimed that it could find no funds to cover the expenses; after discussing the matter, the cabinet decided not to ask Parliament for the money because it might give rise to a controversial debate over the Court. Justice Kerwin reported, 'They [the cabinet ministers] decided that they could not ask for a vote in Parliament in the estimates to cover such expenses as they were afraid that that would give rise to many difficulties, and possibly some unpleasantness.'[1] The considerable attention paid to the Supreme Court over the previous few years and the changes in its structure had opened broader debate on aspects of the Court than the federal government was willing to tolerate. The government accordingly avoided making the Court a subject of special attention, even on the important occasion of its independence. As a result, the Court reverted to a less prominent position in Ottawa, and the status quo ante was confirmed. But the desire to avoid debate about the Court discouraged the possibility of change (and potentially of improvement).

The St Laurent and Diefenbaker appointments during the first decade following termination of appeals showed no apparent recognition of the Court's new status. Both prime ministers, distinguished members of the Canadian bar in their own right – the one as a corporate litigation lawyer, the other as a defence counsel – showed no special sensitivity or concern for the newly won independence of the highest court in the land. The criteria employed by both men in appointing new members to the Supreme Court followed the old established lines; regional considerations prevailed and candidates who demonstrated the traditional legal conservatism were sought. The fact that termination of appeals to the Judicial Committee constituted the end of judicial colonialism and potentially, at least, the beginning of a genuinely indigenous Canadian jurisprudence seems not to have entered the mind of either prime minister. Termination of appeals appears to have been seen as an end in itself rather than as a means to a new beginning. This view, however prominent throughout the Canadian bar, was confusing to the layman. Why abolish appeals if in doing so nothing was to change? The expectation that a truly Canadian final court of appeal might strike out in new directions was unquestionably naïve, for the Court was by now deeply entrenched in the conservative jurisprudence of the Judicial Committee and the House of Lords. Nevertheless, some members of the Canadian bar and the general public expressed the hope that a court free of the immediate institutional dominance of the Judicial Committee would be able to exercise a more independent role in keeping with the peculiar conditions of North America.[2]

Prime Minister St Laurent was confronted in 1950 with a Supreme Court led by Chief Justice Thibaudeau Rinfret, who had served over twenty-five years on the Ottawa bench and who tended to show his impatience in court. Robert Taschereau, the second justice from Quebec, was noted for his insistence on precision from counsel. The senior puisne justice was Patrick Kerwin, a kindly and able man who had been on the Supreme Court bench since 1935. Roy Kellock, who, like Kerwin, was from Ontario, was known for his industriousness and for the tenacity with which he held a viewpoint once arrived at. To all observers, Ivan Rand, the justice from the maritimes, was marked by his intellectual ability and his probing questions. Respect for his repeated and penetrating queries in Court led him to be the justice most feared by counsel; one observer reported that Rand 'uses the word "why" like a machine gun.' In 1944 the able J.W. Estey had come to the Supreme Court from the prairies. The most recently arrived justice was Charles Locke, 'a rugged, solid man who listened impassively' to counsel.[3] These seven justices were joined by two more judges in late December 1949.

According to the terms of the recently revised Supreme Court Act, one of these two new posts was to be filled from the Quebec bar. Since there were already two francophone justices from Quebec, some representatives of English Canadians in Quebec pressured Prime Minister St Laurent to make the appointment from among their members. The minister of finance, Douglas Abbott, suggested that the three civil-law posts be divided according to a ratio of two francophones to one anglophone, so that there would always be an English-speaking Quebec justice on the Supreme Court. But St Laurent would have none of the proposal:

The Quebec Bar is the only one from which it can be expected that French speaking lawyers will ever be appointed to the Supreme Court. A proportion of 1/3 is not exaggerated. To appoint now one English speaking lawyer from Quebec would set a precedent that it then follows would be regarded as inviolate. At some later date it would be done not as a matter of right for English speaking residents of Quebec, but as a matter which happened to suit the conveniences of the moment. We should create the impression that there can be three French speaking members but that there need not always be three.[4]

It was thus certain that the third Quebec position would go in 1949 to a French Canadian.

The choice fell on Joseph Honoré Gérald Fauteux. Born in St Hyacinthe, Fauteux, though not active in politics himself, was well connected politically in the Quebec Liberal party. Between 1929 and 1944 he had served as a crown prosecutor and as a professor of criminal law at McGill. In 1947 he was appointed to the Quebec Superior Court; two years later he was elevated to the Supreme Court of Canada. The new Quebec justice brought with him a considerable expertise in criminal law, and at age forty-nine could look forward to a lengthy career on the bench.[5]

The second new position on the Court went to a representative of Ontario in order to balance the number of justices from that province and Quebec. John Robert Cartwright seemed to have been born to the law and to a position of social prominence. He was called to the bar in 1920 and entered private practice in Toronto, acquiring a wide experience in various types of law. After a distinguished career as trial counsel, Cartwright was appointed to the Supreme Court in 1949 at the age of fifty-four.[6] The average age of this first nine-man Court was fifty-nine; the eldest was Rinfret, aged seventy; the youngest was Fauteux, forty-nine. The justices had an average of eight full years of judicial experience, and the range of experience was considerable: Rinfret had been on the bench for twenty-seven years, while Cartwright was a judicial novice.

No further changes occurred in the membership of the Court until 1954. Thibaudeau Rinfret reached the age of mandatory retirement in June of that year and stepped down. The St Laurent government faced a serious problem in naming a new chief justice. By tradition, the post would go to the senior puisne justice, in this case Patrick Kerwin, aged sixty-four. An able judge and a capable administrator, Kerwin would serve the Court well, but his Roman Catholicism was felt to be a barrier to his elevation. Only once in the history of the Supreme Court had a Roman Catholic succeeded a co-religionist as chief justice (Fitzpatrick in 1906). There was a good deal of concern in political circles that Kerwin's appointment would raise Protestant ire, and the issue was discussed in the press. The prime minister consulted Sir Lyman Duff before deciding to promote Kerwin.[7] This concern over religious affiliation is a reminder of how important that criterion remained for many Canadians. The government hoped that its other choice to fill the vacancy among the puisne justices would mollify Protestants. The new justice from Quebec, Douglas Charles Abbott, was Anglican and English-speaking, and the government was clearly indicating in this appointment that a balanced representation could be maintained in various ways and that traditions were flexible.

When appointed to the Supreme Court, Abbott was already a major public figure in Canada, probably the best-known and one of the most highly regarded federal politicians after Louis St Laurent himself. After graduating in law from McGill and a year of graduate study in commercial law at the University of Dijon in France, he entered private practice in Montreal, where he gained a varied professional experience. In 1940 he was elected as a Liberal member of Parliament from Montreal. Five years later, in 1945, he joined the cabinet and soon took on the prestigious and onerous position of minister of finance. But by 1953 he had decided to leave politics, and, although he agreed to stay on briefly, he informed Prime Minister St Laurent of his intention to return to private practice in Montreal. He also hinted strongly that the prime minister might appoint him to the Senate. St Laurent responded with the suggestion that Abbott might prefer instead a place on the Supreme Court because there would soon be a Quebec vacancy. Abbott joined the Court in the summer of 1954 at the age of fifty-five, with no judicial experience and many years away from active legal practice.[8]

Abbott's selection caused a good deal of public reaction. The patronage nature of the appointment shocked many observers, indicating that the government was out of touch with public expectations of how one should be chosen for such an important judicial office.[9] Nomination directly from the cabinet to the Supreme Court of Canada had not occurred since 1911 (when Louis-Philippe Brodeur was appointed) and would not happen again, a clear sign that succeeding prime ministers got the message. Abbott's prominent partisanship was equalled only by that of Sir Charles Fitzpatrick before he joined the Court, and in this sense Abbott's appointment was out of step with trends that had been developing since the turn of the century. More surprising was the government's willingness to risk the wrath of Quebec public leaders. French-Canadian representation on the bench had been reduced; a known 'centralizer' who had directly challenged the provincial rights of Quebec Premier Maurice Duplessis had been appointed to the highest court in the land. Even apart from political considerations, it is disturbing that a lawyer who had been away from active practice for a decade should be named to the Court. Abbott's knowledge of case law must have seriously deteriorated since joining the cabinet, yet he almost immediately began work in chambers.

Finally, the selection of Abbott is surprising because there already existed a current of dissatisfaction regarding judicial appointments in general. In 1952 the president of the Canadian Bar Association had spoken out against the expedient and patronage character of the selection process and had drawn a good deal of support from the press.[10] As rumours spread of Abbott's imminent appointment to the Court, perhaps even to the chief justiceship, complaints increased. Though opinion varied, the Montreal *Gazette* spoke for many: the Court was now the final court of appeal, and appointments to it were even more important than previously. 'The responsibility of the federal Government has now become profoundly great. The judges of this court whom the federal Government appoints will have to sit in judgement not only as a court of last resort: they will have to give final judgement in cases in which the federal Government will itself be a party. For these reasons the principle of separation between the Cabinet and the Bench must be more than ever respected.'[11]

Though an exaggeration of the traditional extent of separation between politics and the judiciary, the comment is a reflection of changing Canadian views and expectations. Despite such attacks, however, once the appointment was made it was quickly accepted by the public and complimented by many. But its partisan nature did little to enhance respect for the Supreme Court. And, given the Court's challenges during the 1950s to the Duplessis government in Quebec and that government's record in civil liberties, the choice of Abbott caused some to question the Supreme Court's neutrality.

In 1956 the St Laurent government made its last appointment to the Supreme Court. Early in the year Justice Estey died. It was assumed by most observers that the vacancy would be filled by someone from the prairies. Some advisers suggested that now was the time for 'new Canadians' to be represented on the Court. Immigration had been so heavy during the twentieth century, it was argued, that non-charter groups now made up a major portion of the Canadian population. Representatives of various ethnic groups were recommended for the post, and the president of Acadia University put the case well: 'May I suggest that if a non-English, non-French person can be found with the necessary qualifications, his appointment would be a matter of vast gratification to these newer communities. Judgements on contentious issues by our country's highest court of appeal would, moreover, be more readily accepted if all three of the major ingredients of our population were represented among the justices.'[12] The suggestion was not accepted by the government, but the idea of representation on the Court of identifiable groups is an important one. Throughout the history of the Supreme Court there have been frequent complaints that the best possible persons are not named to the bench, that as a criterion merit is only one alongside region, religion, ethnicity, and political service or affiliation. Whatever the validity of such a charge, Canadians have demanded that those criteria be used. The west fought to send a justice to Ottawa, or English-speaking Catholics argued for a seat on the bench, in the same way that 'new Canadians' in the mid-1950s and women in the late 1970s claimed the right of representation.[13] Representation of various social groups can be seen as a strength of the Supreme Court of Canada.

At this point the St Laurent government chose to satisfy the demands of Alberta and selected Henry Gratton Nolan to join the Court. In the summer of 1957 a new government took office. Caught up in the demands of administration after an absence from power for twenty years, the Conservative government of John Diefenbaker was too busy for several months to worry about the Supreme Court vacancy that had occurred with the sudden death of Justice Nolan.[14] It was not until January of the following year that action became imperative because a second vacancy occurred unexpectedly. Justice Kellock, aged sixty-four, suddenly resigned from the Court after over thirteen years' service. Officially, Kellock used poor health as an explanation, though rumour suggested that he was unhappy in a Court led by Patrick Kerwin rather than by himself. The uncertainty or instability created by these two vacancies was exacerbated by Chief Justice Kerwin's ill health in 1958 and by false reports that he too would be retiring soon.[15]

In making its appointments to the Supreme Court, the Diefenbaker government maintained existing traditions. The regional, religious, and ethnic composition of the bench was not altered. Two of the four Diefenbaker appointments – Ronald Martland from Alberta and Roland Almon Ritchie from Nova Scotia – were drawn from the practising bar; neither had ever held judicial office. Martland was a prominent corporate lawyer expert in matters relating to natural resources. He joined the Court at age fifty-one without a record of major service to a political party.[16] He was the fourth successive justice (following Cartwright, Abbott, and Nolan) to come to the Court without regular judicial experience. Ritchie replaced a fellow maritimer, Ivan Rand, who had reached compulsory retirement age. After serving with the judge advocate-general's branch during the Second World War, Ritchie resumed private practice in Halifax. He was forty-eight years old in 1959 when he joined the Supreme Court.[17]

The two other Diefenbaker appointments – Wilfred Judson from Ontario and Emmett Matthew Hall from Saskatchewan – had judicial experience in their provincial superior courts. After two decades in private practice in Toronto, where he acquired a reputation as a specialist in the equity law of wills and estates, Judson was appointed to the Ontario Supreme Court in 1951. He went to the Supreme Court at age fifty-five with seven years' judicial experience.[18] Emmett Hall was chosen to replace Justice Locke, who had retired in September 1962. (Locke quickly incurred the displeasure of his former judicial colleagues by appearing before the Court as counsel, just as Kellock had five years earlier.) Hall was destined to be Diefenbaker's last selection to the Supreme Court. An old friend and law-school classmate of the prime minister, Hall enjoyed a long and distinguished private practice and had acquired a reputation as a trial counsel and as a champion of civil liberties before being appointed chief justice of the Saskatchewan Court of Queen's Bench in 1957. Hall's long-time interest in public affairs and support for the Conservative party had not been strongly manifested, though he had been defeated in the 1948 provincial general election. Ironically, once on the bench his interest in public affairs was given freer rein. In 1957 Hall became chairman of the Saskatchewan Law Reform Commission, and in 1960 he was named chairman of the federal Royal Commission on Health Services (on which he did not complete his work until several months after his appointment to the Supreme Court).[19] In 1961 he was promoted to chief justice of the Saskatchewan Court of Appeal. Hall's appointment to the Supreme Court in 1962 represented not simply the rewarding of a friend; he shared many of the prime minister's views on civil liberties, and his presence gave Diefenbaker an opportunity to influence the makeup of the Court which soon would be ruling on the legal force of the 1960 Canadian Bill of Rights. The new justice joined the Supreme Court a few days before his sixty-fourth birthday and became the first western Roman Catholic member of the Court.[20]

Less than three months later, in the midst of a cabinet crisis and a parliamentary conflict that would bring down the government, Chief Justice Kerwin died suddenly. During frantic attempts to save the government through restructuring the cabinet, some cabinet rebels viewed the Supreme Court vacancy as a heaven-sent opportunity to remove the prime minister by offering him the post. Diefenbaker resolutely refused.[21] The willingness of cabinet members to use the Court vacancy for political purposes should surprise no one, and Diefenbaker's rejection of the offer does not alter the perceived usefulness of the Court for political purposes.

The same day that Diefenbaker rejected this offer of the chief justice-ship, his government was defeated in the House. The vacancy was not filled until after a general election had confirmed the defeat and a new government had taken office. On the same day that Lester Pearson was sworn into office as prime minister, Robert Taschereau, the senior puisne justice, was elevated to preside over the Court. He was sixty-six years of age and had already served for twenty-three years on the Supreme Court bench. The fact that he was a French Canadian must have made his promotion attractive to Pearson, who was about to undertake a new initiative to give French Canadians a more meaningful role across the country and particularly in Ottawa.

The appointments under St Laurent and Diefenbaker during this first decade after termination of appeals to the Judicial Committee show no departures from previous practice. There is every reason to believe that the appointments would have been no different had appeals not been discontinued. Most of the new justices lacked prior judicial experience; traditional regional considerations were honoured; religious criteria (no more than three Catholics) were maintained. It would take another decade before a Jew was appointed to the high court despite the dramatic increase in the number of outstanding Jewish lawyers throughout Canada following the Second World War, and it would take even longer for a woman to claim a seat on the Supreme Court. The period following termination of appeals was not viewed by either government as a time for innovation. The impression is that federal politicians wanted a truly Canadian final court of appeal, but they were not sure why they wanted it. The only hint that a substantive issue prompted an appointment to the

Supreme Court was contained in Diefenbaker's selection of Emmett Hall. Civil liberties, and especially a statutory bill of rights, had long been the publicly expressed cause of John Diefenbaker. He had promised a bill of rights for Canadians in the 1957 and 1958 campaigns, and he delivered in 1960, two years before Hall's appointment. There is little doubt that Hall was chosen because he championed the same causes.

Not surprisingly, the provinces began to take a new interest in the Supreme Court during this period. The federal government had sought and obtained an end to the overseas appeal process without the consent of the provinces. When the opposition leader, George Drew, attempted to have the St Laurent government obtain provincial consent, the prime minister flatly and unequivocally refused.[22] This refusal did not lie easily with some provincial premiers, such as Maurice Duplessis. Quebec had long been comfortable with Judicial Committee decisions, the Labrador boundary decision notwithstanding. Indeed, all the provinces owed an enormous debt to the Judicial Committee for supporting their claims to strong legislative powers under the terms of the British North America Act. But now the Supreme Court was supreme in fact as well as in name. Above all, the Court was the final arbiter of all constitutional disputes between the two levels of government. Yet the Court was the creature of one of the dominant parties in such disputes; it was established and controlled by a simple statute of the federal Parliament; that statute could be altered at any time and in any way the federal government chose; the Court's membership was determined solely by the federal government, and a frequent criterion for selection, emphasized in 1954 by Douglas Abbott's appointment, was service to the governing federal party. The Supreme Court had long been regarded by provincial governments as being predisposed to favour a centralist or federal point of view. Now there was no recourse from the Court's decisions to any other judicial body, as there had been prior to 1949. The result of this situation and of the conflicts with the Quebec government in particular was an increased public concern regarding the constitutional status of the Court.

One expression of these concerns emanated, not surprisingly, from Quebec in the 1950s. The influential Tremblay Report offered a detailed criticism of the Supreme Court of Canada's position and called for three major reforms. First, the Court, the nature of its jurisdiction, and the manner of appointing its members should be entrenched in the British North America Act, after agreement had been reached on these points between both levels of government. Second, the Court should be 'a court of appeal exercising a right of supervision and reform over the provincial courts of appeal' rather than 'a court dealing through appeal with all legal disputes in Canada.' The Supreme Court's jurisdiction should be limited to federal matters, but failing that it should by statute be required to hear any civil-law cases by a panel of five justices, three of whom must have acquired their legal training in Quebec; to reverse a decision of the highest Quebec court, the judgment of the three Quebec justices in Ottawa should be unanimous. Third, the manner of appointment to the Court must be altered to allow more direct provincial influence, or constitutional issues should be diverted to a separate tribunal designed to deal solely with such matters and whose members were appointed by the two major levels of government. Various formulae might be proposed, but the important point, according to the report,

is that the provinces must not allow the present system to remain a permanent one, as if it were satisfactory. The federal government should understand, moreover, that it is of prime importance that the highest tribunal in the land be shielded from all criticism and enjoy the complete confidence of the people, which unfortunately cannot be said of the Supreme Court of Canada as at present established by Ottawa.[23]

Many of the report's comments and suggestions were fair, but it was unrealistic to expect to shield the Court from 'all criticism.'

In the 1950s and especially in the 1960s a variety of proposals on the constitutional status of the Supreme Court was put forward across the country.[24] However, since federal-provincial relations were at issue and since the extremely contentious and difficult matter of constitutional change was potentially involved, none of these plans came to fruition. The problems at the Court were not immediately serious enough to demand action, other issues, such as medicare in the mid-1960s, were already disruptive enough without opening a contentious debate over the status of the Supreme Court. At the government level, effective deliberation regarding the proposed changes to the Court was postponed indefinitely.

The government did not turn a completely blind eye to Court matters. It was responsive to some extent in the early 1950s when a good deal of concern had re-emerged regarding the Supreme Court Reports, which were becoming increasingly more important to the legal community and the lower courts. Two reporters, A.E. Richard and F. des Rivières, had both been appointed in October 1947. Partly because of their inexperience and lack of training and partly because of the rise in the number of cases handled by the Court, the quality of the reporting was felt to be poor. This time the complaints came not from the public but from the justices themselves, especially the common-law justices. A government official stated that the justices were 'extremely dissatisfied' with the reporters' inability to write good headnotes. Another concern was the presentation of a summary of counsels' argument before the Court, an innovation in the reporting which the justices now sought. The chief justice requested the appointment of a third reporter, but others held that what was needed was one well-qualified reporter.

The problem of the reports was first raised in 1951, and it took a full five years to gain substantive action. Unwilling to remove the existing reporters, the government decided to wait until one of them requested a transfer. When this occurred it was possible to bring in the man who was regarded as the best law reporter in Canada. A.B. Harvey was persuaded to move from Toronto to Ottawa in 1956, enticed by a lucrative salary, a new position (deputy registrar and editor), and the apparent promise of the registrarship when it became vacant. By these actions the government showed itself concerned about the Supreme Court and willing to act in its betterment, but only in ways that would not rock the boat. With Harvey's untimely death in 1960, complaints about the quality of the reports returned, but in general the criticisms were minor.[25]

The actual work of the Court attracted increasing public attention during the 1950s and 1960s. Though sporadic, this attention was a reflection of public awareness that here was a significant Canadian institution which, when given an important public issue such as rights and freedoms, could have far-reaching influence. The post-war period was a time of rising consciousness of civil liberties, and English Canadians were attracted by a series of appeals impugning the record of the Quebec government in that area. Canadians were curious to know how their own Court would handle the important issues of human rights in the Canadian context. They had hopes that the Supreme Court would rise to challenge and emerge as a protector of Canadian citizens against the unlawful intrusion of governments or their agents.

Beginning in 1949 and continuing for the next ten years, a series of cases, generally but not exclusively associated with the Jehovah's Witnesses, came to the Supreme Court from Quebec.[26] At issue in these cases was the power of the state or its agents arbitrarily and without just cause to interfere with the civil liberties of individuals. The Supreme Court justices were asked to find the legal foundation for the protection of individual rights. Their task was enormously complicated by the absence of any reference to civil liberties in the British North America Act. But despite the lack of an explicit statutory basis, the Court rose to the challenge in these cases and thwarted the efforts of the Quebec government to infringe the rights of Jehovah's Witnesses. In the process of reaching their conclusions the justices roamed widely over a broad legal terrain and proved unable to agree on a single legal foundation for the judicial protection of individual rights in Canada. The general result of the Court's judgement in *Saumur v Quebec*, for example, was one of considerable uncertainty if not confusion. As Peter Russell has observed, 'three sharply contrasting views were expressed on the general relationship of civil liberties to the division of powers and not one of these views could command the support of a majority.'[27] Little wonder that proposals for a statutory bill of rights clearing up the confusion over the status of fundamental rights and freedoms in Canada began to be voiced throughout the country as a result of the Court's ambiguous judgments involving press and religion.

Nevertheless, the Supreme Court's handling of these cases stands out for several reasons. First, the cases tended to give the impression that the Court was prepared to stake a claim for the judicial protection of civil liberties despite the inadequate statutory provisions covering these matters. That the Court was in tune with public expectations was confirmed by the widespread public acclaim that greeted the judgments. However unsettling this new activism of the 1950s was to many lawyers throughout Canada, it was a welcome development in the minds of most public commentators. Individual justices such as Ivan Rand were singled out for their willingness to assume leadership in this traditionally grey area of Canadian law.

At least as important was the rising intellectual quality of the decisions. Paul Weiler, for example, pointed out that in *Boucher v The King* the Court handled the substantive legal issue by 'subjecting the whole area [of seditious libel] to searching re-examination ... and carried it off with several opinions of great scholarship and wisdom'; the case was 'a text-book example of judicial craftsmanship and demonstrates that Canadian judges are perfectly capable of it.'[28] Coming so soon after the Supreme Court became the final court of appeal, these civil liberties decisions suggested that Canadians could expect more intellectually cogent judgments from the Court.

The disputes in Quebec regarding the Jehovah's Witnesses had long since ended by the time the cases were completed; the Supreme Court merely confirmed the result. In the later cases of the 1950s there was an increasingly direct conflict between the provincial government of Maurice Duplessis and a centralist institution, the Supreme Court, as to the character of the state and the values that would prevail in the province of Quebec. This conflict was underlined by the tendency in these cases for the French-Canadian justices to be in dissent. The obvious differences of opinion between the two contestants and the power of the Court to impose its will on the province heightened the tensions already associated with Quebec's relations with Ottawa. The public attention attracted by these judicial contests simply underlined the tension and the sense of conflict. The *Toronto Daily Star* pointed to the conflict and to the Supreme Court's role in it: 'Premier Duplessis of Quebec said in effect: "I am the law." The Supreme Court of Canada ruled otherwise.' In Quebec, however, the judgments 'confirmed Duplessis in his autonomist position and lent credibility to his claim that Ottawa was meddling ignorantly and recklessly in Quebec's affairs.'[29]

The Supreme Court emerged from these civil liberties cases with an uncertain reputation. Most commentators throughout Canada applauded the justices for their results, but many, after close scrutiny of the supporting reasons, were critical of the quality of the jurisprudence. At best it was confusing and inconclusive. The justices appeared uncomfortable in such a public role; they also appeared unprepared by training and experience for the kinds of issues involved. The Court was being challenged to rethink its role and assume a greater public prominence, and it did not know how to cope. The temper of the times and the expectations of Canadians would not permit it to retreat to the old anonymity. Whether the justices liked it or not, the Supreme Court was the final and highest court in the land and it would have to adjust to its new position and the country's rising expectations.

Significant internal tension existed between Cartwright and Fauteux during this period. Cartwright, the former defence counsel, rarely saw eye-to-eye with Fauteux, the former crown prosecutor, in important matters of criminal jurisprudence. As early as 1956 the lines were drawn between the two justices. The central issue that divided them was the contentious matter of criminal intention, or mens rea. Fauteux avoided whenever possible any discussion of mens rea, whereas Cartwright resolutely insisted upon proof of criminal intention; where there was any doubt, Cartwright ruled in favour of the accused. Cartwright emerges from these cases as inflexibly determined to prot.:ct the criminal accused; Fauteux emerges as the staunch defender of public order.

Contained implicity in this tension was the clash of the two legal traditions. Fauteux tended to disregard precedent and applied the terms of the Criminal Code as if they were extensions of the Civil Code. He appeared unwilling to grant mens rea even in the most obvious circumstances. Cartwright appeared ready to extend the defence of mens rea to the most doubtful matters. Paul Weiler observed of a major criminal judgment, 'Fauteux J. does not debate with Cartwright J. the established legal significance of the principle of *mens rea,* nor does he meet the arguments relating to the word "knowingly" and the structure of section 138(1). He simply assumes that child protection legislation is an overriding goal which must be pursued to the exclusion of the claims of *mens rea.*'[30] The conflict between these two justices caused the Court to fail to meet the expectations of the legal community in an essential area of the criminal law. Criminal appeals increased considerably toward the end of this period owing principally to the Bill of Rights and the introduction of legal aid. Yet the Court appeared incapable of handling the new challenge; at times it appeared hopelessly locked in battle between the antithetical positions of two strong-minded justices. The result was a confusing criminal jurisprudence.

Most of these cases did not attract much public attention; the issues were difficult for laymen to grasp. But the trial of Wilbert Coffin caught the attention of the media and prompted the federal government to intrude into the normal judicial process, reviving the old fears of political intervention. The Coffin case attracted considerable public interest for over two years and continued long after his execution. Coffin, a Gaspé prospector, was convicted of murdering one of three American hunters in the Quebec bush in 1953 and was sentenced to be hanged. His conviction was affirmed unanimously by the Quebec Court of Queen's Bench. In the summer of 1954 an application for leave to appeal to the Supreme Court of Canada reached Ottawa; Justice Abbott, newly arrived from the cabinet – and thus with no judicial experience and with only limited recent legal experience – heard the application in chambers and dismissed it on the ground that no substantial issue of law was involved. That such a publicly contentious case should have fallen to Abbott was unfortunate and caused public doubts about the quality of justice in the high court. The new judge had admitted to a Toronto journalist shortly before the case arose that he had very limited experience in criminal matters and that he would therefore avoid writing judgments in this area until he had acquired more experience.[31] Many viewed this as a specific and substantive example of the weakness of patronage appointments to the Supreme Court. On appeal to the Court as a whole, Abbott's dismissal was upheld on the narrow technical ground that the Court had no jurisdiction to change the decision of a justice when the original application had been properly heard.

Despite the seeming unanimity of the courts regarding the justice of Coffin's trial and conviction, public outcry continued. Interest was increased by the accused's escape from jail in 1955 and by rumours that some of the Supreme Court justices disagreed with Abbott's ruling. The minister of justice took the extraordinary step of asking the Supreme Court, on reference, to hear Coffin's appeal. This direct political intrusion into the criminal process was unprecedented and illustrates the vulnerability of the judicial process in general and the Supreme Court of Canada in particular to public pressure and political interference. In January 1956 the justices held, 5–2, that an appeal by Coffin would have been dismissed. With this advice the cabinet decided not to intervene further and to allow Coffin to be executed some three weeks later. While the Coffin case was not legally significant, it was instructive; it showed that the government would not hesitate to interfere directly in the criminal process at the highest level.

During this period the Court was confronted with a relatively new set of problems accompanying the rise of the positive state in the post-war period. As Frank Scott observed at the time, 'The wide and rapid growth in the functions and powers of public authorities ... and in particular the entrusting of judicial functions to government departments and agencies, have so enlarged the area of public administration, and so increased the daily relations between the individual and the state, that we now accept the body of applicable rules as a distinct legal category and recognize it as a major field of law.'[32] The Supreme Court soon found itself obliged to oversee the exercise of this new major field of law. In addition, it was required to superintend the fairness of the procedures employed by the new public boards and agencies. In these matters the Court emerges with a better reputation than it did in either civil liberties or mens rea cases.

The new function was embraced uneasily by the Court. Justices of the Supreme Court had been trained to give deference to the legislative authority; it was not an easy matter for many of them to resist the wishes of Parliament or provincial legislatures. Cartwright's rulings in several of the Quebec civil liberties cases, for example, can be explained as part of the traditional deference to legislative supremacy.

The first major contentious issue for the Court arose out of the attempt of legislatures and Parliament to restrict access to courts of law in certain matters. In an effort to prevent judicial review of certain kinds of administrative decisions, Parliament and the provincial legislatures began to incorporate privative clauses in many statutes establishing administrative boards. Legislators attempted to do this in a variety of ways: by inserting a no-certiorari clause (a clause stating that certiorari and other forms of judicial review of administrative action were not available); by appending a clause declaring that the agency's decision was final; or by affirming that the agency had exclusive jurisdiction. While the language often varied, the legislative purpose was the same: to deny access to the courts.

That intention constituted a basic problem for the strict constructionism of many members of the Court. It had long been a central tenet of the common-law tradition that superior courts were obliged to oversee the exercise of administrative authority, but many academic commentators supported the new trend toward privative clauses.[33] Professor Bora Laskin, for example, wrote that the superior courts possessed no constitutional support for the claim that they are bound to review administrative board decisions. The courts, he said, 'must bow to the higher authority of a legislature to withdraw this function from them.'[34] The Supreme Court justices disagreed. Their new position as members of a final court of appeal encouraged a more activist view of the Court's role than they had previously contemplated. The justices tended to resist legislative encroachment on judicial review, thus causing some frustration. A good example was the case of *Attorney-General of Canada* v *Brent* (1956).[35] Shirley Kathleen Brent, an American citizen visiting Toronto, applied for permanent residence in Canada. Her application was heard by a special immigration officer, who ordered her deported. Brent appealed eventually to the Ontario Court of Appeal, where the deportation order was quashed.[36] The attorney-general of Canada appealed the order to the Supreme Court of Canada.

A unanimous Supreme Court, through Chief Justice Kerwin, dismissed the appeal on the ground that the Immigration Act did not delegate to immigration officers the authority to deport. The chief justice cited the explicit terms of the privative clause in the act but dismissed it with the observation that since the deportation order had not been validly made, the privative clause did not prevent the Court from reviewing the deportation order. This hardly exhausted the issues involved, but it did illustrate the clear unwillingness of the Supreme Court to abandon its traditional common-law responsibility to review administrative decisions.

Defenders of privative clauses claimed that the new character of administrative law demanded that the old common law be superseded by a modern conception of administrative authority. They viewed privative clauses as the legitimate extension of parliamentary or legislative sovereignty. For the courts to deny force to privative clauses was viewed as tantamount to invading legislative jurisdiction. As Peter Hogg has written, 'the almost total futility of absolute privative clauses in the immigration and labour cases cannot be defended, for it is nothing short of defiance to the command of the legislature.'[37]

Justice Ivan Rand stands out as the most articulate if not the most influential judicial proponent of privative clauses in labour cases of the 1950s. He was frequently in dissent from a Court majority that ignored or circumvented privative clauses. In *Toronto Newspaper Guild* v *Globe Printing Co.* (1953),[38] for example, the Supreme Court majority quashed a decision of the Ontario Labour Relations Board; Justice Rand dissented on the ground that in such matters the privative clause should bar judicial review. The Labour Relations Board was a specialized board empowered by the legislature to perform a specialized function; its members were recognized experts in labour relations matters. Rand believed that the courts should only review decisions protected by privative clauses if the decisions were not 'within any rational compass that can be attributed to the statutory language.'

By the end of this period it was becoming clear to the Court that its judicial function had changed. Since the abolition of appeals to the Judicial Committee, the Supreme Court had acquired a greater responsiblity in public-law matters. However slow the justices were to respond to these new demands, it was clear that they could not avoid meeting their new responsibilities. It was evident to all observers that the post-1949 Court could not lapse back into the comfort of the old anonymity – sitting in judgment on private-law disputes, relying on the Judicial Committee for instructions. The members of the Court were now dependent on their own intellectual resources.

Thus, it was encouraging that the members of the Court in the 1950s occasionally demonstrated a refreshing, albeit sporadic, willingness to meet the challenges of their new position of primacy or to break new ground. *Boucher* (1951) was one example of this, and *Beaver* v *The Queen* (1957)[39] was similarly singled out for the quality of reasoning. In *Fleming* v *Atkinson* (1959),[40] a majority of the Court, led by Wilfred Judson, broke away from the traditional influence of the House of Lords and examined searchingly the legal principles of tort liability.

But this new activism was not destined to survive into the 1960s. The decline was manifested in *Brodie, Dansky and Rubin* v *The Queen* (1962),[41] a case which involved *Lady Chatterley's Lover* and the definition of obscenity (newly defined in the 1959 Criminal Code). A full Court decided in a 5–4 decision that the book was not obscene. The reasoning of the majority was very restricted; in three separate judgments only one justice (Ritchie) chose to examine in a limited manner the definition of obscenity; the other four justices accepted the new statutory definition and ruled that the courts were controlled by a narrow interpretation of the statute in this manner.

One can only speculate on why the justices had uncharacteristically flirted with judicial activism in the 1950s. The separation from the Judicial Committee achieved in 1949 may have induced the justices to assert their intellectual independence to prove to themselves and others that they were now the dominant judicial force in Canadian law. The easiest way to do this was to strike out in new directions. At times the desire to establish the Court's separate identity became quite open. One reporter recounted hearing Chief Justice Rinfret early in 1952 interrupt counsel: 'You are citing English cases, Mr. Dorion. This is the Supreme Court of Canada and has been the final court of appeal in criminal matters since 1935. Why don't you cite Canadian cases in support of your contention.'[42] While there was a potential for intellectual parochialism in such a reaction, it had its positive side. By the end of the decade the motivation to establish judicial independence was weakening, and the inherent conservatism of the Canadian judiciary began to reassert itself.

Finally, the tendency toward judicial innovation evident in the 1950s can perhaps be understood as a result of the growing self-confidence of the justices. Throughout those years the Supreme Court contained men such as Rand and Kellock, who had by the end of the decade served many years on the bench. They were intellectually self-confident men prepared to insert that confidence into their work. One thing is certain: conservatism returned to the Court as these men were replaced by younger justices with limited judicial experience.

9

Changing Expectations
1963–1974

One of the most significant developments of the decade following the adoption of the Bill of Rights was the change in public expectations regarding the role of the Supreme Court within the nation. Canadians began to look to the Supreme Court for leadership after John Diefenbaker's boast that their rights and freedoms were now judicially enforceable. The much-publicized climate of judicial activism in the United States was beginning to make Canadians think about their own Supreme Court. Prior to this time most people were barely aware of the Court's existence; it had truly been a quiet court in a quiet country. The Court itself, however, had difficulty living up to these new expectations. Most of the justices had been on the bench for many years and were clearly unsympathetic with or ignorant of the public's changing expectations. The Diefenbaker government took an early, if in some ways tentative, lead in giving substance to this new role for the court by the passage of the Canadian Bill of Rights in 1960. But the Conservative government went no further. In four appointments to the Supreme Court, the government gave no indication of leadership or new direction. Both the Diefenbaker government and its 1963 successor, led by Lester Pearson, continued to name to the Court justices who fitted into the traditional mould. In 1963 Pearson named Wishart Flett Spence to replace Patrick Kerwin, who had retired. Pearson not only upheld the traditional character of the Supreme Court but also redressed the regional balance, reverting to the earlier distribution of seats at the Court: one from the maritimes, three from Ontario, three from Quebec, and two from the west.

Spence had been called to the bar in 1928. He completed graduate studies at Harvard Law School before taking up private practice in Toronto. In 1950 he was named to the Ontario Supreme Court and while there served as chairman of the Royal Commission on Coastal Trade (1955). After thirteen years' judicial experience he joined the Supreme Court at age fifty-nine.

From the time of Patrick Kerwin's death early in 1963 until the appointment of Bora Laskin to the chief justiceship late in 1973, the Supreme Court of Canada experienced an instability in leadership. In those eleven years there were five chief justices. The three intervening chief justices averaged just three years and six months at the post before retiring. The best leader of the three, John Cartwright, had the shortest term (two and a half years).

Robert Taschereau had joined the Supreme Court of Canada in 1940. Twenty-three years later (and eleven weeks after Kerwin's death had left the Court without a chief justice) he was named to head the institution. Aged sixty-six at the time, Taschereau could reasonably look forward to almost a decade at the Court's helm. But within just a few years it became apparent, at least to observers inside the Court, that such an expectation was no longer realistic. The chief justice's struggle with alcoholism became pronounced. His conduct on the bench was affected and, presumably, his ability to act as a positive force in leading the Supreme Court declined. Taschereau talked about resigning for several months, thus adding to the instability, before finally resigning in August 1967.[1]

The Pearson government could have been faced with a minor dilemma in selecting a replacement, although there is in fact no evidence that the government even perceived the dilemma. The senior puisne justice, to whom the chief justiceship would normally go, was John Cartwright. He was already seventy-two years of age and would be required to retire from the Court in less than three years. Given the short time in which he would be able to exercise his influence in the post, and given the inevitable confusion that would occur in the turnover of the chief justiceship two and a half years hence, it would certainly have been possible and perhaps even advisable to pass over Cartwright for a younger man. But Pearson seems to have seen the chief justiceship simply as a post to be filled. To violate tradition would be to attract attention and debate to the Court, something Pearson wanted to avoid. Thus, when one Québecois recommended the selection of Gérald Fauteux for the office, Pearson replied that although Cartwright had already been appointed, the post would soon be vacant again, at which time Fauteux would surely be considered.[2]

John Cartwright became the twelfth chief justice of Canada on 1 September 1967. As it turned out, he was an excellent choice. He was able in a short time to make a significant impact on the Court owing to his attractive personality. He was an effective administrator, and he was able to succeed where several other chief justices had failed in establishing a firm pattern of judicial conferences at the Court.[3]

The vacancy at the puisne level was, of course, filled from the province of Quebec, the first of six openings among the Quebec seats at the Court in the period 1967–81. The new minister of justice, P.E. Trudeau, chose Louis-Philippe Pigeon. The son of a lawyer in southwestern Quebec, Pigeon studied law at Laval University. He was called to the bar in 1928 and practised with various Quebec City law firms, developing an expertise in civil law and at various times working with Louis St Laurent and Jean Lesage. If such ties left any doubt, Pigeon's sympathy with the Liberal party was confirmed by his appointment as law clerk of the Quebec legislature from 1940 to 1944. In 1942 his scholarly interest in the law was manifested in his acceptance of a professorship in constitutional law at Laval, a post he retained until 1967. Returning from the provincial legislature to private practice in 1944, Pigeon's ties to the political sphere were not broken. From 1960 to 1966 he was legal adviser to the Liberal premier of Quebec. Pigeon's national stature was growing. He was chairman of the National Council on the Administration of Justice from 1963 to 1967, and a leader in the provincial and national bar associations. He was sixty-two years of age when he joined the Supreme Court.[4]

Pigeon's appointment to the Supreme Court of Canada in 1967 was a good one. Though known for his connections with the Liberal party, his reputation as a legislative draftsman and as a constitutional expert reflected a growing desire for a more scholarly Court role to meet the constitutional cases that seemed inevitable in the coming years. Pigeon's was the first appointment by the then justice minister, Pierre Trudeau, to the Supreme Court. It was the first indication of the type of person who would be sent to the Court over the next fifteen or more years. Pigeon was a legal scholar and a constitutional expert with extensive experience as a legislative draftsman. The constitutional conflicts of the 1960s and Pierre Trudeau's ambitions for constitutional change made it reasonable to expect a series of major constitutional cases before the Court in the near future. Pigeon's pragmatic and incisive mind would be a major asset to the Supreme Court over the next thirteen years, during which time he was the dominant civil-law jurist. His years on the high bench confirmed his reputation as a lawyer's lawyer; he was painstaking and meticulous in his work if somewhat ponderous.

In March 1970 Chief Justice Cartwright retired, and the third in a series of short-term chief justices took office. There is no indication as to how much Prime Minister Trudeau or his cabinet debated this appointment, but it is obvious that the tradition of promoting the senior puisne justice was maintained. Even though Gérald Fauteux would have to retire in less than four years, he was named chief justice immediately on Cartwright's departure. The selection was not a strong one and clashed with the sense of Trudeau's design to make the Court more scholarly and to give it a sense of legal direction. However, in the context of the prime minister's desire to give French Canadians a more prominent role in Ottawa, Fauteux's elevation was logical.

The vacancy on the Supreme Court was filled so as to compensate for whatever was staid or traditional in Fauteux's selection. Indeed, this might be a further explanation of the choice of Fauteux: a means of balancing the novelty of the appointment of Bora Laskin to the Court. Born in Fort William, Ontario, Laskin was the son of Russian Jewish immigrants. He studied at the University of Toronto and Osgoode Hall Law School, and then moved on to Harvard Law School for graduate studies. Laskin was called to the bar in 1937. Instead of entering private practice, he chose to teach law. He was a full-time professor of law at the University of Toronto (1940–5), at Osgoode Hall Law School (1945–9), and again at the University of Toronto (1949–65). His legal interests were many. He was associate editor of the Dominion Law Reports and Canadian Criminal Cases from 1943 to 1965. In 1951 he published the first casebook on Canadian constitutional law, a formal and comprehensive statement of the centralist principle for Canada. His centralist leaning was apparent in his 1954 article concerning civil liberties, in which Laskin predicted that when the constitutional issue of control of civil liberties was reconsidered, 'the absence of affirmative Dominion legislation should not militate against making it perfectly clear that civil liberties lie beyond provincial control.'[5] Laskin was known as a leading expert in labour law and had been active as a labour conciliator and arbitrator. He had also taken a considerable interest in the Supreme Court of Canada, demonstrating his own independent frame of mind when, in 1951, he called for the Court to take advantage of its new supremacy to dissociate itself from stare decisis and to develop its own personality: 'What is required is the same free range of inquiry which animated the Court in the early days of its existence, especially in constitutional cases where it took its inspiration from Canadian sources. Empiricism not dogmatism, imagination rather than literalness, are the qualities through which the judges can give their Court the stamp of personality.'[6]

In 1965, Laskin accepted an appointment to the Ontario Court of Appeal.

There he became known for his often penetrating dissenting judgments. When he moved to Ottawa in 1970 he was fifty-seven years old.[7]

Bora Laskin's elevation to the Supreme Court of Canada was remarkable in several respects. First, he was the first justice not to represent one of the two charter groups. As well, he was the first non-Christian to be named to the court. Second, he was one of Canada's foremost legal scholars and his accession to the Court emphasized Pierre Trudeau's design for the institution. Third, both as a constitutional expert and as someone who was clearly sympathetic to civil liberties and to a strong central government, Laskin had been influential in the formation of the prime minister's philosophical concerns and attitudes in those areas.[8] Fourth, the new justice lacked major experience in private practice. In this he failed to meet an assumed essential requirement for a position in the senior judiciary, and his appointment was greeted with criticism in some quarters. Perhaps partly for this reason and partly out of envy at his national reputation for scholarship, Laskin allegedly received a chilly reception from his new colleagues.[9]

The most important new demand placed on the Court during this period arose out of the Canadian Bill of Rights, which was passed by Parliament in 1960.[10] The climate of expectations regarding the role of the Court anticipated a degree of initiative on the part of Canadian judges. Rather than applying the Bill to Canadian law, the new statute imposed upon the Court an ambiguous obligation to 'construe and apply' all laws of Canada as to ensure that they did not abrogate, abridge, or infringe any of the rights and freedoms declared in the Bill. The Supreme Court quickly showed that it was ill-prepared by disposition and training to meet either the changing expectations or this new function, which many members of the legal profession viewed as American intrusions.

In the light of the record of the justices in civil liberties cases throughout the 1950s, some Canadian civil libertarians anticipated a continuation of that trend into the 1960s with the formal adoption of the Bill of Rights. But the members of the Court shied away from further activism. However, the mere enactment of the Canadian Bill of Rights did not occasion the flood of litigation that some observers had predicted. Indeed, it was several years before the Supreme Court had an opportunity to pronounce on the force of its provisions.

The first occasion on which the Supreme Court gave explicit attention to the Bill of Rights occurred in the case of *Robertson and Rosetanni* v *The Queen* (1963).[11] That attention was of no consequence, however. Justice Cartwright, in dissent, was the only member of the Court to relate the issues to the Bill of Rights. The case involved the operation of a bowling alley on Sunday in contravention of the Lord's Day Act. The defendants appealed their conviction on the ground that the Canadian Bill of Rights had in effect repealed or rendered the act inoperative.

In a 4–1 judgment the Supreme Court ruled that the appeal should be dismissed. The majority held that the Canadian Bill of Rights was not concerned with human rights and fundamental freedoms in any abstract sense, but rather with such rights and freedoms as they existed in Canada immediately before the Bill of Rights was enacted. Since legislation such as the Lord's Day Act had been in existence in Canada from the earliest times and had not been considered a violation of that kind of freedom of religion guaranteed by the Bill of Rights, it was not to be considered as violating the terms of the Bill; the Bill of Rights did not create new rights but merely affirmed existing ones. In the opinion of the majority the effect of the act was 'purely secular,' not in any way affecting the liberty of religious practice. In their reasoning the majority retreated to a traditional conservatism and refused the invitation to judicial activism implied by the Bill of Rights.

Justice Cartwright dissented with a strong endorsement of the Bill of Rights. To his mind the Lord's Day Act was a clear and unambiguous infringement of the Bill of Rights. He claimed in his judgment that where there was an irreconcilable conflict between an act of Parliament and the Bill of Rights, the latter must prevail. Given a clear statutory authority, Cartwright rose to the occasion and wrote an aggressive judgment in defence of civil liberties. It was the first time that a justice of the highest court in the land had given such a ringing endorsement of the Bill of Rights (albeit in a dissenting judgment). Cartwright's dissent in *Robertson and Rosetanni* encouraged civil libertarians throughout Canada. Many saw it as the thin edge of the wedge; given time, they hoped, the entire Bill of Rights would one day win approval from the Supreme Court.

Not until almost ten years after the enactment of the Canadian Bill of Rights did the Supreme Court of Canada successfully apply the Bill of Rights to federal legislation. In *The Queen v Drybones* (1970),[12] the Supreme Court ruled section 94 of the 1947 Indian Act inoperative on the ground that it conflicted with section 5 of the Canadian Bill of Rights, which guarantee equality before the law.

The *Drybones* case contained all the elements destined to capture the attention of the Canadian public. Joseph Drybones, a Canadian Indian, had been arrested for drunkenness in Yellowknife. He was charged with violating section 94(b) of the Indian Act, that is, 'being an Indian ...

unlawfully intoxicated off a reserve.' Drybones pleaded guilty; he was convicted and fined the minimum of ten dollars plus costs.

The central dispute in the case arose out of the difference in treatment accorded Indians under the Indian Act and others under the North West Territories Liquor Ordinance. The Indian Act provided for a minimum fine, whereas the ordinance did not; the maximum term of imprisonment under the Indian Act was three months, and under the ordinance it was thirty days; and, most important, because there are no reserves in the Northwest Territories, an Indian living in the territories could be convicted for being intoxicated in the privacy of his own home, whereas others, non-Indians, could be convicted under the liquor ordinance only for being intoxicated 'in a public place.'

The issue was clear: there were two laws in Canada – one for Indians and one for all others. The Supreme Court in a 6–3 decision (Cartwright, Abbott, and Pigeon dissenting) ruled that a sensible interpretation of the terms of the Bill of Rights led them to the conclusion that any federal law that conflicted with the Bill of Rights was inoperative to the extent of the conflict.

Many newspapers throughout the country applauded the Court and greeted the *Drybones* decision as the harbinger of greater things to come. To many editorial writers and civil libertarians, the decision removed any lingering doubts: the Bill of Rights had force and the Court was prepared to invoke it. But rather than resolving once and for all the authority of the Supreme Court to strike down or to declare inoperative federal legislation that violated the Bill of Rights, the *Drybones* decision revealed that the Court was just as deeply divided as ever over the nature of the new judicial activism.

By far the most surprising judgment came from Chief Justice Cartwright. In the most astonishing and most open reversal in the history of the Supreme Court, the chief justice repudiated his dissent in *Robertson and Rosetanni* with the confession that he had erred in his reasoning in that case. After having thought about the implications of his *Robertson and Rosetanni* judgment, Cartwright drew back in horror. It became clear to him, he wrote, that the implications of his judgment in *Robertson and Rosetanni* would be to impose an enormous new burden upon 'every justice of the peace, magistrate and judge of any court in the country' to render all federal statutes inoperative on the basis of a normal act of Parliament which imposed that task under the vague instruction to 'construe and apply.' Those implications could not be what Parliament intended. The judgment said little for a judge of Cartwright's stature. His dissent in *Drybones* was an open admission that he had not thought through his judgment in *Robertson and Rosetanni* in 1963. In the light of Ritchie's majority judgment in that case, which made the same basic points Cartwright was now making in *Drybones* and which he must have read, Cartwright's dissent was more than a little puzzling. It gave the clear impression that members of the Supreme Court were not communicating with one another on the most important judicial matters. Ironically, Cartwright was the one who had introduced regular judicial conferences. The purpose of those conferences was to permit the justices to exchange opinions and make themselves aware of the views of other members of the Court. Perhaps Cartwright would not have written as he did in *Robertson and Rosetanni* if he had had the advantage of Ritchie's views in judicial conference. Small wonder that Cartwright took steps to formalize the judicial conference shortly after becoming chief justice.

The excitement the *Drybones* decision engendered was to be short-lived. What many hoped would be the beginning of a trend in the direction of judicial activism turned out to be an aberration, more remarkable for its uniqueness than for its application of the Bill of Rights.[13]

The Supreme Court revealed more about its hesitancy to use the Canadian Bill of Rights in the breathalyser reference of 1970.[14] Shortly after *Drybones* the Court was required to pass on the legality of an order-in-council that proclaimed only parts of section 16 of the Criminal Law Amendment Act, 1968–69. The order-in-council refrained from promulgating that portion of the act which required the police to provide in an approved container a sample of the breath of an accused taken by a qualified police technician for purposes of self-defence. The Supreme Court of Canada ruled (Ritchie and Martland dissenting) that the order-in-council was intra vires even though it excluded a major provision of the act.

This decision disappointed many Canadians because it obscured the fact that a judgment on the validity of the order-in-council had been handed down in the Supreme Court of British Columbia. This case would probably have come on appeal to the Supreme Court, but the normal process was circumvented because the attorney-general of Canada, John Turner, aborted the process by interposing a reference to the Supreme Court. Civil libertarians were annoyed by Turner's failure to ask the Supreme Court of Canada to apply the terms of the Bill of Rights relating to self-defence to the order-in-council. This was no incidental or accidental oversight; Turner wanted the order-in-council sustained, for he was primarily responsible for its promulgation. The importance of this overt manipulation of the Court emerges when it is recalled that the Bill of Rights was the basis for declaring the breathalyser law inoperative in British Columbia.

But even the failure of the attorney-general to put the question to the Supreme Court did not exonerate the Court itself from assessing the order-in-council against the terms of the Bill of Rights. The Bill of Rights directly instructs the courts to apply the Bill in all cases that come before it. As Professor Bora Laskin, as he then was, had written, the Canadian Bill of Rights 'is addressed to parliament itself and to the Courts, admonishing the former not to enact, and the latter not to construe, federal legislation in the derogation of the declared rights.'[15] Section 3 of the Bill of Rights specifically enjoins the minister of justice to 'examine every proposed regulation submitted in draft form to the Clerk of the Privy Council pursuant to the House of Commons, in order to ascertain whether any of the provisions thereof are inconsistent with the purposes and provisions of this Part.' Professor Laskin predicted that that section would turn out to be 'the strongest feature of the Canadian Bill of Rights.' A reasonable extension of this injunction seems to suggest that the minister of justice was obliged to ask the Court whether the Criminal Law Amendment Act as proclaimed did in fact constitute in its application an abridgement or infringement of the rights declared in the Canadian Bill of Rights. This the minister of justice failed to do, even though Justice Monroe of the British Columbia Supreme Court had agreed that the act as proclaimed denied an accused adequate counsel as assured by the Bill of Rights.

Nevertheless, the majority chose to ignore the Bill of Rights. Justice Laskin concurred with the majority in his first Supreme Court judgment and dismissed the Bill of Rights with the laconic comment that it 'had been insufficiently elaborated.' Curiously, even the leading civil libertarian on the bench, Emmett Hall, avoided applying the Bill of Rights. Concurring with the majority, Justice Hall said: 'Notwithstanding that in my view the Order-in-Council proclaiming parts only of section 1(6) of the Criminal Law Amendment Act, 1968–69, c. 38, may indicate on the part of the executive a failure to live up to the spirit of what was intended by Parliament, I am nevertheless bound to hold that the remedy does not lie with the Courts.' A mere slap on the wrist for an 'executive failure' was truly uncharacteristic of Emmett Hall.

Despite the fact that Justice Laskin joined the Court majority in the breathalyser reference, he believed that the Bill of Rights was designed to give judges a special basis for judicial activism. Indeed, he viewed the Bill of Rights as a 'quasi-constitutional document,' qualitatively different from other acts of Parliament. But Laskin was unable to nudge a Court majority into a more activist role even after he became chief justice. The majority of justices held firmly to the tradition of legislative deference; they wanted a more explicit invitation to judicial activism than the Bill of Rights contained.[16] In this respect the hesitancy and uncertainty were shared with those outside the Court. If expectations, both among the public and the political leaders, were changing in the direction of broader responsibility and a more prominent role for the Court, those expectations were at no time clearly stated or defined. In such an environment the justices' response was typically cautious; the Court would feel its way very slowly as it coped with change.

Only in one area could the government be said to be taking any initiative in encouraging the Court, and that was in the area of personnel. There were signs that a new kind of justice was being appointed to the highest court in the land. Justices Laskin and Pigeon, for example, were intellectually inclined; both men had written extensively on a variety of major issues in the law journals. The public was beginning to demand that the Supreme Court provide a measure of leadership – how much is not clear – and this required a more innovative membership on the Court.

The desirability of a more intellectual Court was also reflected in the government's decision to appoint law clerks to the justices. This idea had been put forward by Justice Locke in 1948 and in 1953. Locke proposed that several law graduates, one for each justice, be hired to carry out background research on cases being considered. Other justices, such as Ivan Rand, added their support to the scheme, arguing that many cases 'are quite inadequately argued' before the Court and that law clerks could be used to provide the judges with additional material on points the justices felt to be important. But the St Laurent government's response was negative. In the mid-1960s the proposal surfaced again, this time as a labour-saving device in the face of the enormous workload now facing the justices. The scheme was adopted and nine law clerks began work at the Court in 1968. Clerks are appointed for one year; at present each justice is assigned two clerks. That law clerks would be rejected as a means of improving the quality of the Court's work but accepted as a means of dealing with the quantity of work is not only ironic but in keeping with the general history of the institution. The rationale for this change has not lessened the positive impact of the clerks' presence, however.

According to one of the justices, a conference procedure now began to develop:

... following discussions, the Chief Justice usually inquires as to who wishes to write, if he had not announced his own intention to write. He sometimes indicates that it would be desirable for a particular judge to write the first reasons, but he does not direct any judge to write. The usual format is: 'Would you be willing to write reasons in this case?'

I would say that conferences changed in character when Chief Justice Cartwright took over. The conferences, which I recall, all involved a discussion of the issues and the proper disposition of an appeal. The judges presented their opinions and the reasons for such opinions, and, if there were differences of view, there would be a debate about the matter.[17]

This procedure, initiated by the justices themselves, addressed the nation's changing expectations for the institution.

In 1973, after a decade at the Court, Emmett Hall retired. He was replaced by another westerner, Robert George Brian Dickson. Born in Yorkton, Saskatchewan, Dickson was raised in that province before leaving for Winnipeg to further his education. He attended the University of Manitoba and the Manitoba Law School and was called to the bar in 1940. His entrance into private practice was delayed by wartime service in the Royal Canadian Artillery, but in 1945 he returned to Winnipeg, where he specialized in corporate law. In 1963 he joined the Manitoba Court of Queen's Bench, and in 1967 was elevated to the provincial Court of Appeal. At age fifty-six, he brought to the Supreme Court extensive experience before the bar and as both a trial and an appellate judge.[18]

Before 1973 was finished, there was three more changes in the personnel of the Supreme Court. In December both Gérald Fauteux and Douglas Abbott retired early, by five months and twenty-two months respectively. What induced these early departures is unknown. The prime minister, however, took advantage of the opportunity to move the Supreme Court further in the direction of an intellectually rigorous bench.

Most dramatic was the selection of Bora Laskin as chief justice. He was the second most junior puisne justice, outranked in seniority by five other members of the Court, led by Ronald Martland. On only two other occasions (1906 and 1924) in the history of the Supreme Court had the senior puisne justice been passed over for the chief justiceship; the tradition of automatic promotion had seemed to be well in place. But it was typical of Trudeau, an activist prime minister (at least in areas of personal interest or concern) to challenge that tradition directly. Laskin would provide the Supreme Court, it was hoped, with a much-needed intellectual vigour and with a philosophical position in constitutional law and civil liberties much akin to the prime minister's.

The surprise elevation of Laskin created a good deal of reaction. Much of the commentary in the press was favourable, reflecting the public's enhanced expectations for the Court. But at the same time there were unconfirmed reports of discontent. Laskin was described as an 'academic lawyer' by some members of the bar. The other justices were allegedly annoyed at not being consulted about the appointment. Justice Martland reportedly was given very little warning that he would be passed over, and was upset. The finance minister, John Turner, was said to be furious at the break with tradition, and sensitive Albertans were reported to be taking the rejection of Martland as a slight against the west.[19]

Amid the controversy two new justices were also appointed, both from the province of Quebec as required. Douglas Abbott had an interview with the minister of justice, Otto Lang, in an attempt to persuade the government (again) that one of the Quebec seats on the Court should be given to a representative of the English-speaking community.[20] The idea had already been rejected in 1949, and it was even less likely to be adopted in 1973.

Jean-Marie Philémon Joseph Beetz was born and educated in Montreal. He studied at the University of Montreal before going to Oxford University on a Rhodes scholarship. Called to the Quebec bar in 1950, he remained in private practice only for a short time. In 1953 he joined the faculty of law at the University of Montreal, where he taught for the next twenty years; from 1968 to 1970 he was doyen du droit. A one-time colleague and close friend of Pierre Trudeau, Beetz supplemented his teaching responsibilities by becoming assistant secretary to the federal cabinet (1966–68) and special counsel to the prime minister on constitutional matters (1968–71). In 1973 he was appointed to the Quebec Court of Queen's Bench. With less than a year's judicial experience, Beetz, another 'academic lawyer,' joined the Supreme Court of Canada at age forty-six.[21]

The second vacancy went to Louis-Philippe de Grandpré. Born and educated in Montreal, he was called to the bar in 1938 and practised law in his native city until the end of 1973. De Grandpré was fifty-six years of age when he joined the Supreme Court.[22] His solid thirty-five years' experience before the bar helped to compensate for the absence of such experience in both Beetz and the new chief justice.

The two appointments were greeted with a good deal of support in Quebec. An editorial in Le Devoir headlined the news: 'Une présence québecoise plus forte à la Cour suprême.'[23] But the truth of that claim is not so clear a decade later. Beetz was an academic and a constitutional expert, and his selection fitted the Laskin pattern. Moreover, Beetz was a known supporter of provincial rights; his appointment balanced Laskin's promotion and helped to deflect any charges that the prime minister was 'packing the court.' But his lack of experience at the bar might be taken as a weakness; there were now two members of the Supreme Court who had had virtually no training as counsel. Beetz quickly began to develop a reputation for indecisiveness.[24] De Grandpré soon evinced a dislike of his new position. Like J.-T. Taschereau, Nesbitt, and Hughes before him, he resigned from the Court less than four years after joining it.[25]

The selection of Beetz and de Grandpré was a disappointment to those who had hoped for more provincial participation in Supreme Court appointments. At the Victoria constitutional conference in 1971 the federal government had agreed that appointments to that Court would be subject to provincial consultation. No method for this consultation was laid down, and since no general agreement on constitutional reform was reached, agreement on individual points was not binding. With the selection of Beetz and de Grandpré the Trudeau government missed an opportunity to create an atmosphere of co-operation and a sense that the composition of the Supreme Court of Canada was the proper concern of more than just one level of government.[26]

In the 1960s Canadians were inundated with accounts of how the Supreme Court of the United States was applying the terms of the American Bill of Rights in dramatic ways.[27] In contrast, the Canadian Bill of Rights and Supreme Court appeared weak and ineffective. As Walter Tarnopolsky observed, 'by 1967 there appeared to be a considerable waning of public interest in the Bill of Rights and some considerable cynicism amongst the legal profession as to its effectiveness.'[28]

At the height of the euphoria surrounding the celebration of the Confederation centennial and the success of Expo '67, the liberal press of Canada focused critical attention on the Supreme Court. The *Toronto Daily Star*, for example, published a series of lead editorials entitled 'The Troubled Bench.'[29] In answer to its first question, 'what's wrong with our Supreme Court?' the newspaper held up the activist example of the United States Supreme Court and lamented 'the weakness and timidity of our highest court.' The second editorial emphasized the same themes, and the final editorial urged that reforms be undertaken 'to make our Supreme Court a stronger and more constructive force in our national life.' The editorial concluded, 'The weakness in the Supreme Court of Canada has aggravated many problems of our national life.' The *Star* urged the Court to become an important and influential element in Confederation's second century. The *Star's* concern was to some extent (though by no means exclusively) the alleged failure of the Court in prominent criminal cases.

The public outrage over the Court had reached a new high a year before the *Star* editorials. The ruling in the highly publicized Truscott case unleashed a fresh onslaught of criticism upon the Court. This case had all the potential for a dramatic decision. Canadians had been reading accounts of how during the early 1960s the Supreme Court in the United States had decisively upheld individual rights. Many hoped that their own Supreme Court would prove to be as effective in a comparably dramatic way in the Truscott case. But such was not to be.

In the fall of 1959 Steven Truscott, aged fourteen, had been tried, convicted, and sentenced to death for the rape-murder of a young girl. An appeal to the Ontario Court of Appeal was dismissed, and an application for leave to appeal to the Supreme Court of Canada was rejected. Truscott's sentence was commuted to life imprisonment. There the matter seemed to rest until the publication in March 1966 of Isobel LeBourdais's book, *The Trial of Steven Truscott*, which argued strongly that a miscarriage of justice had occurred. The book quickly appeared on national bestseller lists and created considerable public doubt regarding Truscott's guilt. Many members of Parliament took an interest in the case; one suggested that the original trial might have been 'a community lynching bee.'[30] By the end of April public doubts had become so vocal and strong that the governor-in-council sent the case on reference to the Supreme Court. The reference conferred on the court the ability to hear new evidence, something heretofore not possible. New, direct testimony, including that of Truscott himself, was presented to a full panel of the Court, which effectively was being asked to overrule itself. After four days of hearings the Court held 8–1 that the conviction should stand unaltered.

That opinion did little to allay public doubts about the fairness of the initial trial. Citing Justice Hall's lengthy dissenting opinion, which claimed that the original trial had been a 'bad trial' and that the only remedy was a new trial, many observers suggested that enough questions remained concerning Truscott's innocence that further government action was called for. It seemed that considerable uncertainty now existed regarding the quality of justice administered by the Supreme Court. The *Toronto Daily Star*, for example, lionized Emmett Hall and found it difficult to believe that the original verdict had been confirmed by the other justices, given the alleged weaknesses in the first trial and the import of most of the new evidence. 'One thing is clear enough,' the paper concluded. 'This case has done damage to public confidence in the administration of justice.'[31] Most editorial comments on the Court's ruling on the Truscott case were unfair and unfounded. A Court majority composed of men as sensitive in criminal matters as John Cartwright and Wishart Spence, to single out two, simply cannot be categorized as heartless. The general public, never versed in the fine points of the law, saw the Truscott judgment as a failure to meet the expectations of the times. Many people could not help wondering how Truscott would have fared in another jurisdiction, such as the United States. Others, principally from the legal community, said that the public expectations were unrealistic. The force of the Hall dissent, however, tended to add to the general sense of disappointment.

Throughout the decade an unofficial agreement emerged throughout the Quebec bar to decide civil-law cases within the provincial court structure. This could never become a firm and official rule of practice, because a dissatisfied client could always insist that his case be appealed to the Supreme Court of Canada. Nevertheless, the growing tide of nationalism in Quebec during the post-Duplessis years prompted the move to resolve civil-law disputes in Quebec by Quebec judges.

Few Quebec lawyers believed more firmly than Louis-Phillipe Pigeon that civil-law cases were properly to be resolved in the Quebec courts. When he joined the Supreme Court in 1967 he brought with him the reputation as a staunch defender of the Civil Code. If and when civil-law cases came before the Court, the Quebec bar could be certain that it had a sympathetic and knowledgeable defender among the justices. Pigeon was present for almost every civil-law case that came to the Court during his tenure on the bench; he often wrote the sole judgment of the Court, but occasionally dissented from his civil-law colleagues. A review of the reported judgments reveals an alliance and compatibility between Pigeon and Laskin; Laskin was almost always in agreement with Pigeon when Pigeon wrote for the Court or the majority. On several occasions Laskin dissented with Pigeon. Only rarely was Laskin in the majority while Pigeon was in dissent; one of the few occasions was in *City of Lachine* v *Industrial Glass* (1978),[32] where both dissenters – Pigeon and de Grand-pré – were civil-law members of the Court; the common-law members combined to dismiss the appeal from the Quebec Court of Appeal. The result was ironic because the majority, led by Judson, ruled that there was no good reason to overturn the unanimous judgment of the Quebec Court of Appeal; in this case the common-law justices seemed more willing to give a greater deference to the Quebec Court of Appeal than the two Quebec justices on the Court. What is curious about de Grandpré's dissenting opinion is that it was based firmly on past precedents of the Supreme Court; it has the appearance of a common-law judgment rather than a civil-law judgment.

Justice Pigeon emerged during his tenure as a strong voice in defense of the Civil Code tradition. He was prepared and willing to speak out in matters touching that tradition without being sympathetic to the strong nationalist voices raised in Quebec throughout his term on the bench. He was both a passionate champion of Quebec and a committed Canadian. His contribution to the development of Canadian law, however, went well beyond the Civil Code; he played an especially important role in constitutional cases throughout those years.

The Supreme Court justices continued to serve the state extrajudicially. Justice Fauteux, a specialist in criminal law, was a member of the royal commission charged with revision of the Criminal Code from 1949 to 1952. In 1953 he was chosen to head a committee of inquiry into the methods and principles under which the remissions branch of the Justice Department operated; when the committee reported in 1956 it urged both the creation of a national parole board and general reform in the corrections field. In 1952 Roy Kellock was named chairman of a federal conciliation board involving disputes between management and the non-operating railway unions; in 1957 he was appointed chairman of the royal commission investigating employment of firemen on diesel locomotives on the Canadian Pacific Railway, an assignment involving the impact of new technology on job security. Emmett Hall was already chairman of the Royal Commission on Health Services when he was elevated to the Supreme Court in 1962. Shortly after completing that task in 1964, the Ontario government appointed him chairman of the provincial Committee on the Aims and Objectives of Education in the Schools of Ontario, which produced the controversial Hall-Dennis Report in 1968. Members of the Court frowned on Hall's role in this commission; many justices felt that it distracted him from his judicial responsibilities. There can be no question that Hall wrote fewer judgments during his involvement with the Ontario education commission.[33] One can sympathize with the other members of the Court, for almost six of Hall's ten years on the Court had been spent serving on two royal commissions, neither of which had any relation to law or judicial problems.

The federal government made use of retired Supreme Court justices along similar lines. Ivan Rand headed a one-man Royal Commission on Coal from 1959 to 1960. More important and certainly more appropriate to his experience was Rand's appointment in 1966 as the sole commissioner to inquire into the alleged misconduct of Judge Leo Landreville of the Ontario Supreme Court. Here was a particularly sensitive problem for the government and especially for the Canadian judiciary. It was both sensible and politically attractive to have Judge Landreville's actions investigated by a highly respected jurist who, being retired, was not beholden to any interested party, even indirectly. (Rand's report was very critical of Landreville and facilitated government action to impeach him.) Finally, in 1967, eight years after his retirement, Ivan Rand led a provincial royal commission studying Ontario's labour laws, an area of his special expertise.

If that use of Rand's services can be argued to be particularly (or at least relatively) appropriate after his compulsory retirement, the same cannot be said for the selection in 1966 of Justice Spence to lead a one-man inquiry into the Gerda Munsinger affair. This appointment had all of the worst possible elements of judicial involvement in political commissions. From the fall of 1964 to the spring of 1966 the Liberal government of Lester Pearson had been wracked by a 'procession of grubby revelations and scandalous allegations that clouded the Ottawa scene for ... many months.'[34] A number of political careers were harmed by the scandal, including that of the senior cabinet minister, Guy Favreau. By early 1966 the partisan animosity created by the Munsinger controversy and its results was intense. In retaliation against the Conservatives – one writer called it 'a willful act of political vengeance' – leading Liberals disclosed details of what was known as the Munsinger affair. Members of the Conservative cabinet were accused of having had liaisons with Gerda Munsinger, who was alleged to be a prostitute and a known security risk; it was alleged that the cabinet ministers had jeopardized the security of Canada and its allies, and that the Diefenbaker government had known of the ministers' conduct yet had not removed them.

The public and the media had a field day with titillating stories and headlines, and the affair blossomed into a major and potentially destructive issue politically. Several days of riotous and often vicious debate in the House seemed to threaten the parliamentary system. To solve the problem and to dampen the volatile political atmosphere, the Liberal government decided to appoint a commission of inquiry to examine the Conservative government's handling of the issue. An official inquiry into a past government's political decisions and actions had never before occurred in Canadian history; in a democracy such matters are judged by the electorate. Against the vehement objections of Conservatives, the Liberal government drew up restricted terms of reference and chose Wishart Spence, the most recent Liberal appointee to the Supreme Court of Canada and a man with long-time Liberal credentials, to head the inquiry.

Thus, a Supreme Court justice, whose political neutrality could be questioned, was asked to conduct an investigation of past political decisions. Nothing could have been more inappropriate. Spence at first refused the assignment, and acquiesced only after considerable pressure was applied. As distressing as the involvement of the Supreme Court in partisan conflict was Spence's actual handling of the inquiry. One legal expert commented:

Mr. Justice Spence has accepted the most flimsy, uncorroborated hearsay evidence, which no respectable court of law would accept for more than one moment, as pointing to existence of wide-scale espionage activity in which prominent people in public life might be involved. Guilt by association, however indirect or far-fetched the association may be, is also not excluded from the ambit of the report.[35]

This incident was as disturbing in its way as the 1946 espionage inquiry had been. Among the losers in the affair was the reputation of the Supreme Court of Canada.

It is clear that by the end of the decade the federal government had begun to take a different view of the Court and its membership. Lester Pearson's appointments at the beginning of the decade departed very little from previous practice. The Trudeau appointments, while continuing to accord consideration to regional interests, were of a different character and quality. After 1968, the academic credentials of potential appointees became important. Both the prime minister and at least one of his ministers of justice, Otto Lang, were academic lawyers. The intellectual kinship between Pierre Trudeau and Chief Justice Laskin can be seen clearly in their shared views of a statutory charter of rights. The new Court members in general tended to have impressive scholarly credentials. This fact alone accounts for the greater willingness of the Court to assume a more creative role toward the end of the decade. The perception of the judicial function in the highest court was destined to change appreciably.

Finally, after 1966 the government began to put a greater distance between itself and the Court. The public outcry over the Spence inquiry began to strike home. The Supreme Court justices were at last being accorded a greater institutional independence. The process was far from complete by 1974, but a solid beginning had been made.

10

A New Beginning
1975–1982

No previous statutory enactments had greater impact on the institutional development of the Supreme Court than the two that occurred during the years between 1975 and 1982. The first, in 1975, was the culmination of a long series of amendments to the Supreme Court Act eliminating appeals as of right and granting the Court almost complete control over its docket. The second was the historic adoption in 1982 of a new constitution in which the Court was virtually entrenched and given a vital new mandate. The first development had been sought eagerly by the Court for many years; the second event was thrust upon the justices by federal and provincial politicians.

Throughout these years the Supreme Court was caught in the crossfires of federal-provincial disputes more frequently than in any previous period. As well, the composition of the Court changed with the departure of several justices. Between the summer of 1977 and the winter of 1980 five members of the Court retired or resigned. Prime Minister Trudeau gave little indication in the selection of the replacements that he was particularly sensitive to the Court's emerging new public-law mandate. The appointments followed traditional regional considerations. Wilfred Judson, an Ontario representative, was replaced by Willard Z. Estey from Toronto;[1] and Yves Pratte of Quebec City replaced Louis-Philippe de Grandpré. Estey was born and educated in Saskatchewan; after completing graduate studies at Harvard, he practised law in Toronto. He quickly achieved prominence in corporate litigation, but left the practice in 1973 for a position on the Ontario Court of Appeal. He became chief justice of the High Court (Supreme Court of Ontario) in 1975. One year later he was named chief justice of Ontario. In this capacity he attracted considerable attention throughout the Ontario bar with his wide-ranging proposals for the reform of the judicial process. To the surprise of many members of the bar, Èstey abandoned this high position and his reform program for a puisne judgeship on the Supreme Court of Canada barely one year after becoming chief justice of Ontario. Only the second provincial chief justice to accept a transfer to Ottawa since A.C. Killam in 1903, Estey, aged fifty-seven, brought to the Supreme Court of Canada added prestige and energy.

Yves Pratte was called to the Quebec bar in 1947 after legal studies at Laval University and graduate studies at the University of Toronto. After becoming well ensconced in his legal career, he began to take on additional and more public tasks. In the fall of 1977, in the midst of a varied career in private practice and public service, he decided, at the age of fifty-two, to leave the practice of law and accept an appointment to the Supreme Court.[2]

Both of these 1977 appointments broke with the apparent pattern of earlier Trudeau selections. Estey's and Pratte's academic credentials are impressive, but their careers as law professors were limited and their legal expertise was in the field of corporate law. Estey not only enhanced the prestige of the Court but soon became an important popularizer, speaking more openly and more frequently than other justices about the Court's work. But Pratte's was not a propitious appointment. The press hinted at patronage, and the government exhibited questionable judgment in placing him on the same bench with Estey, who, just two years earlier had been so critical of Pratte's management of Air Canada. After less than two years Pratte resigned from the Court for health reasons and returned to the corporate world, accepting directorships in such major companies as Domtar and Power Corporation. His resignation and Wishart Spence's retirement in the winter of 1978 created two further vacancies.

In replacing Justice Spence the Trudeau government reportedly sought a specialist in criminal law. Perhaps concerned as well about the declining popularity of the Liberal party in the west, the government chose William Rogers McIntyre to fill the post. McIntyre, a native of Quebec, attended the University of Saskatchewan and then served in the Canadian Army in Europe until 1946. He was called to the bars of Saskatchewan and British Columbia in 1947 and entered private practice in Victoria, specializing in criminal law. In 1967 he was named to the Supreme Court of British

Columbia; he moved to the Court of Appeal in 1973. McIntyre came to Ottawa in 1979 at age sixty with over eleven years' judicial experience.[3]

It fell to the short-lived Conservative government of Joe Clark to fill the Quebec seat vacated by Yves Pratte. The opening offered a welcome opportunity for the young government to establish its political credentials in a region where the Conservative party had long been weak. Not surprisingly, the government selected a known party supporter, but fortunately one with strong legal experience. Julien Chouinard was born in Quebec City and graduated in law from Laval. As a Rhodes scholar he continued his studies at Oxford University before being called to the bar in 1953. From 1965 to 1968 Chouinard served two Quebec governments as deputy minister of justice before resigning to run for the Conservative party in the federal election. After his defeat he returned to the provincial government and served as secretary-general of the executive council from 1968 to 1975. In 1975 he was appointed by the Trudeau government to the Quebec Court of Appeal, and in the following year agreed to head a federal commission of inquiry into the Gens de l'air controversy.[4] In its search for meaningful representation from the province of Quebec, the Clark government reportedly tried hard to entice Chouinard into the federal cabinet during the summer of 1979. Failing that, he was named to the Supreme Court at the relatively young age of fifty.[5]

Early in 1980 Justice Pigeon, who had provided such strength and stability among the civil-law justices throughout the 1970s, reached the age of compulsory retirement. The newly re-elected Trudeau government named Antonio Lamer in his place. Born in Montreal, Lamer graduated from the University of Montreal and entered private practice in his native city. A criminal defence lawyer, he was also active in the Liberal party. In 1969 Lamer was appointed to the Quebec Superior Court. He joined the Law Reform Commission of Canada in 1971 as vice-chairman, and in 1975 was appointed chairman. Lamer was named to the Quebec Court of Appeal in 1978. Along with his varied experience and his concern for the law, Lamer at age forty-seven brought a youthful vigour to the Supreme Court of Canada.[6]

Ronald Martland retired from the Court early in 1982 after a distinguished career of twenty-four years. Sandra Day O'Connor had recently been appointed to the Supreme Court of the United States, and the media exerted pressure on the government to appoint a woman as Martland's replacement. Newspapers profiled female judges across the country, discussing their strengths and weaknesses. More interest and speculation regarding this vacancy was exhibited in the country than ever before in the history of the Supreme Court of Canada – perhaps partly because, after the constitutional decision of 1981, Canadians were aware of how important and influential the justices of the Court could be.[7]

The Trudeau government acknowledged this pressure by naming Justice Bertha Wilson of the Ontario Court of Appeal. In doing so, the government demonstrated that public opinion could have some influence on judicial appointments. Born and educated in Scotland, Bertha Wilson emigrated to Canada after the Second World War. She graduated from Dalhousie Law School in 1958 and practised law in Toronto until her appointment to the Ontario Court of Appeal in 1975. Wilson had an incisive legal mind and brought to the Supreme Court of Canada a reputation for meticulous research in the law. Her appointment also redressed the regional distribution of seats, altered in 1979 by the elevation of William McIntyre.

What can be said of the general trend in appointments to the Supreme Court over the past decade? First, one is struck by the extent of Pierre Trudeau's influence. Including Pigeon, chosen when Trudeau was minister of justice, he or his government appointed ten justices and two chief justices, equalling the record of Sir Wilfrid Laurier and exceeded only by Mackenzie King. Second, the eleven recently appointed justices tend to share several characteristics. Five justices did graduate study in law, and seven of eleven justices (including five of six from Quebec) taught law at the university level; judging by these criteria, this was the most learned and scholarly group of justices ever to join the Supreme Court. Eight of the appointees came to Ottawa with prior judicial experience, including all of the common-law justices; of the three civil-law justices who came directly from private practice, two resigned within a short time. This was a group of justices with judicial training and a healthy respect for the courts below. Although none of the justices had held elected office, a proliferation of non-elected government experience was reflected in the careers of five of the six civil-law appointees. The average age of the new justices was just over fifty-four (higher for the common-law members).

Speaking generally, the criteria for selection in this period were an improvement over the past. A better-educated, more experienced judiciary is a pleasing prospect, but with an average of twenty years ahead of each member at the Supreme Court there is a danger in the potential lack of rejuvenation and diversity. While the regional balance has been maintained, there have been some welcome signs of flexibility. The nominations of Laskin and Wilson make it apparent that the pool from which selections can be made has been broadened to include new groups, creating the potential for better appointments. Finally, there has been no apparent move to try to 'pack' the Supreme Court in any one identifiable direction. At the same time, the process of judicial selection has been improved. Under a series of justice ministers – Trudeau, Turner, and Lang – a system was established of submitting names to the Committee on the Judiciary of the Canadian Bar Association to obtain its views on prospective appointees prior to appointment. This procedure has been maintained by succeeding ministers and further improvements have been made.[8] This system has likely helped to raise the quality of the judiciary and to reassure the often critical legal profession.

Changes in the salary structure and pension benefits over the years enabled justices to be paid at a level consistent with their responsibilities and their earning power elsewhere. In the early 1950s, the chief justice received $25,000 and puisne justices $20,000; the salaries rose steadily, to $27,500 and $22,500 in 1955, $40,000 and $35,000 in 1967, and to $81,000 and $74,000 by 1980, when they were indexed to provide for annual increases.[9] Nevertheless, the increased salary and pension benefits (including survivor benefits) have not been sufficient to attract many leading lawyers to high judicial office. A top lawyer in any of the major metropolitan centres of Canada can today command an annual income of $300,000.[10] If such a lawyer wished to accept a puisne judgeship on the Supreme Court of Canada, he or she would have to take a 66 per cent reduction in salary. Most lawyers are not inclined to do so. One group of lawyers, however, would not be required to make such an enormous sacrifice. Full-time law professors, who emerged as a sizeable group beginning in the 1950s with the transfer of legal education to the universities, could not expect to make the income of a leading corporate lawyer. But an appointment to the bench with tenure to age seventy (superior courts) or seventy-five (the Supreme Court) and a good pension at a salary close to academic levels is attractive to academics. In addition, academic lawyers tend by profession to be drawn to the kind of work done in appeal courts. Law professors are constantly reading court judgments and critically seeking ways to improve the quality of the search for principles and the development of the law; hence the number of academics who accept appointments to the courts. The fact that Prime Minister Trudeau, Justice Minister Otto Lang, and Justice Minister Mark MacGuigan were law professors before entering politics made them amenable to appointing academics. Nevertheless, the appointment of academic lawyers to high judicial office is sometimes viewed critically by some members of the provincial bars because professors often lack practical legal experience.

Important changes were made to the Supreme Court Act and to the Court's jurisdiction under the Trudeau government. The previous Liberal government had declined to introduce such legislation for fear of opening the door to widespread attacks on the Court; as justice minister, Pierre Trudeau had accepted that decision. As soon as he became prime minister, however, the proposed amendments were brought forward.[11] In an atmosphere in which changes were positively considered, one of the most significant developments in the history of the Court's jurisdiction occurred.

By the early 1970s the workload at the Court had become overwhelming. In 1970 judgments were handed down in 137 cases (compared with 62 in 1950), and the increase was continuing. In the fall of 1971 it was announced that a record-breaking 115 cases were on the Supreme Court docket, many of which would have to be postponed until the following year for hearing. A number of these cases were arriving at the Court as a matter of right, involving no important issue of law but meeting the basic monetary requirement. Under the old act, any civil case involving more than $10,000 could be appealed to the Supreme Court as of right. The justices were required to spend much of their time (one estimate was over 70 per cent) on unimportant issues, and the large number of cases deprived the justices of much-needed time to give due consideration to the issues arising in the few major appeals. As well, the workload pressures forced the justices to deal summarily with many minor cases; in 1973, for example, one-third of all cases were disposed of orally from the bench at the conclusion of argument.[12]

The effort to find ways of limiting appeals was hampered by the Supreme Court's duty to supervise the provincial courts of appeal; that responsibility cannot be restricted to cases of public importance. The Court also has a duty to grant leave to appeal in civil-law cases that are not of general importance throughout Canada. Finally, there are areas of law (such as tort, damages, contract, and wills and trusts) that are rarely touched by legislation and in which review by the Supreme Court is especially important. In short, the Court could not function as a general court of appeal for Canada if access to it was limited drastically.

Various proposals were put forward to deal with the problem. The government chose to begin to limit access to the Court for less important cases judged from the point of view of the law. In 1970 an amendment ended appeals by right in cases involving questions of fact alone, but broadened access otherwise.[13] This did not have a major impact.

The justice minister, John Turner, began to mention publicly the possibility of ending all appeals as of right. As in the case of the 1970 changes, Turner consulted leading members of the Canadian Bar Association. By the end of 1974 a new minister of justice was ready to pilot through the House legislation ending appeal to the Supreme Court as of right (except in criminal cases where there was a dissent in the Court of Appeal)[14] and withdrawing all monetary criteria for access to the Supreme Court. Instead, the justices were given authority to grant leave to appeal on the basis of whether in their judgment the case involved an issue of public importance or of legal significance. Section 55 of the Supreme Court Act obliging the justices to hear reference cases remained intact. While aimed at solving the workload problem, such changes in the Supreme Court's jurisdiction had great potential for the quality and import of the judgments handed down. The most noticeable result of the revised act is a dramatic decrease in private-law appeals; there has been scarcely any change in public-law cases. One characteristic of this development has been a reduction of Civil Code appeals from Quebec, since such cases are private-law disputes.[15]

In response to this new freedom to determine its own docket, the Court has adopted a set of informal guidelines. Criminal appeals, even of cases in which there was no dissent in the Court of Appeal, are deemed to be of public importance. This practice, coupled with the introduction of legal aid throughout Canada, has caused the number of criminal cases to rise over the past few years. In 1977, for example, the Court heard thirty-two criminal appeals; in 1975 only two were heard.

If the appeal involves constitutional law, leave is granted almost automatically. If the Court has not had an opportunity to consider the point of law at issue, it grants leave. In civil matters the justices tend to require that the statute in dispute exist in more than one province or be of such importance that it is likely to have implications for other provinces.

Finally, the Court is especially vigilant in cases involving House of Lords precedents. If the House of Lords reverses itself on a case that has been relied upon in the lower courts or in the Supreme Court, then the justices grant leave in order to give themselves an opportunity to bring Canadian law into line with the new development.[16] The Supreme Court justices continue to grant special deference to the senior appellate tribunal in the common-law world.

Unfortunately, the evidence so far is that this control over appeals has not substantially altered the number of cases being considered by the judges. Apart from the fact that motions for leave have naturally increased in number,[17] the total number of cases heard has declined by more than 30 per cent between 1975 and 1980. However, it appears that the number of cases is now beginning to rise once again.[18] This raises the question as to whether the justices are being firm enough in insisting on the presence of significant issues; are their standards of importance high enough? The statistics of recent years indicate that the Court grants between 25 and 30 per cent of the applications for leave.[19]

The first sign that the justices of the Supreme Court were taking some advantage of these developments came with changes in the internal decision-making process. Although the idea of regular judicial conferences had been put forward over the years by several chief justices, their influence and powers of persuasion were insufficient to overcome the strong sense of individualism among many of the justices. Under the leadership of John Cartwright this changed. Ever since his brief term as chief justice, a system of regular judicial conferences has become the practice. At the end of argument in a case, the justices usually retire to consider the appeal. The issues are discussed briefly – the most junior justice speaking first – and a straw vote taken; one justice volunteers to write the initial reasons for judgment; where there is no obvious choice the chief justice designates the writer. The draft judgment is circulated for comments and possible alterations, by which time other members of the Court are able to decide with some certainty whether a separate judgment (either concurring or dissenting) is necessary.[20]

Another positive sign was the justices' increasing awareness and thoughtfulness regarding the judicial function and their role as judges. This is evident, for example, in the writings of Emmett Hall, L.-P. Pigeon, Bora Laskin, and Brian Dickson.[21]

On the whole, the judgments written during the 1970s were simply of higher quality than earlier judgments. The justices have demonstrated a greater (though by no means complete) willingness to come to grips with the basic issues and principles involved in cases, rather than limiting themselves to technicalities or to superficial issues. Paul Weiler, who was so critical of the Court's judicial craftsmanship during the 1960s, was far more positive about the Supreme Court by 1979, pointing particularly to the improvement in 'the entire intellectual tone of the court.' Weiler attributed this largely to Chief Justice Laskin, but the source was broader than that.[22] Without denying the chief justice's important influence, several of the other new justices also have impressive academic backgrounds and are sensitive to the search for principles rather than the mechanical application of rules. As a result, some justices (Dickson, Estey, and Lamer, for example), have given every indication that they are aware of the creative role of the judicial function in the Supreme Court. There is a greater sense of intellectual self-confidence among the justices. Stare decisis is no longer the crutch it once was; the justices are willing to acknowledge that previous decisions of their own or of others should no longer be followed.[23] In *McNamara Construction* (1977)[24] for example, the Court explicitly overruled an 1894 judgment it had relied upon during the intervening years.

This is not to imply that the Court as a whole had jettisoned its past conservatism. A basic deep-seated judicial conservatism remains. Chief Justice Laskin, for example, because of his propensity for bolder juris-prudence, was frequently in dissent. His creative efforts often came into conflict with the Court majority in cases such as in *Murdoch* v *Murdoch* (1975)[25] before he became chief justice. In that case an Alberta rancher's wife claimed a half-interest in the real property (not just the homestead) acquired through the work of both spouses over twenty-five years of marriage. Justice Martland, writing for the 4–1 majority, held that the wife had failed to prove a financial contribution to the growth of her husband's assets and that her claims on the basis of a contribution of physical labour were unacceptable. To the lay person the Court seemed to be saying that twenty-five years' work as a rancher's wife was of no value in law. What the majority actually said was that such work did not alter the conception of marriage as a simple legal contract.

Justice Laskin, in dissent, showed a genuinely imaginative approach to the issues which at this time were on the minds of many women throughout Canada. In a clear and crisp tone readily picked up by the media, Laskin argued that the common-law tradition urged courts to be innovative in such circumstances:

No doubt, legislative action may be the better way to lay down policies and prescribe conditions under which and the extent to which spouses should share in property acquired by either or both during marriage. But the better way is not the only way; and if the exercise of a traditional jurisdiction by the Courts can conduce to equitable sharing, it should not be withheld merely because difficulties in particular cases and the making of distinctions may result in a slower and perhaps more painful evolution of principle.[26]

This was the kind of logic the average person could understand. One CBC radio reporter hailed Laskin as a 'jurisprudential folk hero.'[27]

The Murdoch decision brought the Supreme Court under the full scrutiny of public opinion. Laskin fared well, but the Court as a whole was widely assailed as being out of step with the times. Unable to appreciate the legal complexities of Martland's majority judgment, the general public – especially women – disapproved of the decision; several feminists compared it to the famous *Persons* case decided a half-century earlier. Once again, the Court had 'failed' to live up to public expectations. The public was unable to understand fine legal distinctions, and the Supreme Court was made to appear reactionary and anti-feminist. One magazine headlined its story about the decision, 'The Law as Male Chauvinist Pig.'[28] The justices were blamed for the weaknesses of provincial legislation in the area of family law and for their own traditional unwillingness to give leadership in solving legislative problems.

Not many months after *Murdoch*, Laskin again found himself in dissent on the important question of admissible evidence. In *Hogan* v *The Queen* (1975)[29] the Court majority, led by Ritchie, ruled that evidence obtained in contravention of the terms of the Canadian Bill of Rights was admissible in court. Laskin, in dissent with Spence, argued for the absolute exclusionary rule.[30] 'The American exclusionary rule, in enforcement of constitutional guarantees, is as much a judicial creation,' Laskin argued, 'as the common law of admissibility.' As in *Murdoch*, Laskin was inviting his colleagues to adopt a more activist understanding of the judicial function. But the majority was too firmly entrenched in the older common-law view that all relevant evidence, no matter how obtained, was to be admitted against an accused.

In criminal law the conservatism of the mid-1970s was also manifest. It was apparent in several cases,[31] but nowhere was it more evident to the public than in the highly publicized case of *Morgentaler* v *The Queen* (1976).[32] Henry Morgentaler, a Montreal physician, had been charged with performing an illegal abortion on a seventeen-year old female in violation of section 251 of the Criminal Code. The doctor freely admitted performing the operation, but cited the common-law defence of necessity and the statutory defence of section 45 of the Criminal Code. A jury acquitted Morgentaler, but the Quebec Court of Appeal unanimously set aside the verdict; instead of ordering a retrial, the Court entered a conviction of the doctor and ordered that sentence be passed. In the Supreme Court of Canada, three dissenting justices (led once again by Chief Justice Bora Laskin) held that there was evidence the jury could interpret to support Morgentaler's defence and that the verdict should properly be left to the jury. The six-person majority, however, denied that the two basic grounds of defence were available to him in this instance;

the justices also found the entry of a verdict of guilty by an appeal court to have been permitted by statute, though this was 'obviously a power to be used with great circumspection.' The Supreme Court majority found that Parliament had explicitly provided by statute for both issues, that of abortion and that of substitution of a verdict by jury. Given the past history of the Court and the strength of the statutory terms, it is not surprising that most of the justices could not find a way to interpret the statute in a manner more favourable to Morgentaler. In a typically perceptive majority judgment, Justice Dickson made it clear that the Court was not called upon 'to decide, or even to enter, the loud and continuous public debate on abortion.' The case before the Court revolved around the technical provisions of the Criminal Code relating to necessity as a defence for a medical practitioner.

For the public, however, the issue was far less technical. Abortion was a sensitive issue and emotions ran high. For those supporting more permissive abortion laws, Dr Morgentaler was a martyr to the cause; feminists in this group could see a link between this decision and others, such as *Lavell*, *Bédard*,[33] and *Murdoch*. Some observers saw Morgentaler as a victim of an aggressive and persecuting state; he was perceived as 'the little guy,' harassed in jail, driven to a heart attack and bankruptcy, and hounded with further criminal charges. One headline read: 'Condamné aujourd'hui par la Cour suprême, le Dr. Morgentaler sera demain un héros.'[34] In this scenario the Supreme Court was clearly viewed as one of several state instruments being used to persecute the doctor and to preserve a sexist and illiberal law.

Justice Brian Dickson's majority judgment in *Morgentaler* was carefully crafted, and described what the Court was and was not being asked to do. This and other judgments have earned for Dickson respect and admiration from the Canadian bench and bar. Although he frequently joined in dissent with Laskin and Spence, Dickson demonstrated an independence of judgment in the important areas of constitutional and criminal law. His dissenting judgment in *Canadian Industrial Gas and Oil Limited*[35] showed him at his best in tough constitutional matters. His judgment there, as elsewhere, was meticulously researched, cogently reasoned, and written with a clarity and economy of style rarely found in the Supreme Court Reports.

Justice Dickson stands out as the best criminal-law mind on the Ottawa bench. His contribution to criminal jurisprudence has been nothing short of outstanding. It was Dickson who in *The Queen* v *Sault Ste Marie* (1978)[36] untangled the many knots in the law of mens rea.[37] Writing for a full nine-man Court, Dickson charted a new course in the difficult matter of liability in public-welfare offences such as pollution. After acknowledging that public-welfare offences were the product of judicial creation and now firmly imbedded in Canadian jurisprudence, Dickson reviewed the arguments for and against absolute liability. The past tendency was for courts to adopt a requirement of mens rea in every instance (which was most difficult to substantiate) or to impose absolute liability on the defendant and convict simply upon proof of the offence without regard to intention to commit the actus reus. Dickson felt that these 'two stark alternatives' were unfair. A half-way house must accommodate a valid public effort to prohibit public-welfare offences. And since the category of public-welfare offence as well as the concept of absolute liability were products of the judiciary, the courts need not wait for legislative remedies. Between mens rea offences and absolute liability offences, Dickson inserted a third category: 'Offences in which there is no necessity for the prosecution to prove the existence of *mens rea*; the doing of the prohibited act *prima facie* imports the offence, leaving it open to the accused to avoid liability by proving that he took all reasonable care.' This new category permits consideration of what a reasonable man would do in the circumstances. The Court settled a nagging problem for governments, who were attempting to impose strict environmental standards, and for the lower courts in their effort to apply the law. Dickson was widely applauded for his leadership in this important issue.[38]

The Supreme Court as a whole emerges in *Sault Ste Marie* as a mature and sophisticated institution, and demonstrates that it has the capacity to respond when there is effective leadership. Justice Dickson represents the cautious transition from the older conservatism to a bolder jurisprudence. He is not as bold as Laskin, yet he is prepared to strike out in new directions when required to do so. It is not an exaggeration to say that Brian Dickson, not Bora Laskin, was the most influential justice on the Ottawa bench during Laskin's stewardship. Chief Justice Laskin appeared to go too far too fast for most members of the Court. It is too early, however, to say how influential over time his dissenting judgments will prove to be. There can be no doubt that his influence on other justices has not been as strong as many in 1973 expected it would be.

The Supreme Court was caught in the crossfires of intense federal-provincial rivalry many times throughout the late 1970s, especially in matters relating to natural resources and trade. Several contentious cases arose out of private litigation, and a few were the result of federal or provincial references to the Court. In the 1976 *Anti-Inflation* case,[39] the federal government asked the Supreme Court whether the Anti-Inflation Act was in whole or in part ultra vires the power of Parliament. Chief Justice Laskin led a majority of seven in finding the act intra vires, although the reasons of the majority differed. (Laskin found the act intra vires on the ground that the crisis was temporary. Three members of the majority – Ritchie, Martland, and Pigeon – sided with Beetz and de Grandpré in dissent on the legal point that the federal government could legislate under the head of peace, order, and good government in times of emergency. The three in majority found that an emergency existed, while the two dissenting justices held that double-digit inflation did not constitute an emergency.)

The federal government won the day in that judgment, but the Court's restriction of the power of Parliament under the head of peace, order, and good government in times of emergency was hailed as a victory by the provinces. Provinces such as Quebec, British Columbia, and Saskatchewan welcomed the decision. They applauded wage and price controls, but they did not want the federal government to enter such areas of activity easily. The victory for the federal government, however, cannot be underestimated. It was the first time the Court had held valid the exercise of broad federal economic regulation in peacetime. The Court placed the burden on those who challenged the federal government in this instance and in the future to prove that the conditions did not require emergency legislation.

The Laskin majority pointedly set aside the testimony of thirty-nine leading Canadian economists who argued in facta (written submissions to the Court) that a 10 per cent inflation rate did not call for an emergency response. The economists also rejected wage and price controls as an ineffective and economically unwise measure, but Chief Justice Laskin dismissed this assessment as irrelevant to the legal and constitutional issues of the case. The fact that the government had resolutely refused to call the measure emergency legislation had no impact on the seven justices in the majority.

The Court suffered in the press accounts of this judgment. Some economists charged that the justices had substituted their views of economic policy for that of Canadian economists.[40] In addition, several provinces expressed fears that the decision gave Parliament too-easy access to emergency legislation. In sum, the case did much to confirm Laskin in the minds of many as being pro-centralist.

Two years after the *Anti-Inflation* decision, the Supreme Court found itself in a heated dispute between the federal government and the province of Saskatchewan. The New Democratic government of Alan Blakeney attempted to reap the benefit of the windfall profits destined for oil-company coffers following the OPEC increase in oil prices in 1973. The Saskatchewan legislature imposed a 'royalty surcharge' on oil and gas production equal to the difference between the old price and the new world price set by the international oil cartel. Several provincial governments intervened in the Supreme Court on behalf of Saskatchewan; the federal government intervened on behalf of the Canadian Industrial Gas and Oil Company. What started out as a private dispute between one provincial government and a small oil and natural gas company became a battleground of major proportions involving important constitutional matters.

In a 7–2 decision, the Court ruled against Saskatchewan. All nine justices agreed that the surcharge was in fact a tax. Seven of the justices led by Justice Martland concluded that the tax was indirect and hence ultra vires the legislature. The majority held that since 98 per cent of the oil was exported abroad or to other parts of Canada, the taxes constituted an invasion of the federal authority over international and interprovincial trade.

Justice Dickson, in a typically systematic judgment, argued in dissent that the province had plenary power over natural resources 'subject to limits imposed by the Canadian constitution.' He reasoned that the flow of gas and oil in interprovincial and international trade was not impeded by the surcharge; the tax does not set the price, 'price sets the tax.' He concluded that the surcharge and minimal income tax imposed by Saskatchewan were actually direct taxes and hence within the competence of the provincial legislature.

Dickson's dissenting judgment in this case was imaginative and cogent. To many observers his arguments were more persuasive than the majority's, but they were of small comfort to Premier Blakeney. Both Saskatchewan and Alberta called for changes in the Supreme Court and for new constitutional concessions in regulating non-renewable natural resources. Subsequent events in Parliament, however, brought partial consolation to the provinces. In order to secure the support of the federal NDP, the Liberal government consented to incorporate into the new constitutional resolution an amendment empowering the provinces to impose 'any mode or system of taxation' on non-renewable natural resources.

Scarcely a year after this decision the province of Saskatchewan was back in the Supreme Court, but this time the federal government joined the suit as a co-plaintiff along with the Central Potash Company. In *Central Potash Co. and The Attorney-General of Canada* v *The Government of Saskatchewan* (1979),[41] the Supreme Court ruled unanimously that the province of Saskatchewan's potash prorationing scheme was unconstitutional. Five other provinces – Quebec, New Brunswick, Manitoba, Alberta, and Newfoundland – intervened on behalf of Saskatchewan. The Supreme Court ruled that the scheme constituted an invasion of the federal legislative authority over interprovincial and international trade in part on the basis of the *Canadian Industrial Gas and Oil* precedent. The judgment was a culmination of a line of Supreme Court judgments going back to 1957 and the *Ontario Farm Products Reference*[42] in which the Court resolutely refused the provinces access into international and interprovincial trade.

Not surprisingly, the public reaction to this judgment of the central government's strong position, coming so fast upon the heels of the *Canadian Industrial Gas and Oil* judgment, was one of censure. The Court once again was perceived as incapable of altering its pro-Ottawa stance. Charges of bias were openly levelled against the Court after it ruled against the provinces in two broadcasting cases the same year as the *Canadian Industrial Gas and Oil* case. The criticisms became so strident that the chief justice took the unusual course of responding through the *Law Society of Upper Canada Gazette*.[43] Professor Peter W. Hogg explored the charges in the *Canadian Bar Review*. He concluded after a review of the cases that 'the Supreme Court has generally adhered to the doctrine laid down by the Privy Council precedents ... the choices between competing lines of reasoning have favoured the provincial interest at least as often as they have the federal interest.'[44]

Two judgments in 1980 favouring the provinces tend to support Hogg's review of the issue.[45] Peter Russell, after discussing the most recent cases and those cases in which the Supreme Court upheld provincial incursions into the domain of criminal law, concluded that the Court had demonstrated 'a considerable balance in [its] approach to the division of powers.'[46]

The public perception of the Court as an instrument of central power persisted and was reinforced by the federal government's use of the reference procedure in such contentious matters as offshore resources ownership. The government of Newfoundland, for example, in an effort to ascertain its legal rights over offshore minerals, referred its claim to the Newfoundland Supreme Court in 1982. The Ottawa government attempted to short-circuit this process by referring essentially the same issues directly to the Supreme Court of Canada. This created the impression of a provincial appellate court being played off against the central court of appeal. An inappropriate sense of conflict within the judicial structure was perceived, and the impression was given that the courts at each level were the instruments of the governments at that level. This compounded an existing feeling among the provinces that the Supreme Court of Canada was a federal political instrument to be used against the provinces.[47] Such a perception could seriously inhibit the Supreme Court's effective pursuit of its role as constitutional umpire. The Court, fully aware of these potential problems, adopted ways of meeting them. For example, the Court has declined to hear a reference or has delayed a judgment until the provincial court of appeal has ruled on an issue. In short, it has devised internal procedures to reduce the possibility of political manipulation. Unfortunately, the justices cannot refuse to hear reference cases; the best they can do is delay or rephrase the questions put to them in order to minimize their involvement in political issues.

As if the cases involving trade and commerce were not sufficient to draw the Supreme Court into the vortex of federal-provincial conflict, worse was yet to come. The acrimonious debate in Parliament over the newly returned Trudeau government's determination to pursue unilateral amendment of the constitution eventually shifted to the Court. The prime minister resolutely refused to send the 'patriation resolution' on reference to the Supreme Court. Trudeau consistently claimed that there was no need to test its constitutionality. The Conservative opposition just as stubbornly insisted that it ought to be tested. The opposition charged that the intention to proceed without the consent of the provinces was a violation of Canadian constitutional practice.

A variety of political groups, from native peoples to provincial governments, all espousing different causes, turned to the Court to put an end to a political impasse. The justices were soon thrust into the midst of political controversy. Manitoba,[48] Quebec,[49] and Newfoundland [50] initiated reference procedures in provincial Courts of Appeal. The results of those judgments were split: the Manitoba court (3–2) and the Quebec court (4–1) ruled that provincial consent was not required, while the Newfoundland court ruled unanimously that provincial consent was required. A total of seven provincial appeal court judges had ruled the unilateral patriation route valid, and six members of the same provincial courts had ruled the process invalid. The narrow division of opinion prompted the Conservatives to increase their pressure on the government to postpone patriation until the Supreme Court of Canada heard the three appeals. This the Trudeau government reluctantly agreed to do. The public pressure through the Conservatives and the press was simply too strong for the government to resist. As well, reports from London indicated that some members of the British government were disposed to balk at the request for patriation if Trudeau proceeded unilaterally. These reports added weight to the domestic opposition . At length the Trudeau government bowed to the pressures and referred the patriation resolution to the Supreme Court.[51]

The case came to the Supreme Court as of right in the spring of 1981. No fewer than thirty-eight lawyers representing the federal and provincial governments and interested parties (such as the Four Nations Confederacy) marshalled arguments for and against the essential point of the case: was consent of the provinces required before the federal government could seek an amendment to the constitution in matters touching provincial powers? For five days the eyes and ears of the country were focused on the Supreme Court. Never before in its history – not even during the Bennett New Deal cases or the Truscott trial – had the Court received such concentrated public attention; newspapers and television cameras reported at length the arguments for and against unilateral patriation. A parade of experts appeared on television and in the press, all attempting to second-guess the outcome. Most observers confidently predicted a 'win' for the federal government. Some experts drew attention to the chief justice's alleged tendency to support the federal course in most disputes with the provinces, and almost all noted that six of the nine justices owed their places on the Court to Prime Minister Trudeau. No one was more aware of the views of the press and the commentators than the justices themselves. The issue of patriation had been debated heatedly in public and private for many months. Members of the Court were conscious of the invidious position in which they had been placed, and their judgment was a reflection of the clarity of that understanding.

After taking the entire summer to consider the arguments, the judgment was handed down at the end of September 1981. The Court showed that it would not be hurried by expressions of impatience on the part of a few politicians and members of the media. The results were not nearly as unequivocal as either side would have wished, but they were sufficiently acceptable to both that each claimed the ruling a victory for its cause. In an effort to reduce any possibility of partisanship, the individual authorship of the various judgments was deliberately unstated.

The Supreme Court ruled unanimously that the patriation resolution affected federal-provincial relations and the powers of the provincial legislatures. On the central issue of whether constitutional practice or convention imposed the requirement of provincial consent, the Court's ruling was mixed and confusing. Six of the justices held that a constitutional convention existed requiring 'a substantial degree of provincial consent' for federal requests to amend the British North America Act. The justices refused to say how many provinces constituted 'a substantial degree.' A larger majority (7–2) ruled that constitutional conventions were enforceable in the political forum, not in the courts. The six justices reached this conclusion after a lengthy discussion of what constituted a constitutional convention. The majority – consisting of Martland, Ritchie, Dickson, Beetz, Chouinard, and Lamer – reasoned that the federal character of the Canadian constitution militated against unilateral modification of provincial powers. Yet they drew back from legally enforcing this federal principle.

The minority, consisting of Chief Justice Laskin, Justice Estey, and Justice McIntyre, said that they were required to answer whether unanimous consent of the provinces was necessary. They found that there was no basis for unanimous consent. They implied that the majority's finding that a 'substantial degree of provincial consent' was required amounted to an agreement that unanimous consent was not required. The dissenters also disagreed with the federal principle emphasized by the majority. They found that the overriding power of the federal government under the British North America Act was too strong to permit a restraint of provincial prior consent.

The results of this judgment were relayed to the general public in such headlines as, 'PM's bid "offends" but is legal'.[52] How, many wondered, could something be legal and yet unconstitutional? There can be no denying that the judgment was difficult for the average citizen to understand, especially when many anti-Trudeau politicians insisted that the Court had ruled against the patriation proposal. What the Court actually said was that the unilateral request for amendment was legal (no law was being violated) but unconstitutional in the conventional sense (the government was violating a rule of constitutional practice). The Court held that such practices or rules of behaviour in constitutional matters are not enforceable in law.

The reaction of the academic commentators to the judgment was severe. Peter Russell, for example, acknowledged the boldness of the statecraft in the judgment but questioned the quality of the jurisprudence.[53] Russell and others also questioned the propriety of a court providing a judicial determination of a subject that had just been pronounced non-judicial. As well, the Court's absolute divorce between law and convention was, at best, strained. It was not an impressive collective effort. For a case that was hailed as the most momentous in the Court's history and the most important opinion in one hundred years, it was a great disappointment jurisprudentially.

The judgment sent the federal and provincial constitutional experts back to the drawing-board five weeks after it was rendered. The renewed negotiations resulted in several significant modifications and the eventual endorsement of nine of the ten provinces. To that vital extent the Supreme Court played an important role in solving a highly contentious public issue. In 1972 Richard Simeon had criticized the Court for its weakness as a federal-provincial arbitrator or mediator.[54] The Supreme Court's role in the constitutional crisis of 1981 and the increasing frequency with which politicians of all parties and governments were referring political problems to the courts seemed to indicate that the Supreme Court of Canada was beginning to play a major role in the Canadian federal system. The question remains, however, whether it was proper for the Court to play such a role, at least in this instance. The Court is saved future embarrassment over this judgment for the simple reason that the issues it dealt with will never arise again. The new constitution incorporates an amendment formula, taking the matter out of the realm of convention and placing it in the category of law.

The constitutional reference ended one era and ushered in a new one: the era of the Charter of Rights and Freedoms. It is no exaggeration to say that the Constitution Act, 1982, will prove to be the most significant development in the history of the Supreme Court of Canada. There can be no doubt that this act constitutes a major change in the way Canadians will be governed in the future. Not only does the new constitution retreat from the traditional reliance on the political process and politicians, it imposes on the Canadian courts – and especially on the Supreme Court – a policy-making role in the areas of social justice and minority-language rights. Under the new Charter of Rights and Freedoms the Supreme Court is required to supervise any action on the part of the federal and provincial governments to restrict basic rights and freedoms.[55] Any restrictions must be 'reasonable' and 'demonstrably justified in a free and democratic society.' Since the written constitution (including the old British North America Act as amended) now encompasses so much of the fundamental law of the land, the Supreme Court faces a greater responsibility in seeing that that law is maintained. No previous constitutional act relating to Canada has transferred such sweeping powers to the judiciary as the Constitution Act, 1982.

The Charter of Rights and Freedoms provision (in section 24) encourages private citizens to seek redress of grievances in the courts, and will inevitably result in an increase in litigation in the lower courts. Many of these cases will eventually reach the Supreme Court.[56] In the first fifteen months of the Charter's existence, more than six hundred lower-court cases involved Charter provisions. Several of the more important of those cases are on their way to the Supreme Court. In effect, the Constitution Act, 1982, comes as close as possible, without explicitly doing so, to entrenching the Supreme Court of Canada because so wide a range of issues has now become justiciable. The Court is now called upon to determine the limits of the constitutionally enshrined values in the Charter of Rights and Freedoms.

As a result of this new judicial power, there will undoubtedly be calls for changes to the method of appointment to the Supreme Court in order to provide provincial input. The amendment formula specifically provides that the composition of the Supreme Court can be altered only with the unanimous consent of the federal Parliament and the ten provincial legislative assemblies.[57] The general jurisdiction of the Court can be altered with the consent of the federal Parliament and two-thirds of the legislatures constituting 50 per cent of the population of the country. Formerly, Parliament could alter the size and jurisdiction without consulting the provinces.

This is not to ignore the constitutional provision for legislative override. Under section 33 the federal Parliament and the provincial legislatures may expressly exempt a legislative provision from the terms of the Charter relating to fundamental political freedoms and legal and equality rights. (The override expires after five years but can be renewed.) Some commentators feel that this process is too uncertain and cumbersome to serve as a way of avoiding judicial power. The Quebec government of René Lévesque has attached the 'notwithstanding' clause to every piece of provincial legislation since the adoption of the new constitution (which Quebec refused to endorse). It remains to be seen whether the Supreme Court will allow such a general application of the override provision. Under the terms of the Charter's general grant of standing to sue (section 24) a private citizen could challenge this Quebec procedure.[58]

The Supreme Court has been catapulted into a prominence unsurpassed in its previous history. Under the new constitution the Court is implicitly mandated to impose uniform national rights and liberties. Grave reservations arise as to the capacity or desirability of judges to play this important role. The history of the Canadian Supreme Court reveals a deeply conservative judiciary; only the rare justice – such as Chief Justice Bora Laskin – falls easily into the category of judicial innovator. This invitation to judicial change has been viewed as politicizing the courts. Russell calls the Charter 'a tendency to judicialize politics and politicize the judiciary.' The essential problem posed by the new Charter, according to Russell, is the potential for over-judicializing. 'The danger here is not so much that non-elected judges will impose their own will on a democratic majority, but that questions of social and political justice will be transformed into technical legal questions and the bulk of the citizenry who are not judges and lawyers will abdicate their responsibility for working out reasonable and mutually acceptable resolutions of the issues which divide them.'[59]

It is clear that the new Charter makes many more issues litigious and increases the pressure on Canadian courts to provide judicially enforceable judgments in matters that are not easily amenable to such enforcement. The Charter increases the need for litigation at a time when governments are attempting to use privative clauses and conciliation forums to avoid the courts in disputes involving social issues such as labor relations and human-rights conflicts. It is conceivable that the new Charter will negate much of this effort to bypass the courts. Canadians, in short, run the risk under the new constitution of becoming as litigious as Americans.

A closer scrutiny of appointments to the Court and a fuller understanding of its judgments will be required in future years. The Court has been forced by the Constitution Act to become more active in supervising the content of public policy. Many issues that were private now become public. And since many of the contentious issues of the Charter of Rights and Freedoms already have been litigated in the United States Supreme Court, Canadians can expect American civil liberties jurisprudence to enter Canadian law.

The justices on the present Court will constitute the high bench in the crucial first decades of the new Charter. Are they prepared by training and disposition to assume the new responsibilities given them? Perhaps more important, are the politicians who redefined the judicial function so radically in the Charter of Rights and Freedoms prepared to accept the restraints these non-elected public officials will surely impose? Only one thing is certain: the prologue is over. The Supreme Court has achieved a degree of institutional independence and a broad mandate unequalled by any other judicial body in the Western world. In every sense of the term, the post-Charter years will be a new era for the Supreme Court of Canada and the Canadian political system.

Epilogue

The year 1982 ended a period of change and development that had been underway at the Supreme Court of Canada at least since 1949. Freed from binding colonial influences, the Court slowly came to be regarded as an institution of national significance. Well aware of the stature and influence of the United States Supreme Court, particularly under Chief Justice Earl Warren, Canadians became more comfortable with the idea of an activist court defending various rights and liberties while not actually having to live in the unsettling environment produced by such activism. This period of acclimatization at a distance paved the way for two major adjustments in the Canadian Supreme Court. In 1975, the Court gained control over its own docket, allowing it to focus attention on more important legal issues. In 1982, the Charter of Rights and Freedoms was enacted, holding out to Canadians the promise that the Supreme Court would provide greater judicial protection of fundamental rights and liberties. The ambiguity and confusion concerning the role of the Supreme Court of Canada had finally been resolved.

By 1984 it had become clear that the Charter was having an important impact on the work and the decisions of the Canadian judicial system. During the two years after the adoption of the Charter of Rights and Freedoms, the lower courts of Canada had heard more than 1,000 cases involving the Charter. The result has been a diversity of interpretation in important matters; this diversity will eventually have to be resolved by the Supreme Court of Canada. At present both lawyers and lower-court judges are free to test their understanding of the Charter provisions. In this environment it is incumbent on the Supreme Court of Canada to provide the leadership and guidance so badly needed by the Canadian judicial and legal systems.

To the end of 1984, the Supreme Court had handed down only two decisions relating to the Charter. In *Skapinker* v *Law Society of Upper Canada* (1984),[1] the first Charter case, a unanimous Supreme Court declined to use the Charter to strike down the section of the Law Society Act requiring that a lawyer be a Canadian citizen before being admitted to practice in Ontario. Skapinker had argued that the mobility provision of the Charter negated the citizenship requirement of the Ontario act. The Supreme Court refused to interpret the mobility provisions of the Charter as guaranteeing the 'right to work,' as Skapinker had argued. While prepared to adopt the 'living tree' approach of the Judicial Committee, the justices revealed a cautious disposition toward the Charter; they explicitly affirmed the need to balance 'flexibility ... with certainty'[2] in its interpretation. In *Hunter* v *Southam* (1984)[3] a unanimous Court struck down the search-and-seizure provisions of the Combines Investigation Act. The Court ruled that searches conducted without a warrant are prima facie unreasonable under the Charter of Rights. Chief Justice Dickson seemed to serve notice that the Court was assigning the Charter a major place in the law of the land. 'The Constitution of Canada, which includes the Canadian Charter of Rights and Freedoms, is the supreme law of Canada. Any law inconsistent with the provisions of the constitution is, to the extent of the inconsistency, of no force or effect.'

As the Court faced the initial influx of Charter cases, the chief justiceship became vacant following the death of Bora Laskin in March 1984. Laskin, who had not been well for some time, had been unable to provide the sort of administrative leadership he might have wished. In his place, Prime Minister Pierre Trudeau named Brian Dickson, who had been a prominent and positive influence on the Court for the past decade. Highly regarded by the bar for his sensitively reasoned, articulate judgments, Dickson was well qualified to lead the Court through its first decade of Charter law.

In May 1984, shortly before leaving office, the Trudeau government filled the remaining vacancy by appointing Gerald LeDain of the Federal Court of Canada a puisne justice of the Supreme Court. LeDain was born and educated in Montreal; he graduated from McGill University Law School in 1949. After graduate studies at the University of Lyon, LeDain returned to Montreal, where he spent several years in private practice and as professor of law at McGill University. In 1967 he became dean of law at Osgoode Hall Law School in Toronto. During this time he served as chairman of the Federal Commission of Inquiry into the Non-medical Use of Drugs. He was appointed to the Federal Court of Appeal in 1975. LeDain brought to the Ottawa bench nine years of court experience and a solid reputation in constitutional and administrative-law scholarship.[4]

In November 1984, after twenty-five years on the bench, Justice Ritchie retired from the Court owing to poor health. The new Conservative government of Brian Mulroney named Gérard Vincent LaForest to fill this vacancy. Born and raised in New Brunswick, LaForest brought to the Supreme Court a wide experience in the law. Several years as counsel were complemented by considerable scholarly work, both as a member of university law faculties and as author of a number of highly regarded publications, particularly in constitutional and administrative law. He was an official of the federal Department of Justice (1952–5 and 1970–4) and a member of the Law Reform Commission of Canada (1974–9). In June 1981 he was appointed to the New Brunswick Court of Appeal.[5]

Justice LaForest was executive vice-chairman and director of research for a Canadian Bar Foundation study entitled *Towards a New Canada*. In the section of that study dealing with the judicial power, the authors recommended that all appointments to the Supreme Court of Canada should be made 'with the consent of a Judiciary Committee of a reconstituted Upper House working in camera.'[6] As well, the study urged that formal consultation with the provinces be undertaken before anyone was appointed to the Supreme Court. The report goes into detail about the kinds of cases the Court ought to hear and counsels strongly against its moving in the direction of becoming a constitutional court. In short, few new members of the Court have had the benefit of prior reflection on as many issues relating to the work of the Supreme Court as Justice LaForest.

Although the opportunity of appointing the first Newfoundlander to the Supreme Court was missed, LaForest's appointment maintained the traditional regional balance on the Court and provided the sort of expertise thought to be needed in the face of the wave of Charter cases. The rising intellectual quality of the appointments made by the Trudeau government was maintained.

It is hoped that the reinvigorated bench will assist in dealing more efficiently with the Supreme Court's increasing workload. Motions for leave to appeal have been growing in number. In the decade from 1970–1 to 1980–1, the number rose from 158 motions to 431, largely under the impact of the amendments to the Supreme Court Act in 1975. But that number continues to increase; there were 501 motions for leave to appeal in 1983.[7] In 1983 the Court heard and rendered judgment in just eighty-nine cases, a 25 per cent decrease from the average over the previous five years.[8] Reduced efficiency, the rising number of motions for leave, the additional impact of the large number of Charter-related cases, and the recent trend toward a system that relies heavily on a full panel of judges together create an important administrative problem for the Supreme Court. As Peter Russell has commented:

As the Supreme Court of Canada enters the new era of the Charter it appears to be an institution under stress. The significance of its work is approaching that of the United States Supreme Court. As Canadians observe a decline in its decision-making capacity they may well question its modus operandi and ask why it has so much difficulty handling the demands placed upon it when the same number of Supreme Court justices in the United States can process over 4,000 applications to be heard, decide well over 100 cases a year and follow a decision-making system in which all nine judges participate in every case.[9]

For many decades the Canadian public and political leaders neither expected nor allowed the Supreme Court of Canada to become a conspicuous and influential institution. Viewed in our political and legal culture as a body subsidiary to the legislature and the political executive, the Court occupied an ambiguous place in the judicial hierarchy and was used as a minor political instrument at the disposal of the federal government. Gradually, the Canadian public and bar came to demand greater independence for the judiciary and to expect a more important contribution to the character and quality of society by a more capable group of judges. These changing expectations have had an influence on all judges and courts, but nowhere more than on the Supreme Court of Canada. That institution is now in a position not just to meet those expectations, but to make itself a truly significant participant in the Canadian polity.

Appendix

JUDGES OF THE SUPREME COURT OF CANADA

CHIEF JUSTICES

Hon. Sir William Buell Richards [Ont.]	8 Oct. 1875 to 9 Jan. 1879
Hon. Sir William Johnston Ritchie [NB]	11 Jan. 1879 to 23 Sept. 1892
Rt Hon. Sir Samuel Henry Strong [Ont.]	13 Dec. 1892 to 18 Nov. 1902
Rt Hon. Sir Henri Elzéar Taschereau [Que.]	21 Nov. 1902 to 2 May 1906
Rt Hon. Sir Charles Fitzpatrick [Que.]	4 June 1906 to 21 Oct. 1918
Rt Hon. Sir Louis Henry Davies [PEI]	23 Oct. 1918 to 1 May 1924
Rt Hon. Francis Alexander Anglin [Ont.]	16 Sept. 1924 to 28 Feb. 1933
Rt Hon. Sir Lyman Poore Duff [BC]	17 Mar. 1933 to 7 Jan. 1944
Rt Hon. Thibaudeau Rinfret [Que.]	8 Jan. 1944 to 21 June 1954
Hon. Patrick Kerwin [Ont.]	1 July 1954 to 2 Feb. 1963
Rt Hon. Robert Taschereau [Que.]	22 Apr. 1963 to 31 Aug. 1967
Rt Hon. J.R. Cartwright [Ont.]	1 Sept. 1967 to 22 Mar. 1970
Rt Hon. Joseph Honoré Gérald Fauteux [Que.]	23 Mar. 1970 to 22 Dec. 1973
Rt Hon. Bora Laskin [Ont.]	27 Dec. 1973 to 26 Mar. 1984
Rt Hon. Brian Dickson [Man.]	19 Apr. 1984 –

PUISNE JUDGES

Hon. William Johnston Ritchie [NB]	8 Oct. 1875 to 10 Jan. 1879
Hon. Samuel Henry Strong [Ont.]	8 Oct. 1875 to 12 Dec. 1892
Hon. Jean Thomas Taschereau [Que.]	8 Oct. 1875 to 5 Oct. 1878

Hon. Télesphore Fournier [Que.]	8 Oct. 1875 to 11 Sept. 1895	
Hon. William Alexander Henry [NS]	8 Oct. 1875 to 3 May 1888	
Hon. Henri Elzéar Taschereau [Que.]	7 Oct. 1878 to 20 Nov. 1902	
Hon. John Wellington Gwynne [Ont.]	14 Jan. 1879 to 7 Jan. 1902	
Hon. Christopher Salmon Patterson [Ont.]	27 Oct. 1888 to 24 July 1893	
Hon. Robert Sedgewick [NS]	18 Feb. 1893 to 4 Aug. 1906	
Hon. George Edwin King [NB]	21 Sept. 1893 to 8 May 1901	
Hon. Désiré Girouard [Que.]	28 Sept. 1895 to 22 Mar. 1911	
Hon. Sir Louis Henry Davies [PEI]	25 Sept. 1901 to 23 Oct. 1918	
Hon. David Mills [Ont.]	8 Feb. 1902 to 8 May 1903	
Hon. John Douglas Armour [Ont.]	21 Nov. 1902 to 11 July 1903	
Hon. Wallace Nesbitt [Ont.]	16 May 1903 to 4 Oct. 1905	
Hon. Albert Clements Killam [Man.]	8 Aug. 1903 to 6 Feb. 1905	
Hon. John Idington [Ont.]	10 Feb. 1905 to 31 Mar. 1927	
Hon. James Maclennan [Ont.]	5 Oct. 1905 to 12 Feb. 1909	
Hon. Lyman Poore Duff [BC]	27 Sept. 1906 to 16 Mar. 1933	
Hon. Francis Alexander Anglin [Ont.]	16 Feb. 1909 to 15 Sept. 1924	
Hon. Louis-Philippe Brodeur [Que.]	11 Aug. 1911 to 10 Oct. 1923	
Hon. Pierre Basile Mignault [Que.]	25 Oct. 1918 to 30 Sept. 1929	
Hon. Arthur Cyrille Albert Malouin [Que.]	30 Jan. 1924 to 1 Oct. 1924	
Hon. Edmund Leslie Newcombe [NS]	20 Sept. 1924 to 9 Dec. 1931	
Hon. Thibaudeau Rinfret [Que.]	1 Oct. 1924 to 7 Jan. 1944	
Hon. John Henderson Lamont [Sask.]	2 Apr. 1927 to 10 Mar. 1936	
Hon. Robert Smith [Ont.]	18 May 1927 to 7 Dec. 1933	
Hon. Lawrence Arthur Dumoulin Cannon [Que.]	14 Jan. 1930 to 25 Dec. 1939	
Hon. Oswald Smith Crocket [NB]	21 Sept. 1932 to 13 Apr. 1943	
Hon. Frank Joseph Hughes [Ont.]	17 Mar. 1933 to 13 Feb. 1935	
Hon. Henry Hague Davis [Ont.]	31 Jan. 1935 to 30 June 1944	
Hon. Patrick Kerwin [Ont.]	20 July 1935 to 1 July 1954	
Hon. Albert Blelloch Hudson [Man.]	24 Mar. 1936 to 6 Jan. 1947	
Hon. Robert Taschereau [Que.]	9 Feb. 1940 to 21 Apr. 1963	
Hon. Ivan Cleveland Rand [NB]	22 Apr. 1943 to 27 Apr. 1959	
Hon. Roy Lindsay Kellock [Ont.]	3 Oct. 1944 to 15 Jan. 1958	
Hon. James Wilfred Estey [Sask.]	6 Oct. 1944 to 22 Jan. 1956	
Hon. Charles Holland Locke [BC]	3 June 1947 to 16 Sept. 1962	
Hon. John Robert Cartwright [Ont.]	22 Dec. 1949 to 31 Aug. 1967	
Hon. Joseph Honoré Gérald Fauteux [Que.]	22 Dec. 1949 to 22 Mar. 1970	
Hon. Douglas Charles Abbott [Que.]	1 July 1954 to 22 Dec. 1973	
Hon. Henry Gratton Nolan [Alta.]	1 Mar. 1956 to 8 July 1957	
Hon. Ronald Martland [Alta.]	15 Jan. 1958 to 10 Feb. 1982	

Hon. Wilfred Judson [Ont.]	5 Feb. 1958 to 20 July 1977
Hon. Roland Almon Ritchie [NS]	5 May 1959 to 1 Nov. 1984
Hon. Emmett Matthew Hall [Sask.]	23 Nov. 1962 to 28 Feb. 1973
Hon. Wishart Flett Spence [Ont.]	30 May 1963 to 29 Dec. 1978
Hon. Louis-Philippe Pigeon [Que.]	21 Sept. 1967 to 7 Feb. 1980
Hon. Bora Laskin [Ont.]	23 Mar. 1970 to 26 Dec. 1973
Hon. Robert George Brian Dickson [Man.]	26 Mar. 1973 to 18 Apr. 1984
Hon. Jean Beetz [Que.]	1 Jan. 1974 –
Hon. Louis-Philippe de Grandpré [Que.]	1 Jan. 1974 to 1 Oct. 1977
Hon. Willard Z. Estey [Ont.]	29 Sept. 1977 –
Hon. Yves Pratte [Que.]	1 Oct. 1977 to 30 June 1979
Hon. William Rogers McIntyre [BC]	1 Jan. 1979 –
Hon. Julien Chouinard [Que.]	24 Sept. 1979 –
Hon. Antonio Lamer [Que.]	28 Mar. 1980 –
Hon. Bertha Wilson [Ont.]	4 Mar. 1982 –
Hon. Gerald LeDain [Ont.]	29 May 1984 –
Hon. Gérard Vincent LaForest [NB]	16 Jan. 1985 –

Notes

AC   Appeal Cases
DLR   Dominion Law Reports
OAR   Ontario Appeal Reports
NR   National Reports
NBR   New Brunswick Reports
OR   Ontario Reports
PAC   Public Archives of Canada
QLR   Quebec Law Reports
SCC   Supreme Court of Canada, Records Section
SCR   Supreme Court Reports
UCCP   Upper Canada Common Pleas Reports
UCQB   Upper Canada Queen's Bench Reports
UWO   University of Western Ontario, Regional History Collection

PREFACE

1 See J. Nedelsky 'Judicial Conservatism in an Age of Innovation' in *Essays in the History of Canadian Law* vol. 1, edited by D.H. Flaherty (Toronto: Osgoode Society 1982) 281.
2 A.C. Cairns 'The Judicial Committee and Its Critics' *Canadian Journal of Political Science* 4 (1971) 331
3 P. Home 'Legal Education in Ontario' *Canadian Bar Review* 1 (1923) 685–6
4 T.E. Brown 'Dr Ernest Jones, Psychoanalysis, and the Canadian Medical

Profession, 1908–1913' in *Medicine in Canadian Society: Historical Perspectives* edited by S.E.D. Shortt (Montreal: McGill-Queen's University Press 1981) 322

5 Consultative Group on Research and Education in Law *Law and Learning: Report to the Social Sciences and Humanities Research Council of Canada* (Ottawa: The Council 1983)

6 B. Laskin, quoted in *Le Devoir* 26 August 1975; L.-P. Pigeon, quoted in *The Financial Post* 22 March 1980

CHAPTER 1

1 O.D. Skelton *Life and Times of Sir Alexander Tilloch Galt* (Toronto: McClelland and Stewart 1966) 97; W.F. O'Connor *Report to the Senate Relating to the Enactment of the British North America Act, 1867* (Ottawa 1961 [1939]) annex no. 4, 52, 61; Province of Canada *Parliamentary Debates on Confederation* (Quebec 1965 [1865]) 690; PAC Sir J.A. Macdonald Papers, vol. 46, Quebec Conference minutes and notes taken at the Quebec Conference by A.A. Macdonald, 44

2 S.M. Lipset *The First New Nation* (New York: Basic Books 1963) 15–60

3 House of Commons *Debates* (1879) 1374; (1880) 248. The Conservative minister of justice referred to the Court as 'so essential a feature of our constitution': (1880) 237.

4 PAC Sir J.A. Macdonald Papers no. 64614–9, S.H. Strong to Macdonald 20 December 1868

5 Ibid. no. 64610

6 Library of Parliament, House of Commons Bills, Bill 80 (1869) 'An Act to establish a Supreme Court for the Dominion of Canada'

7 House of Commons *Debates* (1870) 523

8 PAC Sir J.A. Macdonald Papers no. 64622–41, O. Mowat to Macdonald 3 September 1869

9 The procedure was one by which the government could refer a legal issue, a question, or a proposed statute to the Supreme Court for the justices' considered opinion; see chapter 5 for a fuller discussion.

10 Library of Parliament, House of Commons Bills, Bill 48 (1870) 'An Act to establish a Supreme Court in Canada'

11 The reasons for withdrawal are unclear. The bill passed first reading on 18 March 1870, but seven weeks later (on 11 May) it was formally withdrawn by G.-E. Cartier. Three weeks after introduction (on 6 April) Macdonald moved that 'certain resolutions' regarding the court be considered the next day, but discussion of those resolutions and the bill itself never recurred, despite promises from time to time that debate would be forthcoming.

12 PAC RG7, G18, vol. 68, H. Bernard to Lord Dufferin 5 November 1874 and enclosure
13 House of Commons *Debates* (1875) 285
14 38 Vict. c. 11, s. 17
15 Ibid. ss 4, 17
16 House of Commons *Debates* (1875) 286
17 38 Vict. c. 11, ss 52–56
18 House of Commons *Debates* (1875) 286–7; J. Smith 'The Origins of Judicial Review in Canada' *Canadian Journal of Political Science* 16 (1983) 127–9. For a contrary view see ibid. 125–6, 129.
19 House of Commons *Debates* (1875) 751, 924–5
20 Ibid. 289
21 See chapter 8.
22 *Canada Law Journal* 11 (1875) 236; see also 64–5; UWO D. Mills Papers box 4283 clippings scrapbook 24–5.
23 PAC A. Mackenzie Papers no. 795–7, T. Hodgins to Mackenzie 29 April 1875; J. Schull *Edward Blake* vol. 1 (Toronto: Macmillan 1975) 144–7
24 PAC A. Mackenzie Papers no. 795–7, T. Hodgins to Mackenzie 29 April 1875; E. Blake to Mackenzie 12 November 1875; PAC E. Blake Papers reel M243, no. 234, W.B. Richards to Blake 14 September 1875
25 PAC A. Mackenzie Papers no. 795–7, T. Hodgins to Mackenzie 29 April 1875; PAC H.J. Morgan Papers, vol. 20, 7816–21; PAC E. Blake Papers reel M243, no. 235, T. Moss to Blake 14 September 1875; *Canada Law Journal* 11 (1875) 265–6
26 J. G. Snell 'The Nova Scotia Influence on the Supreme Court of Canada' in *Law in a Colonial Society: The Nova Scotia Experience* edited by P.B. Waite, S.E. Oxner, and T.G. Barnes (Toronto: Carswell 1984) 143–63
27 Ibid.
28 PAC E. Blake Papers reel M248, LB1, 395–402
29 T. Rinfret 'Le juge Télesphore Fournier' *Revue Trimestrielle Canadienne* 12 (1926) 1–16
30 PAC E. Blake Papers reel M239, no. 7, L.H. Holton to Blake 12 September 1875; no. 9, Blake to Holton 14 September 1875; reel M243, no. 269–70, R. Laflamme to Blake 23 September 1875; reel M248, LB1, 393–4, 465–74; PAC A. Mackenzie Papers no. 630, R. Laflamme to Mackenzie 22 September 1875
31 PAC E. Blake Papers, reel M241, no. 52, A. Mackenzie to Blake 25 September 1875; no. 284, September [1875]; no. 47, 22 September 1875; no. 49; no. 51, 23 September 1875; reel M248, LB1, 477, 553–6
32 *The Legal News* 16 (1893) 343–4
33 PAC A. Mackenzie Papers no. 1039–40; PAC E. Blake Papers reel M244, no. 956
34 *Regina v The Justices of the Peace of the County of Kings* (1873–5) 15 NBR 539, 541

35 *The Queen* v *Taylor* (1876) 36 UCQB 183

36 By reserving the bill the governor-general declined to give royal assent to the legislation; instead the bill was sent to London where it was up to the British cabinet to recommend royal assent by the queen.

37 PAC E. Blake Papers reel M241, no. 52, A. Mackenzie to Blake 25 September 1875; reel M248, LB1, 612–16; reel M249, LB2, 4–6, 587–626; reel M250, LB2, 746–8

38 J.D. Livermore 'Towards "A Union of Hearts": The Early Career of Edward Blake, 1867–1880' PHD thesis, Queen's University 1975, 283, 290–2; D.C. Thomson *Alexander Mackenzie, Clear Grit* (Toronto: Macmillan 1960) 245

39 The justices of the Supreme Court, their replacements on the provincial benches, and the registrar were all gazetted on 9 October 1875. Blake took some care in establishing the order of precedence among the justices; on a draft list, Strong's name had appeared in second place and Ritchie's in third, but the minister of justice reversed the order. The decision was important, given that the chief justiceship would be determined by seniority for the next three decades. See PAC E. Blake Papers reel M248, LB1, 607–9.

40 Ibid. reel M250, LB2, 826–9, Blake to R.W. Scott 5 November 1875; *Canada Law Journal* 12 (1876) 57; *Canada Law Journal* 20 (1884) 234

41 PAC E. Blake Papers reel M248, LB1, 511–14; idem, reel M250, LB2, 767; reel M249, LB1, 678–80; House of Commons *Debates* (1880) 249–50 and (1882) 1265–7

42 See chapter 3.

43 PAC E. Blake Papers reel M248, LB1, 541–2, Blake to R. Cassels 21 September 1875; reel M252, LB4, 98–100, Blake to Taschereau 27 January 1876

44 SCC Letterbook 1, 9–16, 20, 24

45 Ibid., 17, 23, 36, 50; Depatment of Justice, file no. 34/1869, W.J. Ritchie to E. Blake 25 April 1876; PAC E. Blake Papers reel M252, LB4, 234; reel 242, no. 43; reel M244, no. 467; reel M258, LB8, 643– 4

46 Depart of Justice, file no. 34/1869, R. Cassels to H. Bernard 12 November 1875 and 9 December 1875; R.J. Dalton to Bernard 6 December 1875; PAC RG13, A5, vol. 2038, no. 428, memorandum of Chief Justice Ritchie et al. 27 February 1882

47 Christopher Armstrong analyses some aspects of Ontario's impact on the dominion in *The Politics of Federalism: Ontario's Relations with the Federal Government, 1867–1942* (Toronto: University of Toronto Press 1981).

48 PAC E. Blake Papers reel M242, no. 43, O. Mowat to Blake 17 December 1875; House of Commons *Debates* (1878) 1636–7, 2550–1

49 *Canada Gazette* 9 (15 January 1876), 906; *Canada Law Journal* 13 (1877) 133; PAC E. Blake Papers reel M244, no. 478; reel M251, LB3, 935; SCC Minute Book 1,

2; PAC Sir J. Gowan Papers reel M1897, H. Bernard to Gowan 5 January 1876
50 SCC Reports on Bills 1–4; SCC Letterbook 1, 58–9
51 SCC Minute Book 1, 2–39
52 R.C.B. Risk '"This Nuisance of Litigation": The Origins of Workers' Compensation in Ontario' in *Essays in the History of Canadian Law* vol. 2, edited by D.H. Flaherty (Toronto: Osgoode Society 1983) 449
53 SCC Letterbook 1, 422, G. Duval to J.-T. Taschereau, 22 May 1878
54 SCC subject file no. 14, E. Blake [to governor-in-council] 30 December 1876; SCC Letterbook 1, 106–10, 115–16, 143, 185; PAC RG13, A2, vol. 38, no. 1339; *Canada Law Journal* 13 (1877) 341–2. It is regrettable that the linguistic abilities of the justices necessitated the translation of Court submissions. In 1880, it was alleged, only one of the four English-speaking justices '[knew] the French language': see House of Commons *Debates* (1880) 257
55 (1877) 1 SCR 235
56 PAC A. Mackenzie Papers no. 1081 d–e, Lord Dufferin to Mackenzie 16 December 1875; PAC E. Blake Papers reel M238, no. 11, Dufferin to Blake 2 March 1876; PAC Sir W. Laurier Papers no. 71286, Dufferin to Sir M.E. Hicks Beach 19 July 1878
57 PAC RG13, A2, vol. 40, no. 28, R.G. Haliburton to the minister of justice 15 December 1877; 2 January 1878; memorandum of Z.A. Lash to R. Laflamme 3 January 1878; A1, vol. 458, no. 28
58 W.N.T. Wylie, quoted in *Essays in the History of Canadian Law* vol. 1, edited by D.H. Flaherty (Toronto: Osgoode Society 1981) 142
59 PAC RG13, A2, vol. 39, no. 872, W.A. Henry to R. Laflamme 14 August 1877; A1, vol. 456, no. 872; PAC E. Blake Papers reel M261, LB10, 164–5; *Canada Law Journal* 13 (1877) 365; PAC Sir J.A. Macdonald Papers no. 159435–38, D. Girouard to Macdonald 23 November 1877
60 PAC E. Blake Papers reel M241, no. 134, A. Mackenzie to Blake 15 June 1876; no. 126; reel M252, LB4, 98–100, 107–8; reel M253, LB4, 314; reel M256, LB5, 664–7
61 PAC Sir J.R. Gowan Papers reel M1898, Gowan to J.W. Gwynne 14 January 1879
62 *Canada Law Journal* 14 (1878) 5, 307; *Quebec Mercury* 16 October 1878; PAC A. Mackenzie Papers no. 2082–3, J.-T. Taschereau to Mackenzie 18 September 1878. Two days before Taschereau's resignation took effect, his son was appointed to the Quebec Superior Court.
63 Ibid. no. 1580–1, W.B. Richards to Mackenzie 1 May 1877; *The Legal News* 1 (1878) 565; *Ottawa Citizen* 14 October 1878. For some reason H.-E. Taschereau did not take the oath of office for a further five months; see House of Commons *Debates* (1879) 505.

64 I. MacPherson 'Sir William Buell Richards' *Dictionary of Canadian Biography 1881 to 1890* vol. 11 (Toronto: University of Toronto Press 1982) 731

65 *Canada Law Journal* 13 (1877) 285; *Canada Law Journal* 15 (1879) 40–1

66 In an 1875 decision concerning escheats, he held that in 1867 provincial governments had fully ceded to the central government their sovereignty and any privileges or prerogatives (including escheats) attached to that sovereignty. PAC F.-J. Audet Papers, vol. 28, 746–7; *Canada Law Journal* 11 (1875) 118; *Canada Law Journal* 12 (1876) 152–3; H.-E. Taschereau *The Criminal Law Consolidation and Amendment Act of 1869* vol. 1 (Montreal 1874) and vol. 2 (Toronto 1875). When the appointment was attacked in the House of Commons, it was on the grounds of the timing of the appointment and the privileged character of the Taschereau family; see House of Commons *Debates* (1879) 505–6. In *Church v Blake* (1875) 1 QLR 177, H.-E. Taschereau wrote: 'Avant la confédération, chacune des provinces était revêtue de ce caractère de souveraineté; mais, en joignant l'union fédéral, chacune d'elles a fait au gouvernement central une cession complète de cette souveraineté, des priviléges, prérogatives et attributs de cette souveraineté, comme des revenus provenants de l'exercice de ces priviléges, prérogatives et attributs.' A rumour circulated that if the Liberal government had been returned to office in September 1878, J.-T. Taschereau would have been named lieutenant-governor of Quebec and his place on the Court filled by Rodolphe Laflamme, the minister of justice; see House of Commons *Debates* (1879) 505.

67 *Canada Law Journal* 15 (1879) 41; *Re Niagara Election Case* (1879) 29 UCCP 261

68 PAC Sir J.R. Gowan Papers reel M1898, J.W. Gwynne to Gowan 13 January 1879

CHAPTER 2

1 *Canada Law Journal* 15 (1879) 41

2 House of Commons *Debates* (1879) 1376. There were already signs of electoral discontent regarding the Supreme Court; see, for example, P.H. Russell *The Supreme Court of Canada as a Bilingual and Bicultural Institution* (Ottawa: Information Canada 1969) 17, 242, notes 85 and 86; and PAC Sir J.A. Macdonald Papers no. 165085–8, G.H. Perry to Macdonald 24 April 1879.

3 House of Commons *Debates* (1879) 1373

4 Ibid. 1387. It is possible that the bill did not return for second reading because the cabinet had acted behind the scenes to control Keeler; see ibid. 1373–4.

5 The second rationale was hinted at by the minister of justice in 1879; see ibid. 1380.

6 *Canada Law Journal* 15 (1879) 119; *Canada Law Journal* 16 (1880) 313–14; *McKay v Crysler* (1880) 3 SCR 436

7 PAC Sir J.A. Macdonald Papers no. 148652–60, H.-E. Taschereau to Macdonald [1882]

8 *Canada Law Journal* 19 (1883) 81–3, 121, 197; *Canadian Law Times* 3 (1883) 191–2; *The Legal News* 6 (1883) 89–90. In *Grant v Beaudry* (unreported) the grand master of the Orange Order sued the mayor of Montreal for false arrest. Though the point was not at issue on appeal before the Quebec Court of Queen's Bench, the judges gave as their opinion that the Orange Order (known for its hostility to Roman Catholics and French Canadians) was an illegal association. When the case came before the Supreme Court of Canada, Justice Gwynne commented in court that the judges' opinion was 'extra-judicial and unwarranted.' This in turn set the legal journals squabbling over Gwynne's remarks, which aroused Quebec sensitivities.

9 House of Commons *Debates* (1879) 1375–6. Two Ontario Conservatives broke in the opposite direction to support the Court. Russell *A Bilingual and Bicultural Institution* provides a useful account of Quebec complaints (at 20–1).

10 PAC Sir J.A. Macdonald Papers no. 165085–8, G.H. Perry to Macdonald 24 April 1879; no. 163176–80, D. Girouard to Macdonald, 2 January 1879

11 *The Legal News* 2 (1879) 161–2. See also A.I. Silver *The French-Canadian Idea of Confederation 1864–1900* (Toronto: University of Toronto Press 1982) 122–3.

12 PAC Sir J.A. Macdonald Papers no. 148644–7, F. Routhier et al. to Macdonald 24 February 1880 [1881]. Both internal and external evidence indicates that the petition was sent in 1881 rather than in 1880.

13 House of Commons *Debates* (1880) 240, 267–8. Among the twenty-nine men voting 'nay' were seven Liberals and twenty-two Conservatives; of the Conservatives, one was from Nova Scotia, seven were from Ontario, and twenty-one were from Quebec. See also *The Legal News* 3 (1880) 145–6.

14 House of Commons *Debates* (1881) 914–26; (1882) 950. In 1882 the bill received first reading only, but in 1881 the issue was deferred by a six-month hoist in a vote of 88–39. Those thirty-nine negative votes consisted of six Liberals and thirty-three Conservatives; twenty-three were from Quebec, fourteen from Ontario, and one each from British Columbia and Prince Edward Island. Keeler's sponsorship of the bill ended with his death early in 1881.

15 Ibid. 884. Girouard's solution was first mentioned early in 1879 in a letter to the prime minister; see PAC Sir J.A. Macdonald Papers no. 163176–80, D. Girouard to Macdonald 2 January 1879.

16 House of Commons *Debates* (1881) 1295; PAC Sir J.A. Macdonald Papers no. 148649–50, D. Girouard to Macdonald 10 March 1881

17 House of Commons *Debates* (1881) 1296; *The Legal News* 4 (1881) 65, 73–4, 97. The prime minister did claim, however, that his government was considering adoption of such legislation; see House of Commons *Debates* (1883) 29.

18 House of Commons *Debates* (1885) 168

19 House of Commons *Debates* (1879) 166
20 *Valin* v *Langlois* (1880) 3 SCR 1
21 J. Smith 'The Origins of Judicial Review in Canada '*Canadian Journal of Political Science* 16 (1983) 132. Sir John A. Macdonald, for one, had earlier explicitly rejected any claim that the Court could 'in any degree override the Parliament of Canada'; see House of Commons *Debates* (1875) 289.
22 *Canada Law Journal* 16 (1880) 99–100
23 See, for example PAC Sir J.R. Gowan Papers reel M1898, J.W. Gwynne to Gowan 18 July 1880.
24 SCC Letterbook 1, 421, G. Duval to S.H. Strong 22 May 1878
25 *Canada Law Journal* 14 (1878) 98–100; *Canada Law Journal* 16 (1880) 73–5, 154
26 House of Commons *Debates* (1880) 252–3
27 *Canada Law Journal* 13 (1877) 341–3: *Canada Law Journal* 16 (1880) 42; *The Legal News* 4 (1881) 137–8; *Canadian Law Times* 3 (1883) 195
28 *The Legal News* 7 (1884) 350–1
29 *The Legal News* 1 (1878) 140–1; *The Legal News* 7 (1884) 350–1; *Canadian Law Times* 1 (1881) 645, 649; *Canada Law Journal* 14 (1878) 3–4; *Canada Law Journal* 17 (1882) 87–8
30 PAC RG13, A2, vol. 47, no. 828, J. Maclennan to Z.A. Lash 11 May 1880; PAC Sir A. Campbell Papers reel M24, J.E. Rose to Campbell 17 October 1883 and 20 October 1883; Sir W.J. Ritchie to Campbell 23 November 1883
31 In 1886 the reporter noted that prior to 1880 thirty cases had been left unreported, some because the legal points involved were not important enough and others because the formal notes of the judges who had delivered judgments could not be obtained; see PAC RG13, A2, vol. 64, no. 531, G. Duval to G.W. Burbidge 19 April 1886.
32 See, for example, SCC Letterbook 1, 538, 803, 819; Letterbook 2, 60, 201, 340, 351; Letterbook 3, 24–6.
33 *Milloy* v *Kerr* (1884) 8 SCR at 486 (note); PAC RG13, A2, vol. 70, no. 450, G. Duval to R. Sedgewick, 10 April 1888
34 PAG RG13, A2, vol. 65, no. 886, G. Duval to G. Burbidge 25 June 1886; *The Legal News* 9 (1886) 129, 233; *Canada Law Journal* 17 (1881) 177
35 SCC Letterbook 1, 481–2, R. Cassels to Z.A. Lash 31 October 1878; ibid. 483; House of Commons *Debates* (1886) 890–1; PAC RG13, A2, vol. 70, no. 452; A1, vol. 472, no. 126
36 SCC Letterbook 1, 262–3; Letterbook 2, 88–9; PAC RG13, A2, vol. 60, no. 317
37 SCC Letterbook 2, 451–6; ibid. 88–9
38 PAC RG13, A2, vol. 60, no. 317; A1, vol. 462, no. 1166. As well, excess numbers of each volume were accumulating rapidly (there were 1,500 on hand in 1884), creating storage problems.

39 *In re Sproule* (1887) 12 SCR 140; D.R. Williams, '*... The Man for a New Country':*
   Sir Matthew Baillie Begbie (Sydney, BC: Gray's Publishing 1977) 261–2. Williams
   is incorrect in stating that both Henry and Strong issued the original writ.
40 *Milloy* v *Kerr* (1884) 8 SCR 474; the other cases cited are unreported.
41 PAC Sir J.A. Macdonald Papers no. 148624–39, S.H. Strong to Macdonald
   9 February 1880
42 PAC Sir J.S.D. Thompson Papers no. 6040, S.H. Strong to D. McCarthy 11
   May 1887
43 J. Travis 'Travis on Canadian Constitutional Law' *Manitoba Law Journal* 2
   (1885) 43; *Canada Law Journal* 28 (1892) 484
44 PAC W.L.M. King Papers reel C2264, no. 84490, J.S. Ewart to King 6 May
   1924
45 A picture of the courtroom is reproduced in *The Green Bag* 2 (1890) 241,
   and the room is described in *Maclean's Magazine* (March 1914) 13–14.
46 3 SCR 575
47 (1883) 5 SCR 538
48 4 SCR 215
49 (1881–2) 7 AC 96
50 (1881–2) 7 AC 829
51 (1883–4) 9 AC 117
52 14 AC 295
53 *Attorney-General of Ontario* v *Mercer* (1882–3) 8 AC 767
54 13 SCR 577
55 17 SCR 657
56 B. Laskin 'The Supreme Court of Canada: A Final Court of and for
   Canadians' *Canadian Bar Review* 29 (1951) 1057–65
57 8 SCR 1
58 7 SCR 216
59 14 SCR 392
60 A well-regarded Maritime lawyer, Wallace Graham, provided an interesting account of his appearance before the Court in 1884; see J.G. Snell 'The
   Nova Scotia Influence on the Supreme Court of Canada' in *Law in a
   Colonial Society: The Nova Scotia Experience* edited by P.B. Waite, S.E. Oxner,
   and T.G. Barnes (Toronto: Carswell 1984)
61 Calculated from SCC subject file no. 66; see also chapter 7
62 PAC RG13, A1, vol. 470, no. 372, 381, 1097; vol. 480, no. 3G, 3M; Sir J.S.D.
   Thompson Papers nos. 7676, 7717
63 PAC RG13, A1, vol. 460, no. 169; vol. 462, no. 1356; vol. 472, no. 308; vol. 480,
   nos. 31, 1200; vol. 482, nos. 3B, 3F; A5, vol. 2040, no. 705, S.H. Strong to
   Sir J.A. Macdonald 20 August 1888, and minute by Macdonald.

64 See, for example, *Manitoba Law Journal* 1 (1884) 140–1; *Canada Law Journal* 20 (1884) 177.

65 PAC Sir J.S.D. Thompson Papers no. 3007, C.H. Tupper to Thompson [1883]. We are indebted to P.B. Waite for this reference; the 'risk' referred to presumably concerns the attempts to abolish or weaken the Supreme Court.

66 PAC Sir J.A. Macdonald Papers no. 125096–7, Sir J.S.D. Thompson to Macdonald, 20 August 1888

67 Ibid.; no. 229953–62, A.L. Palmer to Macdonald 21 July 1888; PAC Sir J.S.D. Thompson Papers no. 8151, Macdonald to Thompson 7 August 1888

68 *Halifax Morning Herald* 29 October 1888; *Canada Law Journal* 45 (1909) 157; *Manitoba Daily Free Press* 6 and 27 October 1888. It seems that the post was rejected first by Chief Justice Taylor of the Manitoba Supreme Court and second by Justice Osler of the Ontario Court of Appeal. Patterson had been a member of the Ontario Court of Appeal since 1874. For biographical details, see *Canada Law Journal* 29 (1888) 546; *Ottawa Citizen* 29 October 1888; *Toronto Globe* 30 October 1888; *Canadian Law Times* 8 (1888) 277; *Ottawa Citizen* 25 July 1893. Patterson's pro-centralist leanings seemed confirmed by his decisions in *The Queen* v *Hodge* (1881–2) 7 OAR 246; *Attorney-General of Ontario* v *the International Bridge Company* (1880–1) 6 OAR 537; and *Doyle* v *Bell* (1884–5) 11 OAR 326. Compare *Edgar* v *the Central Bank of Canada* (1887–8) 15 OAR 193.

69 PAC Sir J.S.D. Thompson Papers, vol. 70, no. 7694, G.W. Burbidge to Thompson, 8 May 1888; PAC Sir J.R. Gowan Papers, Sir W.R. Richards to Gowan, 21 May 1888; Halifax *Morning Chronicle* 27 and 29 October, 1 November 1888; Halifax *Morning Herald* 29 and 31 October 1888; P.B. Waite to J.G. Snell, 13 June 1981

70 43 Vict. c. 34; *Canada Law Journal* 16 (1880) 71–2. Compare *Canadian Law Times* 10 (1890) 130–9.

71 In the 1882 speech from the throne the government renewed its pledge of legislation reforming the Court. No copy of the bill is extant; its content must be deduced from the commentary on it, especially the debates in the Senate (where the bill was introduced). It is not clear, for example, whether the common-law justices would have continued to sit on civil-law appeals.

72 Senate *Debates* (1882) 242–50; *The Legal News* 5 (1882) 99, 105, 153; PAC Sir J.A. Macdonald Papers no. 81748–52, Sir A. Campbell to Macdonald [1882]; ibid. no. 179329–30, J.A. Ouimet to Macdonald 29 March 1882

73 PAC RG13, A5, vol. 2038, no. 509, memorandum from Z.A. Lash to Sir A. Campbell 20 March 1882. In this memorandum, dated prior to the introduction of the 1882 bill, the deputy minister of justice indicates that in

1880–1 an amendment had been suggested to Sir J.A. Macdonald, 'but owing to the attack which had been made on the Court he thought it better to do nothing about it.'

74 PAC Sir J.A. Macdonald Papers no. 148652–60, H.-E. Taschereau to Macdonald [1882]; no. 148624–39, S.H. Strong to Macdonald 9 February 1880; PAC Sir J.S.D. Thompson Papers, LB6, 466, Thompson to Taschereau 27 April 1887; no. 21981, Strong to Thompson 8 February [1893]; PAC, RG13, A5, vol. 2038, no. 632, J.W. Gwynne to Sir A. Campbell 5 April 1883

75 Other examples of this use of the justices are Strong's close involvement in the drafting of a new Petition of Right Act; Blake's plans in 1876 to use the judges to consolidate Canadian statutes; Fournier's continuing assistance regarding seigneurial claims; and Richards' advice to the minister of justice in answering an opposition query. See PAC E. Blake Papers reel M244, no. 479, W.B. Richards to Blake 17 January 1876; no. 594, 9 March 1876; no. 467, S.H. Strong to Blake 11 January 1876; reel M251, LB3, 841–4; reel M255, LB5, 48–9.

76 PAC Sir A. Campbell Papers reel M24, Sir J.A. Macdonald to Campbell 28 June 1883

77 PAC Sir J.S.D. Thompson Papers no. 8040, H.-E. Taschereau to Thompson 9 July 1888; LB6, 960–2, Thompson to Sir W.J. Ritchie 19 July 1887.

78 PAC Sir J.S.D. Thompson Papers no. 3963, Sir J.A. Macdonald to Thompson 27 April 1886

79 G.V. LaForest *Disallowance and Reservation of Provincial Legislation* (Ottawa: Department of Justice 1955) 59–61

80 *Canada Law Journal* 22 (1887) 376–7; 51 Vict. c. 37; 52 Vict. c. 37

81 PAC RG13, A5, vol. 2038, no. 428, memorandum of Chief Justice Ritchie et al. 25 February 1882; *The Legal News* 5 (1882) 57; *Canada Law Journal* 28 (1882) 115–16

82 PAC RG13, A2, vol. 52, no. 60, F.H. Ennis to Z.A. Lash 23 January 1882; A1, vol. 466, no. 60; SCC Letterbook 2, 725–6, R. Cassels to Lash 2 January 1882

83 PAC RG11, vol. 4328, file no. 2994-1-C 'Excerpts from Reports of the Department of Public Works' 1

84 Most popular accounts incorrectly place the date of this move at approximately 1877.

85 House of Commons *Debates* (1882) 1265–6. At the same time some members of the House expressed approval that the Court had been moved and congestion relieved in the Parliament buildings and in the library.

86 PAC RG13, A5, vol. 2040, no. 568, R. Cassels to G.W. Burbidge 27 May 1887

87 PAC RG11, vol. 4328, file no. 2994-1-C 'Excerpts from Reports of the

Department of Public Works' 2. The explanations in the House of Commons regarding the purchase of the building to which the art gallery was moving carefully avoided stating the real purpose of the purchase, which was to provide more room for the two central courts; see House of Commons *Debates* (1887) 1183.

88 PAC Sir J.S.D. Thompson Papers no. 10302, Sir W.J. Ritchie to Thompson, 3 August 1889. See also no. 10266, T. Fournier to Thompson, 29 July 1889.

89 PAC RG13, A5, vol. 2040, no. 568; *Brassard et al.* v *Langevin* (1877) 1 SCR 145; *London Free Press* 15 March 1933; House of Commons *Debates* (1938) 2031; PAC Sir J.S.D. Thompson Papers no. 10324, R. Sedgewick to Thompson 9 August 1889

90 PAC RG11, vol. 3914, 8

91 Ibid. 6–32; vol. 4328, file no. 2994–1–C 'Excerpts from Reports of the Department of Public Works' 2; PAC RG13, A5, vol. 2042, no. 935

CHAPTER 3

1 PAC RG13, A2, vol. 84, no. 3D, Sir W.J. Ritchie to Sir J.S.D. Thompson 15 September 1892; *Canadian Law Times* 12 (1892) 242, citing the chancellor of Ontario.

2 *Canada Law Journal* 28 (1892) 481; Toronto *Globe* 27 September 1892; Saint John *Daily Telegraph* 27 September 1892; *Canadian Law Times* 13 (1893) 50

3 PAC Sir J.S.D. Thompson Papers no. 20348, J.R. Gowan to Thompson 29 September 1892; no. 20496, 13 October 1892

4 *Canada Law Journal* 28 (1892) 609; *Canada Law Journal* 11 (1875) 266

5 *Halifax Herald* 8 August 1906; *Legal News* 16 (1893) 95; PAC Sir J.S.D. Thompson Papers no. 4134, R. Sedgewick to Thompson 3 June 1886; no. 4305, 9 July 1886

6 Saint John *Daily Telegraph* 8 May 1901; *Saint John Daily Sun* 21 September 1893; House of Commons *Debates* (1901) 4672–4; PAC Sir J.S.D. Thompson Papers no. 21118, G.E. King to Thompson 5 December 1892; Halifax *Morning Chronicle* 29 October 1888; *Canadian Law Times* 21 (1901) 285

7 The cabinet did consider applying the idea to the justices: House of Commons *Debates* (1894) 4962.

8 Ibid. 4889–90, 4955–5013. The existing pension rights amounted to two-thirds of salary at retirement.

9 PAC Sir C.H. Tupper Papers no. 1376–7, Tupper to Sir S.H. Strong 15 February 1895; no. 1378, Tupper to R. Cassels

10 Ibid. no. 1379–84, R. Cassels to Sir C.H. Tupper, 16 February 1895

11 Ibid. no. 1385–9, Sir S.H. Strong to Sir C.H. Tupper, 19 February 1895
12 Ibid. One year later, when Tupper stepped down as minister of justice, Strong reiterated his support of 'the beneficial changes which ... you contemplated in the composition of the Court'; see ibid. no. 1636–8, 16 January 1896; no. 1639–41, 18 January 1896.
13 Tupper had suggested that the two men would retire with their two-thirds pensions, that the government would submit to Parliament with the next estimates a vote for the difference between pension and salary, and that if Parliament approved the vote the government would submit the item each succeeding year for Parliament's approval, 'Parliament being free, of course, to act regardless of the item being considered an ordinary item' in supply; see ibid. no. 1392–4, Tupper to T. Fournier, 24 February 1895.
14 Ibid. no. 1385–9, Sir S.H. Strong to Tupper 19 February 1895
15 Of the forty reported cases argued in the winter term of 1895, Fournier participated in only nineteen and wrote no judgments at all.
16 Ibid.; PAC RG13, A5, vol. 2044, no. 821, Tupper to Fournier 4 September 1895; no. 837, 10 and 11 September 1895; Fournier to Tupper 9 September 1895; Tupper to the governor-in-council 10 September 1895
17 Quebec *Daily Mercury* 28 September 1895. Angers had been solicitor-general of Quebec (1874–6), attorney-general of Quebec (1876–8), puisne justice of the Quebec Superior Court (1880–7), lieutenant-governor of Quebec (1887– 92), and a member of the federal cabinet (1892–5, 1896). The best analysis of the government's political problems at this time is found in J.T. Saywell 'Introduction' *The Canadian Journal of Lady Aberdeen 1893–1898* (Toronto: Champlain Society 1960).
18 Favourable reviews of both books appeared in legal journals; see *The Lower Canada Law Journal* 1 (1865) 50–1; *The Legal News* 14 (1891) 146.
19 The McGreevy-Langevin scandal involved major charges of corruption and influence-peddling against an influential federal minister (Sir H.-L. Langevin) and a Conservative member of Parliament (Thomas McGreevy); see L. LaPierre 'Joseph Israel Tarte and the McGreevy-Langevin Scandal' *Canadian Historical Association Annual Report, 1961* 47– 57.
20 *The Legal News* 18 (1895) 291–2; Montreal *Daily Star* 22 March 1911; PAC F-J. Audet Papers, vol. 14
21 PAC Sir C.H. Tupper Papers no. 1390–1, Tupper to J.W. Gwynne 23 February 1895; no. 1474, 27 September 1895; no. 1475, 30 September 1895. There were also rumours circulating that efforts were being made to persuade Justice Taschereau to resign, but no evidence was uncovered to confirm or deny this; see Quebec *L'Electeur* 27 September 1895.
22 *Canada Law Journal* 32 (1896) 648

23 Edward Cameron remained registrar until 1930. He was not only an effective and influential administrator, but a legal scholar committed to a national role for the Supreme Court.

24 PAC E. Blake Papers reel M247, no. 1860, J. Cameron to Blake 19 October 1896; *Canadian Law Times* 16 (1896) 271–3; UWO D. Mills Papers box 4282, undated material file, Mills to L.H. Davies [1900?]

25 PAC Sir C.H. Tupper Papers no. 1711–4, Tupper to J.W. Gwynne 10 April 1896; no. 1715, 15 April 1896; PAC RG13, A1, vol. 494, no. 3E; PAC Lord Minto Papers vol. 5, 66–7, Sir W. Laurier to Minto 26 November 1900

26 PAC E. Blake Papers reel 242, no. 175, Sir O. Mowat to Blake 24 November 1896; no. 182, 25 September 1897; no. 184, 30 September 1897; no. 183, Blake to Mowat 27 September 1897

27 *Halifax Herald* 6 August 1906. See also M. Bader and E. Burstein 'The Supreme Court of Canada 1892–1902: A Study of the Men and the Times' *Osgoode Hall Law Journal* 8 (1970) 509.

28 *Canadian Green Bag* 1 (1895) 1–2

29 PAC RG13, A5, vol. 2047, no. 35, W.H. Bartram to D. Mills 16 November 1901; Mills to the governor-in-council, 15 January 1902; *The King v Love* (unreported)

30 PAC RG13, A5, vol. 2047, no. 16; Toronto *World* 9 December 1901

31 SCC Letterbook 14, 523–4, E.R. Cameron to C. Fitzpatrick 19 October 1898

32 Ottawa *Citizen* 17 October 1898. See also Quebec *L'Evénement* 2 and 7 November 1898; and Ottawa *Free Press* 17 October 1898.

33 Toronto *Globe* 9 June 1898; *Canadian Law Times* 18 (1898) 143–4, 164–6

34 Quebec *L'Evénement* 25 October 1898; UWO D. Mills Papers box 4287, Letterbook 3 279, Mills to C. Robinson 9 June 1898

35 *Stephens v McArthur* (1892) 19 SCR 446; *Western Law Times* 2 (1891) 188–9

36 PAC E. Blake Papers reel M242, no. 187, Sir O. Mowat to Blake 15 October 1897; no. 186, Blake to Mowat 14 October 1897; PAC RG13 A5, vol. 2046, no. 752; PAC Sir W. Laurier Papers no. 63728a, Sir S.H. Strong to the solicitor-general 16 March [1902]

37 PAC E. Blake Papers reel M242, no. 187, Sir O. Mowat to Blake 15 October 1897; PAC D. Girouard Papers vol. 1, Sir S.H. Strong to Girouard 22 April 1900; vol. 5, file 2, p. 213, no. 94

38 PAC RG13, A2, vol. 87, no. 883; vol. 89, no. 139; vol. 118, no. 309

39 PAC Sir J.A. Macdonald Papers no. 125096-7, Sir J.S.D. Thompson to Macdonald 20 August 1888

40 PAC E. Blake Papers reel M242, no. 187, Sir O. Mowat to Blake 15 October 1897; no. 175, 24 November 1896

41 PAC RG13, A1, vol. 496, no. 559; A2, vol. 117, no. 3A, H.-E. Taschereau to D. Mills 23 March 1901

42 Ibid. A1, vol. 503, no. 3A; uwo D. Mills Papers box 4287, Letterbook 7, 221; House of Commons *Debates* (1902) 2224-5

43 PAC Sir W. Laurier Papers no. 55288, [Laurier] to Sir O. Mowat 13 May 1901; no. 55285-7, Mowat to Laurier 11 April 1901; no. 62044-5, J.M. Gibson to Laurier 28 January 1902; PAC E. Blake Papers reel M242, no. 187, Mowat to Blake 15 October 1897

44 *Canada Law Journal* 26 (1890) 163. The chief justice of Victoria earned $17,500 and the puisne justices $15,000 each; in New South Wales, the figures were $17,500 and $13,000, and in New Zealand $8,500 and $7,500.

45 O.J. Firestone *Industry and Education* (Ottawa: University of Ottawa Press 1969) 261-2

46 PAC Sir J.S.D. Thompson Papers no. 26719, J.W. Gwynne to Thompson 20 June 1894. A successful lawyer in a major city could earn far more than the puisne justices' salary at this time ($7,000). Robert Borden, senior partner in a Halifax law firm, had an annual income from his law practice in the early 1890s of approximately $30,000; see R.C. Brown *Robert Laird Borden 1854-1914* (Toronto: Macmillan 1975) 86.

47 Canada Sessional Papers (1881) no. 8, 55; (1891) no. 1A, 18-19; (1901) no. 1, M8-9, 12

48 uwo D. Mills Papers box 4287, Letterbook 7, 29, Mills to C. Fitzpatrick 19 December 1900

49 House of Commons *Debates* (1888) 964, 1402

50 PAC RG13, A2, vol. 86, no. 524, R. Cassels to R. Sedgewick 2 May 1892; S.H. Strong to Sedgewick 2 May 1892

51 PAC Sir J.S.D. Thompson Papers no. 21981, S.H. Strong to Thompson 8 February [1893]; no. 22158, G.W. Burbidge to Thompson 21 February 1893; no. 22174, 22 February 1893

52 59 Vict. c. 14. In 1889, by 52 Vict. c. 37, s. 1, a four-judge Court was permitted if the fifth judge had taken part in earlier proceedings.

53 *Canadian Law times* 16 (1896) 246-7; *Canada Law Journal* 32 (1896) 647-8; *Legal News* 19 (1896) 257-8; PAC Sir W. Laurier Papers no. 224390, C. Fitzpatrick to Laurier 30 September 1896

54 PAC Sir C. Fitzpatrick Papers no. 1269, Fitzpatrick to Sir W. Laurier 6 March 1902; House of Commons *Debates* (1902) 1673-4, 4264-5, 5054. The chief justice had been consulted as to this bill; see PAC, RG13, A1, vol. 505, no. 245.

55 PAC Sir W. Laurier Papers no. 10086-9, H.-E. Taschereau to Laurier 27 December 1896

56 59 Vict. c. 14; Senate *Debates* (1896) 252

57 PAC Sir W. Laurier Papers no. 9230-1, Sir O. Mowat to Laurier 28 November 1896

58 PAC RG13, A5, vol. 2044, no. 279; uwo D. Mills Papers box 4287, Letterbook

3, 72, Mills to Sir S.H. Strong 25 April 1898; PAC Sir W. Laurier Papers no.
34766–7, Strong to C. Fitzpatrick 21 June 1899; no. 40632–4 [22 June 1899]

59 PAC Sir W. Laurier Papers no. 42207, C. Fitzpatrick to Laurier 9 February
1900

60 UWO D. Mills Papers box 4287, Letterbook 2, 600–2, 673–9; PAC Sir W.
Laurier Papers nos. 47370–2, 71032, and 71283–5

61 See, for example, PAC Sir J.S.D. Thompson Papers nos. 24848, 22156; UWO D.
Mills Papers box 4287, Letterbook 5, 147; J.G. Snell 'The Deputy Head in
the Canadian Bureaucracy' *Canadian Public Administration* 24 (1981) 302– 5.

62 PAC Sir J.S.D. Thompson Papers LB39, 470, Thompson to Sir S. H. Strong 24
October 1893; no. 23689, Strong to Thompson 31 October [1893]; no.
23764, 7 November [1893].

63 PAC RG13, A2, vol. 121, no. 3K; *The New York Times* 9 May 1902

64 PAC Sir C.H. Tupper Papers no. 1636–8, Sir S. H. Strong to Tupper 16
January 1896; no. 1639–41, 18 January 1896; no. 1726–30, 25 April 1896;
no. 1731–4, [n.d.]. See also no. 1348 [n.d.].

65 *Canada Law Journal* 24 (1888) 391–2. See also *Canada Law Journal* 11 (1875)
118, and 12 (1876) 152–3; *Canadian Law Times* 8 (1888) 148; *Legal News* 11
(1888) 105–6; PAC Sir J.S.D. Thompson Papers no. 6854, H.-E. Taschereau to Thompson 2 November 1887; ibid. LB8, 320–2, Thompson to
Taschereau 21 November 1887

66 PAC Sir J.S.D. Thompson Papers no. 10758, H.-E. Taschereau to Thompson
23 October 1889

67 H.-E. Taschereau to Sir J.S.D. Thompson 20 January 1893, reprinted in
Legal News 16 (1893) 36–45

68 *Canada Law Journal* 29 (1893) 94–5; PAC Sir J.R. Gowan Papers reel M1939, A5,
draft memorandum in response to Justice Taschereau's open letter; Toronto *World* 18 February 1893. Compare for example: *Western Law Times* 4 (1893)
43; *Ottawa Free Press* 26 September 1893; *Legal News* 16 (1893) 66.

69 House of Commons *Debates* (1893) 723, 1550. There was no mention of the
incident in the Senate.

70 Brief favourable reviews of the book can be found in: *Legal News* 16 (1893)
215–16; *Canadian Laws Times* 13 (1893) 182; *Western Law Times* 4 (1893) 100.
Justice Girouard was also busy writing books and articles in this period, but
his interest was the history of the St Lawrence Valley; see, for example,
Review of Historical Publications Relating to Canada 5 (1900) 30–2, and 7 (1903)
123–4.

71 RSC 1906, c. 139, s. 36

72 The Supreme Court took judicial notice of this provision in *Viau* v *The Queen*
(1898) 29 SCR 90. See also *Rice* v *The King* (1902) 32 SCR 480.

73 Province of Canada *Parliamentary Debates on the Confederation of British North America* (Quebec 1865) 41
74 50–51 Vict. c. 50, s. 1; 51 Vict. c. 43, s. 1. See also chapter 7.
75 A.W. Mewett 'Criminal Law 1867–1967' *Canadian Bar Review* 45 (1967) 737
76 For an account of the origin of the Canadian Criminal Code, see G. Parker 'The Origins of the Canadian Criminal Code' in *Essays in Canadian Legal History* vol. 1, edited by D.H. Flaherty (Toronto: Osgoode Society 1981) 249–80; see also R.C. Macleod 'The Shaping of Canadian Criminal Law, 1892–1902' in Canadian Historical Association *Historical Papers 1978* 64–75.
77 See, for example, PAC, RG13, A2, vol. 83, no. 1373, R.L. Borden to R. Sedgewick 2 December 1891; *Canada Law Journal* 26 (1890) 34, 393–9; House of Commons *Debates* (1895) 3108–9, and (1896) 637–8.
78 *Canada Law Journal* 27 (1891) 573–4; PAC RG13, A2, vol. 92, no. 942; A1, vol. 498, no. 1013
79 House of Commons *Debates* (1883) 835
80 PAC RG13, A2, vol. 71, no. 784; vol. 72, no. 6
81 House of Commons *Debates* (1890) 479–81; (1892) 312–13; PAC RG13, A2, vol. 84, no. 179; vol. 89, no. 5
82 Ibid. vol. 73, no. 481; vol. 77, no. 416; SCC Letterbook 14, 512–13, 822–4, 868; House of Commons *Debates* (1894) 3345; (1900) 6436
83 House of Commons *Debates* (1894) 3345
84 Calculated from SCC subject file no. 66. See also chapter 7.
85 PAC RG13, A2, vol. 100, no. 20., S.H. Strong to E.L. Newcombe 16 January 1896
86 PAC D. Girouard Papers vol. 1, J.W. Gwynne to Girouard 22 January 1896, 11 January 1897
87 *Canada Law Journal* 30 (1894) 51. For a scalogram analysis of the Court's decisions in this period, see Bader and Burstein 'The Supreme Court of Canada 1892–1902' 503– 47.
88 *Attorney-General of Manitoba* v *Forest* [1979] 2 SCR 1032
89 P.B. Waite *Canada, 1874–1896: Arduous Destiny* (Toronto: McClelland and Stewart 1971) 246; *Canadian Advance* 26 June 1889
90 (1892) 19 SCR 374
91 *Western Law Times* 2 (1891) 88, 175, 189–91. Strong had concurred with Ritchie; the comment on the value of a judgment written by Strong is a distinct compliment and a reflection of the man's perceived intellectual ability.
92 *Western Law Times* 3 (1892) 82
93 Saywell 'Introduction' 36–7; Waite *Arduous Destiny* 246
94 *Western Law Times* 4 (1893) 123–4; *In re Certain Statutes of the Province of Manitoba relating to Education* (1894) 22 SCR 577

95 *Fraser* v *Drew* (1900) 30 SCR 241
96 *Ontario Mining Company* v *Seybold* (1902) 32 SCR 1
97 PAC Sir J.R. Gowan Papers reel M1899, H. O'Brien to [Gowan] [189?]; D. McMaster 'The Supreme Court of Canada in' *Canada: An Encyclopedia of the Country* vol. 6, edited by J.C. Hopkins (Toronto: Linscott 1900) 341; *Canadian Law Times* 15 (1895) 108–10; *Legal News* 18 (1895) 91–3
98 House of Commons *Debates* (1902) 219–20, 225, 1063; (1903) 283, 2351–73
99 *Canada Law Journal* 38 (1902) 61–5; Bader and Burstein 'The Supreme Court of Canada 1892–1902' 508–9; *Queen's Quarterly* 10 (1902–3) 416
100 *Canada Law Journal* 34 (1898) 1; *Canadian Law Review* 2 (1902–3) 127, 527, 627; *Canadian Law Review* 3 (1904) 283, 485
101 PAC RG13, A1, vol. 503, no. 495; UWO D. Mills Papers box 4287, Letterbook 7 375

CHAPTER 4

1 *Ottawa Valley Journal* 24 September 1901; Toronto *Globe* 25 September 1901; PAC F.-J. Audet Papers vol. 10, 5–9; PAC H.J. Morgan Papers vol. 6, 2158, 2161; PAC Sir J.R. Gowan Papers reel M1900, Sir J.S.D. Thompson to Gowan 1 June 1892
2 *Canada Law Journal* 37 (1901) 677, 758
3 UWO D. Mills Papers box 4286, Clippings Scrapbook; box 4287, Letterbook 1897–8, 189; Letterbook 1898, 437–8
4 PAC E. Blake Papers reel M247, no. 1860, J. Cameron to Blake 19 October 1896; F. Landon 'A Canadian Cabinet Episode of 1897' Royal Society of Canada *Transactions* (3d series) 32 (1938) 49–56
5 See, for example, *Canadian Law Times* 16 (1896) 271–3; PAC Sir W. Laurier Papers no. 51389–98 'The Supreme Court and David Mills' by 'Q.C.' May 1897
6 UWO D. Mills Papers box 4287, Letterbook 1900, 940–1, Mills to Sir W. Laurier 4 December 1900; 815–16, Mills to J.V. Teetzel 14 November 1900; box 4282, file of undated material, Mills to L.H. Davies [early 1897?]
7 *Canada Law Journal* 38 (1902) 65; *Canadian Law Times* 22 (1902) 106; *Canadian Law Times* 23 (1903) 219; London *Daily Free Press* 7 and 13 February 1902
8 Changing public attitudes were beginning to affect not just the judiciary but also patronage-related posts in general, the civil service, and the character and experience of politicians; see J. English *The Decline of Politics* (Toronto: University of Toronto Press 1977) chap. 1.
9 *Canadian Law Times* 22 (1902) 107

10 PAC H.J. Morgan Papers vol. 18, no. 247; *Canadian Law Times* 23 (1903) 319–21; Montreal *Star* 11 July 1903. Armour was already seventy-two years of age, however.

11 J.G. Descôteux *Faculté de Droit Université d'Ottawa 1953–1978* (Ottawa; University of Ottawa Press 1979) 26, 33–4. Justice Fournier had been vice-dean of the law faculty from 1892 to 1895; see ibid. 16–17, 33.

12 *Canadian Law Times* 22 (1902) 428

13 *Fortnightly Law Journal* 2 (1932) 13–14; *Canada Law Journal* 39 (1903) 338; *Saturday Night* 23 May 1903; PAC Sir R.L. Borden papers no. 5980ff; nos. 24563 and 142056–7

14 *Toronto Star* 7 February 1905. Chief Justice Falconbridge of Ontario expressed the usual reaction of chief justices when he commented on rumours that he was moving to the Supreme Court: 'I would not take it if it were offered me. I am chief in my own court here while in the Supreme Court I would be junior judge. I would have to leave my home in Toronto to go to Ottawa and my salary, even, would not be increased.' It is presumably a credit to the Laurier government's powers of persuasion that it was able to prevail upon not one but two provincial chief justices to accept Supreme Court appointments. After Killam was nominated, no provincial chief justice moved to the Supreme Court until 1962.

15 *Canadian Law Review* 2 (1902–3) 656–7; *Manitoba Law Journal* 2 (1885) 32; *Western Law Times* 1 (1890) 235–6

16 PAC Sir C. Fitzpatrick Papers no. 1851–2, A.C. Killam to Fitzpatrick 23 December 1902; no. 1918–20, 27 January 1903; no. 1921, Fitzpatrick to Killam 28 January 1903; Montreal *Star* 10 August 1903

17 *Manitoba Free Press* 10 and 11 August 1903; Montreal *Star* 10 August 1903; Toronto *Globe* 10 August 1903; Vancouver *Province* 10 August 1903

18 *The Canadian Annual Review of Public Affairs 1903* edited by J.C. Hopkins (Toronto: The Canadian Review 1904) 430–1; RSC 1906, c. 37, ss. 10 (2), 13 (2). Killam may have been attracted to the new post by the salary – $10,000, compared with the $7,000 salary of a puisne justice of the Supreme Court of Canada.

19 PAC Sir W. Laurier Papers no. 95895, W. Nesbitt to Laurier 21 March 1905; PAC RG13, A5, vol. 2050, no. 1002, Nesbitt to C.Fitzpatrick 3 October 1905; *Canadian Law Times* 25 (1905) 517, 562–3

20 *Canadian Law Review* 3 (1904) 226; *Canada Law Journal* 40 (1904) 209–10; London *Free Press* 6 May 1944, 32; *Maclean's Magazine* March 1914, 14

21 *Canadian Law Times* 25 (1905) 164; *Canadian Law Review* 4 (1905) 209

22 Ottawa *Citizen* 29 October 1888; PAC Sir J.S.D. Thompson Papers no. 8434, Sir J.A. Macdonald to [Thompson] [October 1888]; *Canada Law Journal* 24

(1888) 546–7; *Canadian Law Review* 4 (1905) 500. The assessments of Maclennan's judicial career to 1905 all emphasized his courteous behaviour and his industry; he too joined the Supreme Court at age seventy-two.

23 PAC Sir C. Fitzpatrick Papers no. 4088–9, memo from Sir H.-E. Taschereau [n.d.]; no. 4812, Fitzpatrick to Taschereau 30 April 1906; no. 4771, [Fitzpatrick] to D. Girouard 9 April 1906; PAC Sir W. Laurier Papers no. 103102–3, Laurier to E. Blake 11 November 1905

24 PAC RG13, A5, vol. 2050, no. 1067, R. Sedgewick to C. Fitzpatrick 16 October 1905

25 PAC Sir W. Laurier Papers no. 103102–3, Laurier to E. Blake 11 November 1905; no. 103482–4A, Blake to Laurier 20 November 1905

26 Ibid. no. 99871, E.H. McAlpine to Laurier 21 July 1905; no. 99872 [Laurier] to McAlpine 24 July 1905.

27 PAC F.-J. Audet Papers vol. 12, 842–4; *Revue du Barreau* 2 (1942) 371–3

28 See, for example, *Canada Law Journal* 42 (1906) 409–10; *Canadian Law Times* 26 (1906) 436; *Montreal Star* 4 June 1906; Quebec *L'Evénement* 4 June 1906; *Toronto Star* 4 June 1906

29 Reports in the press indicated that the post had been declined by E.P. Davis, a Vancouver lawyer, and that the government had considered J.S. Ewart, a famous Winnipeg lawyer, as a candidate for the position; see *Vancouver Province* 3 October 1906; *Ottawa Valley Journal* 28 September 1906, 4; PAC Sir L.P. Duff Papers file D, Duff to G. Davis 6 April 1940.

30 *Canadian Law Times* 26 (1906) 701–2; *Canada Law Journal* 40 (1904) 169; *Canada Law Journal* 42 (1906) 623; R. Gosse 'The Four Courts of Sir Lyman Duff' *Canadian Bar Review* 53 (1975) 484–91

31 PAC RG13, A5, vol. 2050, no. 168, J. Maclennan to A.B. Aylesworth, 29 January 1909

32 *Canada Law Journal* 45 (1909) 156

33 F.A. Anglin *Limitation of Actions against Trustees and Relief from Liability for Technical Breaches of Trust* (Toronto: Canada Law Book 1900); F.A. Anglin 'Mortgagee, Mortgagor and Assignee of the Equity of Redemption' *Canadian Law Times* 14 (1894) 57–77, 98–115; *Canadian Law Times* 20 (1900) 49; *Canada Law Journal* 36 (1900) 144

34 PAC F.-J. Audet Papers vol. 2 315–16; J.G. Snell 'Frank Anglin Joins the Bench: A Study of Judicial Patronage' *Osgoode Hall Law Journal* 18 (1980) 664–73; *Canadian Law Review* (1904) 226–7. Anglin had appeared as co-counsel in cases with A.B. Aylesworth, who by 1909 was minister of justice.

35 *Saturday Night* 6 October 1923; P.-G. Roy *Les Juges de la Province de Québec* (Quebec: R. Paradis 1933) 79; P.-B. Mignault 'Le Juge Brodeur' *Revue du Droit* 2 (1923–4) 241–7

36 *The Canadian Annual Review of Public Affairs 1903* 57
37 *In Re Marriage Laws* (1912) 46 SCR 132. On the background of the *ne temere* issue, see J.S. Moir 'Canadian Protestant Reaction to the *Ne Temere* Decree' Canadian Catholic Historical Association *Study Sessions* (1981) 79–90.
38 UWO D. Mills Papers box 4282, file 1902, Mills to [C. Fitzpatrick] 13 March 1902
39 See, for example, ibid. J. Willson (?) to Mills 14 November 1899.
40 See, for example, PAC D. Girouard Papers vol. 1, J.M. Kirkhoffer to Girouard 5 November 1902 and C. Fitzpatrick to Girouard 30 March 1903.
41 PAC M.J. Griffin Papers vol. 2, D. Mills to Griffin 9 July 1902
42 For examples of Sir Louis Davies' activities, see PAC Sir W. Laurier Papers no. 188648, Davies to Laurier 17 August 1911; House of Commons *Debates* (1906) 67.
43 Halifax *Herald* 3 October 1906; PAC Sir W. Laurier Papers no. 113203, C. Fitzpatrick to Laurier 28 August 1906; J.A. Charlebois to Laurier 4 May 1908; no. 141745, P.B. Dumoulin to Laurier, 20 June 1908
44 Halifax *Herald* 3 October 1906; PAC Sir R. L. Borden Papers no. 581; no. 8540–8613; ibid. vol. 25; PAC Sir W. Laurier Papers no. 113203. We are grateful to J. English for drawing some of this information to our attention.
45 PAC RG7, G21, vol. 579, no. 17943; *Saturday Night* 16 August 1913, 1; R.C. Brown *Robert Laird Borden* (Toronto: Macmillan 1980) vol. 2, 52, 91; PAC Sir C. Fitzpatrick Papers no. 7981
46 See chapter 3.
47 PAC Sir W. Laurier Papers no. 134486–7, L.P. Duff to Laurier [n.d.]; no. 134737–8; Gosse 'Four Courts of Duff' 493–4
48 Lord Dundonald, the general officer commanding the Canadian militia, had long chafed at the political control over himself and his forces. In June 1904 he took his complaints about 'political interference' before the Canadian public. Dundonald was dismissed by order-in-council and, supported by Canadian imperialists, for a time considered offering himself as a Conservative candidate in the upcoming federal election before leaving the country in July.
49 House of Commons *Debates* (1904) 7020–2, 7361–2
50 PAC RG13, A2, vol. 1914, no. 201
51 *Saturday Night* 31 May 1913; PAC Sir C. Fitzpatrick Papers no. 6836, Sir J. Pope to Fitzpatrick 28 June 1915
52 The Shell Committee was organized in the fall of 1914 by the Canadian minister of militia and defence to handle any munitions orders the British government wished to place in Canada.
53 7–8 Geo. V c. 19; J.L. Granatstein and J.M. Hitsman *Broken Promises: A*

History of Conscription in Canada (Toronto: Oxford University Press 1977) 83–98; D.R. Williams *Duff: A Life in the Law* (Vancouver: University of British Columbia Press 1984) 90–3

54 PAC Sir R. L. Borden Papers no. 135912–3, A. Meighen to Borden 17 June 1919. As a result of the demands of the appointment, Duff was frequently absent from the Supreme Court; in the second and third terms of 1918, for example, he was absent for a total of thirty-nine days while busy as Central Court of Appeal judge (see PAC RG13, A2, vol. 312, no. 754).

55 PAC Sir R.L. Borden Papers no. 39402, L.P. Duff to Borden 1 January 1917

56 Brown *Robert Laird Borden* vol. 2, 102–4; Gosse 'Four Courts of Duff' 494–8

57 PAC Sir R.L. Borden Papers no. 47377–9, L.P. Duff to Sir T. White 16 July 1916; no. 135912–3, A. Meighen to Borden 17 June 1919; PAC Sir L.P. Duff Papers file B2, Borden to Duff 1 January 1916 [1917]

58 (1918) 57 SCR 152

59 *Re Lewis* (1918) 41 DLR 1; *Canada Gazette* 20 July 1918, 252

60 PAC Sir C. Fitzpatrick Papers no. 7986, H. O'Brien to Fitzpatrick 29 July 1918; no. 7999–8000, G.H. Pownall to Fitzpatrick 1 August 1918; no. 8016, [Fitzpatrick] to E.R. Cameron 5 August 1918

61 Peter W. Hogg *Constitutional Law of Canada* (Toronto: Carswell 1977) 215–6

62 (1911) 45 SCR 95; PAC Sir L.P. Duff Papers file H [Duff to Lord Haldane (?) February 1925]; A.B. McKillop 'Introduction' in W.D. LeSueur *William Lyon Mackenzie: A Reinterpretation* (Toronto: Macmillan 1979). Duff held for the author, while Anglin in dissent supported the publishing company (and thus Mackenzie King). It is interesting to speculate as to whether this result influenced King, even subconsciously, in his selection of a chief justice in 1924.

63 *Canada Law Journal* 40 (1904) 1–2; PAC Sir C. Fitzpatrick Papers no. 8141, Fitzpatrick to F.A. Anglin 10 September 1918; *Maclean's Magazine* March 1916, 16

64 *Canada Law Journal* 43 (1907) 607. The registrar reported that the time limit on oral argument materially reduced the amount of time occupied by counsel in presenting their arguments; nevertheless the rule became inoperative in 1929. See E.R. Cameron *The Supreme Court of Canada, Practice and Rules* supplement to the 3rd ed. (Toronto: Carswell 1931) 104–17.

65 PAC D. Girouard Papers vol. 1, W. Nesbitt to Girouard 24 November 1906

66 PAC Sir W. Laurier Papers no. 167733, Sir C. Fitzpatrick to Laurier 3 March 1910; PAC Sir C. Fitzpatrick Papers no. 6502–3, L.P. Brodeur to Fitzpatrick 29 March 1913

67 PAC Sir C. Fitzpatrick Papers no. 8111, Fitzpatrick to G.H. Pownall 6 Septem-

ber 1918; no. 7999–8000, Pownall to Fitzpatrick 1 August 1918; no. 8140,
Fitzpatrick to Sir L. Davies 10 September 1918; no. 8153, [Fitzpatrick] to F.A.
Anglin 16 September 1918; *Maclean's Magazine* March 1914, 15

68 See, for example, C.H. Masters 'Supreme Court Practice' *Canada Law Journal* 36 (1900) 324–5; L.H. Coutlée 'Drainage Works and the Supreme Court' *Canada Law Journal* 37 (1901) 221–2.

69 *Stuart* v *the Bank of Montreal* (1909) 41 SCR 516; *Canada Law Journal* 45 653–6; A. Joanes 'Stare Decisis in the Supreme Court of Canada' *Canadian Bar Review* 36 (1958) 178–83

70 (1908) 40 SCR 313; *Saturday Night* 3 January 1914

71 [1914] AC 651, unreported in SCR

72 *Cunningham* v *Tomey Homma* [1903] AC 152

73 (1914) 49 SCR 440

74 Administrative law was not a particularly active area of the Supreme Court's jurisdiction prior to the Second World War. In the period 1903–39 the Court heard forty-six reported appeals from the Board of Railway Commissioners or its successor, but otherwise few such cases came to it. For example, in the same period there were only twelve reported appeals from provincial boards or commissions.

75 *In Re Canadian Northern Railway* (1910) 42 SCR 443

76 J. Nedelsky 'Judicial Conservatism in an Age of Innovation: Comparative Perspectives on Canadian Nuisance law 1880–1930' in *Essays in the History of Canadian Law* Vol. 1, edited by D.H. Flaherty (Toronto: Osgoode Society 1981) 281– 322

77 Ibid. 295–8; 63 SCR 243

78 See R.C.B. Risk '"This Nuisance of Litigation": The Origins of Workers' Compensation in Ontario' in *Essays in the History of Canadian Law* vol. 2, edited by D.H. Flaherty (Toronto: Osgoode Society 1983) 459–60.

79 *Montreal Rolling Mills Co.* v *Corcoran* (1897) 26 SCR 595; *Canadian Coloured Cotton Mills Co.* v *Kervin* (1899) 29 SCR 478. For an analysis of the law in Ontario in this matter, see Risk '"This Nuisance of Litigation"'

80 Williams *Duff* 150–1, 158, 175

81 Calculated from SCC subject file no. 66

82 Department of Justice file no. 110/1903, E.R. Cameron to C. Fitzpatrick 19 January 1903

83 *Canadian Law Review* 3 (1904) 377–83, 403– 22; *Canadian Law Times* 24 (1904) 243

84 *Canadian Law Times* 24 (1904) 381–2

85 *The Rules of the Supreme Court of Canada* edited by E.R. Cameron (Toronto: Poole & Co. 1907) 1– 8

86 60–61 Vict. c. 34, s. 1; 2 Edw. VII c. 35, s. 4
87 *Kent* v *Ellis* (1900) 31 SCR 113; *Gorman* v *Dixon* (1897) 26 SCR 91
88 Why Manitoba, Saskatchewan, and Alberta were left out is unclear; Manitoba seems to have been completely ignored, while it was explicit that no stated criteria were applied to the other two prairie provinces.
89 *Canadian Law Review* 3 (1904) 413; PAC RG13, A2, vol. 156, no. 834, J.J. Foy to A.B. Aylesworth 16 March 1909 and enclosure
90 PAC RG13, A5, vol. 2050, no. 953, Sir H.-E. Taschereau to Sir W. Laurier 8 January 1903 and 16 September 1906; A2, vol. 144, no. 3-H1, C. Fitzpatrick to E.L. Newcombe 18 October 1907; A.B. Aylesworth to governor-general in council 19 October 1907; vol. 2052, no. 563, F.A. Anglin to Aylesworth 15 March 1910 and enclosure; PAC Sir W. Laurier Papers no. 110221–2, E.R. Cameron to Fitzpatrick, 9 May 1906; House of Commons *Debates* (1906) 1103, 3068, 3910; (1907) 2978
91 There was a strong tendency, of course, to appoint geographically proximate jurists, that is, ones resident in Ontario and Quebec. Thus, in June 1918, when Fitzpatrick and Duff were absent, the chief justice of Ontario was asked to provide a replacement, though neither of the absent justice was from Ontario; see PAC RG13, A2, vol. 218, no. 3M.
92 PAC Sir R.L. Borden Papers no. 49412, Borden to Sir T. White 16 December 1918.
93 For an example of that sensitivity, see UWO D. Mills Papers box 4287, Letterbook 8 (1901–2), 471, Mills to Sir S.H. Strong 30 January 1902.
94 PAC Sir W. Laurier Papers no. 225739–41, Sir L.H. Davies to Laurier 7 June 1902.
95 PAC Sir C. Fitzpatrick Papers no. 5125–8
96 C. Miller *The Canadian Career of the Fourth Earl of Minto* (Waterloo: Wilfrid Laurier University Press 1980) 160; PAC Sir R.W. Scott Papers no. 2008–10, Sir S.H. Strong to Scott 21 November 1901
97 PAC Sir J. Pope Papers vol. 15, no. 11T; vol. 14, no. 3M; vol. 22, nos. 370, 376
98 PAC Sir C. Fitzpatrick Papers no. 5386, A. Shortt to Fitzpatrick 16 June 1908; no. 6359, Lord Grey to [Duke of Connaught] 23 May 1913; no. 6376, [Fitzpatrick] to R.L. Borden 30 June 1913; PAC Sir W. Laurier Papers no. 159490, Fitzpatrick to Laurier 3 September 1909
99 PAC RG13, A2, vol. 199, no. 146, R.J. Maclennan to C.J. Doherty 21 January 1916; Sir J. Aikins to Doherty 19 January 1916; A1, vol. 527, no. 840; House of Commons *Debates* (1905) 1398
100 PAC RG13, A2, vol. 197, no. 146, E.R. Cameron to W.S. Edwards 7 Febru-

ary 1916. For an example of delay, see PAC Sir L.P. Duff Papers file G, A. Grenier to Duff 6 February 1918 and memorandum to Duff 22 April 1926.

101 *The King* v *Stewart* (1902) 32 SCR 483; *McKee* v *Philip* (1916) 55 SCR 286; PAC RG13, A2, vol. 123, no. 343, E.L. Newcombe to E.R. Cameron 8 April 1902

102 *Canadian Law Times* 32 (1912) 971–3. Although thirteen of the decisions had been unanimous, in only two of those cases had there been just a single judgment. Of the twenty-four total appeals reported, two had one judgment, three had two, four had three, eight had four, five had five, and two had a full six judgments.

103 PAC RG13, A2, vol. 123, no. 343, E.R. Cameron to E.L. Newcombe 20 March 1902, and enclosure; vol. 214, no. 1394, Newcombe to Cameron 18 and 31 August 1917

104 PAC Sir W. Laurier Papers no. 132246–7, Sir C. Fitzpatrick to Laurier 16 November 1907; no. 120860, H. Gervais to Laurier 1 March 1907; PAC RG13, A2, vol. 145, no. 311, E.R. Cameron to A.B. Aylesworth 21 February 1907; 6 March 1907

105 This did not prevent Sir H.-E. Taschereau, who had retired on a 100 per cent annuity, from attempting to increase his income by seeking to avoid paying municipal income taxes; see PAC Sir W. Laurier Papers no. 161367, Taschereau to Laurier 26 October 1909.

106 House of Commons *Debates* (1911) 547; (1915) 2055; Senate *Debates* (1917) 263–7; PAC RG13, A2, vol. 212, no. 791

107 Calculated from SCC subject file no. 66

108 *Canada Law Journal* 52 (1916) 420

109 *Ottawa Citizen* 21 January 1913. See also, for example, *Canada Law Journal* 52 (1916) 419; *Canadian Law Review* 2 (1903) 589; *Maclean's Magazine* March 1914, 137–8; House of Commons *Debates* (1949) 18. Early in 1920 the attorney-general of Ontario wrote to the minister of justice: 'Has your Government considered whether or not the time has now come for the abolition of that [prerogative] appeal [to the Judicial Committee]? Most Ontario people who have considered the subject are, I think, agreed that it ought to be abolished as to ordinary litigation. Some of our judges and lawyers, however, as you will be aware, still hold to the view that the right of appeal ought to be retained as to constitutional questions. My own view is that the appeal to the Judicial Committee of the Privy Council ought to be abolished altogether. I think the people of Canada are as competent to manage their own affairs, including their law

courts, as are the people of Great Britain or the United States.' See PAO
RG4, C3, 1910/3876.

110 (1904) 35 SCR 197 at 200 (per Nesbitt J.)

CHAPTER 5

1 PAC RG13, A2, vol. 190, no. 3G, Sir C. Fitzpatrick to C.J. Doherty 19 March
1915; vol. 218, no. 3M, 31 May 1918; A5, vol. 2056, no. 2290, Fitzpatrick to Sir
R. L. Borden 21 October 1918. Interestingly, though he had not completed
the required fifteen years' service in the judiciary, Fitzpatrick was granted
a pension of two-thirds of his salary, which pension he renounced for the
duration of his term as lieutenant-governor; see PAC RG13, A5, vol. 2056,
no. 2290.

2 PAC Sir R.L. Borden Papers no. 85809, Sir C. Fitzpatrick to Borden 20 June
[1918]; no. 3598–99, memorandum [by Borden] 25 July 1918

3 House of Commons *Debates* (1918) 1976; PAC Sir R.L. Borden Papers no.
45855–74

4 House of Commons *Debates* (1918) (1896–7) 1976, 2478–9; (1919) 850. See also
(1917) 6049–51.

5 House of Commons Debates (1919) 850–79, 977

6 PAC RG13, A5, vol. 2057, no. 293, Sir H. Drayton to C.J. Doherty
22 January 1920; Doherty to Drayton 30 January 1920; Montreal
Star 27 March 1919, 4; PAC A. Meighen Papers no. 910–11, A.E.
Barbour to Meighen 27 March 1919; no. 914, J.L. Johnson to Meighen
8 April 1919

7 *Ottawa Farm Journal* 22 October 1918; Ottawa *Citizen* 22 October 1918;
Toronto Star 19 October 1918; Montreal *Star* 21 October 1918

8 PAC RG13, A2, vol. 183, no. 3C; PAC Sir R.L. Borden Papers no. 75953, Sir
L.H. Davies to Borden 1 September 1918; no. 75955, 6 September 1918;
no. 75954, Borden to Davies 3 September 1918; R. Gosse 'The Four Courts of
Sir Lyman Duff' *Canadian Bar Review* 53 (1975) 498

9 *Toronto Star* 19 and 23 October; Montreal *Star* 21 and 23 October 1918;
Ottawa *Citizen* 22 October; Gosse 'Four Courts' 499

10 A. Marin *L'Honorable Pierre-Basile Mignault* (Montreal: Fides 1946); *Revue du
Barreau* 5 (1945) 503–12; *Revue du Barreau* 7 (1947) 61–6; P.-G. Roy *Les Juges de
la province de Québec* (Quebec: R. Paradis 1933) 375; PAC F.-J. Audet Papers
vol. 21, 676–7; Montreal *Star* 24 October 1918

11 PAC RG13, A5, vol. 2058, no. 1596, L.P. Brodeur to R. Dandurand 10
September 1923, and passim; PAC W.L.M. King Papers reel C2251, no.
71220–7, Brodeur to King 27 September 1923; Diary vol. 1924, 2 January, at 1

12 Malouin practiced law in Quebec City, where he was for a time crown prosecutor. A member of Parliament from 1898 to 1905, he joined the Quebec court in 1905. He was sixty-six years old at the time of his appointment to Ottawa. See Roy *Les Juges* 339; *The Canadian Directory of Parliament, 1867– 1967* edited by J.K. Johnson (Ottawa: Public Archives of Canada 1968) 348–9.

13 PAC Sir L.P. Duff Papers file J, Duff to N. Jeffrey 7 February 1924. See also PAC W.L.M. King Papers reel C2252, no. 75320–1, Sir L. Gouin to King 31 December 1923. Early in March 1924 Malouin was reported to be severely ill and was forced to be absent for nine sitting days; see PAC RG13, A5, vol. 2058, no. 845.

14 R.M. Dawson *William Lyon Mackenzie King: A Political Biography, 1874–1923* (Toronto: University of Toronto Press 1958) 362, 387–8; F.W. Gibson 'The Cabinet of 1921' in *Cabinet Formation and Bicultural Relations* edited by F. Gibson (Ottawa: Information Canada 1970) 63–104

15 PAC W.L.M. King Papers MG26 J2, vol. 57, file Y-2600, M.L.L. Malouin to King 16 December 1923. In his diary the prime minister recounted a blatant example of a similarly partisan process associated with the Court (Diary vol. 1924, 18 January, at 18): 'This morning I spent clearing up correspondence ... Among appointments was a young man named Jones who came to ask if the next appt. to the Supreme Court Bench cld. not go to New Brunswick & to say he had been speaking in Eng.[land] on [tariff] preference was a student of economics at McGill, was deciding now which party he would belong to ... was at the "parting of the ways" & that decision of Govt. in apptg. his father to the Supreme Court would be the deciding factor. I never encountered such an insufferably conceited & arrogant & corrupt [?] young man.'

16 See, for example, Montreal *Star* 25 January 1924.

17 PAC W.L.M. King Papers, Diary vol. 1924, 1 May at 83; reel C2252, no. 73319, Sir L. Gouin to King 8 December 1923; reel C2701, C71115–6; reel C2244, no. 61311–5; MG26 J1, no. 72206–7, King to R. Dandurand 19 September 1923; no. 72224–6, Sir L. Davies to King 20 September 1923; Montreal *Star* 1 May 1924; PAC RG13, A5, vol. 2058, no. 845; vol. 2056, no. 2302; PAC A. Meighen Papers no. 18178–9, Davies to Meighen 30 March 1921, and enclosure; no. 18161–6, 25 February 1921

18 PAC W.L.M. King Papers, MG26 J1, no. 72206–7, King to R. Dandurand 19 September 1923; Diary vol. 1924, 4 January, at 4

19 Diary vol. 1924 5 May, at 85 and 11 May, at 88

20 PAC W.L.M. King Papers vol. 57, file Y-2600-Q-S-T, King to T. Eakin 28 July 1924; MG26 J1, no. 86521, King to E. Lafleur, 8 September 1924;

no. 86523–4, 9 September 1924; no. 86522, Lafleur to King 9 September 1924

21 See, for example, ibid. no. 83811, R.R. Cromarty to King 1 May 1924; PAC A.K. Cameron Papers vol. 22, Cameron to A.B. Hudson 25 March 1936.

22 R. Brossard 'Eugene Lafleur' *Canadian Bar Review* 11 (1933) 367–75; Montreal *Star* 30 April 1930; Montreal *La Presse* 30 April 1930

23 See, for example, PAC A.K. Cameron Papers vol. 22, Cameron to A.B. Hudson 25 March 1936; PAC W.L.M. King Papers MG26 J1, no. 90964–5, N.W. Rowell to King 12 May 1924; 83872–3, J.A. Cross to King 12 September 1924; reel C2261, no. 81595–6, Sir J.A.M. Aikins to King 10 September 1924.

24 PAC W.L.M. King Papers, Diary vol. 1924, 1 May, at 83–4 3 May, at 83–4; reel C2263, no. 83268, E.R. Cameron to King 1 May 1924. Another candidate, W.N. Tilley, was ruled out because his Liberal credentials were weak and, as chief counsel for the Canadian Pacific Railway, he was felt to be too influenced by that politically active, Conservative-leaning company; see ibid. reel C2266, King to P.C. Larkin 6 September 1924.

25 *Halifax Herald* 2 May 1924; PAC C. Murphy Papers vol. 23, no. 10120–5, J.F. Orde to Murphy 26 February 1927; PAC W.L.M. King Papers MG26 J2, vol. 57, file Y-2600, L. Harstone to King 12 May 1924; reel C2267, E.M. Macdonald to King 28 August 1924; Diary vol. 1924, 12 September at 114

26 PAC Sir L.P. Duff Papers file S, T. Sweatman to Duff 5 September 1924.

27 Ibid. 26 September 1924; Gosse 'Four Courts,' 501

28 PAC Sir C. Fitzpatrick Papers no. 8018, Fitzpatrick to E.W. Beatty, 8 August 1918; no. 8023, Fitzpatrick to E.R. Cameron, 10 August 1918; no. 8026, Fitzpatrick to A.C. Hill, 10 August 1918; Gosse 'Four Courts' 498

29 PAC W.L.M. King Papers, Diary vol. 1924, 4 May, at 84; authors' interview with D.C. Abbott, 18 April 1980

30 Toronto *Globe* 18 September 1924; PAC W.L.M. King Papers reel C2261, no. 81835–6, Sir A.B. Aylesworth to King 1 May 1924; reel C1933, no. 37098–9, Mrs H.I. Anglin to King 19 August 1919; reel C1944, no. 49301–2 [December 1921]; no. 49299–300, F.A. Anglin to King 7 December 1921.

31 PAC W.L.M. King Papers, Diary vol. 1924, 12 September, at 114

32 Ibid. reel C2267, no. 88308–9, E.M. Macdonald to King 28 August 1924; Diary vol. 1925, 9 March, at 49; authors' interview with D.C. Abbott, 18 April 1980; Snell's interview with W.K. Campbell, 16 July 1980.

33 *Canada Law Journal* 36 (1900) 473–4; *Fortnightly Law Journal* 1 (1931) 134; PAC Sir J. Pope Papers vol. 31, no. 1002, W.W. Cory to Pope 14 October 1924; E.L. Newcombe *The British North America Acts, as Interpreted by the Judicial Committee of the Privy Council* (Ottawa: S.E. Dawson 1908); House of Commons *Debates* (1909) 254–5 and (1910) 1014–16

34 PAC W.L.M. King Papers reel c2267, no. 88308–9, E.M. Macdonald to King 28 August 1924; reel c2263, no. 83660; no. 83688, J. Connor to King 18 September 1924; Diary vol. 1924, 12 September, at 114, and 15 September, at 117; MG26 J1, no. 89618–21, Sir W. Mulock to King 1 July 1924

35 *Revue du Barreau* 22 (1962) 563–72; Roy *Les Juges* 463; PAC L. St Laurent Papers vol. 239, file 'Hon. T. Rinfret'; PAC W.L.M. King Papers, Diary vol. 1924, 12 September, at 114

36 Under section 99 of the British North America Act, 1867, Superior Court judges held office during good behaviour and could be removed by the governor-general on address of the Senate and House of Commons. Superior Court judges were thus protected from compulsory retirement until the British North America Act was amended in 1960. But this protection did not cover county court judges, who were affected by compulsory retirement legislation as early as 1903 (3 Edw. VII c. 29, s. 3), or the members of the Supreme Court of Canada.

37 PAC RG13, A5, vol. 2059, no. 278 [E. Lapointe] to J. Idington 20 February 1926, and passim; A2, vol. 312, no. 754; vol. 296, no. 624; A1, vol. 537, no. 278

38 The best list of these cases is contained in R. Boult 'Ad Hoc Judges of the Supreme Court of Canada' *Chitty's Law Journal* 26 (1978) 289–95. However, a memorandum from the Justice Department lists fourteen cases not mentioned by Boult; see PAC, RG13, A2, vol. 312, no. 755.

39 *Canadian Bar Review* 1 (1923) 211

40 PAC W.L.M. King Papers MG26 J2, vol. 57, file Y-2600, J.H. Spence to King 4 August 1924; J.H. Lindsay to King 9 June 1924; P.M. Anderson to King 4 July 1924; J.E. Friesen to King 27 June 1924

41 On the Maritimes' rights movement in the 1920s see E.R. Forbes *The Maritimes Rights Movement, 1919–1927* (Montreal: McGill-Queen's University Press 1979).

42 Regina *Leader-Post* 10 March 1936; ibid. 4 April 1927; *Canadian Directory of Parliament* 317; *Fortnightly Law Journal* 2 (1932) 28–9

43 PAC W.L.M. King Papers MG26 J2, vol. 57, file Y-2600, J.H. Spence to King 4 August 1924

44 PAC C. Murphy Papers no. 10120–5, J.F. Orde to Murphy 26 February 1927

45 *Canadian Directory of Parliament* 539; PAC W.L.M. King Papers reel c2248, no. 66762–3, C. Murphy to King 4 October 1922, and enclosure; reel c2259, no. 80512, R. Smith to King 21 December 1923; MG26 J1, no. 125703–4, N.W. Rowell to King 8 April 1927

46 PAC W.L.M. King Papers MG26 J2, vol. 15, file J-1100, A.N. Smith to King 21 October 1926; 17 February 1927; 25 March 1927; J1, no. 127176–7,

R. Smith to King March 12 1927; reel c2301, no. 127179, 9 May
1927

47 Ibid. J2, vol. 15, file J-1100, A.N. Smith to King 21 October 1926; 17
February 1927. The population figures are calculated from the *Census of
Canada, 1921* vol. 1, 3 568.

48 There were letters discussing the retiremennt, but they have been lost
and their contents are unknown: see PAC, RG13, A1, vol. 540, no. 989.

49 See, for example, *Dupuy* v *Ducondu* (1882) 6 SCR 425; *Canadian Pacific Railway*
v *Robinson* (1888) 14 SCR 105; *Wadsworth* v *McCord* (1887) 12 SCR 466; *Ross*
v *The King* (1902) 32 SCR 532.

50 *Montreal Street Railway* v *Boudreau* (1905) 36 SCR 329 involved a claim for
negligence. The common-law justices (Davies, Nesbitt, and Idington)
combined to view the case as a matter of tort law and disposed of it on the
appropriate common-law precedents. The two Quebec justices agreed
with the Court of Appeal that this as a strict Civil Code case and that
damages should be awarded for negligence.

51 See, for example, *Saint Lawrence Terminal Company* v *Hallé* (1908) 39 SCR
47; *Audette* v *O'Cain* (1908) 39 SCR 103; *Tanguay* v *Canadian General
Electric* (1908) 40 SCR 1.

52 P.B. Mignault 'L'Avenir de notre droit civil' *La Revue du Droit* 1 (1922)
104–16

53 For a useful account of Mignault's career as defender of the Civil Code, see
J.-G. Castel 'Le juge Mignault defenseur de l'intégreté du droit civil
québécois' *Canadian Bar Review* 53 (1975) 544–57.

54 60 SCR 105

55 60 SCR 131. Justice Duff does not take up the essential issue in either of
these cases; he disposes of both cases with a single sentence and appears
insensitive to or unaware of the importance of the matter.

56 Mignault elaborated on these issues five years later in 'The Authority of
Decided Cases' *Canadian Bar Review* 3 (1925) 1–14.

57 Those two cases were *Kierman* v *Metropolitan Life Insurance* [1925] SCR 600
and *Regent Taxi* v *Congregation des Petits Frères de Marie* [1929] SCR 650.

58 Those three cases were *Brilliant Silk Company* v *Kaufman* [1925] SCR 249;
Larue v *Royal Bank of Canada* [1926] SCR 218; *Attorney-General of Canada* v
Attorney-General of Quebec [1929] SCR 557.

59 PAC E. Lapointe Papers no. 1975, W.L.M. King to Lapointe 4 October
1929; vol. 19, file no. 49, Lapointe to King 7 October 1929

60 Montreal *Le Devoir* 1 October 1929. There had also been speculation that
Lapointe himself was interested in the post, but this was likely just
partisan gossip; see *Saturday Night* 8 September 1928.

61 Quebec *Le Soleil* 3 January 1930; *Ottawa Journal* 26 December 1929

62 PAC RG13, A2, vol. 374, no. 1562, memorandum to the minister of justice, 7 October 1932

63 PAC W.L.M. King Papers, Diary vol. 1929, 26 November, at 262; vol. 1933, 1 March at 70, and 3 March at 72

64 PAC Sir R.L. Borden Papers no. 53281, Sir L.H. Davies to Borden 31 July 1919; no. 53284, F.A. Anglin to Borden 3 August 1919; B.F. Hogan 'The Guelph Novitiate Raid' Canadian Catholic Historical Association *Study Sessions* (1978) 57–80

65 D.R. Williams *Duff: A Life in the Law* (Vancouver: University of British Columbia Press 1984) 156. Duff was used in a somewhat similar manner at the Judicial Committee, being involved in 1924 in the Irish Boundary Commission.

66 PAC Sir R.L. Borden Papers, nos. 104433–47, 104481–3; nos. 80396, 80407–8; PAC Sir L.P. Duff Papers file R-S [Duff] to W.E. Raney 7 March 1923

67 See, for example, Department of Justice file no. 920/1919; file no. 157/1925; file no. 267/1927; file no. 779/1927; file no. 420/1930.

68 American Supreme Court justices were receiving $20,000 ($20,500 for the chief justice) by 1927, for example; see, House of Commons *Debates* (1927) 1561–2. In 1917 one member of Parliament estimated that 'a lawyer in a good practice in Canada can earn twice or three times as much as the salary of the Chief Justice, and a gentleman of the eminence of the Chief Justice could easily earn at the Bar from $25,000 to $50,000 per annum in the larger cities'; see House of Commons *Debates* (1917) 6051.

69 Annual Departmental Reports: Department of Justice 1929–30 (Ottawa 1930) vol. 1, part L-5,7

70 B.L. Strayer *Judicial Review of Legislation in Canada* (Toronto: University of Toronto Press 1968) 183

71 Ibid. 183–4. This strengthening of the process was paralleled by provincial legislation at this time providing for references to the highest court of appeal within the provinces; see ibid. 186–7.

72 The federal Conservative governments of the 1890s sent five reported cases to the Court on reference, followed by a hiatus in the early years of the Laurier government.

73 *In re Certain Statutes of the Province of Manitoba Relating to Education* (1894) 22 SCR 677

74 *Attorney-General of Ontario v Hamilton Street Railway* [1903] AC 524

75 *In re References by Governor-General in Council* (1910) 43 SCR 561

76 Nevertheless, the justices continued to insist on the distinction between a reference and a stated case. See *In re Board of Commerce* (1920) 60 SCR 456;

G. Rubin 'The Nature, Use and Effect of Reference Cases in Canadian Constitutional Law' *McGill Law Journal* 6 (1959–60) 169–70. The Judicial Committee upheld the constitutionality of the reference system in 1912; see Strayer *Judicial Review* 185.

77 RSC 1906 c. 37, s. 55; *In re Branch Lines of Canadian Pacific Railway* (1905) 36 SCR 42

78 9–10 Geo. V c. 37, s. 32; *In re Board of Commerce* (1920) 60 SCR 456; Rubin 'Reference Cases' 169–70

79 Strayer *Judicial Review* 187–8; *Hirsch* v *Protestant Board of School Commissioners* [1926] SCR 246; *In re Meaning of the Word 'Persons'* [1928] SCR 276. Some popular accounts of the latter case contain erroneous assertions that section 60 of the Supreme Court Act (RSC 1906 c. 139) permitted any five interested persons to petition the government for such an order-in-council but section 60 actually included no such wording. See, for example, C.L. Cleverdon *The Woman Suffrage Movement in Canada* (Toronto: University of Toronto Press 1950) 145.

80 Toronto *Globe* 4 November 1927. Water power refers to the energy source potentially convertible to electricity.

81 H.B. Neatby *William Lyon Mackenzie King: 1924–1932, The Lonely Heights* (Toronto: University of Toronto Press 1963) 255–63. A good example of the use of references as a delaying tactic is *In re the Constitutional Validity of Section 17 of the Alberta Act* [1927] SCR 364, where, despite a unanimous decision in the Supreme Court unopposed by any government, Ottawa chose to appeal the decision to the Judicial Committee.

82 *Saturday Night* 13 October 1928; *Reference re Waters and Water-Powers* [1928] SCR 200

83 In the *Water-powers Reference* the costs of the five counsel representing the attorney-general of Canada alone in the case were $60,179.50, and eleven days were consumed in hearing argument. The cost of the eleven counsel representing six other parties is unknown.

84 PAC Sir L.P. Duff Papers file H [Duff to Lord Haldane (?) February 1925]; *Gold Seal Ltd* v *Attorney-General of Alberta* (1921) 62 SCR 424

85 As a member of the Judicial Committee Duff participated in sixteen reported Canadian constitutional cases and wrote the opinion in three of them.

86 Duff's views on the federal character of the British North America Act appear to have impressed the Judicial Committee in *City of Montreal* v *Montreal Street Railway* [1912] AC 333.

87 [L.P. Duff] to W.F. MacLean [early 1925]; letter in possession of David R. Williams.

88 L.P. Duff 'The Privy Council' *Canadian Bar Review* 3 (1925) 273–81

89 For a useful review of Duff's contribution in constitutional cases, see
   G. LeDain 'Sir Lyman Duff and the Constitution' *Osgoode Hall Law Journal* 12
   (1974) 261–338.
90 *In the Matter of Sections Four and Seventy of the Canadian 'Insurance Act, 1910'*
   (1913) 48 SCR 260
91 *Attorney-General of Ontario* v *Attorney-General of Canada* [1896] AC 348
92 [1922] AC 191
93 *In re Board of Commerce* (1920) 60 SCR 456
94 For a discussion of Duff's judgment in *Board of Commerce*, See B. Laskin
   'Peace, Order and Good Government Re-examined' *Canadian Bar Review*
   25 (1947) 1054–87. Similarly federalist jurisprudence was developing in this
   period related to the trade and commerce power. Most of the justices readily
   accepted the leadership of the Judicial Committee and Duff in constitutional law. Chief Justice Anglin, however, perhaps spurred by his personality conflict with Duff, voiced some discontent in *The King* v *Eastern
   Terminal Elevator* [1925] SCR 434.
95 Since the Court kept no complete record of caseloads and since the Reports
   were still selective in their criteria for reporting, it is necessary to rely on
   outside or subjective observations for such comments. For the 1920s the
   absence of comment on workload leads us to assume that there was no
   significant change.
96 Williams *Duff* 146; *In re Meaning of the Word 'Persons'* [1928] SCR 276; *Edwards*
   v *Attorney-General of Canada* [1930] AC 125
97 PAC Sir L.P. Duff Papers file D, Duff to Sir L.H. Davies 28 April 1923; file
   M, P.B. Mignault to Duff 24 September 1924
98 *Proceedings of the Fifth Annual Meeting of the Canadian Bar Association, 1920*
   (Winnipeg 1920) 259; ... *Sixth* ... *1921* (Toronto 1922), 250; ... *Seventh* ... *1922*
   (Toronto 1923) 267; ... *Twelfth* ... *1927* (Toronto 1928) 66–9, 250; *Canadian Bar
   Review* 4 (1926), 102–3
99 PAC Sir L.P. Duff Papers file Q-R, T. Rinfret to Duff 10 January [1925]; file
   A, F.A. Anglin to Duff 30 September 1926, 4 December 1926, and 24
   January 1927; file M [Duff] to P.B. Mignault 20 September 1928; file Q-R
   [Duff] to Rinfret 20 September 1928. It is not known how often these
   judicial conferences were held.
100 PAC RG13, A2, vol. 215, no. 228 [E.L. Newcombe] to E.R. Cameron 6
   February 1917, 14 February 1917; Cameron to Newcombe 8 February and
   5 April 1917; PAC Sir L.P. Duff Papers file C, Duff to R.R. Cromarty 15
   June 1923
101 PAC RG13, A2, vol. 222, no. 892
102 *Proceedings of the Seventh Annual Meeting of the Canadian Bar Association, 1922*

(Toronto 1923) 71; PAC RG13, A2, vol. 283, no. 1944; vol. 341, no. 1068; Public Archives of New Brunswick, Barristers' Society of New Brunswick, *Council Minute Book* 9 April 1921. By way of contrast with the distribution in the 1880s, the provincial distribution in 1930 was as follows: Prince Edward Island 41, Nova Scotia 56, New Brunswick 182, Quebec 697, Ontario 2,513, Manitoba 689, Saskatchewan 608.5, Alberta 576.5, British Columbia 179.

103 *Canadian Bar Review* 1 (1923) 108

104 *Minutes of Proceedings of the Eleventh Annual Meeting of the Canadian Bar Association 1926* (Toronto 1927) 61–63; ... *Twelfth* ... *1927* (Toronto 1928) 249; PAC Sir L.P. Duff Papers file C, R.R. Cromarty to Duff 24 March 1926; G.W. Howell 'A Slice of Canadian Legal History – 156 Years of Law Reporting in Ontario' unpublished paper 47–8, 56; PAC RG13, A1, vol. 535, no. 1166

105 House of Commons *Debates* (1925) 130–2, 283–341; (1927) 1054, 1755; (1929) 25; M. Prang *N.W. Rowell* (Toronto: University of Toronto Press 1975) 441–2; PAC Sir L.P. Duff Papers file H [Duff to Lord Haldane (?) February 1925]. See also chapter 7.

106 See, for example, PAC RG13, A2, vol. 316, no. 1610, A. McConnell to E. Lapointe 19 October 1927.

107 PAC Sir L.P. Duff Papers file A, F.A. Anglin to Duff 30 September 1926; *Canadian Bar Review* 8 (1930) 681–2

CHAPTER 6

1 PAC W.L.M. King Papers, Diary vol. 1932, 11 January, at 339

2 Ibid. vol. 1929, 28 September, at 211; PAC RG13, A5, vol. 2063, no. 3A; vol. 2061, no. 3C

3 PAC W.L.M. King Papers, Diary vol. 1933, 2 January, at 3, and 11 January, at 14. In July 1930, Anglin was so incapacitated that he could not conduct his own correspondence; see Bodleian, Lord Sankey Papers, c507, no. 96, F.A. Anglin to Sankey 2 July [1930]; no. 97, H.I. Anglin to Sankey [circa July 1930].

4 PAC W.L.M. King Papers, Diary vol. 1933, 11 January, at 14; PAC RG13, A5, vol. 2063, no. 3 A.

5 D.R. Williams *Duff: A Life in the Law* (Vancouver: University of British Columbia Press 1984) 138–42, 153, 157–9, 316–17; *Saturday Night* 11 April 1931; PAC A. Meighen Papers no. 109480, E.H. Finlayson to Meighen 15 November 1932 Duff's alcoholism was exacerbated by the death of his wife in 1926.

6 Williams *Duff* 157–62. The selection was influenced by Duff's close friendship with W.D. Herridge, Bennett's brother-in-law and close adviser.

7 Windsor *Border Cities Star* 18 March 1933; *Ottawa Morning Journal* 21
March 1933; *Fortnightly Law Journal* 2 (1933) 285, 295–6; *Vancouver Province* 13
February 1933; PAC Sir L.P. Duff Papers file U, W.P.M. Kennedy to
Duff 18 March 1933

8 PAC R.B. Bennett Papers no. 251760–1, Bennett to C.D. Richards 28 January
1932; Toronto *Globe* 18 May 1932

9 PAC A. Meighen Papers no. 103437–40, O.S. Crocket to Meighen 16
February 1932; University of New Brunswick, O.S. Crocket Papers box 7,
file 10; Saint John *Telegraph-Journal* 13 April 1943, 3, 11; *Fortnightly Law
Journal* 2 (1933) 106–7

10 PAC A. Meighen Papers no. 36240, O.S. Crocket to Meighen 14 March 1924;
no. 42555–7, 31 August 1925; no. 103437–40, 16 February 1932, 4 April
1935; no. 141048–50 11 July 1936; no. 141042, Meighen to Crocket 22 September 1932; W.H. McConnell 'The Judicial Review of Prime Minister
Bennett's "New Deal"' *Osgoode Hall Law Journal* 6 (1968) 53–4

11 Snell's interview with W.K. Campbell, 16 July 1980

12 *Fortnightly Law Journal* 2 (1933) 285–6, 310–11; *Winnipeg Free Press* 18 March
1933

13 PAC RG13, A5, vol. 2066, no. 135295, F.J. Hughes to H. Guthrie 27 August
1934; PAC Sir L.P. Duff Papers file H, Hughes to Duff 25 July 1935

14 *Ottawa Journal* 1 July 1944 5; *Maclean's Magazine* 1 April 1936 46–7; *Fortnightly Law Journal* 4 (1935) 209, 233–4

15 PAC A. Meighen Papers no. 120783, R.A. Reid to Meighen 19 May 1935;
Fortnightly Law Journal 5 (1935) 55–6

16 PAC W.L.M. King Papers MG26 J2, vol. 158, files J-200 and J-200-H

17 *Fortnightly Law Journal* 5 (1936), 294–5; *Winnipeg Free Press* 26 March 1926
3, 6; PAC W.L.M. King Papers reel C2301, no. 127411, H.T. Symington to
King 3 April 1927; R.M. Dawson *W.L.M. King, 1874–1923* (Toronto:
University of Toronto Press 1958) 361–70, 450

18 PAC A.K. Cameron Papers vol. 22, Cameron to A.B. Hudson 25 March 1936

19 PAC W.L.M. King Papers MG26 J2, vol. 158, file J-200, R. Taschereau to King
16 February 1940; *Fortnightly Law Journal* 9 (1940) 247–8; B. Lee 'The
Amazing Taschereaus' *The Globe Magazine* 2 November 1963, 6–8, 15; Department of Justice, file no. 141312 [W.S. Edwards], memorandum to the minister
of justice, 29 January 1940

20 *Fortnightly Law Journal* 13 (1943) 6–7; *Canadian Bar Review* 47 (1969) 155–60

21 PAC W.L.M. King Papers MG26 J2, vol. 158, file J-200-7

22 Ibid. Diary vol. 1939, 9 March, at 300; MG26 J2, vol. 158, file

J-200-1; House of Commons *Debates* (1939) 3104–5; (1943) 63–74, 107

23 PAC Sir L.P. Duff Papers file A, Duff to Sir D. Alexander 14 February 1943; J.W. Pickersgill *The Mackenzie King Record 1939–1944* (Toronto: University of Toronto Press 1960) 74

24 PAC L. St Laurent Papers, vol. 4, file 35–3, speech by Duff 15 December 1943

25 PAC W.L.M. King Papers, Diary vol. 1944, 5–7 January at 11, 13, and 16; MG26 J2, vol. 158, file J-200-1, A. de la Rochelle to [King] 27 November 1942; *Fortnightly Law Journal* 13 (1944) 177

26 Toronto *Globe and Mail* 13 December 1975

27 PAC W.L.M. King Papers MG26 J2, vol. 158, file J-200-1, Senator A. Blais to King 4 January 1943. See also files J-200-1 and J-200-7. Frank Ford of the provincial Supreme Court was recommended almost unanimously by those supporting Alberta's claims.

28 Ibid. file J-200-7, J.G. Gardiner to King 4 July 1944, and passim

29 *Saskatoon Star-Phoenix* 23 January 1956; *Regina Leader-Post* 23 January 1956; *Toronto Daily Star* 23 January 1956

30 PAC W.L.M. King Papers, Diary vol. 1947, 22 May; MG26 J2, vol. 436, file J-20, I. Mackenzie to King, 26 May 1947; authors' interview with D.C. Abbott 18 April 1980

31 PAC RG13, A1, vol. 544, nos. 634 and 953; R.M. Dawson *Constitutional Issues in Canada 1900–1931* (London: Oxford University Press 1933) 325–32

32 8 Geo. VI c. 45; 10 Geo. VI c. 56; 13 Geo. VI c. 27. It is estimated that a leading lawyer in Saskatchewan during the Second World War would have had an income of $10,000–$12,000; this made appointment to the Court economically attractive (W.Z. Estey to F. Vaughan 4 May 1983).

33 House of Commons *Debates* (1946) 2717; *Canadian Bar Review* 11 (1933) 27–40

34 *Winnipeg Free Press* 4 June 1947; SCC biographical directory, at 13, and judges' files; PAC A. Meighen Papers no. 103762, C.H. Locke to Meighen 15 August 1933

35 PAC W.L.M. King Papers, Diary 7 July 1947, 26 January 1948, 28 May 1948, at 5. According to Ilsley, Rand was either 'anxious to get back to N.B.' or considering a return to private practice.

36 *Proceedings of the Fifth Annual Meeting of the Canadian Bar Association, 1920* (Winnipeg 1920) 120–2; House of Commons *Debates* (1932) 2999

37 See, for example, *Fortnightly Law Journal* 12 (1942) 162; *Fortnightly Law Journal* 13 (1943) 33–4, 177, 226; House of Commons *Debates* (1947) 4927

38 PAC W.L.M. King Papers MG26 J4, reel C4279, NO. C141860-1

39 PAC Sir L.P. Duff Papers file D, Duff to H.H. Davis 18 February 1942; J.L. Granatstein *The Politics of Survival* (Toronto: University of Toronto Press

1967) 119–22; House of Commons *Debates* (1943) 63–74; Williams *Duff*
221–39, 255–61

40 House of Commons *Debates* (1942) 521; PAC W.L.M. King Papers, Diary
vol. 1942, 4 February, at 115

41 J.L. Granatstein *A Man of Influence* (Ottawa: Deneau 1981) 177–9; J.W.
Pickersgill and D.F. Forster *The Mackenzie King Record 1945–1946* (Toronto:
University of Toronto Press 1970) 133–58; M.H. Fyfe 'Some Legal Aspects of
the Report of the Royal Commission on Espionage' *Canadian Bar Review*
24 (1946) 777–84. In addition to the two justices, Gérald Fauteux was
commission counsel.

42 See, for example, PAC Sir L.P. Duff Papers file A, Duff to C.H.A. Armstrong
15 March 1934, 8 June 1935; file G, Duff to H. Guthrie 15 March 1934, 20
May 1935, 16 February 1935; file K [Duff] to S.C.S. Kerr 20 September 1935;
file L, E. Lapointe to Duff 29 May 1936.

43 Williams *Duff* 94–5; J.W. Pickersgill and D.F. Forster *The Mackenzie King
Record 1944–1945* (Toronto: University of Toronto Press 1968) 222. Duff's
membership in the Ottawa-based political élite is underlined by his leadership of the Dining Club in the early 1940s, an exclusive club in which
leading Ottawa figures met monthly for good food and good gossip; see
Granatstein *Man of Influence* 112 note.

44 Department of Justice file no. 137743, Sir L.P. Duff to W.S. Edwards 20
February 1937, and passim; file no 139048, Edwards to Duff 4 April 1938,
and passim

45 PAC R.B. Bennett Papers no. 251858, J.C. Mahaffy to Bennett 15 February
1933

46 House of Commons *Debates* (1946) 2717

47 *Canadian Bar Review* 8 (1930) 675–6

48 PAC RG13, A2, vol. 401, no. 614, P.G. Thomson to H. Guthrie 21 May 1934

49 Ibid. Guthrie to Thomson 23 July 1934. This final point was rewritten within
the Justice Department so as to avoid any implication that the Supreme
Court was not held in the highest possible regard everywhere; see ibid.
W.S. Edwards to Mr Plaxton 26 July 1934.

50 Ibid. Thomson to Guthrie 7 August 1934

51 Ibid.

52 In this case, however, most of the public criticism seems to have been
levelled not at the Supreme Court but at the quality of the Manitoba
court. These complaints offer an interesting contrast to the 1890s,
when there were also criticisms of the rate of reversal suffered by Manitoba courts in Ottawa. In the earlier instance the criticism had pointed to
bias and weakness in the Supreme Court; by the 1940s, however the

Supreme Court was perceived as a neutral, accurate, and valued arbiter of the law. Over the years the Court had acquired a respected place in the eyes of lay observers. The lead editorial of the *Winnipeg Free Press* of 15 February 1944 detailed the Manitoba Court of Appeal's 'incapacity,' weakness, and reversal rate; see also the issue of 17 February 1944.

53 PAC Sir L.P. Duff Papers, file M [Duff] to H. Mercier 5 March 1935. See also, for example, file D [Duff] to A.K. Dysart 16 January 1936; file Q-R, Duff to Justice Rivard 23 May 1933.

54 Authors' interview with D.C. Abbott 18 April 1980; Snell's interview with W.K. Campbell 16 July 1980

55 See, for example, PAC Sir L.P. Duff Papers file S, Duff to Justice St Germain 13 November 1934; W.K. Campbell 'The Right Honourable John Cartwright' *Law Society of Upper Canada Gazette* 12 (1978) 338.

56 PAC Sir L.P. Duff Papers file D, H.H. Davis to Duff 9 December 1935; compare *Fortnightly Law Journal* 5 (1936) 209.

57 PAC Sir L.P. Duff Papers file S, Duff to Justice St Germain 22 November 1934; [1935] SCR 53

58 *Reference re the Jurisdiction of the Tariff Board* [1934] SCR 538; *Reference re the Constitutional Validity of Section 110 of the Dominion Companies Act* [1934] SCR 653; *Reference re the Constitutional Validity of the Companies' Creditors Arrangement Act* [1934] SCR 659

59 J.R.H. Wilbur *The Bennett New Deal: Fraud or Portent* (Toronto: Copp Clark 1968) is the most useful work on this subject.

60 H.B. Neatby *W.L.M. King 1932–1939* (Toronto: University of Toronto Press 1976) 94–5; House of Commons *Debates* (1935) 157–8, 281, 2064–5

61 PAC Sir L.P. Duff Papers file D [Duff] to A.K. Dysart 10 January 1936

62 McConnell 'Judicial Review of Bennett's "New Deal"' 50, 82–3

63 PAC W.L.M. King Papers MG26 J2, vol. 158, file J-200-M, E.M. Macdonald to King 15 February 1936. These references to the Supreme Court and to the JCPC cost the federal government $66,042.64; see House of Commons *Debates* (1943) 683.

64 Neatby *King 1932–1939* 225–31. On the contest between the Social Credit Government and Ottawa, see J.R. Mallory *Social Credit and the Federal Power in Canada* (Toronto: University of Toronto Press 1954).

65 *Reference re the Power of the Governor-General in Council to Disallow Provincial Legislation and the Power of Reservation of a Lieutenant-Governor of a Province* [1938] SCR 71

66 *Reference re Alberta Statutes* [1938] SCR 100

67 PAC Sir L.P. Duff Papers file Q-R [Duff] to N.W. Rowell 11 March 1938

68 Montreal *Star* 5 March 1938; *Vancouver Province* 9 March 1938; *Canadian Bar Review* 16 (1938) 215–16

69 *Reference as to Whether Members of the Military or Naval Forces of the United States of America Are Exempt from Criminal Proceedings in Canadian Criminal Courts* [1943] SCR 483

70 Neatby *King 1932–1939* 235–6, 267–8; C.P. Wright 'To Finance Padlock Appeals' *Canadian Forum* 14 (1939) 215–20; House of Commons *Debates* (1938) 3421

71 *Christie* v *York Corporation* [1940] SCR 139

72 *Reference Relating to Persons of the Japanese Race* [1946] SCR 248. See also *Fortnightly Law Journal* 16 (1946) 30–9.

73 *Financial Post* 4 May 1946

CHAPTER 7

1 SCC Letterbook 13, 200–2, R. Cassels to E.L. Newcombe 25 February 1897

2 Ibid.; SCC Letterbook 15, 660–1, E.R. Cameron to E.L. Newcombe 11 December 1899

3 PAC RG13, A2, vol. 122, no. 263; PAC Sir W. Laurier Papers no. 83859–60, E.R. Cameron to C. Fitzpatrick 28 March 1904

4 SCC Letterbook 1900–1, 3, E.R. Cameron to E.L. Newcombe 29 May 1900; PAC RG11, vol. 4327, file no. 2994-1-B, Cameron to C. Fitzpatrick 12 April 1904

5 PAC Sir W. Laurier Papers no. 225761-62, E.R. Cameron to C. Fitzpatrick 12 January 1903; PAC RG13, A2, vol. 122, no. 263

6 House of Commons *Debates* (1903) 3404; (1906) 7036

7 PAC RG11, vol. 4328, file no. 2994-1-C, 'Excerpts from Reports of the Department of Public Works'

8 *Maclean's* March 1914, 13; PAC RG13, A2, vol. 164, no. 1538

9 PAC RG11, vol. 4327, file no. 2994-1-B; vol. 4328, file no. 2994-1-C

10 SCC Judges' Files, L.A.D. Cannon, E.R. Cameron to W.S. Edwards 23 January 1930

11 PAC RG11, vol. 4328, file no. 2994-1-C, T.W. Fuller, memo to the deputy minister 29 August 1931; ibid. Supplementary Public Works Estimates 1934–5

12 PAC Sir L.P. Duff Papers file C, J.J. Heagerty to Dr Woodhouse 9 December 1935; ibid. 'Report re Building Occupied by the Supreme Court of Canada'; PAC RG11, vol. 4328, file no. 2994-1-C, 'Report re Building Occupied by the Supreme Court of Canada'

13 PAC E. Lapointe Papers vol. 19, file no. 49, W.L.M. King to Lapointe 11 April 1936; PAC RG11, vol. 4328, file no. 2994-1-C

14 V. Tomovcik 'Reconstruction of Ottawa-Hull: The Gréber Era' MA thesis, University of Waterloo 1977

15 PAC RG11, vol. 4328, file no. 2994-1-C

16 Ibid. PAC W.L.M. King Papers MG26 J2, vol. 158, file J-200-S (1936); House of Commons Debates (1937) 292

17 Montreal Gazette 3 January 1980, 49; Saturday Night 28 August 1954, 25 Ottawa Citizen 28 December 1979; W. Chevalier 'Entretien avec Ernest Cormier' Vie des Arts 20 (1975–6), 14–19, 87–9; 'Plans by Cormier' Canadian Business 24 (1951) 26–7, 84–7

18 PAC RG11, vol. 4328, file no. 2994-1-C-D-F; Snell's interview with W.K. Campbell, 16 July 1980; SCC building file

19 Ottawa Journal 23 November 1940; Toronto Globe and Mail 5 April 1980

20 PAC RG11, vol. 4331, file no. 2994-26

21 PAC W.L.M. King Papers MG26 J2, vol. 436, file J-15-7, E. Cormier to King 21 September 1945; SCC building file; PAC RG11, vol. 4330, file no. 2994-1-0

22 There is much literature on this controversy. See F.H. Underhill 'Edward Blake, the Supreme Court Act, and the Appeal to the Privy Council, 1875–6' Canadian Historical Review 19 (1938) 245–63, 292–4; F. Mackinnon 'The Establishment of the Supreme Court of Canada' Canadian Historical Review 26 (1946) 258–74; J.D. Livermore 'Towards "A Union of Hearts": The Early Career of Edward Blake, 1867–1880' PH D thesis, Queen's University 1975, 290–316.

23 Johnston v St Andrews (1877) App. Cas. 159; Canada Central Railway Co. v Murray (1883) 8 App. Cas. 574; Prince v Gagnon (1883) 8 App. Cas. 103

24 See especially C. Berger The Sense of Power (Toronto: University of Toronto Press 1970)

25 PAC Sir J.A. Macdonald Papers no. 125325–32, Sir J.S.D. Thompson to Macdonald 25 July 1890

26 Ibid.; PAC Sir J.A. Macdonald Papers no. 125387, 15 December 1890; no. 125838-41, 4 August 1890; no. 8151, Macdonald to Thompson 7 August 1888

27 Technically, two other Canadians also became members of the committee. On 1 January 1920, in recognition of their work at the Versailles Peace Conference, C.J. Doherty and A.L. Sifton were both appointed to the imperial Privy Council. Since both were retired judges, they were both ipso facto members of the Judicial Committee. Neither, however, ever sat on the committee, but their appointment inadvertently created some confusion about the number of colonial members on the committee.

28 R. Gosse 'Random Thoughts of a Would-Be Judicial Biographer' University of Toronto Law Journal 19 (1969) 604

29 PAC Sir W. Laurier Papers no. 115079, A.B. Aylesworth to Laurier 29 October 1906; PAC RG13, A2, vol. 146, no. 555, E.L. Newcombe to C. Russell & Co. 22 April 1907

30 Frank Hodgins in *Saturday Night* 23 March 1912

31 *Clergue* v *Murray* [1903] AC 521; *Canadian Pacific Railway Company* v *Blain* [1904] AC 453; PAC Sir C. Fitzpatrick Papers no. 6385-6, R.B. Haldane to Fitzpatrick 13 October 1913; *Albright* v *Hydro-Electric Power Commission* [1923] AC 169. In the period 1903–18, 'putting aside those cases settled by consent,' there were 192 petitions for leave to appeal from Supreme Court of Canada judgments, 97 of which were granted; see *Canada Law Journal* 56 (1920) 94–5.

32 PAC W.L.M. King Papers MG26 J2, no. 108215-20. The registrar of the Court made a similar case; ibid. J1, no. 109583-7, E.R. Cameron to King 29 September 1926.

33 House of Commons *Debates* (1927) 1055. See also, for example, PAC S.W. Jacobs Papers no. 1010 [Jacobs] to F.A. Anglin 19 September 1924.

34 [1935] AC 500

35 F.R. Scott 'The Privy Council and Minority Rights' *Queen's Quarterly* 37 (1930) 677–8

36 J.L. Granatstein *The Ottawa Men* (Toronto: Oxford University Press 1982) 273

37 *La Revue du Droit* 10 (1931–2) 379–80

38 [1940] SCR at 76

39 [1947] AC 127

40 R. Bothwell, I. Drummond, and J. English *Canada since 1945* (Toronto: University of Toronto Press 1981) 91–9 provides a useful survey of the developments.

41 PAC W.L.M. King Papers, Diary 30 January, 3 February, and 5 March 1948

42 D.O. Carrigan *Canadian Party Platforms 1867–1968* (Toronto: Copp Clark 1968) 185

43 13 Geo. VI c. 37, s. 3

44 Department of Justice file no. 159285, 'Abolition of Appeals to the Privy Council' 24 December 1948

45 Ibid. file no. 152966; PAC RG13, A5, vol. 2073, no. 156794. The lawyers' recommendations were largely repeated in a Canadian Bar Association resolution in the late summer of 1949.

46 Ibid. no. 156794

47 House of Commons *Debates* (1949) 2d session, 312–3

48 *The Advocate* 7 (1949) 97; Department of Justice file no. 157279; House of Commons *Debates* (1949) 2d session, 881-4; Montreal *Le Devoir* 20 Septem-

ber 1949; *Saturday Night* reprinted in *Montreal Gazette* 4 February
1949

49 Since the first statute in 1875, apart from various amendments to the Judges
Act, thirty-one different statutes had been passed containing many alterations of various clauses in the Supreme Court Act.

50 PAC A. Meighen Papers no. 147899-900, Justice P.H. Gordon to Meighen 8
February 1949; *Saturday Night* 24 May 1947; Department of Justice file no.
153000-1

51 Department of Justice file no. 153000-1; House of Commons *Debates* (1949)
2d session, 493

52 Department of Justice, file no. 153000-1; R. Boult 'Ad Hoc Judges of the
Supreme Court of Canada' *Chitty's Law Journal* 26 (1978) 289–95; House of
Commons *Debates* (1949) 2d session, 660–5

53 Ibid 665–6; 13 Geo. VI c. 37, ss 2, 6; W.G. How 'The Too-Limited Jurisdiction of the Supreme Court of Canada' *Canadian Bar Review* 25 (1947) 573–86

CHAPTER 8

1 SCC Judges' Files, T. Rinfret, [P. Kerwin] to Rinfret 4 April 1950. Rinfret
was able to organize a dinner in the fall of 1950, attended by representatives of the bench, the bar, and federal and provincial governments;
see PAC, L. St Laurent Papers vol. 118, file J-20-S.

2 See Bora Laskin 'The Supreme Court of Canada: A Final Court of and for
Canadians' *Canadian Bar Review* 29 (1951) 1038

3 Ottawa *Morning Citizen* 31 January 1950; I.N. Smith *The Supreme Court of
Canada* (Ottawa: The Journal 1952)

4 PAC L. St Laurent Papers vol. 118, file J-20, memorandum 12 November 1949;
authors' interview with D.C. Abbott 18 April 1980

5 SCC Judges' Files, G. Fauteux; J.G. Descôteaux *Faculté de Droit, Université
d'Ottawa 1953–1978* (Ottawa: University of Ottawa 1979) 85; Toronto
Globe and Mail 17 September 1980

6 W.K. Campbell 'The Right Honourable John Cartwright' *The Law Society of
Upper Canada Gazette* 12 (1978) 326–43; PAC W.L.M. King Papers MG26, J2,
vol. 158, file J-200

7 W.K. Campbell 'The Right Honourable Lyman Poore Duff' *Osgoode Hall
Law Journal* 12 (1974) 258; PAC L. St Laurent Papers vol. 187, file J-20-3,
J.W. de B. Farris to St Laurent 7 June 1954

8 PAC D.C. Abbott Papers vol. 1, 'Biographical Sketches;' Toronto *Star
Weekly* 16 July 1955; authors' interview with D.C. Abbott 18 April 1980

9 Toronto *Globe and Mail* 1 July 1954; *Ottawa Journal* 27 February 1954; PAC

Abbott Papers vol. 22; PAC L. St Laurent Papers vol. 187, file J-20-3; Senator J.W. de B. Farris to St Laurent 7 June 1954

10 Department of Justice file no. 164045; *Chitty's Law Journal* 2 (1952) 138–9
11 Montreal *Gazette* 14 June 1954
12 PAC L. St Laurent Papers vol. 186, file J-20-1, W. Kirkconnell to St Laurent 1 February 1956 and passim
13 Another example of such criteria at work is the early 1960s proposal that academics be represented on the Supreme Court; one law professor recommended that the Pearson government begin a tradition of always having one legal scholar on the Court and put forward the names of Cecil Wright and Bora Laskin for consideration. See PAC L.B. Pearson Papers vol. 158, file 341.3, A.M. Linden to Pearson, 22 April 1963.
14 Harry Grattan Nolan, the first Supreme Court justice from Alberta, died suddenly sixteen months after his appointment: SCC Judges' Files, H.G. Nolan
15 J.G. Snell's interview with W.K. Campbell 16 July 1980; Ottawa *Citizen* 7 November 1958 Kellock's fellow justices and the profession were upset that after returning to private practice he soon reappeared at the Supreme Court as counsel.
16 *Canadian Who's Who 1955–1957*, (Toronto: Trans-Canada Press 1957) 708; *Time Canada* 25 May 1959 13
17 See SCC Judges' Files, R.A. Ritchie; *Who's Who in Canada, 1966–1968* (Toronto: International Press 1968).
18 SCC Judges' Files, W. Judson; *Time Canada* 25 May 1959 13; Toronto *Globe and Mail* 19 June 1980
19 See F. Vaughan 'Emmett Matthew Hall: The Activist as Justice' *Osgoode Hall Law Journal* 10 (1972) 411–28.
20 SCC Judges' Files, E.M. Hall; Regina *Leader Post* 24 November 1962; W. Stewart 'The Good Works of Emmett Hall' *Maclean's Magazine* July 1975, 35–9
21 The account of this offer is incorrectly reported in Peter Newman *Renegade in Power* (Toronto: McClelland and Stewart 1963) at 370–1. This proposal was raised on an earlier occasion. The authors are grateful to the Hon. Gordon Churchill for his diary notes relating to this event.
22 See House of Commons *Debates* (1949) 2d session, 193, where Drew raised this objection. For St Laurent's reply, see 196. A brief account of this debate is contained in a Publex from P.A. Clutterbuck, British high commissioner to Canada, to the Rt Hon. Noel Baker, MP, secretary of state for commonwealth relations, 21 March 1949 (no. 92) Privy Council Office PC 8-1639, Public Record Office, London.

23 *Report of the Royal Commission of Inquiry on Constitutional Problems* vol. 3, book 1 (Quebec: Province of Quebec 1956) 288–96

24 Peter H. Russell *The Supreme Court of Canada as a Bilingual and a Bicultural Institution* (Ottawa: Queen's Printer 1969) points to several of these proposals (43–55).

25 Department of Justice file no. 165858, F.P. Varcoe, 'Memorandum for the File Re: Supreme Court Reporters' 24 February 1953, and passim; *The 1961 Year Book of the Canadian Bar Association and the Minutes of Proceedings of the Forty-third Annual Meeting,* (Ottawa: National Printers 1961) 184–5

26 See *Boucher* v *The King* [1951] SCR 265; *Saumur* v *Quebec* [1953] SCR 299; *Switzman* v *Elbling* [1957] SCR 285; and *Roncarelli* v *Duplessis* [1959] SCR 121.

27 Peter H. Russell *Leading Constitutional Decisions* 3rd ed. (Ottawa: Carleton University Press 1982) 319

28 Paul Weiler *In The Last Resort* (Toronto: Carswell 1974) 191

29 *Toronto Daily Star* quoted in Penton *Witnesses* 222; Conrad Black *Duplessis* (Toronto: McClelland and Stewart 1977) 386

30 Weiler *In the Last Resort* 306

31 J. Hébert *I Accuse the Assassins of Coffin* (Montreal: Les Éditions du Jour 1964) 103

32 Frank Scott 'Administrative Law: 1923–1947' *Canadian Bar Review* 25 (1948) 268

33 See Peter W. Hogg 'The Supreme Court of Canada and Administrative Law: 1949–1971' *Osgoode Hall Law Journal* 11 (1973) 197

34 Bora Laskin 'Certiorari to Labour Boards: The Apparent Futility of Privative Clauses' *Canadian Bar Review* 30 (1952) 989

35 [1956] SCR 318

36 *Ex parte Brent* [1955] OR 480; 3 DLR 587

37 Hogg 'The Supreme Court and Administrative Law' 202

38 [1953] 2 SCR 18

39 [1957] SCR 531

40 [1959] SCR 513

41 [1962] SCR 681

42 Ottawa *Evening Journal* 4 April 1962

CHAPTER 9

1 Vaughan's interview with W.K. Campbell 21 June 1974

2 PAC L.B. Pearson Papers vol. 136, file 343, Pearson to E. Marquis 28 August 1967

3 Snell's interview with W.K. Campbell 7 July 1980

4 SCC Judges' Biographies 17

5 B. Laskin 'Our Civil Liberties: The Role of the Supreme Court' *Queen's Quarterly* 61 (1954) 471

6 Ibid.; 'The Supreme Court of Canada: A Final Court of an for Canadians' *Canadian Bar Review* 29 (1951) 1076

7 SCC Judges' Biographies 17; *Toronto Daily Star* 29 December 1973; J. Gault 'Doing Justice to Bora Laskin' *Maclean's* July 1974, 19, 62–8

8 Contrast Laskin's 'An Inquiry into the Diefenbaker Bill of Rights' *Canadian Bar Review* 37 (1959) 77 with Trudeau's *A Canadian Charter of Human Rights* (Ottawa: Queen's Printer 1968).

9 Vaughan's interview with W.K. Campbell 21 June 1974

10 Canadian Bill of Rights (1960) 8–9 Eliz. II c. 44

11 [1963] SCR 651

12 [1970] SCR 282

13 Despite the initial success in *Drybones* the Bill of rights has not been a significant aid to Canadian Indians before the Court.

14 *In the Matter of a Reference by the Governor-General in Council Concerning the Proclamation of Section 16 of the Criminal Law Amendment Act 1968–69* (1970) SCR 777

15 Bora Laskin *Canadian Constitutional Law* 3rd ed. (Toronto: Carswell 1966) 976

16 For an interesting comment on the Canadian judiciary's deference to the legislature under the Bill of Rights, see Peter W. Hogg 'A Comparison of the Canadian Charter of Rights and Freedoms with the Canadian Bill of Rights' *The Canadian Charter of Rights and Freedoms* edited by Walter Tarnopolsky and Louis Beaudoin (Toronto: Carswell 1982) 2. Hogg writes, 'The Canadian Bill of Rights was potentially capable, when enacted, of shielding civil liberties much more effectively than it has. The primary reason for the failure is the [failure of] the Canadian judiciary, steeped in the tradition of legislative supremacy, to make law-makers comply with the Bill.'

17 Hon. Ronald Martland to Vaughan 14 May 1984

18 D. Gibson 'Unobtrusive Justice' *Osgoode Hall Law Journal* 12 (1974) 339–55

19 Quebec *Le Soleil* 31 December 1973; Halifax *Chronicle World* 31 December 1973; Gault 'Laskin' 19

20 Snell's interview with L.W. Abbott 16 September 1980.

21 SCC Judges' Biographies 19; *Who's Who in Canada, 1977–78* (Toronto: International Press 1977), 818–19; Toronto *Globe and Mail* 29 September 1981

22 *Who's Who in Canada, 1977–78* 2

23 Montreal *Le Devoir* 28 December 1973

24 Vaughan's interview with Pierre Patenaude 4 November 1976

25 *Maclean's* 15 October 1979, 34

26 House of Commons *Debates* (1973–4) 9098–9
27 The extent to which some elements of Canadian society were attracted to American developments is perhaps evidenced by the fact that following the successful procedure of Clarence Earle Gideon before the Supreme Court of the United States, a large number of Canadian prisoners began to file habeas corpus applications, written 'largely in an unintelliglble form' and to complain about the unlawfulness of their incarceration. See Department of Justice, file no. 195183; for a complete account of Gideon's case, see Anthony Lewis *Gideon's Trumpet* (New York: Random House 1967).
28 Walter Tarnopolsky 'Civil Liberties during the Post-centennial Decade' in *Decade of Adjustment* edited by Julio Menezes (Toronto: Butterworths 1980)
29 *Toronto Daily Star* 29 July, 31 July, and 2 August 1967
30 *Time Canada* 1 April 1966, 10; *Toronto Daily Star* 20 April 1966
31 *Toronto Daily Star* 3 and 8 May 1967; Toronto *Globe and Mail* 5 May 1967; *Montreal Star* 5 May 1967; *Time Canada* 12 May 1967, 17–8
32 [1978] 1 SCR 988
33 See F. Vaughan 'Mr Justice Emmett Hall as Royal Commissioner' *University of Western Ontario Law Review* 17 (1978–9) 223. See especially the statistical account at 249.
34 Peter Newman *The Distemper of Our Times* (Toronto: McClelland and Stewart 1968) 286, 389; see passim for details of these scandals.
35 Edward McWhinney, quoted ibid. at 406

CHAPTER 10

1 *Canadian Who's Who 1981* (Toronto: University of Toronto Press 1981) 298. According to one report (*Maclean's* 15 October 1979, 35), Chief Justice Laskin took the extraordinary step of recommending the appointment of Justice Charles Dubin of the Ontario Court of Appeal to this seat.
2 *Canadian Who's Who 1981* 806; *Canadian News Facts* 9 (1975) 1487–8, 1495.
3 *Canadian Who's Who 1981* 806
4 Quebec air-traffic controllers resented the federal regulation making it mandatory for them to converse with French-speaking pilots in English. For a full account of this controversy, see Sanford Borins *The Language of the Skies* (Montreal: McGill-Queen's University Press 1983).
5 Ibid. 173; *Canadian Parliamentary Guide 1981* (Ottawa: Normandin 1981) 1007–8; Toronto *Globe and Mail* 29 September 1981
6 *Canadian Who's Who 1981* 544–5; Toronto *Globe and Mail* 29 March 1980
7 See, for example, *Kitchener-Waterloo Record* 14 March 1981; *Toronto Daily*

Star 17 March 1981; Toronto *Globe and Mail* 13 January 1982; *Today Magazine* 2 January 1982, 7; Ontario Committee on the Status of Women 'Women and the Charter of Rights and Freedoms' (November 1980).

8 E. Ratushny 'Judicial Appointments: The Lang Legacy' *Advocates' Quarterly* 1 (1977–8) 2–17

9 3–4 Eliz. II c. 48, s. 1; 12 Eliz. II c. 8, s. 1; 14–15–16 Eliz. II c. 76, s. 1, 23–24 Eliz. II c. 48, s. 1; 29–30 Eliz. II c. 50, ss 9, 19.2

10 The authors are grateful to Mr Justice Estey for this information; Estey to Vaughan 17 April 1983.

11 Department of Justice file no. 195183

12 Paul Weiler *In the Last Resort* (Toronto: Carswell 1974) 8; PAC E.M. Hall Papers vol. 9, file 110; Bora Laskin 'The Supreme Court of Canada' *The Law Society of Upper Canada Gazette* 8 (1974) 251

13 18–19 Eliz. II c. 44, s. 1

14 Between 1975 and 1980 the Court heard 127 criminal appeals as of right. During this period the justices heard a total of 216 criminal cases: statistics compiled by the registrar, the Supreme Court of Canada. The authors are grateful to Mr Brian Crane, QC for making these statistics available to them.

15 In 1975, before the changes became operative, the Court heard thirty-one Civil Code appeals. By 1980 the number had dropped to four.

16 Interview with Mr Justice Estey 24 December 1979. We are grateful to Mr Justice Estey and the Osgoode Society for permitting us to use this material.

17 From 333 in 1976 to 419 in 1982

18 The number of appeals in 1975 was 160; in 1979, 107; in 1982, 129.

19 Authors' interview with Mr Justice Estey 24 December 1979, confirmed by registrar's statistics.

20 Authors' interview with D.C. Abbott 18 April 1980

21 L.-P. Pigeon 'The Human Element in the Judicial Process' *Alberta Law Review* 7 (1970) 301–21; Laskin 'Institutional Character' 329–48; E.M. Hall 'Law Reform and the Judiciary's Role' *Osgoode Hall Law Journal* 10 (1972) 399–409; Brian Dickson 'The Judiciary: Law Interpreters or Law-Makers' *Manitoba Law Journal* 12 (1982) 1–8

22 B. Amiel 'Nine Men in Search of Even-handed Justice' *Maclean's* 12 February 1979, 39

23 G. Bale 'Stare Decisis, the Supreme Court and Law Reform' *Chitty's Law Journal* 26 (1978) 337–40

24 [1977] 2 SCR 655

25 [1975] 1 SCR 423

26 Ibid. at 450–1
27 Cited by Paul Weiler in 'Of Judges and Scholars: Reflections on a Centennial Year' *Canadian Bar Review* 53 (1975) 568
28 *Time Canada* 24 March 1974 6
29 [1975] 2 SCR 574
30 For a good discussion of the exclusionary rule, see Malcolm Wilkey 'The Exclusionary Rule: Why Suppress Valid Evidence?' *Judicature* 62 (1978) 215, and Craig Bradley 'The Exclusionary Rule in Germany' *Harvard Law Review* 96 (1983) 1032.
31 See, for example, *The Queen* v *Pierce Fisheries Ltd.* [1971] SCR 5; and Weiler *In the Last Resort* 97–104.
32 [1976] 1 SCR 616
33 [1974] SCR 1349
34 Montreal *Le Devoir* 3 April 1975
35 [1978] 2 SCR 545
36 [1978] 2 SCR 1299
37 See the discussion of mens rea in chapter 8.
38 For a critical assessment of this judgment, see A.C. Hutchinson 'Sault Ste Marie, *Mens Rea* and the Halfway House: Public Welfare Offences Get a Home of Their Own' *Osgoode Hall Law Journal* 17 (1979) 415
39 [1976] 2 SCR 373
40 For two different legal assessments of this decision, see Albert Abel 'The Anti-Inflation Judgment: Right Answer to the Wrong Question' *University of Toronto Law Journal* 26 (1976) 409; and Pierre Patenaude 'The Anti-Inflation Case: The Shutters Are Closed but the Back Door Is Wide Open' *Osgoode Hall Law Journal* 15 (1977) 397.
41 [1979] 1 SCR 42
42 [1957] SCR 198
43 Chief Justice Bora Laskin 'Judicial Integrity and the Supreme Court' *Law Society of Upper Canada Gazette*, (1978) 116
44 Peter W. Hogg 'Is the Supreme Court Biased in Constitutional Cases?' *Canadian Bar Review* 57 (1979) 721
45 See *Dominion Stores* v *The Queen* [1980] 1 SCR 844; and *Labatt Breweries Ltd* v *A.-G. of Canada* [1980] 1 SCR 914.
46 Peter H. Russell *Leading Constitutional Decisions* 3d ed. (Ottawa: Carleton University Press 1980) 295
47 See, for example, *Canadian Annual Review 1972* edited by J. Saywell (Toronto: University of Toronto Press 1974) 107.
48 (1981) 117 DLR (3d) 1
49 [1981] CA 80; (1981) 120 DLR (3d) 385

50 (1981) 118 DLR (3d) 1
51 *Re: Resolution to Amend the Constitution* [1981] 1 SCR 754
52 Toronto *Globe and Mail* 29 September 1981; the headline in *Le Devoir* read:
    'Le projet de résolution est légal mais inconstitutionnel': 29 September
    1981.
53 See Russell 'The Supreme Court Decision: Bold Statecraft Based on Ques-
    tionable Jurisprudence' in Institute of Intergovernmental Relations *The Court
    and the Constitution* (Kingston: Queen's University 1982).
54 Richard Simeon *Federal-Provincial Diplomacy* (Toronto: University of
    Toronto Press 1972) 30, 287
55 See David C. McDonald *Legal Rights in the Canadian Charter of Rights and
    Freedoms* (Toronto: Carswell 1983).
56 For an account of the Charter cases during the first year of its operation,
    see F.L. Morton 'Charting the Charter – Year One: A Statistical
    Analysis', paper prepared for the 1984 annual meeting of the Canadian
    Political Science Association held at Guelph, Ontario (June 1984).
57 Constitution Act, 1982, 41(d)
58 See Peter Russell's misgiving in 'The Political Process of the Canadian
    Charter of Rights and Freedoms' *Canadian Bar Review* 61 (1983) 30–54.
59 Ibid. 52

EPILOGUE

1 *Skapinker* v *Law Society of Upper Canada* [1984] 1 SCR 357
2 Ibid. at 366.
3 *Hunter* v *Southam* (as yet unreported)
4 For an account of the reaction to Le Dain's appointment, see David
   Vinneau *Toronto Daily Star* 30 May 1984
5 *Canadian Who's Who 1984* (Toronto: University of Toronto Press 1984) 659
6 *Towards a New Canada* (Ottawa: Canadian Bar Foundation 1978) 55
7 S.I. Bushnell 'Leave to Appeal Applications to the Supreme Court of
   Canada' *Supreme Court Review* 3 (1983) 479–558; P.H. Russell 'The First Two
   Years in Charter Land' paper presented to the 1984 annual meeting of the
   Canadian Political Science Association, Guelph, Ontario (June 1984) 5
8 Ibid. 4
9 Ibid. 6

Index